ALONG THE EDGE OF
THE FOREST

ANTHONY BAILEY

ALONG THE EDGE OF THE FOREST

AN IRON CURTAIN JOURNEY

faber and faber
LONDON · BOSTON

First published in the USA and Canada in 1983
by Random House Inc, New York
and Random House of Canada Ltd, Toronto
First published in Great Britain in 1983
by Faber and Faber Limited
3 Queen Square London WC1N 3AU
Printed in Great Britain by
Redwood Burn Limited, Trowbridge, Wiltshire
All rights reserved

Portions of this work were originally published in the *New Yorker*

British Library Cataloguing in Publication Data

Bailey, Anthony
   Along the edge of the forest.
   1. Europe, Eastern—Description and travel
   I. Title
   914.7'04853   DJK18

ISBN 0-571-13195-6

But it was primarily against people's methods
rather than against their objectives that
[my] indignation mounted in such moments.
Objectives were normally vainglorious, unreal,
extravagant, even pathetic—little likely to be
realized, scarcely to be taken seriously.
People had to have them, or to believe they
had them. It was part of their weakness as
human beings. But methods were another matter.
These were real. It was out of their immediate
effects that the quality of life was really
molded. In war as in peace I found myself
concerned less with what people thought they
were striving for than with the manner in
which they strove for it.

    —George F. Kennan, *Memoirs 1925–1950*

Before I built a wall I'd ask to know
What I was walling in or walling out,
And to whom I was like to give offense.
Something there is that doesn't love a wall,
That wants it down.

    —Robert Frost, *Mending Wall*

Their holy places are the woods and groves.

    —Tacitus, *Germania*

AUTHOR'S NOTE

In a number of places in this book I have changed
certain details—personal names and attributes,
occupations, and the locations of meetings and
incidents—in order to conceal the identities of
informants and participants who desired anonymity.
I owe a great deal to several persons who are not
listed below. But as well as by people who are given
their real names in the text, and to whom my debt
is evident, I was much helped by Carol Carl-Sime;
Heidi Foster; Alwin Strecker; the staff of Inter
Nationes, particularly Frau Simons, Frau Heibey,
Frau Frölich and Frau Hederer; Eva Hartmann; the
staff of the Goethe Institute, London; C. J. Fox;
Hildegard Jablonski; Paul Modich; and Eugen
Freund. I was in mid-journey when I discovered
David Shear's pioneer work, *The Ugly Frontier*
(Chatto, London, 1970), many of whose facts and
perceptions remain valuable. *Stern*'s account of the
Strelzyk-Wetzel balloon escape (in three issues in
1979) was useful to me, as were various articles in
GDR Monitor, *New German Critique*, *Die Zeit*,
Die Welt, *Der Spiegel*, and innumerable other
European, British and American newspapers and
periodicals, to whose reporters and editors I am
grateful.

CHRONOLOGY

Potsdam conference: treaty to ensure "that never more should a war be started from German soil"

Founding of United Nations

1946   Churchill "Iron Curtain" speech at Fulton, Missouri

1947   Truman Doctrine: U.S. announces it will help resist Russian encroachment on Europe

Marshall Plan to assist European recovery

Cominform of East-bloc nations established

1948   Communist government takes over in Czechoslovakia

Yugoslavia expelled from Cominform

1948–49   West Berlin blockaded by USSR; Allied airlift

1949   Communist takeover in Hungary

North Atlantic Treaty Organization founded

Federal Republic of Germany founded

German Democratic Republic founded

1949   USSR explodes its first atomic weapon

1950–53   Korean War

1952   East Germany hardens border with West Germany

1953   Stalin's death

Strikes and uprising in East Germany crushed by USSR

1954   West Germany admitted to NATO

USSR declares East Germany to be sovereign state

1955   Warsaw Pact established

Austrian State Treaty

1956   USSR 20th Party Congress: Khrushchev denounces Stalin's policies

Hungarian Revolution put down by USSR

1957   Treaty of Rome: EEC established

1958   Moratorium on nuclear testing by U.S.A., U.K. and USSR

1959   Castro takes over in Cuba

1961   USSR first manned space flight

Berlin Wall created

1962   Cuban missile crisis

1963   Nuclear test ban treaty

JFK assassination

1965   Death of Churchill

1966   Ceauşescu declares Rumania recognizes no supreme authority within Communist movement

1968   "The Prague Spring"; Russian-led invasion of Czechoslovakia

1970   Brandt and Stoph, heads of the two Germanys, have first such meeting since division of their country

1971   Four-Power agreements on Berlin

1972   West Germany and East Germany recognize each other: the Basic Treaty

1973   West Germany and East Germany become members of the United Nations

1974   West Germany and East Germany exchange permanent representatives

Alexander Solzhenitsyn expelled from USSR to West Germany

1975   Helsinki Accords intended to end Cold War and ensure human rights

First joint U.S./USSR space venture

1977   Czechoslovakia: Charter 77 civil rights movement

1978   Moscow: Yuri Orlov, Helsinki Accords monitoring group leader, sentenced to seven years' labor-camp term plus five years' exile

1979   Soviet invasion of Afghanistan

U.S.A. and China establish diplomatic relations

1980   Death of Tito

Formation of independent trade unions in Poland

1981   Massive anti-nuclear protests in European cities

Martial law and government clamp-down in Poland

1982   Death of Brezhnev

U.S.A./USSR arms limitation talks continue

CONTENTS

ALONG THE EDGE OF THE FOREST

1. THE BEACH AND THE SEA

At twilight on the north coast of Germany, facing out on what we call the Baltic and the Germans call the East Sea, the thickening darkness where sky and water merge is brought into focus by lights—small, wavering pinpricks of light where ships are. Among such vessels are East German patrol boats, forced by the rules of the sea to announce their watchful presence not only to other ships but to anyone along the northern shore of the German Democratic Republic who might be thinking of that expanse—that seemingly open, free element—as a way of escape.

In daylight the gray patrol boats are less visible. I sat one cool Sunday afternoon in early autumn on the beach of the Priwall peninsula, opposite Travemünde, a seaside resort, harbor for ferries to Scandinavia, and yachting port, at the mouth of the Trave River, which has the old Hansa city of Lübeck a few miles upstream. Priwall is an arm of West German land attached to East Germany: an enclave of boatyards, small summer cottages and beach whose connection to Travemünde is by a pair of ferries. One ferry, just for foot passengers, lands close by the jetty where the *Passat*, one of the last of the great square-rigged grain ships, is moored. From where I sat, I could see beyond the four masts of the *Passat* the thirty-story white tower of the Maritim hotel and apartment complex at the north end of Travemünde and then the low West German coast of Schleswig-

Holstein curving northward past Timmendorfer Strand. A number of yachts were out sailing on Lübeck Bay, though the wind was a strong southeasterly. Priwall Strand had a score or so of visitors; in midsummer it would have been packed. The eastern section of the beach is reserved for nude bathing and sunbathing, what in Germany is called *Freikörper-kultur*. Several signs announced this, though the few people in this section, including me, were fully clothed.

At the far end of the beach is the border between the two Germanys. It is marked, on the West German side, by a line of metal poles, ten feet or so apart, sticking up out of the sand. The poles are painted in red and white bands and are joined by a red-and-white-painted chain—dangling in a way that seems to tempt one to jump over it. A little beyond this line are a row of half a dozen placards set on posts that declare HALT! HIER GRENZE. The three words are one above the other, *Halt* in blue, *Hier* in red, *Grenze* in black. At the bottom, in smaller lettering, is the name BUNDESGRENZSCHUTZ, the Federal German Frontier Police, the authority that has set up these signs most of the way along the frontier—*die Grenze*—between West and East Germany. The beach here is about fifty paces wide from the water's edge to the low dunes. There, in the dune grass, a few meters east of the West German posts, stands a square concrete post, about the height of a short man, painted in chevron stripes of black, red and gold, and bearing an aluminum plaque with the name and symbol of the German Democratic Republic. The sand on the beach is brown-gray and is carpeted in many places with fragments of gray and white mussel shells. A series of yellow buoys continues the demarcation line for half a mile out to sea and is brought to the attention of sailors and swimmers by two orange-tipped range markers on the dunes.

It is the same sort of sand and shells across the posts and chain, though there the East German beach gradually narrows, the dunes still low, until it vanishes at a wooded headland about a mile distant. The main differ-ence is that there is not a soul on it, the other beach, only pigeons and gulls. Over there, about two hundred meters away, a tall fence can be seen through the dune shrubbery. The fence arrives from the south, from inland, and then makes a right-angled turn to run eastward along the dunes behind the beach. It is accompanied by lamp standards every twenty meters or so. Near the corner is a small shed and a concrete watchtower. On the beach itself I can just make out two angled metal posts and what looks like a trip wire, perhaps some sort of warning system, strung between them. The watchtower is light-gray, its octagonal observation room set on a con-crete column, and with a searchlight on its roof. I detect a slight move-ment behind the glass windows, and what looks like the shape made when a man has his arms up, elbows out, holding binoculars to his eyes. (And when I raise my own binoculars I see that is what he is doing, looking—through binoculars—at me.) In summer, with all the free body culture going on, he must get an eyeful.

Gray clouds—and what looks like a veil of rain falling behind the East German headland. A pair of ducks. A tired or dying swan, head buried in its back feathers, sits on the sand a few feet from the water's edge. Four boys throwing a ball. People walking dogs. Three immensely high-sided ferries coming in from Scandinavia in line astern. I have my coat collar turned up to deflect the wind past my ears. The dune grass bends, the wind whirrs. I can hear blackbirds chirping in the East German shrubbery and smell the seaweed or old mussel shells, upwind, on the West German beach. This is where the border begins, what we still sometimes call the Iron Curtain. The long dividing line between us and them.

I turn inland from the beach and follow the border for its first kilometer or so south—first across the thin neck of the Priwall peninsula, summer cottages on one side, border markers and thick East German scrub on the other. Good rabbit country, I would judge. Some of the summer people have been dumping their disused kitchen pots in the East German bushes. I come to an untenanted watch cabin, like a garden shed, with an adjacent kennel, also empty. A notice board put up by the *Bundesgrenzschutz* gives details about the location of the border, and the importance of observing the signs and markers. There is a sandy parking lot with three or four cars, and then a view out over an inland bay formed by a broadening of the Trave River behind the peninsula. The bay is called the Pötenitzer Wiek, and one can walk along its shore, sometimes only a foot or so wide, between the green water and the border posts. The East German fence is very close here, up on a grassy slope, but the signs remind one not to imagine that the fence marks the border—the signs mark the border; the fence is back on East German soil. Another East German watchtower comes into view, giving me sudden reason to be glad I'd refrained from stepping over the border. I walk as far as I can go; further progress to the south would mean shoes off, and paddling. Back near the parking lot I pass a family out on a Sunday-afternoon excursion. The father is saying to his small son, pointing just beyond the marker posts, "That is the DDR"—as if to say, touring the edge of the Inferno, That is Hell.

I was here on Priwall beach at the start of a journey. I intended to travel the length of the Iron Curtain—a name that gained wide currency after Winston Churchill's speech at Fulton, Missouri, on March 5, 1946: "From

Stettin in the Baltic to Trieste in the Adriatic, an iron curtain has descended across the Continent . . . All these famous cities and the populations around them lie in what I must call the Soviet sphere, and all are subject in one form or another not only to Soviet influence, but to a very high, and, in many cases, increasing measure of control from Moscow." To choose Stettin, even then, as the northern terminus of the Iron Curtain was either cavalier or optimistic, since the Soviet zone of Germany extended well west of that city—to the Trave, in fact. And thirty-five years later it is at the mouth of the Trave that the Iron Curtain still begins. My own, I hoped well-founded, optimism was that the curtain now became a good deal less iron in its southern reaches, approaching Trieste.

My idea was to look as closely as I could at what is still the dividing line between two power blocks and two states formed out of one people, the Germans. I thought the border, running through the heart of Europe, warranted attention for what it was and what it did; and also, perhaps, for what it could not do, what it failed to keep apart, prevent and divide. I meant to look at the ground and at the people living along the border. I was curious about the effects of living close to what might almost seem to be a geological fault line—certainly a geographical and perhaps a metaphysical one. I thought that since this was the frontier of what we loosely refer to as "the free world" or "the West," and since I was interested in the facts lying beneath the rhetoric and in what will be thought on the subject in time to come, it would be good to make a reconnaissance along the frontier and try to fit together my impressions of land and people and what has happened in recent history. My means of travel was to be for the most part car—my 1973 Saab station wagon, which carried books, clothes, umbrella and two pairs of walking boots. I had sent word of my plans to several agencies of the West German and Austrian governments and to a few friends and acquaintances along the way. Six weeks before setting forth I had asked the London embassy of the German Democratic Republic for a journalist's visa to spend a little while in East Germany, as close to the border as would be allowed, continuing my journey south on the other side through small East German towns and villages, and coming back into West Germany again. When I left my home in London there had been no answer to this request, although an official at the embassy assured me that it had been dispatched to East Berlin, and followed up by a reminder.

There were no doubt other, personal motives. This journey was partly prompted by restlessness, by dissatisfaction after a long spell of domesticity, and by a feeling that I ought to try to relate the ups and downs of my own existence to the greater issues of the age—which may be what has impelled men in other times to go on pilgrimages, crusades, explorations. Then, too, I am a child of the 1930s. I was born in the year that Hitler came to power. Germany, Austria, Czechoslovakia; Munich and Prague; these were the names that I heard, aged seven, as my mind began to open to the world. For the next four years the Germans were the enemy—the Jerries, the Boche, the Huns—and for some time after that they remained people one did not trust and felt no generous impulse toward. For a long time I was one of those people who could not consider buying a Volkswagen. The image of the concentration camp gas chambers rose alongside those of Bach, Beethoven and Brahms when Germany was mentioned. And yet I knew very little about Germany or the Germans. When the earlier feelings of animosity faded—in the way that they did for most people in Europe, as an older generation of Germans passed away and a new pair of Germanys rose in a different Europe—I was left with the vacuum of my own ignorance, which I felt needed to be filled.

I was on the public jetty next to Travemünde yacht club the following morning to join the West German patrol boat *Uelzen* for a short voyage in Lübeck Bay. The *Uelzen* is one of eight boats operated by the Bundesgrenzschutz (BGS) in its Zee Commando division, patrolling the 238 kilometers of coastline between Flensburg (on the West German border with Denmark) and Travemünde, and the offshore waters. Something like a larger version of the PT and motor torpedo boats of World War II, the *Uelzen* had a crew of twenty-four, could do thirty knots and had two 40mm Bofors guns on deck, neither of which had ever been fired in anger. The BGS boats are named after towns where the frontier police have bases, and Uelzen, in Lower Saxony, is such a town.

The senior officer on board the *Uelzen* was Johannes Kühne, his rank Erster Polizeihauptkommissar—which I will call captain. Captain Kühne was an old sea dog with a modern look; out of uniform, he might have been taken for a lawyer or banker. There were no sea wrinkles, no weathered skin. On the other hand, the senior officers of the *Scharnhorst* and *Graf Spee* had not been Cape Horners, and it was a little while before these discordant thoughts, provoked by the act of listening to a German officer in naval uniform, began to settle.

Captain Kühne took me to one side of the crowded wheelhouse and pointed out the old Travemünde lighthouse. "You can read about it in Thomas Mann's novels," he said.

Mann was born in Lübeck. I noted that his lighthouse had been overshadowed as a landmark by the new Maritim skyscraper, on which beacon lights for the harbor entrance had also been installed. It was a calm day, overcast. The line of yellow buoys stood out clearly. Captain Kühne showed me on the chart how the DDR border angled out into the Baltic from the seamost buoy and then ran eastward roughly three miles off their coast. Just east of the buoys is a small area of DDR water where up to one hundred and ten Lübeck fishermen are allowed to fish, the only West Germans allowed to work regularly on East German territory. Two small boats, not much bigger than skiffs, were inside the buoys, fishing. The right to fish there had been disputed by the DDR for a long time, and Lübeck fishermen had been arrested, fined and otherwise harassed, but negotiations between the two German states had finally sorted the matter out.

"This has been a border for a very long time," said Captain Kühne. "It was the border between Schleswig-Holstein and Mecklenburg. The Lübeck fishermen first had their privilege to fish in Mecklenburg water ratified in 1128, in the time of the Emperor Frederick Barbarossa."

However, beyond the two small fishing boats the East German beach remained empty. Captain Kühne said that there was a barrier zone along the coast, roughly five kilometers deep, where people were not allowed without special permission. Those who live within this zone have been vetted to establish that they are reliable citizens, not likely to flee the DDR; they have to carry a special registration pass. A similar zone exists all the way down the intra-German border, behind the East German fence. On the coast there are also severe restrictions as to who may use boats. Canoes, row boats, sailboats may only be used in daylight hours, after the authorities have been properly notified about each voyage. People who come on holiday to the East German Baltic resorts are generally there through official travel agencies and trips arranged by their places of work or trade unions. Foreign vessels must follow a prescribed approach to DDR ports and have advance permission to enter DDR waters. A yacht that by accident, bad navigation or ignorance crossed into the five-kilometer zone was likely to be sternly warned off by DDR patrol boats if not seized.

Captain Kühne pointed out a faint blur on the horizon—one of the patrol boats of the other side. He said, "When we meet them out there their men never wave at ours—which is something seamen do all over the world when they encounter one another."

I tried to imagine this; it would be like the meeting of ghost ships.

The *Uelzen* had spotted a boat not far away with which it wanted to make friendly contact. The big diesels roared, spray flew, and in a few minutes we were near one of the main fairway buoys, where a Travemünde fishing boat was hauling its nets. There was shouting, waving. The *Uelzen* stood off until a net had been emptied on deck, and then it came alongside to purchase a tray of codling for the evening meal.

I knew that despite the coastal watchtowers, the restricted zone and the East German patrol boats, people had occasionally got away from the DDR by sea. In the 1960s a young man from the small town of Neustadt-Glewe, about fifty kilometers east of the border and roughly the same distance south of the coast, used to practice skin diving in a lake near the town with snorkel or oxygen tank, and no one thought anything of it. One summer day he went to Boltenhagen, the first sizable place on the sparsely settled coast east of Lübeck, and at nightfall went into the water there. His parents then received a telegram from West Germany, saying he'd arrived safely; he had swum at least twenty-five kilometers across Lübeck Bay. Another man designed and built his own underwater propulsion device—a moped motor harnessed to a propeller, getting its air via a snorkel tube. This took him to Denmark in five hours. A West German firm marketed a production model of the device in 1973—but the market was in the other Germany, and not exactly accessible. In September 1979 an East German family—father, mother, baby—escaped in a folding boat powered by a small outboard motor; they came from Grevesmühlen, a little way inland from Boltenshagen, and managed to elude the patrol boats and reach Travemünde. Some East Germans have jumped down onto jetties in Scandinavian ports from the decks of East German ships. Some have jumped overboard and were picked up by West German vessels that had been warned to stand by. Two years ago, an East German swam from the Mecklenburg coast near the village of Klutzhoved a distance of twenty-five kilometers at night to the Schleswig-Holstein coast, taking his course from a lighthouse. Captain Kühne told me that several swimmers have been found hanging on to buoys, at the end of their strength. A few years ago a sailmaker from an East German port fled with his wife and child in a small yacht. As they approached the five-kilometer limit an East German patrol boat came in hot pursuit, but fortunately a message had been sent to West Germany alerting the authorities to their plans, and the patrol boat *Duderstadt* was waiting for them. It took the yacht in tow just outside the limit; sailmaker, wife and child were hurriedly welcomed on the patrol boat, and a BGS crewman put at the helm of the yacht—a dangerous position, so it seemed for a while, as the East Germans appeared to want a battle or collision. The sailmaker now makes sails and lives with his family in the *Uelzen*'s homeport of Neustadt-Holstein; he sails his yacht on the western, unrestricted side of Lübeck Bay.

2. THE BORDER

In Lübeck you are made to remember that the Middle Ages were not only plague, war and devastation. Here is a medieval city of close-packed merchant houses with high gables, tall church towers and spires, and narrow streets, set on an oval island encircled as with mirrors by the calm Trave. Despite having lost its eastern hinterland, the city still has a quietly prosperous and independent air. Lübeck once flourished on the export of salt and the import of wine; the association that mattered most to Lübeck for several centuries was neither with province nor country but with the Hanseatic League of North German and Netherlandish towns that traded with Russia and Scandinavia; shipyards and docks are still busy in Lübeck. The Marienkirche, the tall twin-towered cathedral, can be seen from well out to sea, a building whose Gothic proportions nicely combine with local materials—dark brick without; and within, red brick floors and white chalky stone columns picked out with a terra-cotta mortar between the stones. Overhead, the vaulting is decorated like fine china. On the floor of a small chapel below the south tower, huge pieces of bell are lying in a deep dent in the paving, just where they fell when the tower was hit during a British air raid in 1942. The tower has been dedicated as a memorial to Germans buried in other lands, and the church itself is a sort of reminder for many Germans of the churches of lost German territory in Eastern Europe. Lübeck took in nearly a hundred thousand refugees from those Eastern lands in 1945.

In the course of a stroll around the town I paused to look at the Baroque façade of Thomas Mann's birthplace, the Buddenbrooks house; the Buddenbrooks were bankers and the house is appropriately now a branch of the Volksbank. I dined at a small quayside inn on fish soup "Marseilles"—a sort of bouillabaisse made with local, Baltic ingredients and none the worse for it. I took the opportunity of the large table I had to myself to spread out a map and look at some of the places on the border where I would be in the next few days. I had been told that many West Germans considered the border with East Germany to be different from other international frontiers. In fact, West German officialdom has tended to regard it as legally nonexistent, to be there as a kind of emblem of East German authoritarian rule, with the legal consequence in West Germany that any East German who makes his way there is in almost every case treated as a citizen of the Bundesrepublik, the Federal Republic—a German. Thus the education ministers of the seven West German *Länder*, or Federal states, recently decided that national maps should show the frontier between West and East Germany in a different manner from other frontiers, using a form of marking described as "a string of pearls." The German Tourist Office road map I was looking at while eating my fish soup had not caught up with this decision but used the same Morse code dot-dash-dot line for all of West Germany's borders. The education ministers had also recommended that on maps showing both states, they were to be labeled "Federal Republic of Germany" and "German Democratic Republic," but the entire area they covered was to be called Germany. Further defining these prickly matters, the ministers said that where lack of space was a problem in maps and school texts, the abbreviation DDR for Deutsche Demokratische Republik could be used. (All European cars that travel abroad are supposed to carry a label or badge showing where they come from; the West Germans use a simple D for Deutschland, the East Germans have DDR.) The right-wing–tending newspapers of the West German publishing magnate Axel Springer usually print DDR in quotation marks, as if it were a slang term that had no real authority to it. In both countries, people allude to the other as *drüben*—"over there."

The land border between the two German states is 1,390 kilometers long—that is, roughly 870 miles. From the air—seen, say, from a plane on the way from West Berlin to Hanover—the border looks like earth that has just been prepared for a new road, much lighter than the surrounding ground of fields and forests. At night those parts of it close to frequented places, near towns and villages and the few permitted road and railway crossings, are illuminated by powerful lights. To learn about the border fortification system, and how either side guards the border, I went to the Bundesgrenzschutz barracks in a modern suburb outside Lübeck. The BGS looks after all German frontiers, though naturally less rigorously on the borders with Austria, Switzerland, France, Luxembourg, Belgium, the Netherlands and Denmark than with East Germany. The BGS also guards airports, German embassies abroad and high federal officials; they provide backup power for the police in each *Land* in the event of civil emergency, riot and insurrection. On the intra-German border the BGS conducts daily patrols, keeping an eye on DDR border activities. In this they are assisted by the West German Customs Service, the *Zoll*, which has little actual customs duties on most of the intra-German border but provides men who do much of the footwork in keeping watch along it. In Bavaria, the *Land* which works hardest to preserve itself as an independent state within Federal Germany, the Bavarian Frontier Police also patrol the borders with East Germany and Czechoslovakia.

There is clearly duplication if not triplication of efforts here; but these organizations have their separate origins and historic associations with the border, and an element of competition between them may make for efficiency. Even so, their combined numbers are much less than the force which the DDR has permanently manning its border with West Germany. On the eastern side, Soviet forces stationed in the DDR are generally well back from the border, except for those stationed at some of the crossing points. On the western side, Britain and the United States retain a border role in their respective postwar zones of occupation, and send out military patrols to gain intelligence and demonstrate a presence. The British, moreover, maintain a small outfit called the British Frontier Service, a little group of for the most part rather elderly veterans of border duty who wear a semi-naval uniform and accompany all British patrols whether in helicopter, jeep or armored car. Somewhere or other along the line, I intended to visit all these border-watching organizations, talking to them as I would have done, say, to guides before crossing a mountain range or to coast guards in the course of walking along an unfamiliar shore.

At the BGS barracks near Lübeck a young sandy-haired officer named Peter Lemke gave me a briefing on the DDR border with the help of various diagrams and displays. He said that I should note (as I had in fact already noted) that the DDR fence was not the actual borderline—*that* was marked by border stones and posts. The DDR chevron-striped columns were also on DDR territory. It was a good idea, he said, to use only paved roads and proper paths where the border could be easily discerned, and to contact BGS or Zoll personnel for information and assistance. DDR law was different from West German law. "DDR border troops have orders to practice their control functions most rigidly," he said. "Even if you violate DDR territory accidentally, you run a great risk."

Between the actual border and the DDR fence there was generally a cleared strip of ground, of varying width. There were also usually two fences, with an area of ground between that was often sown with mines. The fences were roughly three meters tall, and made of metal cut and then stretched into a grid pattern, with small diamond-shaped holes, too small to get one's fingers in—and too sharp to hold on to even if one could. Three panels of this metal grid are fastened together one above the other and supported on concrete posts; the bottom panel is let well into the ground so a person cannot crawl under. On the inner side of the inner fence is a plowed strip, which is kept well raked and shows up footprints; and inside this strip, a deep ditch intended as a vehicle barrier; inside this, a concrete track for troop patrol vehicles. Apart from lights and electric- and sound-alarm systems, the DDR relied on observation towers for de- tecting escapers: the towers were of two types, the sort I'd seen at Priwall, with an enclosed watch post set on a cylindrical column, and a newer type, a square tower with windows made of pinkish-brown reflecting glass that made it difficult to see what those inside the observation post were doing. In various places where the East German authorities feel there is a great risk of escape attempts being made, dog runs are installed; there are at least a thousand dogs helping guard the DDR border. Informers also keep an eye open for strange faces in the five-kilometer restricted zone within the fence system. In many places along the border, houses and farm buildings have been demolished to give the border guards a clearer view or better field of fire. This is the third generation DDR fence and barrier system, and though it might seem as effective as can be, the DDR au- thorities show no signs of thinking they have perfected it. It is believed to have cost the East German regime in building and maintenance some- thing like 12 billion Deutschmarks—$6 billion.

Peter Lemke introduced me to some BGS noncommissioned officers who were also having their first introduction to the East German border. I asked one what he had thought when he first saw the watchtowers, the wire, the minefields.

"It's a strange feeling," he said. "They tell us that over there is Germany, too, but you wonder in what way. I know the East Germans tell their people that the fences are to keep us out, to stop us invading them, and prevent us from sending in our spies. But when you take a close look at the border you see that it isn't like that at all. All the devices and defenses are aimed to stop their own people. The DDR has built a barrier to keep its own people in."

Lemke and I drove in a dark-green BGS Passat station wagon to the small town of Schlutup, which is on the border not far from Lübeck. Here a main road crosses the border, a transit route to Rostock, East Berlin and Gdansk. This is one of the nine *Grenzübergänge*, or border crossings, which are all that are left of hundreds of major roads and thousands of minor ones that used to go across where the border now cuts them off. Just east of the West German checkpoint, where the BGS examines vehicle and driver documents and the Zoll checks on foreign goods being imported, a white house stands on the north side of the road, right next to the border. This building has had a difficult recent history, since it stands in the province of Mecklenburg. However, unlike the rest of the province (which was occupied by the Soviets and became part of East Germany), this house was generously handed over to the British by a friendly local Soviet army commander who knew that the British needed a military police guardroom at the border. The original owners of the house, who had fled to the West, eventually got their house back but found they were expected to pay property taxes to Mecklenburg still. Perhaps Mecklenburg and the DDR would reclaim the house. While its future was cloudy the house became run-down, but its position in the West has now been firmly established. It has been given new windows and a new coat of white paint, and gleams optimistically over the border pole that stands right outside the front door.

At this date the border seems so fixed that it is hard to realize it was not always so. The present dividing line between East and West Germany was to all intents and purposes arrived at in London in January and February of 1944. A common wartime assumption among the Western Allies had been that after an interim period of postwar occupation, Germany would be restored to international life as a sovereign state. However, a division of Germany had been contemplated by some as a desirable outcome of the war. The possibility of dismembering Germany had been discussed, without any decision being taken, at the meeting of Allied foreign ministers in Moscow in October 1943. At the three-power conference in Teheran in November-December 1943 the leaders agreed that Germany should be split up: Roosevelt and Stalin at that point thought it should be divided into five parts; Churchill wanted it in three—one of Prussia, the second of Austria and Bavaria; and the third of the Ruhr and Westphalia (the latter to remain under international control). Anyone with a knowledge of the way German is spoken, as High German and Low German particularly, would have plumped for a more logical way of dividing Germany as horizontal rather than vertical. In any event, as a result of the foreign ministers' get-together in Moscow of Eden, Cordell Hull and Molotov, it was decided to set up a body, the European Advisory Commission, to prepare recommendations for the terms of surrender to be imposed on Germany, the zones of occupation, and the machinery of control. The commission sat at Lancaster House in London; its first formal session took place on January 4, 1944. The British representative was Sir William Strang, later Lord Strang, a Foreign Office official, whose main job this became; the United States and the Soviet Union made their ambassadors in London their delegates to the commission, John Winant and F. T. Gusev. Among Winant's close advisers were George F. Kennan and Philip Mosely, who both later wrote about the experience—as did Strang.

It was a difficult time. The British and Americans often found their Soviet partner an obdurate negotiator—deadlock in discussions sometimes lasted weeks. As for the Americans, they had problems too. According to Strang, "It was often patent that Winant was being placed in an embarrassing position by cross-currents of opinion and unresolved disagreements as to policy or jurisdiction among governmental agencies in Washington." According to Kennan, the British were well prepared with a plan for zonal borders, which they presented on January 15. The Americans had no instructions; they sent the British plan to Washington and waited for a reaction. The British proposals put the western border of the Soviet zone of Germany almost exactly where it is today. On February 18 the Soviets accepted the British plan for zones of occupation more or less without change. The U.S. delegation informed Washington of this but still had no instructions. Kennan wrote later: "Our British colleagues became restive, we ourselves acutely embarrassed."

There were, it seemed, rivalries between the U.S. State Department and the U.S. military. No one in London knew that the British proposals had already been discussed by President Roosevelt and the American Joint Chiefs of Staff, and it appeared that the State Department didn't know this either. The point of view of the U.S. War Department's Civil Affairs division was that occupation zones were a purely military matter, of no concern to the European Advisory Commission; the zones should be determined by the position of troops at the time of Germany's defeat. A good idea, possibly, if one could have been sure the Russians weren't going to get very far west; but the idea was certainly carried forward now in a counterproductive way. The War Department blocked the dispatch of instructions to Winant until March 8; then he was sent a memorandum and sketch maps produced by the Joint Chiefs. It proposed a much reduced Soviet zone and a vast U.S. zone, whose frontiers touched Berlin, Leipzig and Bayreuth.

The American delegation was bewildered by this proposal. Kennan wrote: "The eastern border of this zone, so far as we could reconstruct it from the cryptic description given, was one that made no sense at all. It cut, apparently without rhyme or reason, across geographic and administrative boundaries. Since it failed to extend as far as the Czechoslovak frontier, there was left an entire area the intended disposition of which was unclear." Washington had sent no arguments to persuade the Russians to accept a boundary so much less advantageous to themselves than the one they had already agreed to with the British. The plan was not, it seems, put to the British or Russians, Kennan with Winant's military adviser flew to Washington to try to straighten out the confusion and gain a coherent and defensible point of view. Kennan went to the White House, where the President said with a laugh that the Joint Chiefs' proposal was "just something I once drew on the back of an envelope"—apparently while en route to the Cairo Conference. Roosevelt, according to Kennan, was more concerned at that point as to whether the British or Americans would get the northernmost of the two Western zones.

FDR, in any event, said he would deal with the mixup. On May 1 Winant was instructed to approve the boundaries of the Eastern zone as proposed by the British and accepted by the Soviets. The result was forthcoming in the London Protocol of September 14, 1944, which laid down the specifications for the Soviet zone of occupied Germany. It was to be

The territory of Germany (including the province of East Prussia) situated to the east of a line drawn from a point on Lübeck Bay where the frontiers of Schleswig-Holstein and Mecklenburg meet, along the western frontier of Mecklenburg to the province of Hanover, thence along the eastern frontier of Hanover to the frontier of Brunswick, thence along the western frontier of the Prussian province of Saxony to the western frontier of Anhalt; thence along the western frontier of Anhalt; thence along the western frontier of the Prussian province of Saxony and the western frontier of Thuringia to where the latter meets the Bavarian border; thence eastwards along the northern border of Bavaria to the 1937 Czechoslovak frontier . . . with the exception of the Berlin area, for which a special system of occupation is provided below.

According to Strang, "the western boundary of the Soviet zone was agreed upon without great difficulty"—at least, one assumes, as far as the Russians were concerned. He wrote, in his memoir *Home and Abroad*: "It is often asked why the limits of the Soviet zone . . . were set so far to the west." The answers he gave were several. The European Advisory Commission began meeting six months before D-Day. No one had any idea at the time that Western armies would necessarily get deep into Germany. Some thought, in fact, that the Russians might control all Germany up to the Rhine. Others thought that the Russians might not enter Germany at all but stop at its eastern borders, perhaps concluding a separate peace, and leaving the German Eastern Front armies free to help defend the Western Front—where static trench warfare might once again occur. And it was therefore politic to induce the Soviets to participate in the invasion of the German fatherland with consequent rewards. Few people, as Kennan later noted, understood Soviet ambitions.*

Strang thought the proposed British subdivision of the spoils "as fair as any"—and if it erred in generosity to the Soviet zone (which was to have 40 percent of the area of Germany, 36 percent of the population, and 33 percent of its productive resources), "this was in line with the desire of our military authorities, who had preoccupations about postwar shortages of manpower, not to take on a larger area of occupation than need be." There was also the possibility that the Soviet zone might be reduced in the east by postwar alterations in German territory in favor of Poland. Furthermore (wrote Strang), "had there been no agreement by the time the Western forces met the Soviet forces at Torgau on the Elbe in 1945, we and the Americans might then have negotiated a settlement fixing the Eastern boundary of our zones on the Elbe, over a hundred miles to the east of the line actually agreed upon; but Berlin, of which the Russians were in occupation, would then assuredly have remained a part of the Soviet zone and would not have come under joint administration." A basic element in the situation was the widespread hope of postwar collaboration with the Russians, a prospect in which a few people like George Kennan had less confidence but which persisted for several years, despite such

* The only way the present dividing line might have been drawn much farther east, beyond Berlin, would have been if the Allied Second Front in northern Europe had been launched earlier and the Western armies had made a much faster advance—and perhaps if there had been no demand for unconditional surrender, announced by Roosevelt at Casablanca (January 1943) and subscribed to by Stalin (May 1943), a peace treaty might have been concluded bringing the war with Germany to an end much sooner. But this notion leaves out various factors, including Hitler himself.

manifestations as the deliberate halting of the Soviet army outside Warsaw in the summer of 1944 while the Germans put down the Warsaw uprising. The Poles, then as now, could well compare their position to that
of Christ, crucified between two thieves. Certainly no one at the Lancaster
House meetings ever seemed to have suspected that the arguments and
deliberations of the commission were forming the structure of the postwar
world for the next forty or fifty years. In postwar Germany it was said of
the division: the Americans got the scenery, the French got the wine, the
British got the ruins, and the Russians got a blank page of history on
which to write what they wanted.

In fact, the British had put some historical thinking into their original
proposals with regard to the influence the proposed borders might have
on any tendencies to separatism that might develop in Germany after its
defeat. The British plan suggested boundaries that tried not to cut across
"areas in which local autonomous movements are likely to take place."
There was hope that if old provincial borders were followed, centrifugal
and decentralizing forces in Germany would be encouraged. "Any such
movements will, however, almost certainly be based on the revival of old
loyalties to States and Provinces with certain natural internal boundaries
dictated by geography, history and economic considerations . . . An anti-
Prussian bias may well develop in certain areas, and there are strong
grounds for weakening the present preponderance of Prussia."

The idea for the line suggested as the western border of the Soviet
zone went back a long way. In many respects it matched the line, following the Elbe, that was reached by the first great Christianizing wave to
flow over middle Europe and that became the eastern frontier of Charlemagne's empire. Beyond it the Slav tribes awaited future missionaries and
colonizing princes. On each side of this line were different systems of land
tenure: large manor-ruled estates in the east, smaller holdings in the west.
And there also came to be a religious split. Golo Mann, the historian son of
Thomas Mann, writes: "Since the eastward-looking, newly German or
colonial parts of Germany—Brandenburg, Pomerania and Prussia—became
Protestant while the old Empire to the South and West remained pre-
dominantly Catholic, the Reformation once again strengthened the dividing line between the two regions of Germany." At the time of Napoleon,
the line was re-emphasized, with a zone on one side strongly influenced by
the French and that on the other by the Russians.

That the division lies atavistically deep is suggested by the possibly fabu-
lous account of Konrad Adenauer, the Rhinelander who became postwar
Chancellor of West Germany, going as a young deputy by train to the

between-the-wars Weimar parliament. As his sleeping car crossed the Elbe, Adenauer was allegedly heard to turn restlessly in his berth and mutter, "*Ach*, Asia."

On April 24, 1945, Hitler asked his minions: "Is it not possible that any day now, any hour, war may break out between the Bolsheviks and the Anglo-Saxons over their prey, Germany?" Although this prophecy of divergences between the Allies was soundly based, it did not come to pass early enough to help the Führer.

When the war ended, two weeks later, the Western armies were deep in what was to be the Soviet zone. In the next few weeks a great number of Germans who had been living in Eastern Europe fled into the area occupied by Anglo-American forces, and halted their flight there. They did not know of the London Protocol, and had only a few days' notice of the withdrawal of the Western Allied troops into their own zones. On July 1 Truman and Stalin agreed in an exchange of telegrams to the pulling back of the Western armies. Many of the refugee Germans suddenly had to move westward once more.

Yet for a while the border between East and West was porous—and just as well, since millions of Germans continued to be on the move. Their movement westward had begun before the approaching wave of Russian armies. It is reckoned that up to the time of the Potsdam Conference in July-August 1945 some 4 million Germans had left their Eastern homes. At Potsdam, the United States, Britain and the Soviet Union agreed that a great deal of former German territory east of the Oder-Neisse rivers should be put under Polish administration. The USSR had seized roughly 200,000 square kilometers of eastern Poland in 1939 and now favored compensating Poland with ex-German territory, comprising East Prussia, Silesia and parts of Pomerania and Brandenburg, all of which land had been inhabited by Germans for many centuries.

The Potsdam Protocol also recognized the necessity of a "transfer" of Germans who had been living in Poland, Czechoslovakia and Hungary. But it scarcely legitimized what happened next—the expulsion of more than 5.5 million Germans living in the former German territories east of the Oder-Neisse line, and 3.5 million Sudeten Germans from Czechoslovakia. Thus, including those who had fled before the Russian armies, 13 million Germans were shunted west, leaving most of their possessions behind. It is thought that more than a million died during this forced migration. History took its revenge for the long German thrust for *Lebens-*

raum in the East, and for Nazi treatment of the Slavs as slave peoples. The majority of the German refugees from the East tried to reach the Western zones of Germany, as did many Germans from the zone they now saw being occupied by the Soviet armies. There was an additional severe strain on the resources of the Western zones, where food, clothing and housing were hard to find. In June 1946 the Allied Control Council acceded to a Soviet request and issued an order "closing" the zonal border between East and West. But this order did not have much effect at first, since the border was unfenced, and crossing from the Soviet to the Western zones was primarily a matter of evading border guards.

In some places the flow from East to West ran fiercely. Helmstedt, a small mining and market town on the main autobahn from Hanover to Berlin, now found itself on the frontier between the British and Soviet zones. Roughly 5 million people are believed to have come west in this vicinity in the two years after the war, nearly half of them in a clandestine way.

In postwar Europe the increasing chilliness that eventually gelled into the Cold War was several years in being fully felt. Many were relieved at the end of the conflict in 1945, and closed their eyes to the fact that the USSR now controlled all of Europe east of the Elbe and the Alps; that, as Hugh Seton-Watson put it, "the danger which all the great wars since the sixteenth century [and until the twentieth century] had been fought to prevent had come to pass." Field Marshal Jan Smuts, Churchill's great South African friend, ignored Churchill's Fulton speech when he said the following October, "There is no fundamental dividing line between East and West." Churchill and Stalin had met in Moscow in October 1944, with Averell Harriman as the American observer, and had agreed to a division of interest in the postwar Balkans. In Rumania, Russia had 90 percent, the Allies 10 percent. In Greece, the Allies had 90 percent, Russia 10 percent. In Bulgaria, Russia had 75 percent, the Allies 25 percent. In Hungary and Yugoslavia the interests were ascribed 50-50. Czechoslovakia and Poland, for which Britain had gone to war, were absent from the agreement. But if the Allies had retained any illusions that these divisions of interest might actually moderate the Soviet appetite for satellite states, they were soon shattered, though the Soviets tightened their hold at different times. In Rumania the Communists took over in February 1945. Hungary had a fairly free election in November 1945, and a coalition government was formed, but by 1948 the Communist party had taken over and established a monopoly. In Poland the Soviets at once installed their own client Poles as a Communist regime. Czechoslovakia, like Hungary, had a three-year period of reprieve before the Communist Party took full control. Finland and Rumania were forced to cede land to the Soviet Union. The Baltic states of Lithuania, Estonia and Latvia, together with the eastern parts of Poland gobbled up in 1939, remained within the newly expanded Soviet empire. The USSR exacted heavy reparations from Rumania, Finland, Hungary, Bulgaria, and of course Germany.

When a theater curtain falls, the action stops, the actors walk away, the stage darkens. Here, perhaps, it might have been more like a movie that suddenly froze still—and the projector made only infrequent, unexpected jerks forward thereafter. As the Soviet grip tightened, the United States felt the need to re-engage its interests in Europe. Truman announced an aid plan for Turkey and Greece in March 1947, and this was soon followed by General Marshall's speech at Harvard announcing a massive program of assistance for those European countries that wanted it. The leaders of many East European countries might have wanted the aid but had to decline it. Czechoslovakia accepted an invitation to the conference called to discuss the plan but then backed out. The Communist Information Bureau, or Cominform, was established by Moscow in September 1947 to counter any Westernizing tendencies and provide a structure within which the countries of Eastern Europe could adapt to Russian hegemony.

In Germany, cooperation between the victors did not last long after the war. Among the divisive elements were the Soviet Union's insistence on stern reparations and a regime of its own choosing in the Eastern zone. Soviet-owned corporations were set up at the same time as Russia continued to dismantle large sections of East German industry, which were shipped to the USSR. The Social Democratic Party was forced to merge with the Communist Party into a Socialist Unity Party, the SED. This received the majority of votes cast in 1946 Soviet-zone elections, the last in which East Germans had a free choice of fairly independent parties. Although the SED proclaimed the desirability of a unified German democratic state, and Stalin for a while gave the impression of favoring a united Germany, his track record in Eastern Europe now made it clear that the Soviet Union intended to have a Communist East German state which it could dominate.

Among the Western powers, France—with a zone in West Germany and a sector of West Berlin—was strongly opposed to the creation of a central government in the western half of Germany and used its veto powers to prevent the establishment of such a central administration. However, political parties were founded, and in 1946-1947, elections took place for *Land* parliaments. In 1947 the U.S. and British zones were merged into one economic area, and councils dealing with the economy and administration became the foundation of a parliament and executive for West Germany. In March 1948 the Soviet Union pulled out of the Allied Control Council; with all hope abandoned of working out the future of Germany in hand with the Russians, the Western powers proposed that a national assembly be set up to work out a constitution for a West German state. Currency reforms were introduced in the Western zones, without consultation with the Soviets. At the same time, the Western powers signed a treaty in Brussels providing for mutual aid against aggression; this led, a year later, to the setting up of the North Atlantic Treaty Organization. But in spring 1948 these steps spurred the Soviet leadership into angry response—a blockade of the Western sectors of Berlin. As the blockade hardened, with all land links cut between the Western zones and the city, 120 miles to the east, the Allies were forced to airlift in the necessities of life to keep their parts of Berlin going. For ten months two million West Berliners were sustained in this way; it was probably not the ground that any Western leader would have chosen for such a battlefield, but once pushed to it, the Allies made it a sticking point. In May 1949 the Soviet Union called off the blockade. Later that year there came into force the Basic Law of the Federal Republic of Germany, by which a West German state was established; the first elections for the Bundestag, the Federal parliament, were held on August 14. In October, to the accompaniment of accusations that West German political parties had betrayed the cause of German unity, the German Democratic Republic had its foundation ceremonies in East Berlin. There would be two Germanys henceforth.

Two particular dates are significant in the ensuing history of the border between East and West Germany. They are May 26, 1952, and August 13, 1961. On the first, the East German government began to barricade the border. Otto Grotewohl's regime announced that a ten-meter-wide "control strip" would be constructed along the entire border, backed to the east by a five-hundred-meter-wide "protective strip" and a five-kilometer-deep "forbidden zone," to be entered only by those with a special pass. Fields in the protective strip were only to be worked in daylight hours; next to the border, all labor was to be supervised by guards. Barbed-wire

fencing began to rise. The DDR government decreed: "Crossing the ten-
meter control strip is forbidden for all persons. . . . Weapons will be used
in case of failure to observe the orders of the border patrols."

The reasons for these measures were spelled out for the East German
public. They were needed, Grotewohl said, to protect the DDR from
"spies, diversionists, terrorists, and smugglers"—all of whom were apparently crossing the border from west to east in increasing numbers. But
few Westerners doubted that the real reason was to prevent what the
DDR authorities termed "flight from the republic"—a crime which hundreds of thousands of East Germans had committed, or were premedi-
tating. In the following months, some eight thousand residents of the
border areas who were termed "unreliable" were removed from their homes
and resettled in places farther away from the border; protests led in some
instances to resistance which was overcome by the People's Police.

Yet in the West at this time—during the last months of Stalin's life
and the first year or so of leadership by his successors—there was some
belief in Soviet minds that the USSR might accept internationally supervised free elections for all of Germany, that Moscow might go along with
a reunited, neutral Germany. But this was never tested to find out if it
was merely a ploy. Certainly, for the next nine years a large loophole
to the West remained in Berlin. Here thousands of daily comings and
goings went on between the Western and Eastern sectors of the city.
Many people lived on one side and worked on the other. Transit facilities
and utilities remained intermingled and interdependent. Although inter-
ruptions and restrictions were gradually introduced—on telephone lines
and bus services; on the number of street crossings; and on access from
the Western sectors to surrounding East German territory by the building
of a fence and mined strip—the overground S-Bahn and underground
U-Bahn railway lines remained open, and refugees from East Germany
could make their way into West Berlin among commuters and shoppers.
Some of the impatience East Germans felt with the increasing severities of
their regime and the spartan way of life imposed on them was manifested
in an uprising on June 17, 1963—a revolt mostly of workers in East Berlin,
quelled by Soviet troops. Many of the people who continued to leave for
the West, via West Berlin, were those East Germany could least afford
to see go: skilled workers, engineers, designers, doctors. From the setting
up of the Federal Republic in 1949 to August 12, 1961, 2.8 million East
Germans fled from the DDR; throughout the 1950s roughly 19,000 escaped into West Berlin every month. On August 13, 1961, the East German government took the ultimate step of sealing off the exits: West
Berlin was completely divided from East Berlin and East Germany. And

thus the life blood that had been pouring from the veins of the East German state was reduced to a barely visible trickle. Though now, when it was visible, it could often be seen to be real human blood, spilt at fence or wall.

Peter Lemke and I stood for a while at the border by the white house where the road crosses into East Germany. Opposite the house, by the roadside, stood a tall stone, megalithic in appearance, with the name SCHLUTUP incised in it, and below the name of the town, the inscription GETRENNT 1945— ; in other words, "Divided in 1945." The date of reunion has been left open.

We could hear dogs barking—*their* dogs, Lemke said, kept in kennels near the East German checkpoint and brought out in teams from time to time to guard stretches of the border near here. Next to the fence on the Western side was a neatly tended garden, belonging to the last in a line of small well-kept houses. Lemke said, "The people who own the garden are glad they have neighbors on one side only."

It was ten-thirty in the morning. The sun was shining, everything seemed peaceful; it could have been a country road anywhere. A faint wind in the trees, a few blackbirds singing. There was little traffic: a single big Polish truck passed, going east; a solitary car with West German plates coming back from East Germany. In the little headquarters office of the West German control point we talked to the BGS noncom in charge, Oberstaffmeister Poser. He told me that there was generally a tide of traffic flowing into East Germany in the early mornings and back again in the evenings, composed for the most part of people making short trips to visit relatives over there. In the height of summer it could be busy all day long with tourists traveling on their way to Poland and Berlin, or to catch ferries from the DDR to Scandinavia. At the East German checkpoint a quarter of a mile down the road, just out of sight behind the trees, the control procedure was strict; sometimes it took an hour and a half to get through the vehicle inspection and documents check. "Some West Germans are not very good at accepting this," said Herr Poser. "Sometimes they protest and argue, and are sent back. Sometimes on the way back they stop here and open their hearts to the first person they meet. They may have strayed off the transit route and been fined by the East German police. They may have had a present confiscated by the border guards. Sometimes they say, 'This is my last trip over there, damn it.' But of course they go again."

On this side the BGS are chiefly interested in drivers having the correct documents and in the roadworthiness of some of the East European trucks, particularly the state of their tires and whether they are overloaded. The Zoll officials are concerned as to whether returning West Germans have more than their duty-free allowance of spirits and tobacco after stocking up in the East German Intershops (one of which is situated at the DDR checkpoint here) where such goods, which have to be purchased with hard currency, are cheap by West German standards.

I asked Herr Poser if he ever talked to his East German counterpart, whom he said he had never seen.

"Every day," he said, patting one of two telephones on his desk. "This is for emergencies only. There are a dozen or so of these telephones along the border so that we can make contact if there is an accident, or something like a forest fire. We test the line once a day to see that it's working properly. Our conversation is very formal and correct, limited more or less to the words needed to say 'Yes, I can hear you.' Though since last September they've been replying to our calls with 'Good morning,' which is an improvement."

One such call last year was because an East German dog—a German shepherd—had turned up here at the checkpoint, dragging a broken chain. It was not given asylum. A phone call to the East German checkpoint brought a pair of *Aufklärer*, the specially trained East German border reconnaissance troops, to the road border crossing, where the dog was handed back to them.

"We're still waiting for the reward," said Herr Poser with a smile.

Lemke and I went next to a house several hundred meters back along the road toward Schlutup. Here we talked to a cheerful middle-aged lady, Frau Wally Hanson. She was wearing a green overall coat and was cleaning house, but she led us to a shed attached to her husband Gerhardt's workshop, where she stores various items that the East Germans refuse to allow travelers from the West to take in. What began as a favor for one person, who was in distress when turned back with a record player, has become a service that people have to resort to nearly every day. The BGS, Zoll and local garages usually send them to her. Some of the items they have when turned back are too large for the shed. A windsurfer, which the East German officials obviously thought might be used for a Baltic escape, lay on the grass behind a nearby garage. In the shed, among Frau Hanson's store of fresh eggs and a pinball machine her husband was planning to repair, were such things as a new bicycle (one is not allowed to ride into the DDR on a bike or enter it on foot), a radiotelephone, two antique oil lamps, several dozen beer glasses with brewery labels on them, and ten tomato plants. Frau Hanson said, pointing to a kitchen-counter unit, "That had a double sink in it, which they allowed in. But they wouldn't let in the wooden counter unit. There's no telling what they will say okay to and what they will reject. They've let in a Siamese cat but turned away a canary."

According to Frau Hanson, people who are refused entry because of such possessions aren't always ready to give up at the first attempt. One man going over with his wife not long ago to attend a niece's confirmation was refused permission to take in an expensive tape recorder. He returned to the Hansons', emptied out clothes from a suitcase on one of the benches, put the tape recorder in the suitcase, returned to the checkpoint and made a successful entry into the DDR. Some people who are told they have too many new clothes with them—obviously intended as gifts for friends and relatives in the DDR—return to the Hansons' and put them on in several layers under whatever they are wearing.

Frau Hanson has by now a vicarious knowledge of the East German checkpoint and those who man it. Her guests, as she thinks of the people who leave things with her, have told her about many of the East German checkpoint personnel. "That Tamara—she's a tough one," she says—Tamara being one woman official whose reputation for absolute diligence has earned her this Russian nickname. Frau Hanson generally charges her guests a nominal fee of one mark per item, but some people insist she take a larger sum. Some, who come after dark or before daylight, have left things on the back step with a note and a coin rather than wake her. The canary that was left fared well, since the Hansons also have a canary. Most of those who leave things pick them up again on their return journey, but sometimes they return by a different route or simply forget that they have left things there. After a decent interval of a year or so, Frau Hanson gives clothes to charities and disposes of other items at church sales. Between such times, what with stuff that is currently stored there or has been forgotten, the shed resembles a small museum of odd objects, curiosities that the Iron Curtain has not let through.

Lemke and I drove on through Schlutup and turned south. In five minutes we reached the village of Eichholz, with suburban houses scattered among trees. A lane led past houses to a field where a young woman was picking dandelions. Beyond was a copse, more thickly planted with trees. The way the lane would have taken into it was barred by a horizontal red-and-white-painted pole, and just beyond this stood the border markers and signs. A small brook ran through the copse. I could make out, thirty meters or so away, the DDR fence. One of the signs said ZONENGRENZE, the term, dating from the occupation period, that still appears on roughly one sign in ten. Another sign said AUCH DRÜBEN IST DEUTSCHLAND (There, too, is Germany) and on its reverse side, which anyone standing in the DDR would more easily read, EINIGKEIT UND RECHT UND FREIHEIT FÜR DAS DEUTSCHE VATERLAND, the words that begin the German national anthem. Lemke said that in October 1980 a captain of the DDR border troops came over the border at this spot, carrying his rifle and field equipment— he had told his men to let him through a gate in the fence and then rushed over into West Germany.

As we stood there, leaning on the barrier pole, looking at where the former lane was being grown over with grass and weeds, listening to the brook ripple over the stones, one of the bushes parted—its branches waved and a green shape rose out of it with what for an instant looked like a single eye. This cyclopean figure, dressed in combat gear, was a member of the *Aufklärer*, DDR border reconnaissance troops. The eye, pointed at Lemke and me, was the telescopic lens of a 35mm Praktika camera. And with this the military scout proceeded to stand and photograph us. The camera made a little whirr as the shutter operated and the film moved on. Lemke straightened up, put his peaked uniform cap at a jaunty rake and gave a broad smile for the camera. "He's delighted to see you here," Lemke said. "He'll get good marks for this—reporting a new face, someone in civilian clothes at the border. They'll start a file on you. I just wonder how they manage to store all the film they shoot."

The *Aufklärer* must have taken a dozen snaps of us. When Lemke brought out a camera of his own and aimed it, the soldier quickly moved back to the bush he had come from and stood half concealed, his back to us, writing in a notebook. In his notes, I imagined, was the word "*Engländer . . .*"

Lemke said, "He probably has a companion hidden in the undergrowth. They invariably work in twos or threes—keeping an eye on one another, since they do most of their work this side of their fence. They don't trust us, and they don't trust one another."

It was a few minutes before I got over the strange feeling of this encounter—a feeling that resulted, I thought, from not being regarded as of quite the same species as the man who had been observing me. As we left, Lemke said "*Auf Wiedersehen*" to the *Aufklärer*, still standing behind his bush. There was no reply.

3. ABSENT FRIENDS

drove to Hamburg to spend the night and talk to some people who work there. On the autobahn from Lübeck it was a fast run, angling southeastward from the border; Hamburg itself is about fifty-five kilometers due west of the border. Its own inclinations, however, are more to the north, west and south, since it is a great port attached by the river Elbe to the North Sea, and to the rest of West Germany by rail, road, canal and air. There is little sense of the border being not far away—even the occasional road sign saying BERLIN seems unexceptional, no different from signs pointing the way to Hanover, Bremen, Kiel and Lübeck. Hamburg was booming, at least to the extent that all its hotels were full. But I found shelter at the Katholische Akademie, a modern hostel near the waterfront, where I was given a suite more spacious than I've ever had in a hotel. A modern wrought-iron crucifix hung over my bed, perhaps to guard me from the temptations of Hamburg's notorious port district, the Reeperbahn, not far away along the Ost-West Strasse.

As it was, I had prior engagements. I took a highway east to Aumühle, a village about twenty kilometers from the border, for tea with the Gruners. Theo Gruner is a lawyer, his wife Sybille a government official, both in their mid-forties. Theo was born on a farm in Thuringia that was briefly in American army hands in 1945 before the U.S. forces had to withdraw from the Soviet zone. Neither he nor any of his family (who left when the Americans did) have ever gone back to it. The Gruners live in an elegant contemporary house, the furniture a thoughtful mixture of up-to-date design and antiques collected in several European countries; it would have been hard to tell, without looking closely at magazines, papers and books that lay around, that the house was in Germany. Nearby is the wooded Bismarck estate, Friedrichsruh, the country retreat of the Iron Chancellor, who unified Germany for the first time, in 1871. There, like royalty, he had his own private station for trains to stop at. The mansion was bombed during the war, and a present generation of Bismarcks live in a new house on the grounds, which form a great park for the locality. Few in Aumühle seem bothered by the nearness of the border. Theo Gruner said with a shrug, "If the Russians invaded, their tanks would be here in less than an hour."

But if the Gruners don't find it worthwhile to worry about the border, they and some others do think often of what is beyond it. Sybille Gruner said, "I believe we have to make a special effort to stay in contact with the East Germans. If we don't, one day there won't be a German nation anymore." I had thought of Germany, divided, united; but the "German nation"—this was new, but heard now not for the last time.

There have been several stages in the postwar relations between East and West Germany that are handily illustrated by the ability of Germans (mostly from the West) to move back and forth between the two states. From the start East Germany has treated with extreme disfavor the idea of its own citizenry visiting the West. The right to leave the DDR, which is stated in the 1949 constitution, is missing in the constitution of 1968, where the citizen's freedom of movement is confined to the area within the state. Those who have been allowed to leave for good, or for a visit, have generally been men over sixty-five and women over sixty—in other words, retired people, who are no longer producing any benefit for the state. If they care to stay in the West, so much the better, since the DDR will not have to pay them pensions. Other exceptions are sometimes made for younger people who have what are called "urgent family grounds"—births, marriages, silver and golden wedding anniversaries, critical illness and death—for visiting close relatives in West Germany. (This list was expanded in February 1982 to include confirmations, first communions and various significant birthdays, in old age, of immediate relatives.) There are also frequent exceptions for trusted party members and for privileged athletes and artists, singers, film directors and writers, whose work or performances abroad acquires prestige and hard currency for the DDR; and for some who have more down-to-earth occupations, too, such as barge crewmen, train personnel and truckdrivers taking cargoes to or from the West (and whose wives and children are safely left behind, almost as hostages, in East Germany).

Theo Gruner said, "There was a long period in the 1960s when even East German pensioners found it hard to get permission to come over here. The DDR was upset by the fact that West Germany wouldn't recognize it as a state in its own right. In those days, journeys into East Germany were difficult and uncertain. There were long queues at the few crossing points. Only West Germans who had close relatives over there were given DDR entry permits, after their relatives had applied to their local police for permission for them to come."

At the beginning of the next decade, however, the Bonn government under Chancellor Willy Brandt announced that it was willing to talk with the DDR on the basis that the DDR was one of two German states. And while Brandt was setting out new principles for intra-German relations and talking with Willi Stoph, chairman of the DDR Council of Ministers, the four powers (United States, Britain, France and Soviet Union), after what had been more or less a twenty-year hiatus, began negotiations on the situation of Berlin. On September 3, 1971, they arrived at the Quadripartite Agreement. This confirmed the ties between West Germany and West Berlin, and assured unimpeded travel between the two for West Berliners, West Germans, and foreigners with transit visas. East Germany three months later signed with West Germany a transit agreement with the same assurances, and in 1972 two further treaties were signed, dealing with travel to East Germany and intrastate relations. In 1974 the two states exchanged permanent representatives, who were not quite ambassadors. In 1975 the Helsinki Agreement helped create an additional framework for less rigid relations and a somewhat more permeable curtain. Application procedures for West Germans wanting to visit East Germany were simplified. Distant relatives, and not just close ones, were allowed to make visits, and so were plain friends; holidays and camping trips in the DDR were permitted for West Germans, as they were for visitors from foreign countries. East German pensioners now got permission to make several trips west a year rather than just one, up to a total (this was unchanged) of thirty days. The result, in 1979, was that there were 3.6 million visits from West to East Germany, 3.1 million from West Berlin to East Berlin or East Germany, and nearly 19 million trips made by travelers between West Berlin and the West.

"Everything looked more and more rosy until October 1980," Theo went on, accepting (as I had just done) a slice of a strawberry *Torte* from his wife. "The day after our federal election the DDR government raised the amount of money which we are compelled to exchange into DDR marks when there. This had been 13 Deutschmarks a day for adults—old people and children being exempt. The new amount was DM 25 per day for everybody. It had the effect of reducing the one-day visitor traffic by sixty percent in the first month, and by about half thereafter. Now people aren't visiting their East German relatives so often, they're leaving the children at home or they are making shorter trips."

Another category of travel is the so-called Near Border Traffic, by which West Germans living in a region roughly fifty kilometers wide next to the border are allowed to make day visits to friends or relatives in the similar zone in the DDR, the theory being that such people are likely to have connections close by the border on the other side from whom they have been parted. To make such a visit—up to nine are permitted every three months—a form must be obtained from one's local town hall, filled out and sent to the DDR, where it has to be approved and stamped by the police in the place one intends to visit. Overnight stays aren't allowed on such visits, and this makes it difficult for those who want to attend, say, a full-blast celebration of a marriage or anniversary. One may drive in one's own car, or take trains and buses which operate for the purpose from ten towns along the border.

Although it is well within the average range of this border zone, Hamburg is not part of the Near Border Traffic program—presumably because the East Germans didn't want to allow such privileges to the 1.7 million people living in the Hamburg metropolitan area. As it is, the West German border zone includes about one fifth of the territory of the Federal Republic and some 7 million people. In 1979 more than 400,000 West Germans availed themselves of the right to make such a short and near visit. There is one restriction for those whose friends or relatives live in the DDR five-kilometer protective zone, where only those East Germans with special registration passes are allowed: the meeting has to take place at a spot farther east, outside the protective zone. The West German government puts out a great deal of literature about travel to East Germany—pamphlets that list all the rules and regulations, the ins and outs, and which are probably helpful to many, but also, I suspect, because they list so comprehensively all the difficulties, are occasionally off-putting.

Apart from the nine road crossing points, there are today eight rail crossings of the border, two waterways for barge traffic, and three air transit corridors between West Germany and West Berlin. Other sorts of links have also been improved in the last ten years or so. The number of

telephone lines has been more than quadrupled between West Germany
and East Germany. Every day about 35,000 calls are made to East Germany. Every year some 75 million letters go from the Federal Republic to
the DDR, and some 100 million in the opposite direction. More parcels
go from west to east than vice versa.

I had dinner with Bernhardt and Emilie Fischer, friends of the Gruners',
in Reinbek, a village between Aumühle and Hamburg. It was hospitality
to a complete stranger, but I felt that it was the sort of thing the Fischers
liked doing. Their house was bigger and older than the Gruners', with a
nice touch of disorder that presumably came from their several small
children. Bernhardt Fischer is in his early forties, square-faced, firm-jawed—
a face you might have thought belligerent until you saw his warm eyes.
He is a senior officer in the Hamburg city government. Two facts he con-
siders important about himself are that his father was killed during World
War II and that as a student, in 1955, he biked around England and got
a tremendous welcome from all sorts of people who didn't know him. In
1976 Bernhardt came to the conclusion—it was almost like a religious
conversion—that more than governmental efforts were needed to bridge
the divide between East and West Germany.

He had no relatives or friends there. He knew that even among those
West Germans who did, the ties were slipping as families aged and close
relations died. Where people had once had brothers or sisters there, they
might now have first or second cousins. Bernhardt at any rate decided to
put into effect his own *Ostpolitik*. He set about it by asking people in
Hamburg whether they knew someone in East Germany who might welcome visitors from the West, who would be prepared to go through the
procedure of inviting him and his wife and sign the necessary forms. In
1976 he made the right contacts, and since then he has made by car at
least two trips a year to the DDR; he feels the importance of speaking
with and being with people, not just sending them parcels or paying income tax which his government may use in various ways to help East
Germans. Because of his position as a city executive he has to make a
pledge, before going to the DDR, that he will not divulge any important
municipal information.

"Now my best friends are in the DDR," Bernhardt said. "When I am
with them we talk all the time. I sleep very little there. It is quite intense.
I realize that I should not be the one who starts talking about politics,
or keep asking them questions. But they ask me about politics and about
West German life, and they tell me about their lives. What they know

about us they have only from television—our television—which is often too highly colored, and which doesn't convey the basic matter of dull everyday existence."

The last time Bernhardt was there, visiting friends in Magdeburg, he told them about a trip he and Emilie had made a few months before to Israel. (Israel and Judaism are subjects somewhat frowned upon by the DDR regime.) On another occasion he talked to twenty students from a nearby technical college about a six-week tour of the United States he had made the previous summer, in company with an engineer, now living in Massachusetts, who had left East Germany via West Berlin in 1960. Bernhardt showed slides of the trip. His Magdeburg friends told him, "You are allowed to make journeys and we are not. Please go on making them and come here and talk to us about them."

"Private person talking to private person," said Bernhardt. "That is the most important thing."

For these visits the Fischers are willing to put up with a lot—with red tape and totalitarian practices at the border, and the nervousness. It is very organized, thorough and depressing. Like most West Germans who go to the DDR frequently, he has at this point an anthology of incidents that have occurred to him at the border. He generally brings in his own photographs, films and slides, and has as yet never been given any trouble by DDR border officials on this score, though he knows they may react in hostile fashion to magazines, newspapers and books—particularly, for some reason, paperbacks. On his first visit to the DDR, in 1976, he had with him a large illustrated book about Hamburg and declared it at the border checkpoint. A woman official, whom he considered good-looking (and therefore tended to feel would be sympathetic), glanced through the book and asked him to wait. She went off with the book. When she returned, twenty minutes later, she said she was sorry, but he couldn't take it in. "Why?" asked Bernhardt.

"Nothing to do with me," she said. "You can pick it up on your way back."

On a later visit he declared another book, *Days of Greatness*, by the German writer Walter Kempowski. The border official, this time male, read part of a page; he turned several pages and read some more. Bernhardt was getting worried. The official began to laugh. Bernhardt noted the number of the page he was reading. The official said, "All right, that's a book you can take in."

Back in the car, Bernhardt saw that on that particular page Kempowski had described a comic beer-drinking scene in Plattdeutsch, or Low German —a language, he was pleased to realize, that crossed the border.

On another occasion Bernhardt said anxiously to his wife, as they approached the border crossing, "Now for goodness' sake behave properly." When they got there, a DDR officer said "*Guten Tag.*" Emilie replied with a big smile, "Yes, it's a lovely day, isn't it?" And Bernhardt's heart pounded —she was being too friendly; they would be suspicious. Occasionally you encounter an official who looks at you in such a way that you know he's human. Mostly they are very coolly correct. They stare into the cars, counting to make sure that the number of passengers matches the number of documents, seeing that you aren't smuggling an extra person out of the DDR. An official snaps, "You have two children?"

"Yes, two children," replies Emilie.

"Two children?" asks the next official.

"Yes, two," says Emilie.

Before what she knew would be the fourth asking of the same question, Emilie says with obvious impatience, "Still only two children."

"*What do you mean*— 'Still only two children'!" The official is furious; no one is allowed to be angry with him.

But the fifth official admires her passport photo, which shows her smiling. It was taken in Denmark, she tells him.

"Ah, that must be a beautiful country," he says.

Bernhardt on that occasion was angry with her for upsetting the fourth official. "You never know what might happen if they arrested us," he said. His wife understands this. When Bernhardt goes alone to the DDR she worries about him; she knows how arbitrary they can be. Will he come back? It is the Iron Curtain. He may be somebody in Hamburg but at the border checkpoints he is just a single being. Will he have any influence against that system if they decide to move against him?

Once, on Bernhardt's way back, a DDR border official searched his wallet and found among other currency a single dollar bill. Bernhardt had forgotten he had this and had not included it on the list of money he had declared on entering the DDR. Now he realized that the single dollar was all they'd need if they wanted to seize him then and there.

"You have not declared this dollar . . ."

But nothing happened.

Another time at the border checkpoint a light went green, a barrier pole was raised and they drove forward. An official shouted and held up his arm for them to stop. "The light was red!" he said.

"The light was green," said Bernhardt, "and the pole went up . . ."

"Your papers," said the official.

He took away Bernhardt's driver's license, registration and passport. After twenty minutes he returned and told Bernhardt he had to pay a

10-mark fine. Bernhardt paid. What else was he to do? How else would he get his papers back?

He has swapped stories with other West German drivers, who have similar experiences and tell of being made to pay for minor infringements. Sometimes the East German police seem to lie in wait for West Germans, like Georgia police in speed traps set up for Florida-bound New Yorkers.

When you leave, searches sometimes include the X-raying of luggage. A long stick may be poked into the fuel tank to make sure that it hasn't been altered to provide hiding room for someone. The back seats are folded down for inspection, and the undercarriage examined with the aid of mirrors set in the road surface. It may take twenty minutes for such an inspection, twenty minutes' wait, and twenty minutes for passport control. In the summer, or on holidays, generally longer.

Many of the people Bernhardt knows over there, *drüben*, are Lutheran, as he is. The Lutheran services he has attended in the DDR are quite frequently more crowded than those in West Germany, though several of the ministers he knows there preach guardedly, as if not to antagonize the regime. But despite worries about going beyond the limits of the unwritten concordat with the state, the Lutheran Church in the DDR has recently been fairly outspoken about the all-prevalent militarism of East Germany, and has suggested, for instance, that community service form an alternative to conscription into the armed forces. The cost of building new churches in the DDR is met from contributions made by West German congregations, and a proportion of the salary of East German ministers is found in the same way. Even so, the ministers earn less than the average East German factory worker.

What worries East Germans most, said Bernhardt, is the simple fact that they can't get out if they want to. They might not want to live permanently in West Germany, but they resent not having the choice. Some would like the chance of experiencing for a little while at first hand the high standard of living in West Germany, which, in the abstract, they feel bound to despise. Bernhardt thinks that the majority of East Germans— if the Soviet army left—would demand a change of government the next day. They don't want to imitate the West, but they want to have a system and government of their own, not imposed by the Russians.

He says, "I share one ambition with my East German friends—that is, to make peace safe. Even so, when I am there I defend the system that gives us the opportunity to make mistakes and then to put them right."

Bernhardt feels, as do many West Germans, that there is more stress in his own part of Germany. Over there, in the DDR, people have closer contact with those who share the same sympathies and opinions. Friends really need their friends. People may help each other more because things are more difficult. Bernhardt knows one East German man, formerly a high agricultural official, who gave up his post a year or so ago. With his wife he is fixing up an old country house as a home for disturbed children. He has no income; he is using up his savings; his wife gets a small salary from a church organization she works for. The state, which suffers a shortage of facilities for such children, is giving them no help. However, a number of young people who live in the area are helping out. Bernhardt is impressed by this couple, who are doing something that would be laudable in West Germany but is exceptional in East Germany, where the state is expected to provide that sort of service and frowns on private interference. Bernhardt in fact seemed to think West Germans would be unlikely to act so altruistically, but I wondered later if he didn't feel a need to compensate for the good life in West Germany by ascribing greater virtue to those who grinned and bore it in the East.

Bernhardt is admired in his office for what he does, Emilie said. His colleagues sometimes ask, How did you get friends in East Germany, and can we do the same? Bernhardt tells them how to go about it. He gives them names and addresses. But they don't get around to it.

He says, "The feeling of connection between here and there is latent, not really alive, except for those who still have close relatives there. I'd say only one in twenty of West Germans have any real idea of what it's like over there. Of course, part of the trouble is that the East German government isn't interested in encouraging contact—rather the reverse. That's why they've increased the compulsory exchange for each day of a visit. Our government does its best with pamphlets and posters to promote knowledge of the DDR and visits to it, but in the end it's up to individuals to reach out and get to know individuals there. It's important to take one's children—to show the East Germans that 'capitalist' children are just like theirs. And our children learn. Our children write to theirs."

When they are in East Germany, Bernhardt and Emilie wear their simplest clothes. They don't want to come across as rich West Germans. "The West German high standard of living is part of the problem now, part of the division," he says, "though it may be leveling out a bit." It's still the case that one of the best things you can do for friends there is to give them Deutschmarks, which they can spend in the Intershops on hard-to-get items—though this may mean seeming like rich uncles. The Gruners told me that the best way to mail Western currency to East Germany was to wrap it in carbon paper inside the envelope so that it is hidden from detecting devices. Whether this is true, or an example of what West Germans think they must do to evade the barriers, I'm not sure. (Later, in Czechoslovakia, I was told that if I wanted to send someone there a paperback by, say, Solzhenitsyn, I should remove the front and back covers and glue the book inside the similar size covers of an innocuous work, like a historical novel or a mystery.)

Many of Bernhardt's recollections of his visits to East Germany have to do with cars. His Volvo station wagon arouses comment in a country where most people, if they have a car at all, feel fortunate to own an austere Trabant, for which there can be a five-year waiting list. On his first trip to Magdeburg, Bernhardt pulled up at the entrance of the drab apartment building where his friends live. He was greeted by their two small sons, whose first words were, "How do you get to have such a fine car?" Bernhardt replied, "When you're bigger perhaps you'll have a car like this." But he wasn't very happy with this answer.

On one occasion as he parked his car there, he saw a man get out of a nearby Trabant and proceed to unscrew his windshield wipers and lock them in the car. Bernhardt's host explained that the stealing of such parts was not thought of as genuine stealing. It is so difficult to get spare parts, and the state owns just about everything, discouraging private possessions—therefore stealing windshield wipers is like stealing from the state.

Bernhardt's host in Magdeburg formerly owned a twelve-year-old Wartburg. He kept it in the open parking lot nearby. Then he heard of a garage for sale five kilometers away and sold the Wartburg to buy the garage. This was a sensible move, Bernhardt's host explained, because although cars were hard to come by, garages were even more difficult to obtain. (To me Bernhardt says, "We take so much for granted here!")

I got the impression that Bernhardt and Emilie enjoyed their visits to the East partly because of this sort of shock, which among other things made them feel fortunate. But they also liked the intensity of conversations and experiences shared. It was as if they were undergraduates again, sitting up late to talk about God, creation and the destiny of mankind: What are we here for? And in other ways to visit East Germany was like going back a generation: steam locomotives on the railways; horse-drawn wagons on farms; coal dust in the streets. Emilie Fischer said, "I think I know now how Allied soldiers felt after the war, handing out cigarettes, toothpaste, chewing gum. We have things now. We take them there. Things like peppercorns. They have no flowers in their houses, though East Germany exports seeds to Holland. Last time we went, we took some bathroom tiles for our friends, who said they couldn't get any there. Bernhardt bought them here in Reinbek. The tiles had no mark of origin on them, but the shopkeeper said they came from the DDR."

When the Fischers return home, they don't stop thinking about their friends in Magdeburg. They write weekly. They send parcels containing chocolate, stockings, shoes, or things for carpentry, like nails. Their friends have a small ceremony when such a parcel arrives—they wait, even for a day or two, until they can get the whole family together. The parcel is then placed on the dining table, and one of the children is given the prized job of opening it, taking out each wrapped item in turn while everyone guesses whom it is for and what it might be.

Bernhardt arrived on a visit before learning about this procedure; he got to Magdeburg the same day as one of his parcels that he had mailed several weeks before. Because he wanted to know if everything had got through intact, he asked if it could be opened right away. His host agreed, but with a reluctance Bernhardt didn't understand. While they were examining the contents (and saw that all was there), his host's small daughter entered the room, looked at what they were doing and burst into tears. Bernhardt's host explained the situation: the parcels were like Christmas presents. So Bernhardt helped wrap things up again and re-tie the parcel, and the ceremony—only slightly dampened—was held the next day.

Some West Germans meet their East German relatives or friends on relatively neutral ground in one of the Eastern-bloc countries like Bulgaria, Rumania or Hungary, to which the East Germans are allowed to travel in tour groups for holidays. When the Gruners went to Budapest several years ago, they didn't have such a meeting in mind, though friendship with some East Germans was a result of the trip. Sybille Gruner asked at the desk of her hotel where she could get tickets for a concert that night; she was told that the only way was by making it worthwhile for someone in the concert-hall box office. At which point a man standing within earshot identified himself as a performer at the concert—a soloist from East Berlin—and offered to get some tickets for the Gruners. They found themselves in the best box in the house, sitting with the soloist's wife. Sybille Gruner's only worry was how they would be able to repay the East German couple—should they reimburse them for the tickets or take them out to dinner? Sybille knew that the East Germans were restricted in the amount of currency they could take out of the DDR. She knew that the generosity of West Germans may create problems. East Germans often feel bound to demonstrate that they aren't seeking West German acquaintance just because the West Germans are better off, and worry that the West Germans may think so. The reverse side of the problem is the embarrassment and guilt that West Germans feel about the East Germans, whom history seems to have made suffer a prolonged dictatorship, and in the postwar period much less good fortune.

In this case, as it happened, there was no cause for anxiety. The Gruners and the East German couple dined together at their local hotel after the concert, and were bound together in cordial detestation of the maître d', who announced when they were halfway through the meal that the restaurant was closing at once. They invited the musician and his wife to visit them in Aumühle whenever he made a trip to the West, and this they have done on several occasions. They have all become good friends.

The musician is one of the class of privileged East Germans who are permitted to make such trips, for professional purposes. Even then, there is no absolute assurance that an exit passport for travel in the west will be issued. On a recent trip the musician's wife learned only the day before her husband was to leave that she would be allowed to accompany him to France and Germany. They, like the Fischers, drive a Volvo—it is one of a thousand that East Germany has imported, and which fairly celebrated people can obtain. On several occasions when the musician has been driving on West German roads, people—seeing a Volvo with DDR plates— have shaken their fists or made rude gestures at him, presumably because they think he is a Communist *apparatchik*—or perhaps because they resent the fact that food parcels and other forms of help are being sent to East Germans who aren't allowed to leave and here is one driving through West Germany in an expensive car. According to Theo and Sybille Gruner, the musician and his wife do not feel uneasy about their special privileges, though others in their circumstances are known to. He plays about twice a year in the West and is allowed to keep in Western currency 20 percent of his earnings—with this he buys, among other things, toys and clothes for his children. His wife doesn't work, which is unusual in East Germany. His children will be going to school wearing Western clothes—looking different from their classmates, who will be outfitted in the modest, recognizable range of East German children's clothing. The Gruners wonder what problems are hereby being stored up. They don't yet feel they know the East German couple well enough to ask.

On their last visit to the West, when they stayed a night with the Gruners in Aumühle, the musician and his wife asked if they could go to one of the louder, more garish nightspots in the Reeperbahn. It wouldn't have been the Gruners' choice, but they could see how living in puritan East Berlin one might get to want such a thing. Anyway, the evening was a success. They've all agreed to go there again the next time the East Germans come west.

4. SALT ROAD

I got up at six-thirty, too early for breakfast at the Katholische Akademie, and set forth for Ratzeburg. This is an old town, smack on the border, twenty kilometers south of Lübeck. People are at work early in West Germany—most offices open at eight and I had to battle out of Hamburg against the incoming traffic. But when I reached the Schleswig-Holstein countryside it was a gentle morning with hazy sunshine. The land was flat at first, almost Dutch. Trees along the edges of watery fields stood in folds of mist. The light was of the pink-gold sort one sees in the paintings of Caspar David Friedrich, the early-nineteenth-century German artist—a light which seemed a little at odds with the fact that the fields were a particularly vivid green. The border came down the east side of a long lake, the Ratzeburger See, and Ratzeburg itself stood on a hilly island at the south end, joined by causeways to the surrounding land, the kind of place that would have been a good subject for woodcut illustrations of Grimms' fairy tales.

I parked the car on the edge of town and walked through quiet cobbled streets to the marketplace. This was surrounded by small shops that seemed prosperous enough, despite the border and the consequent loss of trade from much of the town's hinterland. I had coffee and a doughnut for my postponed breakfast, and then made my way to the north end of the island where Ratzeburg Cathedral stands in a grassy park. Since it was too early for the cathedral to be open, I had to be satisfied with the exterior of the squat Romanesque brick building, which Henry the Lion, Duke of Saxony and Bavaria, caused to be put up in the twelfth century. An old graveyard lay next to the cathedral, full of long wet grass. There was a view northward over the lake: small boats moored to finger piers; camping trailers and holiday caravans parked in a distant field; ducks gliding in on the calm waters.

In 1945 the border ran right through Ratzeburg. The cathedral, like the white house on the road outside Schlutup, was in Mecklenburg. But the local British and Soviet commanders decided to make their own on-the-spot interpretation of the London Protocol, to leave Ratzeburg in one piece inside the British zone and compensate the Soviets with territory outside town. It was one of several such exchanges along the border, by which 12,000 acres of the British zone were swapped for 6,500 acres of the Soviet zone, for the purpose of making local communications on both sides work more smoothly, as they certainly wouldn't have if the old border had been insisted on. Even so, looking on a map today at the border's contortions as it snakes around Ratzeburg and goes through all sorts of bends and bulges to the east of town, you wouldn't think much border rationalizing had been achieved. Many people who fled from Mecklenburg to the West in the early postwar years meet in Ratzeburg every May. They attend a service in the cathedral, eat, drink, dance, sing and talk Plattdeutsch together.

South of Ratzeburg the country rises a little into low, morainic hills, a rolling landscape with small lakes lying in the shallow valleys, and woods separating stretches of fertile farmland. Poplars lined some of the country roads I followed toward Gudow and Buchen, more or less along the route the medieval salt wagons had traversed from Lüneburg to Lübeck. Occasionally a field had become a campsite; a wood was being cleared for a small settlement of holiday cottages. Now and then to the east a gray watchtower appeared among the trees, or over a far hedge, and I knew the border was still there. My road weaved through a big area of road work, where it crossed the track of a new autobahn that was being built between Hamburg and Berlin, and for which West Germany was paying the construction costs. At the small town of Buchen the railway from Hamburg to Berlin crosses the border—Buchen is the last West German stop on the line. Tourists in Hamburg who want to see the border are often told to take the local train to Buchen, where taxi drivers will drive them down to the bank of the Elbe–Trave canal and point out the DDR fence on the far side. Anyone who says that it doesn't look especially dangerous may be told about Michael Gartenschläger and the SM-70s.

Gartenschläger was born in the last year of the war and grew up in East Berlin, unhappy. He set fire to a cooperative-farm building; he wrote on the Berlin Wall as it was being built, "Germany for Germans." He was tried for these offenses, convicted as an agitator against the state and given a life sentence. While in a youth prison he received craft training and qualified as a turner. Twice he tried to escape. Once he climbed up onto a prison roof and protested about the food; he succeeded in getting an increase of rations for those held in solitary confinement. Among his fellow prisoners he won a reputation as one prepared to take a stand.

In 1971, after nearly ten years in jail, he was ransomed out of prison and out of East Germany by the West German government—by a procedure, used to get many out of the DDR, that I found out more about later. But prison life and the forms of survival it had required stayed with Gartenschläger. He needed adventure. He became an "escape helper" in the West, assisting people to get out of East Germany, organizing, for instance, the acquisition of false Libyan passports for East Germans. His life centered on the idea of getting somebody or something out of somewhere; he was obsessed with *die Grenze*.

In 1976 he was living in Barsbüttel, Schleswig-Holstein, when he heard about a new device called the SM-70 that the DDR was installing on the border fences. It was, apparently, a kind of short shotgun, triggered by wires running along the fence, and—it was thought—meant to replace the mines that were not always effective. (Mines decayed; they could be set off by animals or the pressure of snow and by heat: by forest fires, or even by long periods of very warm weather.) It was also thought that the new devices were meant to deter escapes by those who knew the border defense system best, DDR ex-border troops who had served their time and might return to an area where they had been stationed in order to try and get out. The press report which Gartenschläger first read on the SM-70s suggested that the Bundesgrenzschutz didn't as yet know much about them. The device had been developed secretly, a "socialist accomplishment" (as the report sardonically labeled it) that was believed to have had origins in Nazi Germany, where the SS had planned to use it on the fences surrounding concentration camps. Plans for the device had apparently been captured by Soviet troops, and—possibly after a period in which they were refined or modified in the USSR—given to the DDR authorities. They were being installed in various places along the *Grenze*, fastened to the outer fence at ten-meter intervals and at three different heights, each automatically triggered device containing (as it was later discovered) 102.4 grams of explosive and ninety pieces of sharp-edged iron shrapnel. Gartenschläger determined to get one.

In mid-March 1976 he and a friend made several reconnaissance forays along the border at night; they were looking for a likely spot. Gartenschläger found it a few kilometers from Buchen near the village of Bröthen. The woods were relatively thick on both sides of the border. The trees would provide good concealment for anyone approaching the border until he crossed it and stepped onto the cleared strip in front of the fence. The fence—roughly thirty meters beyond the border-marking posts—made several abrupt right-angled jogs within several kilometers, and Gartenschläger decided to capture a SM-70 mounted near such a corner. On a preliminary expedition on the night of March 28 he crawled to the fence, hooked a cable around the trigger wire leading to a SM-70, crawled back toward the shelter of the woods and pulled the cable. The SM-70 went off with a loud explosion. Spotlights came on at an East German watchtower about three hundred meters away, but Gartenschläger and his companion weren't spotted. Nor did they see any DDR border troops. The men in the watchtower may have decided that the automatic firing device had been set off by a bird or an animal. Gartenschläger concluded that the border guards were not particularly alert along this stretch.

Two nights later Gartenschläger and his colleague came back to the border at the place—about a kilometer from this first spot—where it made a right-angled bend. They brought a homemade ladder, a long stick with a cord attached to act as a lifting tool, a fishing line, various hand tools (spanner, clippers, screwdriver) and a first-aid kit. There was no moon. He and his friend parked their car and then blackened their hands and faces. As Gartenschläger walked forward, he sprinkled pepper on his and his colleague's tracks with the hope of deceiving dogs. They also put branches across the path, with the idea of hearing any West German patrol—BGS or Zoll—that might otherwise surprise them. Then they lay for half an hour to see if anything was stirring in the area. At four forty-five Gartenschläger left his companion in hiding, holding one end of the fishing line, which was to be used as a warning signal, and with the other end tied to his waist he crawled to the fence, pushing the ladder ahead of him. He lifted the ladder to rest against a concrete fence post. Then he climbed up and set about disconnecting the topmost of the three SM-70s mounted on that section of fence. He did so by leaning over the top of the fence, first cutting through the cable that carried an electrical charge to the detonator, loosening the bolts that held the device firmly in place, and then turning it so that its funnel-shaped barrel pointed away from him. He disconnected the trigger wire and thought he would then be able to lift the SM-70 free, but it wouldn't budge. He saw that a second trigger wire went from its support bracket to the next topmost SM-70, thirty meters away. At this point he took a short break while he wondered why the other SM-70 hadn't fired when he tried to lift off the first. He then disconnected the wire leading to the second SM-70. It was now getting light, and Gartenschläger quickly finished unfastening the device, scrambled to the ground with it, picked up his ladder and bits of gear, and hastened to rejoin his companion just across the border in the woods. There they made a lot of noise because Gartenschläger wanted to take some photographs of the DDR border troops discovering that an SM-70 was missing. But no one came.

Gartenschläger's SM-70 made a lively story in the West German press; newspapers and magazines such as Der Spiegel gave it coverage. The BGS was presumably pleased to have one for close inspection but didn't think it politic to say so. Whether it was technical expertise, iron nerves or luck, Gartenschläger had got one intact, and got away with it with his life intact. But being the sort of man he was, he couldn't stop there. On April 23 he went back to the same area and obtained another SM-70. His companion on his occasion was Lothar Lienecke, a twenty-eight-year-old former East German who had been in Brandenburg prison with Gartenschläger and then renewed his acquaintance in Hamburg; he greatly admired Gartenschläger's resource and courage. The West German authorities, however, didn't have quite the same unmixed feelings about Gartenschläger's exploits. The local prosecutor called in Gartenschläger for questioning; presumably his people had to demonstrate that they were trying to prevent border incidents and possible bloodshed, as well as trying to preserve the détente of Ostpolitik. Gartenschläger didn't show up for the appointment. Therefore the investigating officers went to his home, quizzed him and warned him not to do it again. Gartenschläger replied that they would hear of him soon enough. He intended to do something notable.

And so he did. The next day he contacted Lienecke and another friend and former DDR prisoner, Dieter Uebe. Gartenschläger told them that they would all drive to the border near Uelzen and get another SM-70. They set off at nine-thirty that evening but first stopped near Buchen at the place where they had left their ladder in the woods. Lienecke told a Spiegel reporter later that it was a dark and chilly night, once again without a moon. When they'd got the ladder, Gartenschläger suddenly changed his mind; instead of going to Uelzen he wanted to go back to the same place where he'd got the previous SM-70s, get another one, and also fire off one. Perhaps it was simply more of a challenge that way. Just before midnight Gartenschläger posted his friends at the border marker opposite the place where the DDR fence made its right-angled turn; Uebe was armed with a shotgun. Gartenschläger crawled again toward the fence. He put up his ladder and began to climb. Lienecke heard movement in the cleared strip near the fence. He shouted out to Gartenschläger, "Halt! This is the Zoll. Come back here at once!"

This was not only a call to warn Gartenschläger but to suggest to the DDR troops that West German customs men were on hand, to take charge, to witness any incident. But of course they weren't. In any case, the reply from the DDR border troops was unspoken. Gartenschläger was illuminated by a spotlight. There were several bursts of automatic-rifle fire. Gartenschläger was hit, dropped, scrambled back a little way, but fell dead eight meters or so from the fence, still well within DDR territory. Dieter Uebe fired his shotgun but apparently without hitting anything. In the morning, sleeping bags and blankets were seen in the cleared strip where DDR troops had stalked out the area, awaiting Gartenschläger's return. On the third time he was unlucky.

Just before noon I reached the Elbe River near Lauenburg, crossed it and traveled along its southern bank to the village of Bleckede. The border for some eighty kilometers along here follows the river—though having said that, one has to add that the facts of the matter are a little less precise, this being the last section of the intra-German border that remains in dispute between the Federal Republic and the DDR. The West Germans claim that the border should run along the northeastern bank of the river—where in fact the East Germans have built their fence system—while the East Germans claim, seemingly with greater modesty, that the border should be taken as running down the center line of the river, which here flows from the southeast toward the northwest. The Elbe is broad, the country flat on either side, with extensive water meadows, great areas of marsh, and plump, grassy riverbanks to keep floodwaters out of the fields behind. But the deepwater channel of the Elbe does not necessarily run along the middle of the river, and the big barges moving by (mostly West German, East German, Polish and Czech) have to follow a course that winds first near one bank, then the other—and is always changing. Even the shallow-draft East German patrol boats are sometimes forced to come over to where the water is deeper on the West German side to avoid running aground on their own.

I learned some of these things that afternoon while cruising on the Elbe in a West German customs patrol boat. I knew from reading I'd done before setting out that the East and West German governments had agreed in 1972 to set up a commission to handle some of the then un-resolved problems of the border: this was a step forward from the lack of cooperation that had marked relations between the two states till then. The *Grenzkommission* got going a year later, worked through initial dis-trust and difficulties, and established a businesslike atmosphere for coping with the practical and technical problems of the border. An early task was to define exactly where the border was. In a number of places, as in Ratzeburg, the occupation forces had altered the frontiers specified in the London Protocol, which had sometimes crudely followed old provincial borders. Sometimes a thick crayon had been used to mark a border on a map, covering several kilometers of ground in a way that left lots of room for disputes. Documents had to be dug out of archives, the ground sur-veyed, and marker posts and stones put up or replaced. Old border stones with old coats of arms, dating from previous centuries, were found some-times deep in undergrowth. Surveyors went out in teams made up of members from both Germanys, and faced occasional problems with slightly different survey methods. But now the only section of the border that re-mains to be fixed is along this part of the Elbe, and both sides have agreed that since no solution seems satisfactory to either of them, they had best shelve the matter. A lecturer in contemporary politics I met later said this was a British solution: "You don't solve the problem, you just live with it."

Yet, generally speaking, the Grenzkommission seems to have found German solutions—by thrashing things out, many practical problems have not become political problems. The commission meets about eight times a year, alternating between places east and west, sometimes close to the border but also farther afield. It has worked out the sharing of water from border rivers, problems of waste disposal, and how to handle open-cast mining in an area traversed by the border. It has introduced fourteen direct telephone connections of the sort I'd seen at Schlutup so that bor-der forces on each side could speedily cooperate in the event of emergen-cies like floods, fires, health hazards or everyday farm problems like loose cows. The East Germans showed some reluctance to use these telephones at first but have gradually accepted them. The Grenzkommission has deliberately kept aloof from most of the life-and-death aspects of the border: it won't discuss escapes or questions of compensation for injuries on the border; it has, however, dealt with the tricky business of river navigation where, as on the Elbe, boats are sometimes forced to cross what one state may consider the dividing line. The DDR has agreed that its forces will not shoot at vessels that are compelled by, say, low water or loss of control, to come on what they consider to be the East German side of a river.

I had talked in Bonn, a little while before I set off on this trip, with Frau von Rottenburg, a West German government lawyer who serves on the Grenzkommission. She said that despite the appearance of stagnation of relations between the two German states, the Grenzkommission had been a real achievement and was continuing to nibble away at all sorts of practical problems. It was, moreover, a peaceful forum where personal contact was made and views developed. Some members of the commission got interested in particular matters—one of her colleagues had devoted himself to maintaining the ancient privileges of the Lübeck fishermen. At commission meetings, members of one state sit opposite members from the other state at a long table, but small, less formal working groups are often set up to handle special issues. The East German government rarely changes its delegation, while the West German side now has only one or two members who have served since the beginning. Camaraderie would be too strong a word for the atmosphere at commission meetings, Frau von Rottenburg said, but the members met not only at working sessions but at dinners given by municipalities in which the commission has sat.

"We don't share many jokes," she said. "I don't think Communists have a very well developed sense of humor, at least that they are prepared to show in front of political opponents. But it is possible to have friendly conversations with them, to talk about hobbies or sport. Sometimes we visit local museums together. I think they enjoy coming over and seeing West German towns, though naturally they don't say so."

In West Berlin I was to meet a little later a former member of the Grenzkommission, Dr. Hansjürgen Schierbaum, who was now serving as the deputy plenipotentiary of the Federal German government to West Berlin. Dr. Schierbaum is a veteran of the 1971–72 border negotiations between North and South Korea, which led to the July 4, 1972, non-aggression declaration. He is an expert on frontier agreements and a firm believer in the power of quiet diplomacy to change things for the better. A tall, scholarly-looking man, Dr. Schierbaum said that he had felt "psychological difficulties" as a West German negotiating border questions, when in the background he always felt the presence of the Berlin Wall, the border-fence system, the inhumanity. He had helped negotiate the West German–East German transit agreements, but this did not prevent his heart beating faster, like that of any ordinary nervous West German, when entering the East German autobahn checkpoints. Yet he had got on pretty well with his East German counterpart on the Grenzkommission— a man who was chief of staff of the DDR border troops but did not (Schierbaum felt) particularly like his job. Dr. Schierbaum belongs to the Christian Democratic Party, which was then in opposition in West Germany, and this mystified his DDR counterpart—he couldn't understand how an opponent of the government party could be allowed to take part in government. "I explained that in Western Europe you could be a member of the opposition and still support the basic beliefs and goals of your country. After a little while he said that he understood this. Which is unusual, since it's by no means the orthodox Communist Party line. But even under Communist surfaces you can sometimes find human beings."

On the river the Zoll boat chugged out of a creek which forms the harbor of Bleckede. It was a sparkling afternoon. On the far side of the river the water was high against the green banks. Beyond was the red-tiled roof of a farm, farmhouse and barn merged together under one roof, as they are also in Friesland and Denmark. A watchtower stood close by the farm, and between farm and the river ran the fence. I had already had several different reactions to the fence. I had been curious; I had been amazed; I had been horrified; now—suddenly—in this place of great beauty, I felt furious. To live in that farm and not to be able to walk down to the water that lapped against the riverbank! Not to be able to paddle, or fish, or skip a stone, or push out a rowing boat, or sit with one's feet at the water's edge! These struck me as deprivations more tangible than anything— worse, at that moment, than not having a genuine vote or the right to travel to Lübeck or New York.

I had been met at Bleckede by a BGS officer, Rainer Leonhardt, who accompanied me on the boat. He said, "The watchtower is occupied during the day, but at night the guards come down and station themselves a little way from the tower so that they can see and hear better."

The boat, a broad-beamed fiberglass thirty-footer, overtook a string of barges pummeling their way upstream; two Czech barges from Prague coasted downstream toward Hamburg. Ducks took off at our approach and flew into the DDR. In some places the fence passed out of sight behind islands and marshes, intersected by creeks into which the wake of the Zoll boat traveled when we were well past. The West German customs officials examine every barge coming out of East Germany near the little town of Schnackenburg, about sixty-five kilometers upriver from Bleckede, and the patrol boat has the job chiefly of coping with emergencies on the river and showing the flag. As we passed the village of Konau on the East German side, one of the customs officials pointed out a place where the fence was down—undermined by recent floods, which had reached the highest level since 1885. Armed guards were watching over the men who were making repairs. The broken fence prompted me to ask about escapes. Leonhardt said that on the 550 kilometers of border in Lower Saxony, the province we were now in, twenty-one people had managed to escape in one way or other in 1980. In this year of 1981, so far only a third of that number had made it.

Between Darchau, the next DDR village, and Neu Darchau, in Lower Saxony, a ferry used to run; now the fence cut off access to the cobbled Darchau ferry slip. Near here I spotted three goats on the East German riverbank—they were on the riverside of the fence, and were presumably West German goats that had swum over for greener pastures. We passed an East German barge named *Potsdam* towing a West German yacht toward West Berlin (the only way a yacht owner wanting his boat on the extensive lakes of West Berlin would be able to get it there, Leonhardt said). We passed one of the new-type square watchtowers, and were watched through binoculars and duly photographed; one of the older cylindrical columned towers was standing nearby. "They had to build the square ones because the others weren't very strong," Leonhardt said. "A few of them have fallen down." He sounded pleased that the DDR's efforts to perfect its border now and again came up against the constant force of human error.

We landed at Hitzaker, a pretty resort. It is the hometown of Prince Claus von Amsberg, who married Princess Beatrix, now Queen of the Netherlands, and is otherwise noteworthy, so Leonhardt told me, for the crowds of West Berliners who come to it on vacation. In a field by the riverbank where we came ashore sat a dark-green BGS helicopter—an Alouette, Leonhardt said. I knew what was going to happen next because my stomach was sinking. The BGS, like all such bodies, assumes that inquisitive people like myself are invariably delighted to be taken up in a helicopter and whizzed over the landscape while the pilot swoops down to points of interest and one wonders at what moment one can properly ask for an airsick bag.

"We thought you would like a short flight along *die Grenze*," Leonhardt said, and of course it was churlish to say no. I climbed in, buckled up and adjusted the headphones, which—I hoped—would not only permit communication but prevent me from being deafened by the Alouette's engine a foot or so over my head. The helicopter rose in a funny sort of crouching forward position. When the ground had dropped away it shot forward, the rotors like a black spinning halo overhead. We flew south at a height of three hundred meters, moving at eighty-five to one hundred knots, and down below there were farms and villages, small hamlets composed of half a dozen farmhouses set in a star-shaped pattern around a church, with little lanes and tracks to the fields radiating from the core. The fields were striped in different shades of green, gold and brown, and various textures, some—unsown—like dark-brown corduroy. In one field a black horse was running. Although all day the sun had been shining till now, we ran into a few showers, the rain drops curving up the plexiglass windshield. We hit the border again where it returns from its travels around a West German bulge to the east, and followed it south, over the villages of Schafwedel, Luben, Ohrdorf, Brome and Zicherie. In some places a single fence ran near the border, with a second fence a long way in the rear; in other places there was the usual double fence, the strip in between. Some of the East German villages right on the border were cut off additionally by a concrete wall, to prevent villagers from waving to one another. The border was always visible because of the plowed strip and the concrete patrolway. I noted a windmill with relief at seeing something both manmade and unmenacing. We flew back over thick woods in which a strange pattern of roads and road surfaces could be discerned. "The Volkswagen testing ground," Leonhardt told me.

I spent the night at Bleckede. I stayed in a small hotel on the riverbank, the Landhaus am Elbe. Before dinner I walked along the riverfront road, by the little haven, to a point with seats and benches where one could look across the river. Two barges were moored near the mouth of the haven. Bleckede has a trade in sand. Flags hung limply from a row of short flagposts. The sky—once again out of early-nineteenth-century German Romantic painting—was calm yet florid: gray above; then a glaring yellow-pink-white. Then a line of poplars, the green bank, the river. A DDR patrol boat, gray too, was going slowly downstream, holding a course in mid-river. I couldn't hear its engines. The only sound was a bird chirping and the river running over some stones. Over there the fence.

There were few other guests at the hotel—a pair of elderly ladies who spent most of the evening playing a German sort of Scrabble with lettered dice, and a middle-aged couple—lovebirds, I thought—who appeared briefly for drinks from the bar and then hastened back to their room. I talked after dinner with Herr Schacht, the proprietor, and his daughter Marion. Herr Schacht was a large cheerful man in his sixties. He and his wife, who was away visiting relatives, had run a hotel in the main street of Bleckede until they bought the Landhaus am Elbe in 1969. The hotel was generally full on weekends and all summer long with people from Hamburg and West Berlin—the Berliners drove like maniacs to get here and relax. He referred to the authorities on the other side of the river as "the Russians." The DDR was still the Soviet zone for him; the border was the *Zonengrenze*. He said that before World War II, Bleckede had been a market town for the other side of the river as well—farm produce was brought over by ferry, and customers from across the river came to buy in Bleckede's shops and cafés. Everyone over here had relatives over there. Bleckede was a good deal less busy now, but visitors—guests of his hotel—came for the quiet and the river view.

When she had finished cooking and helping serve the dinner, Marion Schacht sat down. We had a brandy together. She was in her early twenties, born in Bleckede, and had recently come back from working for six months at the Kensington Hilton in London. Bleckede was beautiful but a bit on the peaceful side. Because they found it drowsy, many young people moved away to larger towns, and so it became quieter still. The only people moving in were Berliners, who after visiting for a while built summer houses and retired here. They saw the water and the grass and somehow didn't see the other side of the river; and perhaps they also wanted to be as close as possible to their other home, Berlin. Marion felt in a similar way about the border. She had grown up with the fence, which all the time was before her eyes—so that she saw it but didn't see it. The other side of the river was like a mysterious foreign country; she had never been there. You heard rumors about who was living in houses you could see on the riverbank, generally officers or party officials or agricultural functionaries, because you had to be highly trusted to live so close to the border. Highly trusted or very old. One house over there called *der Heisterbusch* was burned down by the DDR authorities three years ago when its occupants died. Marion said that people in Bleckede were sure that the DDR authorities knew all about them. "We know they are looking at us all the time through their binoculars, making notes, taking photographs. But we are used to it."

The Schachts asked me to sign their visitors' book, and as I leafed through the entries of the last six years and read the genial and grateful comments of the hotel's guests—"Fine food!" "Excellent company!" "A lovely spot!"—I couldn't find a single mention of or allusion to the border.

5. DIVIDED VILLAGES

got an early start again and drove along the southern bank of the Elbe on a road that wound sometimes near the river and sometimes up and down the forested slopes nearby. There was very little traffic on the Elbuferstrasse, as it is called, apart from a few yellow post-office vans collecting or delivering mail. Along the roadside, signs warned of deer crossing. Like most motorists I'm used to such warnings but have never seen a deer cross a road in the neighborhood of the signs. So I was startled when a blurred brown shape appeared, moving fast across my vision right in front of the car, became recognizable as a young deer, seemed almost to pause in the act of leaping and cast a glance in the direction of the onrushing machine, its one visible astounded eye gleaming bright, and then seemed to gather its resources and bound on. It was fully across the road and running across a field before my foot had retreated from the brake. I took a few deep breaths to pull myself together.

I stopped briefly at the former ferry landing at Neu Darchau. The cobbled lane ran down into the waters of the Elbe. Out in the channel two Czech barges were heading for home. There were swans, willows, a black steel skiff named *Toller* anchored in the reeds. Only the two adjacent watchtowers across the river disturbed the serenity; they were like the gibbets in a landscape by Breughel. I assumed that the man in civilian

clothes sitting near the ferry landing and staring at the reeds with binoculars was a bird watcher, for Marion Schacht had said that the peace and
quiet of the border area was good for wildlife, and particularly along the
Elbe, where some of Europe's rarest species of birds are to be spotted. I
saw a stork, big wings beating slowly, long legs sticking back. The storks
generally arrive in these parts in early April and leave around the end of
August. People continue to fix old wagon wheels to their rooftops to
encourage storks to nest there. The male stork prepares the nest, and
then goes looking for a female to share it with him. But the storks are
said to be declining because frogs, which are a great feature of their diet,
are hard to come by as a result of widespread use of industrial fertilizers
on both West and East German farmland.

I paused in the market town of Dannenburg to buy a local paper and
a new road map, to cover the next part of the journey. Then the road ran
along a low dike lined with chestnuts. I passed through Gorleben, where
in the 1960s there was a confrontation between East and West German
patrol boats, insisting on their river rights, that nearly led to shooting, and
now there is much anxiety about the construction of a nuclear waste-
disposal facility. Outside Gartow, the next village, a group protesting
against this had set up a trestle table by the roadside. The anti–nuclear
power movement is vociferous in West Germany, demonstrating in a
mass rally in Bonn in October 1981 and active in trying to halt the building of nuclear power stations. Here, a young man behind the table said,
they were particularly concerned because the authorities were affecting
to have a period of contemplation and claiming that nothing would
happen for a long time; but all the while (so the protestors felt) plans
for the facility were going ahead. Test drillings at the Gorleben site had
gone down to 1,004 meters. The authorities say the site would only be a
temporary one but local people think that temporary can easily become
permanent; they are scared of the effect on local farms, milk, water, the
Elbe, the wildlife; they don't like the secrecy surrounding it—no one has
a clear idea of how the facility would work, nor do they like the power the
atomic energy authorities have to move and dispose of nuclear waste
without consulting in a meaningful fashion the people of the area.

Schnackenburg was as far east as I could go. It is a village that has seen
more vital days; it gained the right to call itself a *Stadt*, or city, in 1373.
It has six hundred inhabitants and a wealth of picturesque half-timbered
houses, constructed with wooden posts and brick infill (the Germans call
them *Fachwerkhäuser*), many of which were being restored with the help
of state funds. At eleven-thirty in the morning the streets and cobbled

sidewalks of Schnackenburg were deserted save for a few small children playing a game of ball. From the high river wall I looked down a wide stretch of the Elbe to the bend, a kilometer or so distant, where it ceases to form the West German border and becomes East German on both banks.

From Schnackenburg it was back again out of the bulge, west, west-southwest, then south—a long detour through villages whose roads to other places nearby were often cut by the border. Every five minutes or so I had to consult my new map (on which the border was shown as a thick purple line). Now and then the East German watchtowers loomed over the ridge of a rolling field, each time creating a renewed shock. There were frequent belts of trees and small copses, and as I drove farther south the effect of these woods began to accumulate. From a distance there was often the illusion of a forest running behind the fence. Through my half-closed eyes the woods and copses in the foreground and middle distance seemed to merge and I could imagine the old endless Germanic forests, which once covered the interior of this continent, and in which anyone who has had to read Caesar's *Gallic Wars* in school, as I did, can picture as from a relic of race memory all manner of primitive and horrible happenings.

In the early afternoon I reached Brome, a small town that sits at the base of a mitten-shaped bulge into East Germany. In Brome are the modern municipal offices of a district council that looks after eighteen villages and ten thousand people, and I called there to meet Hans Schön-ecke, the council's chief executive. Schönecke, a handsome man in his early thirties, took me on a short walking tour, through a new park with a lake, toward the border. The West German government, aware of the difficulties that face communities along the border, has set aside several hundred million marks a year to help them. Brome has got some of these funds for its park, for restoring its local museum, and for improving schools and roads. Like many such towns it has been cut off since 1952 from communities in the DDR that once formed part of its natural hinterland. The West German government also gives special incentives and subsidies to industries in the border area, but Brome has very little industry to help. Although people go on building new houses here, because land is cheaper than in larger, busier places, most men in Brome drive to work daily in Wolfsburg, twenty kilometers to the south.

Beyond the park we came into a little lane and soon enough the signs —HALT! HIER GRENZE. We walked single file along a narrow track through some thin woods, with the fence just visible, a gray screen. "This is the old border between Hanover and Anhalt-Saxony," Schönecke said. "Now it is the border with Moscow." I could hear a tractor working in a DDR field. "We grow the same crops as they do," Schönecke said; "it's somehow strange to see them in fields side by side, with the border between— corn, sugar beet, potatoes. And we both have the same black-and-white cows."

A small brook wound eastward; where it crossed under the border fence a lifting gate like a portcullis had been installed, clearly at considerable expense. A fixed gate would have got clogged with debris; lack of a gate would have allowed people to escape. Clouds of midges hovered over the path. Schönecke said that he had gone recently to the DDR on a day visit with the idea of driving as close to Brome from the other side as he could get. He felt very nervous as he approached the edge of the five-kilometer protective zone, but got as far as Mellin, a village only three kilometers from the border, when he saw one of the signs saying that no one was allowed farther without special permission. At that point he turned back.

Two Zoll men came by, pushing bicycles, accompanied by German shepherds. We exchanged "Guten Tags." A DDR tractor was working in the area between the border and the fence, and two border guards were keeping an eye on it. "They have to keep clearing the shrubbery and saplings," Schönecke said. "In the strip between the fences they still have mines in places along here, but also SM-70s on the fence. Sometimes in the middle of the night we hear the mines go off. A few years ago there was a little forest fire here that spread in from the DDR—forty-seven mines exploded. But elderly men who've hunted all their lives say that the border has been good from that point of view—there are more pheasants, deer and hares than ever."

A DDR helicopter racketed overhead, following the fence, just inside the border line; a large bird—a stork or a crane (I couldn't tell which)— was stirred by the noise and lifted with great slow wingbeats. We halted at the junction of the track and a lane into Brome—the lane that had once been a country road from Brome to Mellin, and was now closed by the border. On the wooden barrier in front of the West German markers was a little basket, with some empty beer bottles in it.

I pointed to the bottles and asked, "BGS or Zoll?"

"Maybe both. And also for people who come and park their cars here. These closed roads are popular as lovers' lanes."

As we stood there the Aufklärer appeared. It was the same as at Eichholz outside Lübeck, only this time the bushes parted and there were two of them, binoculars around the neck, Kalashnikov over the shoulder.

From a distance of seven meters one of them aimed a camera at us and clicked away. The sound of the camera seemed to exaggerate the rural silence.

Schönecke said to them, "Good day. It's a pity you have to do that sort of nasty job, isn't it?" He turned to me, preparing to continue our walk along the path, and with a wink said loudly enough for them to hear, "When I was over in Mellin the other day . . ."

I took a room for the night in a comfortable pension run by the Jurgens family. It was a large modern house with a small holding attached. I talked for a while with young Jurgens, who works in the Brome post office and with his wife helps his parents run the pension, where business was good. Several salesmen were staying there and so were two long-term guests, Poles who worked in Wolfsburg and whose car, with Polish license plates, was parked in the driveway. The pension was fully booked for the following weekend, when a reunion was being held in Brome and the neighboring village of Zicherie for people who had once lived in the area of the DDR due east of here known as the Altmark. A thousand people were expected. The bands of the local fire brigades would play. There would be singing, dancing and eating, particularly of Altmarker Tiegelbraten, and of course beer drinking. A happy occasion, though some would shed tears. Young Jurgens said that he had first cousins living in the Altmark, at Ristedt eight kilometers east of Brome. Before the border was sealed, Ristedt was twenty minutes away; it took three or four hours to reach it now by way of the nearest border crossing at Helmstedt. It also took three or four weeks to get the required permission using the forms for Near Border visits. He went only once a year now that the trip had become so expensive, though it was worth it for his children to play with his cousin's children.

I talked German with young Jurgens. I was therefore restricted by my limited knowledge of the language to fairly simple subjects: pleasures and regrets, good and bad, ease and difficulty. Where things were. The cost of things. Places and distances. I was glad that I had spent several months, not long before, going every weekday afternoon to the Goethe Institute in Kensington, London, to absorb under the firm direction of Herr Keilbach, Frau Cole and Frau Newns a basis of German, learning something of the German rhythm that causes one unthinkingly to get the right part of the verb at the end of the sentence, and even to enjoy pronouncing German as accurately as I could. My fellow pupils included two male singers of classical music, a woman cellist, a waiter, two engineers, a BBC radio producer and two young women with German boyfriends. The cellist was Russian, the waiter Italian, and one of the young women was Australian; the rest of us were British. We reflected in different ways an interest in Germany. Frau Cole (who like Frau Newns is married to an Englishman) said that we were much easier to teach than schoolchildren because we were all so highly motivated. We were also helped on the way by the expert Goethe Institute teaching methods, which may have taken something from police interrogation techniques: Herr Keilbach coming on as a sort of heavy on Mondays and Tuesdays; Frau Cole surely and benignly instructing on Wednesdays and Thursdays; and young Frau Newns conducting a reviewing, reminding and mopping-up job on Fridays, when her own diffidence made one often feel more knowledgeable than one in fact was. After several weeks of these intensive sessions I found that on the way home by train I was actually thinking German thoughts *in German*. And although once in a while, as Herr Keilbach fired a question at me and I confused *wo* and *wer* (which respectively and confusingly mean "where" and "who") or gave the dative to a preposition that takes the accusative, I was put in mind of the concentrated stare of a U-boat commander examining his prey through the periscope, I was more often made to think of what we, British and Germans, have in common: the roots of words; many customs and institutions. I began to read, albeit in English, the German classics, like Goethe and Mann. From something Herr Keilbach said one afternoon I realized that we were of roughly the same age and that he, perhaps even more indelibly than I, had spent formative hours in an air-raid shelter. Being British did not give one a monopoly of the resentment of war.

In the course of a stroll that evening around Brome I dropped into what appeared to be the most flourishing pub, the Gasthaus Schmidt. According to young Jurgens, this inn and half of Brome had been in Soviet hands at the end of the war until the local commanders made practical adjustments to the old provincial boundaries. Now the Gasthaus was certainly in native hands. I was welcomed in with a barrage of ribald and cheerful remarks; made to declare my place of origin and purpose in Brome, and was soon involved in several rounds of drinks. The drink was beer, from the tap, at DM 1,10 a glass. A one-eyed man who was quite drunk—like several others in the crowded room—kept calling me "Tommy," and alternately slapped me hard between the shoulders and tried to strangle me. Perhaps he, too, had some scene of war in his memory that needed to be expiated or re-created. In any event, no one seemed to regard his behavior as in any way unusual, and while fending him off I talked to one of the customs men whom I'd seen that afternoon with bicycle and dog, and who introduced himself as Norbert Hunting.

In his late thirties, blond and with an incipient portliness, Hunting told me that he had been stationed in Brome for twelve years and liked it. The Zoll had sent him for a little while to the Dutch border, where he had had to keep an eye out for terrorists and drug smugglers, and he was glad to come back to the quietness of Brome. The perfected DDR border meant that not much happened here. The last escapes in this area had been in 1976 when four DDR officers—who had known one another since kindergarten—managed to get across the fence together one night, before SM-70s were installed. Now the busiest time on the border was in the summer, when tourists, flower lovers, mushroom pickers and the like often strayed over the border and were arrested by DDR troops, and generally kept for two or three days before being released—when the BGS would question them about what had happened to them and what they had seen in East Germany. Although he agreed there might seem to be a duplication of effort in border surveillance by the West Germans, he was proud of the feet-on-the-ground and local-knowledge approach of the Zoll. He thought, too, that a possible by-product of all the men looking after border security was that there was less crime in border communities. He wasn't sure the border was so good for wildlife: birds and animals collided with the fence and set off the SM-70s; some were killed by mines; some were shot by the DDR border troops, either for sport or to prevent the birds and animals triggering the static weapons. The DDR troops have a reputation for not talking to West Germans—and indeed have orders not to—but Hunting has found that sometimes they will, on Sundays, when they quietly call over to ask about West German football scores.

He talked, at least when in the Gasthaus Schmidt, with the air of the man on the spot, whose understanding of events is superior to those of the higher-ups in Bonn. Clearly he enjoyed his job. He had liked accompanying one of the DDR officers (now an engineer), who had escaped in 1976, when he recently visited the place on the border in Brome where he had come across. Hunting said, "He just stood there and said, 'How did we ever make it?'" And in Brome itself Hunting was obviously fond of being a kind of village policeman, who could bask in the warm regard of the habitués of the Gasthaus Schmidt. "Hunting's a good fellow, isn't he?" one of them said to me, not insincerely, but with a smile that suggested he knew that Hunting liked to be praised. Hunting was also the manager of the Brome soccer team, which was doing well, and whose coach was a man who actually played for Braunschweig (Brunswick), a team in the main Bundesleague. As for the border—well, Hunting didn't think it was going to go away. It was a fact of life in Brome. It had, he thought, forced people together. The spirit in Brome was good, was cheerful. And perhaps the border wasn't altogether bad for business, either. There was going to be the Altmark reunion this coming weekend. And on summer weekends now, tour buses were beginning to show up from Holland, Belgium, France and various parts of Germany, with parties anxious to see the border.

I had intended to eat dinner at the Gasthaus Schmidt but I wasn't too displeased—after four or five rounds of beer and ever increasing Anglo-German amity—to be told that the owner's wife wasn't cooking this week. She had broken her ankle, the owner said. So I left, to boisterous shouts of *"Auf Wiedersehen,* Tommy!" I drove a few kilometers south toward the next village of Zicherie to a roadhouse Hunting had recommended, where there was game on the menu and a herd of deer in an adjacent paddock. A stuffed deer's head and many sets of antlers decorated the walls. I had broiled trout. I was reading Heinrich Böll's novel *Group Portrait with Lady,* and an incident in the book made me think of the BGS officers I'd met, like Lemke and Leonhardt, who looked very little different from the smartly uniformed German officers of World War II, were pleasant and correct, punctilious even, holding one's raincoat so one could put one's arms in the sleeves. What made them different from the German soldiers in Böll's book who machine-gunned Russian prisoners and Russian children bringing food to Russian prisoners? Could the same thing happen again? Some uniforms seemed to have a strange power to cause people to put their consciences aside and to simplify decisions about who the enemy is. Perhaps, too, uniforms can make one jump to conclusions about those who wear them: the way one looked at those DDR lads and couldn't help thinking of *them* as the Enemy. They, too, were human. What did they think of us? Did they go back to their barracks and liven up things by telling jokes about those they'd seen in the West that day?

Zicherie is well-known in West Germany as a "divided village." The tour buses visit it, West German TV crews film it, and schoolchildren are brought to it from various parts of the Federal Republic to learn about the border. Zicherie lies between the fence and the main road, a small collection of farmhouses, barns, cottages and new houses, with seemingly as many tractors as cars, and chickens wandering in the street. The World War I memorial has been given a thrifty World War II addition. Before the war Zicherie formed one community with the village of Böckwitz, a few hundred meters to the east. Now, where the road to Böckwitz is barred before the border, there are the signboards and display cases that I'd begun to recognize as usual in these circumstances. One says staunchly: "Zicherie-Böckwitz remains in the middle of Germany. The fence system is not a frontier." Zicherie, another placard informs me, had 250 people living in it until 1939; 450 after 1945 (presumably because of the flood of refugees from the East); and 250 again today. Forty-five work in Zicherie, the rest in Wolfsburg. Some still have relatives living in Böchwitz. On a stone set up in 1958 are incised the words DEUTSCHLAND IST UNTEILBAR (Germany is indivisible). Now toilets have been built for visitors coming to see the evidence of divided Germany. Beyond the border-marking posts, empty soft-drink cans lie on the East German grass. There is a newish road sign saying ZICHERIE, as if for traffic coming along the barred road from Böchwitz. Behind the first DDR fence is a concrete wall, running several hundred meters in either direction, and between fence and wall one of the older watchtowers, from which comes the sound of a radio. Now that I know that these older towers have occasionally collapsed, none of them seems to me absolutely vertical.

I walk along a little track beside the border at the foot of various back gardens. Apples on apple trees; rhubarb and flowers; birds singing. An old lady is weeding a flower bed. I say "Good morning" to her, but she ignores me; she looks right through me. Possibly I am associated with the thing which she has managed to put out of her mind; she will not, cannot, see me. A dog looks out from the open door of a barn with greater interest in who is going by. The path is bordered by dandelions and cow parsley. As I come around a bend I see two DDR border soldiers standing right next to the border, looking up a lane between houses into Zicherie; neither sees me. I walk on quietly and have a strong urge to say "Boo!" When they do at last notice me, one grins to himself self-consciously; the other pulls out a camera and takes four or five photographs of me. When he has finished this task, he and his colleague step back a few paces and light cigarettes. From the lane a middle-aged man and woman appear; they approach the red-and-white-painted barrier and stand there talking in English. Suddenly I realize that the woman is walking around the end of the barrier and is setting off toward the fence on a course that will take her right past the DDR men. I call out to her before she has gone a few steps and beckon her back. I explain that the signs that say HALT! HIER GRENZE mean what they say; the fence is well within DDR territory.

She looks at the two border guards. "Oh," she says, "I thought they were ours."

She was born in Wolfsburg; she and her husband, an American, live in the state of Washington; she has brought him here to show him the border for the first time. He is, I think, looking a little pale. He looks at the DDR men and their guns and then at his wife, and starts to say, "What do you think . . . ?"

I say, "Well, I'm told they generally keep you two or three days." I don't mention more serious incidents that I know have occurred.

But he is already convinced I have done something pretty great, maybe even saved his wife's life. He writes out their names and address. He says, "If you ever get to Washington, look us up."

One of the newer buildings in Zicherie is the Haus Altmark. It is on the grounds of what was once Zicherie's school and now forms a center, run by the state of Lower Saxony, for adult groups and school classes to learn about the border. (These visitors—intrusive though they may seem to older residents like the lady in the garden—provide a big boost to Zicherie's frail economy.) I called at the Haus Altmark and talked to some teachers who were accompanying a class of sixteen- and seventeen-year-olds from the town of Hoya, near Bremen. Hoya, I was told, was a long way west of the border in terms of awareness. Adults there wouldn't have the same concerns and anxieties, prompted by the border, as people who lived for example east of the Hamburg–Nuremberg autobahn—and who for the most part had more relatives in the DDR. Without such concerns among adults the children, of course, were more ignorant about border matters. One young man from Hanover who lectured frequently at the Haus Altmark said that most German parents failed to explain to their children the facts of German division, and it was often skirted around in school. Although modern German history was taught, the period after World War II concentrated on West Germany; what knowledge children had of the DDR they gained from TV. Yesterday the Hoya class had arrived; the children walked down the village lane to the barrier and saw the border—the fence and the wall—for the first time. One girl wanted to know if there were mines. Two DDR border guards were at hand and the girl shyly called to them, "May I ask you a question?" They didn't reply. She repeated her question about asking a question. Still no reply, only frozen stares.

The lecturer said, "I don't think she's managed to make sense of it yet."

We went upstairs to a huge barnlike room where a discussion was taking place. A big map of both Germanys was on the wall. There were thirty youngsters of both sexes; names like Anke, Frank, Inga, Thomas, Belinda; one boy chewing gum. I'd had the impression I might be asked to join in the conversation, but when my journey was described to the group it seemed to make me the center of the event. To get myself off the hook of being considered a border authority, I resorted to some quick questioning at large. What were *their* feelings about *die Grenze*, about divided Germany, about the chances of the two Germanys ever joining together again? And when this general barrage had flown over their heads, I asked, more particularly, how many had close relatives in the DDR. Only four hands went up. I continued the poll: how many thought that reunion with East Germany was likely? Six hands went up. The owner of one of these, a boy, volunteered that he thought the reunion would come in about a hundred years, when the two states would be forced to cooperate by such factors as lack of oil. I said that I had gathered that close ties between families east and west were disappearing as people got older and relatives died. What did they think of Bernhardt Fischer's idea of deliberately setting about finding someone to make friends with in East Germany and thereby promote a sense of German neighborliness if not nationhood? Since there were 60 million West Germans and only 17 million East Germans, all it needed was one West German in four to reach over and befriend an East German. What effects might this not have?

But even if these sixteen- and seventeen-year-olds hadn't thought much before this about the division of Germany, they replied now with what seemed to be world-weary experience. My suggestions—Bernhardt's ideas —were no doubt well-intentioned, even idealistic, but in practice, if something like this appeared to be happening, the DDR government would not allow it. Look how they had raised the compulsory amounts of Deutschmarks that had to be exchanged daily on visits to the DDR—with the effect of cutting down such visits. And such proposals as Bernhardt's wouldn't tackle the main problem, one girl said, which was that the DDR regime wouldn't let its people freely come over here and see us.

I asked what some of the other things were that mention of the DDR made them think of. A boy said, "There is no unemployment there. No demonstrations, either, except those wanted by the state." A girl called Annette said, "Over there you are forced to do something if they think you are good at it and it is right for the state. You have no choice."

But as time passed, I said, wouldn't the East Germans become more like the West Germans or even the Poles? Wouldn't they want rights and conditions that they saw that other countries had? It wouldn't matter if they did, many of these young people seemed to feel—the Russians wouldn't allow it.

One older youth who accompanied the class from Hoya was named Michael Richter; he had only recently arrived in West Germany from East Berlin, where he had been a theology student. His father was dead;

his mother, aged sixty, had been allowed to leave several years before; and he had had to wait until this year for permission to join her. In East Berlin they had lived in the district of Treptow, in the Kiefholzstrasse. "The wall was one hundred and fifty meters away," he said. "For us it felt like the end of the world. I couldn't believe that it would be possible ever to get beyond it. And now here I am. It's very curious, almost funny, to be so close to the border—but a world away."

6. WOLFSBURG

Wolfsburg is no longer at the center of Germany. Its location was the reason it was decided to set up a manufacturing plant there in 1938 to build Ferdinand Porsche's People's Car, the Volkswagen, and to build a model town for the plant's workers—a town which the government of the Third Reich had soon rechristened in its own terminology: "Town of the Strength-through-Joy Motor Car." Since 1945 it has again been Wolfsburg, and it was a surprise to find it on the map a few kilometers from the DDR border. In the late morning I drove toward it from Zicherie. Just outside the next village of Croya a lumpy human shape was standing rather perilously out in the road, and as I swerved the car around it, it—an elderly woman—waved a hand up and down. I stopped. She approached the car. Then, having worked out that she could not get in what she had thought was the passenger door, she came around to the other side of my Saab (which has right-hand steering for British roads) and got in. Clearly, I was giving her a lift. She was wearing a sheet of clear plastic over the shoulders of an ancient black dress. (Although the morning was gray, it wasn't raining.) She began to talk and I didn't understand a word. I think that even if my knowledge of German had been magnificent, I would not have understood her. She was speaking or rather barking a country dialect, and it may have been that even in that she wasn't making much sense. Now that she was seated next to me I noticed that she had in her lap an apparently empty shopping bag and wore plastic bags on her hands as if she had been brought up to wear gloves when going out. Bristly black hairs sprouted from her chin and upper lip. Her eyes didn't seem focused on anything external. She was visibly filthy and gave off a strong smell of urine. All in all, she was an absolute shock—there in my relatively clean and tidy car on the well-maintained road running through the prosperous West German countryside; for a few minutes her presence drove all thoughts of the border and the modern world out of my head. Possibly it was a test. If she wasn't Howard Hughes reincarnated as a witch, she was perhaps one of the old gods or goddesses in disguise, checking up to see how friendly people might be to a distressed wayfarer of no obvious charm—rather the opposite. Maybe she had been sent to tell me something I ought to know. But if it was a test, I failed it. I had mentioned Wolfsburg as she got in, and this had produced no sign of disapproval, but now, passing through the small town of Rühen, gallantry and respect for the gods faded before the overpowering smell. I was afraid that I would have to discard or at least steam-clean the front passenger seat if she stayed aboard another minute. I pulled up, said that I was going to the post office and showed her how to open her door. She clambered out, bits of plastic hanging. When I came back from Rühen post office, having made a token purchase of a few stamps, she had walked on, still well out in the road. As I drove past I didn't look at her for fear of meeting those strange vacant eyes. If it was you, Pallas Athene, my apologies.

I had lunch at the Holiday Inn in Wolfsburg with Karl-Heinz Schüling of Volkswagen's public relations office. (VW is pronounced "Fow-Vey" in German, which for the English-speaking takes a little getting used to.) Herr Schüling is a small energetic man, enthusiastic about his job and his company, and with a nicely old-fashioned, schoolmasterly way of speaking English; he had learned the language while staying with a family in Cambridge. Naturally, we talked about cars. I felt the need to say a few loyal words about my Saab, but it was funny, in the light of my past as an avowed nonbuyer of VWs (which tactfully I didn't mention), to hear myself saying to Herr Schüling, "I could not buy a Japanese or Russian car"—the Japanese because they are serious economic competitors, the Russians because they are proprietors of prison labor camps and psychiatric hospitals in which dissidents are held captive. However, this hands-across-the-Channel attitude on my part was not entirely reciprocated by Herr Schüling. He said, "I only buy German products, even when I know another country's product is cheaper. I earn good West German wages and should be prepared to pay higher prices for West German products."

Herr Schüling was a native Berliner; he had been thirteen when the war ended and still felt exceptionally lucky to have survived it. Although he didn't enjoy reading about the war, he had recently read Sebastian Hafner's biography of Hitler. His own family were all in West Germany now, but his mother-in-law lived in Brandenburg in the DDR, and he and his wife made roughly four visits a year over there. He said, "They are short of lots of things—stockings, linen, fresh fruit. Cigarettes are expensive there, except for those you buy with hard currency in the Intershops. My wife's relatives there depend on us to give them Deutschmarks. Yet it is true that there is a great deal of mutual aid over there. When my father-in-law died a few years ago, all the neighbors came around to give his widow a hand—they helped lay out the body and called the undertaker for her."

The border presented no drastic problems for VW, Herr Schüling said. The town was on the Mitteland Kanal—barges brought coal for VW's big power plant, which also provided district heating for three quarters of the people of Wolfsburg—and it also had good railway connections for the shipment of finished cars. However, like any other firm in the border area, VW was able to apply for special subsidies and tax breaks for its plants in Wolfsburg and Salzgitter, thirty kilometers to the southwest. Twenty percent of VW's shares belong to the Federal government, 20 percent to the state of Lower Saxony, and 60 percent to private shareholders. Wolfsburg VW employs about 57,000 people, nearly 10 percent being foreign nationals—Yugoslavs, Tunisians, Spaniards, Greeks, Turks and (the great majority) Italians. There are at least seven Italian restaurants in town. The unemployment rate—though higher than for many years past—is lower in the Wolfsburg area than in most other industrial areas of West Germany, for example North Rhine–Westphalia. But anyone in Wolfsburg who doesn't want to work for VW has the problem that there isn't much else to do there; for most unrelated jobs they'd have to leave town.

Although VW has plants in many countries, in North and South America, Nigeria and Yugoslavia, there are no plans afoot for opening a plant in the DDR. In 1979, however, 10,000 of the VW model called Golf (the Rabbit in America) were sold to the DDR on a "compensation basis"—that is, for payment in industrial goods. Part of the deal involved the delivery to VW of some huge body-panel presses from Erfurt, in East Germany; Herr Schüling said, "They are among the best of their kind."

The DDR also supplied tires for the cars—shipped to Wolfsburg and fitted there to the cars. Another aspect of the transaction was that Volkswagen bought East German astronomical equipment and presented it to the town of Wolfsburg for an observatory. The arrangement had a few drawbacks. One was East German government displeasure at West German press comment on the deal. The Golfs were first of all sold in the DDR for 33,000 marks each, more than twice the price in West Germany. (The average monthly wage in East Germany was then roughly 900 marks; the Trabant, the cheapest East German car, is sold for roughly 9,000 marks.) West German papers condemned the East German regime for making a VW seem as accessible to its people as a Rolls-Royce; and not only did such a price make a VW seem like a luxury but it gave the impression that West Germany was part of a conspiracy to make East Germans pay through the nose for West German products.

After lunch Herr Schüling took me on a tour of the VW plant. We started in the press shop ("the size of sixty-five football fields," said Herr Schüling), where huge machines, four stories high, were stamping out sheet-metal pressings from giant reels of steel, and overhead conveyor belts, part of a system 190 kilometers long ("the distance from Wolfsburg to Berlin," said Herr S.), carried them to the body assembly line. There, for a single Golf, 5,400 different parts have to be assembled; with 3,000 Golfs produced every day, some 16 million parts for just that model are moved within the plant daily. In parts of the plant there is an eerie calm, with robots picking up things and moving them around. In others the noise is deafening and hearing protectors have to be worn. Hydraulic- and pneumatic-powered welding carousels, programmed by computer, weld the body panels together; then, on an assembly line, doors, hoods and fenders are attached; a lift takes the body to the paint shop; it is suspended for a while in a massive marshaling yard under the roof and brought down to final assembly at the right moment to be fitted with all the rest of its equipment: seats, brakes, engine, steering system, exhaust, wheels, wires, cables, lights and instruments.

A number of the assembly-plant buildings are 1938 German contemporary—cleanly designed, using well-balanced masses of brick, glass and tile. But the pace and variety of movements within seemed to me smack up-to-date; one feature which appears archaic but which actually makes for speed and efficiency is the use of bicycles, 3,500 of them, for workers to get around the plant. Herr Schüling said, however, that VW had a way to go before it caught up with the Japanese: in 1979, 2.8 million Toyotas were built by 60,000 workers; 2.5 million VWs by 250,000 workers. VW was investing DM 10 billion in the period 1981–85 on new production processes to speed things up. Only 600 or so of Porsche's People's Car were built in 1940–44, when the plant was given over mainly to war production, but millions were built thereafter until it was phased out (still looking very much like the original model) a few years ago because it required too much time and had become too expensive to make in West Germany. (Some Beetles, or Käfer, as they are called in German, are imported from VW plants in Mexico and Brazil; among other buyers who continue to use them are the Bavarian Frontier Police.)

The average VW assembly-line worker was earning DM 3,000 gross per month (roughly $1,500 or £750), before any fringe benefits. A 4.9 percent wage increase had been awarded in February 1981, but in several places in the plant I saw handmade signs saying "8% Wanted." What the Germans call a works council is generally successful in thrashing out labor and production problems with management before output is interfered with by go-slows or strikes. (Although inflation in Germany was 6 percent, modest by Western standards—unemployment was also 6 percent and rising, which might put a brake on wage demands.) The atmosphere on the line seemed neither hectic nor boisterous. The "cycle time" is 1.45 minutes per worker per assembly operation, which gave one faster-than-average man whom I watched for a while the chance to bolt on his bits and pieces under a car and then sit down and read his newspaper for a few moments before the next car body arrived. There are four 16 minute breaks and one 30-minute break per eight-hour shift. Herr Schüling said that some workers liked to change their jobs from time to time—to move, say, from fitting tires to installing engines. Some, having learned one task, preferred to stick with it. I was impressed by the number of youthful workers—both young men and young women—who were working in teams on various operations, slipping in parts, supervising machines, checking the results. Everywhere I looked there was movement, parts arriving, parts being assembled into cars, cars inching forward along the track. A lot of physical action is required of the workers, even when they can stand on the track as it goes forward. All these bits and pieces end in a machine that is driven off the end of the track to the waiting railroad cars for shipment to various parts of Germany and the world. A new car every fifteen seconds. Wolfsburg's VW plant is the biggest single employer in the border area of West Germany, and the thousands of neat and shiny vehicles it turns out daily will provide mobility and freedom—while consuming energy and polluting the air. The Volkswagen plant, even in this ambivalence, seems as close as any place can be to the center of Western economic life.

Outside the plant, there is the traffic roar of a modern car-dominated town. Since Wolfsburg is a company town, most cars on its wide streets were VWs and Audis, made by a branch of VW. I spotted two brave dealers who were attempting to sell Renaults and Fords. My Saab attracted some wry looks, but elderly cars of any sort are rare in West Germany— except possibly for old Beetles owned by university students and, as one goes south, cars that have the bright mid-green license plates that denote they belong to Americans in U.S. government service or with the armed forces. (Instead of big beat-up old Chevys and Plymouths, the young soldiers drive bargain-priced Opels and Audis, just this side of the junk-yard.) On the autobahns, West Germans still seem to flaunt their cars; if they have a powerful BMW or Mercedes, they will drive it excessively fast. But in towns and cities they tend to settle into more punctilious, less aggressive driving manners, with little of the manic desperation that marks drivers in, say, Italy or Massachusetts.

I spent the night at the Alt Wolf Gasthaus, a picturesque but excellent inn in the village of Old Wolfsburg, now a suburb of the modern town to which it has given its name. A wolf appears in the coat of arms of the von Bartenleben family, who have lived in the area from medieval times, and a wolf was duly incorporated in the arms designed for the town in 1945, showing the animal on the battlements of a castle. A hundred meters or so from my inn stands the castle, with impressive battlements; but the last wolf in these parts was said to have been killed in 1823. From my room I heard the occasional clop of horse's hoofs on the cobbled roadway outside, the animals being ridden to and from a fancy equestrian estab-lishment not far away. But no modern traffic sounds from the main high-way, just beyond the castle, penetrated into the inn restaurant where I was reading Heinrich Böll and tucked into an excellent ragout.

In my room I watched television for a while after dinner. Four West German channels could be received, but the same two programs were on them all—both serious talk shows, with a group of men discussing the problems of youth and unemployment. On the fifth channel, from the DDR, was a boxing match; out of what was on, it won my attention.

7. A WAY THROUGH

had arranged to be in Helmstedt in the early afternoon, so with a morning free I drove first to Braunschweig, which is perhaps better known to English-speaking readers under its Anglicized name of Brunswick, to enjoy the simple pleasures of looking at old buildings and pictures. Brunswick is a bustling place whose old center has been largely pedestrianized, in the way that the centers of many similar sized German cities have been. It makes walking in them a delight. The heart of Brunswick is the twelfth-century cathedral of St. Blaze, a building of yellow-gray stone, capped with a roof of red-brown tiles, forming one slanting flank of an unequal-sided place on which also front the old town hall and the ducal castle. Out in the middle of the place a bronze lion stands on a high plinth. It was erected in 1166 by Henry the Lion, Duke of Saxony and Bavaria, as a token of his power and influence—which in fact soon ran up against the greater power of Frederick Barbarossa; but though Henry lost many of his far-flung domains, he kept Brunswick, his lion and his cathedral. He was buried within it, and so was his consort Mathilda, daughter of the Plantagenet King Henry II of England. The cathedral is now a Lutheran church. Yet even before the Reformation, St. Blaze's must have seemed to have protestant tendencies, its interior untinged by the bright colors of Mediterranean Catholicism. Although the architectural historians say that the rebuilt, Gothic columns in the north aisle—cut with a deep spiral twist in them—are in the Flamboyant style, I thought the mason in charge had picked up the idea from the great wooden crucifix that hangs at the head of the aisle. This, the work of the twelfth-century master Imerward, is a simple, forthright and utterly moving piece, in which the sculptor has done nothing to hide the fact that it is all one piece of wood— Christ and the cross are a single entity. The figure of Christ has a long, hollowed face, and his brown robe has thick seams and ribbed folds that the twisted columns appear to reflect.

I walked from the cathedral and across a small park to the Herzog Anton-Ulrich Museum. The later dukes of Brunswick have done well by the town, too, bequeathing to it a collection of paintings that is particularly strong in old Dutch and German masters. I spent the most time with two works. One, by Rembrandt, was a family portrait which I had admired many times in books on Rembrandt. Now, to see it in the flesh, as it were, in the spacious, wonderfully daylit and uncrowded gallery, was like going to some much praised place for the first time—Greece, for instance— and being not at all disappointed; far from it. The portrait showed father, mother and three small children, the father's face looming happy out of the somber background, the clothes of the woman and children in the foreground mostly in Rembrandt's favorite reds, oranges and golden browns. The youngest child has its fingers splayed out across its mother's breast. The mother puts out a hand that reciprocates the gesture in a way that makes sure that the child will not fall forward off her lap.

The second work was by Lucas Cranach the Elder. I've often found his paintings cold, even when sensual. But this was an Adam and Eve that suggested something like sadness to come; it has a suitably impending melancholy. Both figures are pale against a black background. Adam, standing on the left of the central tree, holds in one hand an apple whose attached leaf and twig cover his private parts, while he puts out his other hand tentatively to accept another apple, out of which Eve has already taken a bite. He is giving her a look that seems to combine doubt and— almost in anticipation—rebuke. "What," he seems to be saying, "are you doing to me?" Eve stands with her legs crossed, also covering herself with her hand. She looks about sixteen: high round forehead, round eyes, round cheeks, round breasts, round tummy. The snake looped down from an overhead branch. And the trunk of the tree itself ran up the middle of the painting—which, I now saw, was in fact two paintings, two joined panels, the seam of the dividing line running up the center of the tree trunk. I obviously hadn't got very far away from the border—the sight of something divided into two parts made the allegorical wheels start turning. It was tempting to see a vision of two Germanys in this thoroughly German picture of grace, sin and the fall. But male and female He created them, and I couldn't determine how one might dispose of West Germany and East Germany in those terms.

I chose the older road, Route 1, rather than the autobahn, as my way eastward to Helmstedt. Flat open countryside rose slowly to low forested hills in the south. Good tank country, I thought as I came around a bend in the village of Abbenrode and saw a pair of British army Chieftain tanks parked beside the road, with their crews on the grass having a midday siesta. In some respects this is still the British zone. There are British military bases in several places in northwestern Germany. The British Army of the Rhine (though stationed east of that river) forms part of NATO land forces which are intended to halt a Warsaw Pact offensive to the west, should it ever come. Just beyond Helmstedt—a market- and coal-mining town that still basks in the fame of having had one of the foremost German universities until 1810, when Napoleon's brother Jerome, King of Westphalia, closed it down—the autobahn crosses the border. It is the main road link between West Germany and Berlin. I joined the autobahn for a kilometer or so and took the turnoff just before the border inspection point. Here, in a dip below the autobahn, was a small group of buildings that included a NAAFI Roadhouse (a restaurant run for the benefit of Allied military personnel) and the headquarters of the Autobahn Control Detachment of 247 (Berlin) Provost Company of the British Royal Military Police.

In my days as a national service conscript in the British Army, in the early 1950s, NAAFIs (the Navy, Army and Air Force Institute—the equivalent of the American PX) were bleak cafeteria-type refuges where soldiers who didn't have access to either an officers' or sergeants' mess could find solace in stale doughnuts, hard rock-cakes, and a murky, intense-tasting drink said to be tea. The NAAFI Roadhouse at Helmstedt was so far evolved from that sort of place as to show no signs of its ancestor. It was a spacious room with armchairs, nicely laid dining tables, and a small bar. I sat at the bar with a ham sandwich and a Heineken and talked to the manager about Dutch beer. He said that he had been a fan of Oranjeboom and before it went out of business—bought up by Amstel?—he had cornered the last supplies of his NAAFI distributor, which kept him going for a year. I was waiting for a representative of the British Frontier Service, and at the appointed hour of 2 P.M. he showed up—a sprightly but somewhat veteran figure in what looked like nautical uniform: navy-blue trousers and jacket, white shirt and a white-topped naval-style peaked cap.

"Tom Jones," he said, introducing himself. "I hope you weren't expecting a helicopter ride, because I couldn't get one for this afternoon."

"Oh, no," I said. No need to affect disappointment.

We climbed into a small dark-blue Ford Escort with sagging springs, driven by an elderly German who seemed to speak no English but apparently got the message when Jones, in a rough-and-ready mixture of German and English, mentioned a place to go to, on the border not far away. On the way there Jones told me that he had been with the British Frontier Service for twenty years and in Helmstedt for the last seven, helping patrol a hundred-kilometer-long sector of the IGB—which is what the British military call the intra-German border. "To avoid incidents, British forces personnel aren't allowed within one kilometer of the IGB unless they have us along," said Jones. "And we know every inch of it. We were formed as part of the Allied Control Commission of Germany in 1946, to patrol and control the German frontiers, stem the flow of refugees, sweep mines in the Elbe, and try to get the German Customs Service restarted. There was a lot of smuggling in those days, of both people and goods. Our first director was a British Navy captain—he dreamed up this naval-type uniform for us, though in fact we're civilian civil servants employed by the Ministry of Defence. The DDR troops call us 'the men in the white hats.' "

We bumped down a rutted lane near the village of Zollecke, north of the autobahn. There, by the familiar border markers, as in a scene specially laid on to demonstrate the full variety of border patrolling, were two members each of the BGS and Zoll on our side of the border and two DDR Aufklärer on the other, one of whom was busy with his camera. Jones greeted one of the BGS: "Long time nicht gesehen. I hope he's saved some of his film for me." He turned to the Aufklärer with the camera: "Guten Tag." But the Aufklärer did not acknowledge the greeting. Jones said more quietly to me, "That's interesting—the senior of these two frozen-faced gentlemen is the equivalent of a sergeant major, the other's only a private. Usually both are senior NCOs or officers. They're real one-hundred-and-fifty percenters. They've got only three steps to make to freedom and they won't take them."

One of the Zoll came over and joined our little huddle. At Jones's behest he told me of an occasion when the Aufklärer had actually spoken. A recent Zoll patrol in this area had temporarily lost control of a dog, a German shepherd, which ran across the border and flushed two *Aufklärer* from behind a bush. They ran off, pursued by the dog. The Zoll called back the dog. A few minutes later the two *Aufklärer* returned; they picked up their automatic rifles from the bush and came to the border where the Zoll men stood. One of the *Aufklärer* said, "Please don't report this. Don't say we ran off without our weapons."

The camera turned away. "I hope you'll send me a snap," said Jones. Then, to the other *Aufklärer*, who was smothering a yawn, "*Zu viel Arbeit* today, eh?" (Too much work today, eh?)

"I really enjoy this job," Jones went on as he took me for a short stroll through the woods along the border, violets growing beside the little path, the fence twenty strides away. "I like taking parties of Allied troops to the border, which they've never seen before, and briefing them on it. In many ways the border doesn't need much explanation. You just have to see it for yourself. It's the worst blunder *they* ever made—the worst advertisement a political system could have." There were SM-70s on the fence. Jones said that in the Harz Mountains, a bit farther south, the DDR had created small animal runs under the fence in a few places so that creatures like hares didn't set off the SM-70s. Occasionally you could see places where sections of fence could be unlocked, bent back, for the *Aufklärer* to come through. He, Jones, liked to take note of such things. We came to a clearing where a disused road, grass growing in cracks of the paving, reached the border. This, said Jones, was Route 1, in pre-autobahn days the main road to Berlin. Several pieces of rusty metal by the roadside were the remains of a bus. It was said to have been carrying German troops, fleeing the Russian advance, when an American plane hit it with gunfire and it overturned here.

In its busiest days just after the war the British Frontier Service had some three hundred men. Now it has sixteen, four of whom are stationed in Helmstedt; the entire outfit is under the wing of a British major general, whose headquarters is in Bonn. With the re-establishment of the Zoll, the setting up of the Bundesgrenzschutz, and the creation of a working relationship between the two German states in the 1970s, the Frontier Service no longer has its old raison d'être. Yet its experienced men are valuable links between the British forces and the West German authorities, as guides and interpreters of the border, and also, I suspected, as something of a puzzle for the East Germans, who must have great difficulty figuring out what the men in white hats are really up to.

"No doubt the border's quieter than it used to be in these parts," said Jones as we walked back. "Before 1970 we had on our sector about thirty deliberate border crossers a month." Now, since the DDR border defenses were tightened up, most of the excitement comes from accidental crossings of the border. Two British soldiers on a recent skiing exercise didn't realize they had crossed the border, were nabbed by the East Germans and kept for a few days before being sent back by train. A young woman from Helmstedt flying her glider was forced down just inside the DDR by East German helicopters; they kept her a week, made sure she hadn't got any photographs and then sent her back. She had to pay for the return shipment of the glider. But in "the old days," 1945 to 1949, smuggling was rife on the border and the pressure of refugees trying to make their way West brought about disorder and crime. Between 1945 and 1947 Helmstedt police recorded seventeen murders, two hundred robberies, and a hundred incidents involving Russian troops in this part of the border. Ten Helmstedt policemen were abducted to the Soviet zone. Cigarettes and coffee were the hard drugs of the time, but the police and Frontier Service were also kept busy looking for basic commodities such as fish, brought down from the North Sea and Baltic ports by train and smuggled across into the Soviet zone to be sold on the black market. From the other direction, refugees paid local people to lead them along the least guarded forest paths and across the border into the British zone. Some of these guides were untrustworthy—they took their fee and abandoned their parties. A few guides were villains.

One such person, who has become part of the shadowy history of the border, was Rudolph Pleil. When in 1947 he was first committed to prison for twelve years on charges of manslaughter and robbery, no one had much idea of Pleil's full career as a malefactor. However, while in prison, Pleil wrote his memoirs. He gave them the previously used title *Mein Kampf*. But when no one would pay attention to them, he began to write confessional letters. He wrote to the mayor of the town of Vienenburg, on the border southwest of Helmstedt, and told him that if people looked in a well near the edge of town they would find the bodies of two refugees he had murdered. "Here they refuse to believe that I can kill so fast and well. Hurry up and find the bodies. Rudolph Pleil, killer."

The bodies were found. Although he admitted to four murders, he said that he had confessed to another five murders because he was in need of food and a smoke, and the police had offered these if he cooperated. But it was believed that he had in fact killed nine women in all—had said he would help them across the border at night, had led them into the forest and there robbed and murdered them. Another court gave him a life sentence. In prison Pleil encouraged the attention of criminal psychologists; he seemed to believe that his disastrous life was a model for mankind. He committed suicide, hanging himself with a towel in his prison cell, in February 1958.

At the Helmstedt military police detachment (to which Jones returned me), the war is not very far away. Neither World War II, whose concluding arrangements created the structure in which the work of the military police goes on, nor the war that might conceivably come. The Helmstedt post would become a forward command post, for however short a time, if the balloon went up. In one corner of the post commander's office lay his pack and steel helmet, at the ready. The commander was Major Philip Smyth, RMP, MBE, known as Paddy Smyth because of some Irish blood, a chunky man who looked like a mixture of James Cagney and Winston Churchill. He had risen from the ranks (where he had spent eighteen years) and had commanded the United Nations military police organization on Cyprus during the Greek-Turkish troubles. Here he ensures that the Allied right to road access to Berlin, agreed to in the Potsdam treaty of 1945, is exercised daily. He is the senior officer of the various Allied troops stationed at the autobahn checkpoint—a military presence largely paid for by the West Berlin government, which is in turn largely funded by the West German government. There is close cooperation from the French, despite their lack of commitment to NATO. (The local French commander has a German wife, and when Mayor Smyth calls on them at home, they all speak German.) The major said that he has a good working relationship with the Russians, who have a similar presence on the other side of the border crossing. "They're correct and precise. Sometimes one wishes for a little human fallibility to show as well. It's pretty boring that they're so predictable. If they make any mistakes, they are the last people to acknowledge it. They're always pushing a bit, seeing how far they can go with you. But if you meet their benchmark of what the job circumstances should be, you can do all right with them. One big problem with them from my point of view is that all their local decisions have to go back to be approved at a very high level. That prevents them from being anything like flexible."

I drove up to the autobahn checkpoint with Major Smyth in an elderly black Ford Taunus with a British military police driver. A large hotel for transients was being built on the West German side of the checkpoint, presumably for the use of drivers who got here late in the day and saw the road signs that said BERLIN 188 KM. The checkpoint resembled a mammoth toll station on an American highway, with booths at which civilian cars and trucks, coming and going, stopped for document and possible customs check. Allied military personnel heading for West Berlin are directed to a separate building, where their papers are examined and they are given a briefing on what to do, and not do, on the autobahn journey. A long counter was staffed by American, British and French personnel. The Allied travelers are given a military movement order, with a translation in Russian; all military dealings in regard to the autobahn are with the Russians, not the East Germans. The drivers are told not to take less than two hours for the journey—a shorter time will involve breaking the 100 km. per hour East German speed limit, and trouble with the autobahn police, who will have to call in the Russians. If the Allied travelers don't turn up within five hours, the British military police will come looking for them.

As we stood on the steps of the military control station, all sorts of traffic streamed through the checkpoint, which the military call Checkpoint Alpha. (Bravo is at the other end, the gate to West Berlin.) A thousand trucks a day go through—some at that moment were East German; a West German truck carrying buttermilk to West Berlin; and a Russian truck pulling a U.S. container. A pair of French tour buses headed east, and, among the many cars, a large old Peugeot, with various possessions wrapped in plastic piled on its roof rack, and the trunk lid tied down. "That's a Pole," said Major Smyth, "taking home as much food as he can carry." I said that I assumed that the control was more rigorous at the other checkpoint, visible half a mile away, where the Russians dealt with the Allied military people, and the East Germans with the civilians. The major said, "Don't assume they're slipshod here. The details of all drivers are punched out for the West German police computer, which comes back in a few seconds with results. Yesterday the BGS here identified a young Britisher as someone who'd been sentenced in West Germany to eighteen months but who'd escaped. He was apparently trying to drive through to friends in West Berlin. A Helmstedt judge has remanded him in custody."

The major led me to the roof of the military control station, in which several rooms are thickly lined with concrete and metal, for protection against Soviet eavesdropping. The actual border was about twenty meters away. "You'll see the sun flash on their binoculars when they spot us up here," said the major. There was a big square-towered DDR watchtower not far off, and I counted eleven others ranged around their checkpoint, where their fences came down to the edge of the autobahn. Here, as at Schlutup, I could hear the dogs. "By now they'll have a camera trained on us too," Major Smyth said. "They keep an eye on our checkpoint all the time, and on roadways leading across the border. If they see a vehicle trying to escape through their checkpoint, they can block the exit with a wagon, a heavy concrete-loaded affair that is shot hydraulically across the roadway. Naturally, at night the whole place is ablaze with lights. The stark reality of it is pretty offensive, don't you think?"

Every day Major Smyth sends two of his men in a Range-Rover up the autobahn to Berlin and back, as Potsdam gave them the right to. They call the round trip out of Helmstedt "the sweep." Most such trips are without incident, but now and then they find an Allied vehicle that has broken down or been involved in an accident. A heavy recovery vehicle and an ambulance are on stand-by. Regimental Sergeant Major Hawksworth of the military police detachment is a Russian-language specialist who will go out to confer with the Russians if needed. Among the instructions Allied personnel are given before setting forth are warnings not to leave the austere four-lane autobahn, and not to stop and park in any areas occupied by Soviet or East German troops. Not long ago the military police kept an eye on a convoy of trucks transporting circus elephants to Berlin for the British Military Tattoo, and they gave the British show jumper Caroline Bradley a hand when her horse transporter broke down not far from the DDR checkpoint at this end, near Marienborn. (They aren't allowed to tow in civilian vehicles but alerted a Helmstedt garage that has permission to go on this section of autobahn, and the garage truck went to get her.)

"On a sunny Sunday," said the major, "you could almost believe that Germany was reunited. There, on the autobahn, are cars from both Germanys. I sometimes think that many of the East German drivers may be driving on it just for the cosmoplitan atmosphere, among the cars and people from other countries. But then none of the people from other countries may leave the autobahn, and the East Germans have to leave it at either end before it reaches West Berlin or the border."

Major Smyth had several interests apart from his job: he kept pet peacocks; he was studying to become a barrister; and he read a great deal of history. In Helmstedt he had found someone with whom to talk about history and modern times—a man called Klaus Lüders who is director of an institute for the study of intra-German relations, housed on a suburban Helmstedt road half a mile from the military police post. (It was, I gathered, a more adult and fuller-time version of the Haus Altmark at Zicherie; individuals and groups came to it, for seminars and discussions, from all over West Germany.) Lüders, a very tall man of about forty, dropped by at the post after dinner; he, Major Smyth and I sat on the verandah of the road house with glasses of Scotch. A new moon was rising. A tall hedge rose between us and the roadway. There was the steady noise of autobahn traffic and the occasional cawing cries of the major's peacocks. We chatted our way through some topics of the moment—an air traffic controllers' strike in London; the consequent nonarrival that day of Mayor Smyth's *Daily Telegraph*; what the peacocks ate—to the matter of Germany. What, I wondered, did Lüders think of the chances of German reunification—and what did West Germans think of it?

"Those questions lead to what Germans think of themselves," said Lüders. "The big question is, Who are the Germans? And as to chances of reunification, how deeply felt and how widespread are feelings about the subject? Polls are taken now and then. Politicians revert to it from time to time. And various groups get together to ponder it. The first article of the West German constitution holds out hopes for a united Germany at some time in the future. June seventeenth, the anniversary of the 1953 workers' demonstrations in East Berlin, is celebrated here as the Day of German Unity—what used to be the western end of the boulevard Unter den Linden in West Berlin has been given the name Strasse des 17. Juni. But in a thousand years of its history, as you must know, Germany has been united for only some seventy-five years."

I had been told by an official in Bonn that the government, following the constitution, took the position that West Germans should work for reunion in perhaps thirty or forty years' time; they should do so by practical methods, for instance by way of the efforts of the Grenzkommission to reduce tensions, by family visits to East Germany, and by subsidizing the trips of East German pensioners to the West. In 1976 a poll found that about two thirds of West Germans thought reunification was important but roughly the same percentage thought it was unlikely to come about. In 1968 Chancellor Kurt Georg Kiesinger talked of "the will of a great people to regain its unity." In 1970 Chancellor Willy Brandt talked of making a fresh start toward the day when "the partition of our nation can . . . be overcome." A few years ago one of the leaders of the Social Democratic Party, Herbert Wehner, suggested in articles in *Der Spiegel* that the two Germanys might be able to draw closer together in a neutral confederation, which would allow for various disparities of development. Meanwhile in East Germany the idea of reunification seemed dead, at least in ruling circles, for most of the last decade: where the 1968 DDR constitution had talked of the two German states approaching each other by stages until their unification, the new 1974 constitution made no reference to the continuing existence of the German nation. Now and again the idea has been used by the East Germans as a weapon for exploiting differences seen to exist in West Germany in regard to defense or policy toward the Eastern bloc. Erich Honecker, the East German leader (who was born in what is now West Germany), suggested at a recent party meeting that once West Germany became socialist, the two German states would be united again. Hard to say if he had his tongue in his cheek.

But what politicians say and what people feel are often far apart. Lüders said, "Our local paper had a report the other day about a stamp-collecting club. It talked of the countries whose stamps members were collecting—'Germany, France, the DDR . . .' If I ask young people from near the Rhine at one of our discussion groups what Germany is, at least half will say 'West Germany.' The rest will say 'The two German states.' I think it is important to ask this question, to make people think about it, and to ask themselves how we reached this point. They must ask, 'How did this come to be, this border, these two states?' And to find an answer they must resume the history of the Cold War, of the Second World War, of Hitler, and of the failure to give sufficient backing to the Weimar Republic. All this can only be explained in terms of the past and what the German people brought upon themselves. The border and the division of Germany represent a kind of nemesis. It is too easy to push all this aside, to repress it. If it was repressed for too long, there could be a sudden surge of interest in it. And if the wrong person made use of such an enthusiasm and hit the right inspirational note, as Hitler did, the results could be dangerous. We must talk about our national identity, rationally, frequently, and not leave the subject to extremists from right or left. There should be no great gaps, no long silences."

Major Smyth returned with our glasses amply replenished; he picked up a few of Lüders' last words—"Gaps? Silences?"

"I suppose what I mean," Lüders said, "is the need for continuity here. In our past we have had serious political breakdowns which have been associated with a breakdown of social values. We have had no continuity of values as Britain has had—you have had severe political problems, too, but your society has managed to adjust to them. In any event, even if people weren't almost deliberately putting the border into a distant corner of their minds, it would be difficult to remain constantly excited about it over twenty or thirty years. So we seem calm. Yet there is a real tension between our everyday response to the border and all it stands for and our response to its grotesqueness. For example—here in Helmstedt lives a man whose grandmother died in a town a few kilometers away in East Germany. He applies for permission to attend her funeral, and he receives per-

mission two days after she was buried. One may think much of the time
that the border is something remote, something maintained by conditions
created and decisions made by politicians in Washington and Moscow—
until you are given a sharp reminder like that of how it affects an individual right here."

"One way it affects me as an individual," said the major, "is that people
in Helmstedt think I'm the person to bring complaints to. Someone called
me yesterday and said, 'A Russian driver has just parked his truck outside
my house. Please send your soldiers at once to take it away.' "

We had shifted to a lighter mood. Lüders said that there were generally
more political jokes in places where political discussion was constrained.
About ten years ago the DDR issued a set of stamps with birds on them.
The ten-pfennig stamp had a vulture. There was also a regular ten-pfennig
stamp showing the portrait of the then party chief, Walter Ulbricht.
People made up the twenty-pfennig postage for a letter by sticking on one
Ulbricht stamp and one vulture stamp, side by side. And then there was
the joke about the present party chief, Erich Honecker. Returning to East
Berlin from a trip abroad, he finds the place deserted. There is a big hole
in the wall and a note pinned up, saying: "Erich, you're last. Don't forget
to turn out the lights."*

I had been given a guest room attached to the Sergeants' Mess. It had a
window, out of which, before it had got dark, I had noticed a West German striped border marker, just visible down a grassy slope in the trees.
Lüders had said, as he left, that the military police post was on the site
of an early monastery; from places such as this, on what was then a religious border, missionaries had gone out to convert the pagan tribes in
the east. I lay in bed listening to the sound of the autobahn—the international sound of traffic. The major's peacocks were silent. Before I fell

---

* It was hard to avoid the impression that West Germans told so many East German
jokes because they had so few of their own. It would have been easy to make a considerable anthology of them. Two others are perhaps worth recounting here. In one, an
East German party official runs into a colleague who is carrying a raincoat and umbrella. The first official asks, "Why the umbrella, Comrade? There isn't a cloud in the
sky." The second official says, "I know, Comrade, but it's raining in Moscow." In the
other story, a car is stopped on the autobahn by the East German police. They make
the driver get out, and ask for his license.
He says, "Sorry, I don't have one."
His wife calls out, "Have they found out you failed the test?"
Grandma in the back says, "Have they discovered Grandpa in the trunk?"
And from the trunk comes a voice, "Are we in the West yet?"

asleep I remembered something that I should have asked the major about—Erich Schliephake's tramp. Erich, a journalist I'd met briefly in Hamburg, had come over from the DDR before the Berlin Wall was built. Erich knows a middle-aged tramp called Kurt who drops in to see him when he's passing through Hamburg on his travels. Kurt often makes his way along the border—he is particularly fond of the Harz Mountains area. On five separate occasions in different places on the border he has pretended to have just escaped from the DDR. He calls this his *Grenztrick*. When he spots the BGS or Zoll approaching he throws his jacket and possessions in such a way that it looks as if they've been hurled over the fence from the other side. His jacket is already torn. He then allows himself to be taken away for debriefing by military intelligence officers and gives them a colorful account of goings on in the DDR, the presence of Soviet panzer divisions, and the like. He claims that once at Helmstedt he received 200 Deutschmarks from each of the Allies—British, Americans, French and West Germans. Erich said that on Kurt's last attempt to play this trick, the British recognized him as having tried it before.

8. THE ISLAND

Among the numerous embassies in Belgrave Square, London, are those of the Federal Republic of Germany and of the German Democratic Republic. They have similar addresses, similar buildings, and confusion can arise. One of the things that an official of the DDR embassy had said to me when I called up one day earlier in the year to ask about the possibilities of traveling for a way along his country's border was, "Are you sure you've got the right German embassy?" When I'd said yes, I was sure, he had asked me to come by later in the week for a talk about my proposed journey.

I rang the buzzer at the immensely stout front door and spoke my name into a wall microphone. I had, I said, an appointment with Mr. Steiner. "A moment," said a voice. I waited several minutes and then the door opened. A man came out, said brusquely, "Please wait," and shut the door firmly behind him. I waited. I leaned against a pillar of the porch and watched the taxis swish around Belgrave Square. A few more minutes passed. Then the door opened and a woman invited me in. Down the stairs came a middle-aged man, thinning hair, big steel-framed spectacles—Mr. Steiner. He apologized for not taking me up to his office; it was being redecorated.* We sat down in a corner of the small ground-floor reception area, where a few chairs were placed around a low table with a base made of perforated panels. (Easily wired for recordings, I thought.) Coffee came and Mr. Steiner made a pleasantry about how even in the midst of emergencies like redecorating the coffee continued to be served. A plump elderly lady sat down nearby, apparently waiting. I wondered if she had a good memory in case the tape recorder wasn't working. "And so?" said Mr. Steiner, genially, his glasses flashing from the overhead light.

I told him of my intention to travel across Europe along, or near to, the dividing line. I didn't use the term Iron Curtain. It would be interesting to drive into the DDR, say at Helmstedt, spend four or five days wandering south as close to the border as was permitted, and come back into West Germany perhaps at Worbis. I was a British citizen. Probably (I said) I had some preconceptions—I might have said "suspicions." I was a product of Western society. But I tried to keep my mind as open as could be.

"Ah," said Mr. Steiner; he did not sound very convinced. He stared at me for a moment. "Well, let me tell you our position. We in the German Democratic Republic deplore the division of Germany very much. It is unnatural, it is dreadful—but it is history now. There has been a separate development of the two German states for more than thirty years now. Despite our common heritage and common language, there is no foreseeable chance of reunification."

He stirred his coffee. We each took a sip from our cups. He said, "We have our problems. We still have to wait for a long time to buy a car. There are some housing shortages. But we are sensitive to being treated as less than equal. We want full recognition by West Germany of the DDR as a state, with its own borders as a state. We want ambassadors exchanged, not just representatives."

Mr. Steiner told me that he had grown up in Thuringia, not far from the Bavarian border town of Coburg. After 1952 it had been difficult for ordinary people to cope with the fact that they couldn't go and spend a weekend in Bavaria anymore. They couldn't understand why this development was necessary. Now most people accept this as necessary, particularly the young who have been born since the separation. Most probably don't want reunification, which might be dangerous.

---

* In February 1982 it was revealed in the *Times* of London that in fact the entire DDR embassy had been demolished bit by bit and rebuilt behind the 1825 façade, despite the rejection by the Greater London Council of an application to make these changes.

He seemed fond of the word "development"—"our socialist development"; "our different development."

He introduced, quite diffidently, the fact that "our way of doing things" made necessary, for what I wanted to do, a journalist's visa and a guide-interpreter who would accompany me and arrange interviews. I would have to stay in approved hotels, though of course these would be international five-star hotels, and I would have to go to East Berlin for a briefing at the International Press Center, where all foreign journalists were received.

I said that I didn't particularly feel the need for a briefing and that going to East Berlin first might interrupt what I thought of as a continuous journey. I didn't make a practice of staying in international five-star hotels anywhere in the world, as they tended to be large and coldly modern, and not much help to one who was interested in locality and conversation.

Mr. Steiner said that he understood my objections to that sort of hotel, but unfortunately the DDR's socialist development had not so far got around to the constructions of smaller and possibly cozier hostelries. The inns of former times had generally been converted into private dwellings. To give me an idea of the DDR, Mr. Steiner handed me some booklets and magazines. Socialist developments seemed to be strongly emphasized in them. He told me what I should include in the letter that I must write when requesting a journalist's visa. "If I were you, I would apply for a longer rather than a shorter visit. That would be more favorably received," he said. I had the impression he wanted me to feel that he was on my side in the forthcoming debate over my application. "I will forward your letter to the International Press Center. We will see what can be done. You have a definite chance. Though it's a pity you've left it a little late."

In fact, I'd gone to see Mr. Steiner six weeks before setting off for Germany. A month later I called him to see if there had been any progress with my application. He had reminded the International Press Center, he said, but there was no news. It was three months after this, after the journey had been completed, that he called to say that my visa was approved. Too late! Fortunately there had been nothing to stop me from crossing East Germany to West Berlin, and this is what I did. Since the car would be a nuisance there, I took the train from Hanover, where the station was thronged with wild-looking *Gastarbeiter* from Turkey and Greece, long-distance travelers, women going shopping, young and old layabouts, and elderly Germans in green loden jackets and feathered hats that indicated their attachment to a rural, possibly feudal, past and its pursuits. On the platform a bunch of youngsters stood singing in an uninhibited way; in Britain a group would either need to be on stage or at a football match (or drunk) to let loose that way. There was also a group of slightly more subdued young men who, from the way they sprang to it when an announcement in English came over the loudspeaker, were evidently British soldiers, catching this train to Braunschweig where they would connect with a special British military train traveling to and from West Berlin every day. Between Hanover and Braunschweig they were frequently in the corridors, lugging their Adidas sports bags, which seem to have replaced duffle bags, and making use of the East German *Mitteleuropa* refreshment car.

The diesel locomotive was East German, and so was the rolling stock. I had a seat in a somewhat faded though comfortable first-class compartment, in which only one seat was unoccupied. My fellow passengers were "older people." Two ladies in what I judged to be their early sixties; one frail old lady in her late seventies; and a distinguished-looking man of perhaps sixty-five. The ladies' handbags and overcoats filled the vacant seat. There was an atmosphere of unspoken friendliness that may have sprung from the fact that we were about to go across East Germany together. At Helmstedt we took aboard East German ticket inspectors, customs and passport officers, and railway guards in uniform. Just before we reached the border a strong pulse of anticipation passed through our compartment. The ladies looked anxiously from window to window. The elderly gentleman went out and stood in the corridor, where he stared forward to catch sight of the *Grenze*. We passed into the area of open-cast coal workings that straddle the border. Over a heap of the brownish excavated coal appeared a watchtower. A fence angled into toward the train, then a second fence. We were in.

The fences turned at right angles and ran along each side of the tracks, forming a fenced corridor in which the train traveled east. There were no gates. The gap needed for the tracks was presumably well sealed by guards and dogs, and well watched from the towers. Tall concrete lamp standards paraded along the fences. And then the fences had ceased and we were in a scrubby, uncared-for forest that lasted for several kilometers, with young trees too closely packed and many dead trees among them. The train pulled to a halt in a station—Marienborn—sealed off from the world beyond by a gray wall topped with barbed wire. One of the ladies from my compartment joined a few other passengers in hastening along the platform to the hard-currency Intershop. When she returned, she stuffed her plump shopping bag into the already crammed overhead rack and sat down, her face showing the strain of feeling that she had acquired some bargains but didn't want to look too pleased about it. On the platform there were only gray-uniformed armed guards, no waiting passengers. This train was not for them.

Beyond Marienborn there was fitful sunshine. The patchwork countryside of woods and fields, sun and shadow, looked not unlike that of Germany to the west. Around the villages and small towns were the same allotment gardens with neat vegetable patches and small sheds often used as summer cottages; church towers or spires lifted the skyline. Houses looked the same except perhaps for being drabber, less well-painted. There were the same waterlogged furrows in field bottoms; ducks on ponds; crops being gathered. And some differences: several horse-drawn wagons moving along farm tracks; and in a siding near Magdeburg, a big black steam locomotive, puffing brown-black smoke into the air as it tugged a freight train.

At Magdeburg, in the late afternoon, armed gray-uniformed men of the DDR Volkspolizei stood between our train, which halted briefly, and a train that stood at a platform filling with commuters. Whom were the Vopos protecting from whom? The old lady sitting opposite me pointed out the twin spires of Magdeburg Cathedral. The elderly man took up the challenge of informing the foreign visitor; he pointed through the other window to a forbidding building. "Prison," he said. "For political prisoners." We crossed the Elbe, and what looked like barracks appeared on the southern side of the tracks. "Engineers of Soviet army," said my guide. A passport control officer came in and checked our documents. He stamped my passport and issued me a transit visa. "West Berlin?" he asked. "Ja," I replied. The train would be going on to a terminus in East Berlin; some of the passengers were retired East Germans returning from visits to relatives in the West. The passport officer wished us all a good journey as he closed the compartment door.

My elderly companion continued to point out occasional landmarks: we flashed by a large rock, close to the track. This and an overhanging tree known as the Biederitz Busch form a monument to the foundation of the DDR. At Kirchmöser were some industrial buildings that he said were Soviet tank-repair workshops. We halted briefly in Brandenburg. At Werder, twenty minutes later, he pointed out a Soviet artillery camp and then an old engine shed. "The Kaiser's personal engine was housed here," he said proudly. "Next is Potsdam."

Approaching Potsdam, I saw an "Inter-Hotel" sign and thought of Mr. Steiner. The ruins of Potsdam Palace appeared, where the August 1945 agreement was signed. We halted for a few minutes again, and I had the impression that the engine was switched and that the guards left the train. It was twilight as we approached West Berlin. This time the entrance was through a walled passage that felt like a trench, concrete panels topped by a concrete-pipe section, impossible to get a handhold on. Watchtowers and bright lights. Griebnitzsee Station, and Vopos on the platforms on each side. Then we had made the jump again ("West Berlin," said the elderly man) and the train was running through the Grunewald forest, extensive for a city. We paused at a suburban station, where I helped the oldest lady to the door with her extremely heavy suitcase. Twenty minutes after coming in through the wall we were amid the lights of the city center and had reached the Zoo Station. My fellow passengers and I said goodbye to one another and the phrase "*Auf Wiedersehen*" seemed right; they spoke almost as if we expected to see one another again.

Insula—the island—West Berliners sometimes call their city. It exists, one hundred and fifteen miles east of the border, as a result of the 1944–45 agreements and Allied determination to stay put despite Soviet pressure. The Soviet representative on the Allied Control Commission withdrew from the meeting that was being held on March 20, 1948, and refused to attend further sessions. The city's administrative and political structure was split in two. The day after a currency reform was announced in the Western sectors (June 24, 1948), the Soviet authorities blockaded all land access to West Berlin. Over the following eleven months the Allies successfully supplied the city by air, demonstrating that the Western powers had the will to fight this fiercest of Cold War battles to a conclusion.

West Berlin remains an act of will or faith. The supporting theology has even been subscribed to by the Soviet Union. In the Quadripartite Agreement, signed in September 1971 and put into effect in June 1972, the USSR agreed no longer to contest the Western powers' presence in West Berlin; the city's ties with the Federal Republic of Germany were accepted; a legal basis was provided for unimpeded traffic between West Germany and West Berlin; and West Berliners regained the right to visit East Berlin and East Germany. However, West Berlin's integration in the political, financial and social system of West Germany is not total. Federal laws are adopted by way of parallel laws, subject to the agreement of the Western Allies. East European countries insist that West Berliners travel to those countries on identity cards rather than on West German passports. Meanwhile the postwar origins of the setup remain evident in the military presence of the Western Allies, who patrol their zones of the city and make occasional sorties into East Berlin (in return for which the Russians are allowed to do the same in West Berlin). No West German airline is allowed to fly to West Berlin. Pan Am and British Airways happily fill the gap with frequent flights from Tegel Airport to various West German cities as well as places abroad. (West Berliners complain that these airlines tend to use their oldest equipment on intra-German routes, perhaps because in the air-transit corridors over East Germany, Allied flights are still confined to Dakota-suitable altitudes of 10,000 feet. A consequence of this is that flights to and from Berlin are often turbulent— though one's ears aren't subjected to great changes of pressure.) The West German government maintains numerous offices in West Berlin, but the West Berlin Senate, the city government, sometimes regards these as representatives of a rival power. Because there is conscription in West Germany but not in West Berlin, many young West Germans come to live in the city to avoid military service.

Their presence helps. Berlin for some time has had an aging and declining population—too many elderly people, too few energetic middle-aged or young ones. So although one visible and apparently anarchic element of the young may be the punk-haired youths and pallid drug addicts who hang out on the Kurfürstendamm (popularly called Kudamm) near the Zoo Station, there are also many students to be seen in galleries, pubs and bookshops, or riding the mostly underground U-Bahn to the university out at Dahlem, new blood for Berlin's tired veins. The city has always depended on immigrants. It was the capital not only of Germany but of Central Europe (and still feels as if it is the latter.) "Most Berliners come from Breslau" was a prewar saying. Like New York, the city took the poor and underprivileged and turned them into something—not necessarily the most polite, but rather pushy, on the make, and quite friendly people, who felt distinguished by the city, wherever they had come from. In Hitler's time they remained a good deal less than Nazi, making a point— as George Kennan noted—of saying *"Guten Morgen"* to one another instead of "Heil Hitler," as they were supposed to, and showing little enthusiasm for the war. They now feel more special than ever, living on their island under the protection of the powers. "Spoiled rotten," some West Germans think.

I liked this special feeling in West Berlin. I walked the boulevards and streets, and felt that fully charged zip in the air which a few cities have and which brings one's nerves and senses alive. Berliners give the impression of knowing not only that they are privileged but that they are moment by moment triumphing over circumstantial adversity. The city floats in space beyond the borders of the West, a hot-air balloon kept aloft by agreements not to shoot it down (or by agreements to suspend the laws of gravity that affect political structures). It is also kept up by West German money, which provides 60 percent of the city's funds, and by tourism.

People are attracted to it as they would be to an island, which is "different," and which gives them a precarious feeling of being in the midst of the Red sea.

Berlin insularity comes out in various ways. Berliners feel the need to get off their island now and then—to drive, if only for a long weekend, to West Germany and sit by the Elbe or walk in the Harz Mountains. A waitress in the canteen of the radio station RIAS told me that she had spent a two-week vacation on Bali in 1981. Berliners feel a pride in their island and feel superior to mainlanders, but they also tend to look at problems from an island point of view—if a problem can't be immediately related to West Berlin, their interest drops fast. And they feel, too, the claustrophobia of an island; the suicide rate is higher than it is in West Germany. In spring, the pent-up drivers of West Berlin get out on the old section of autobahn that runs through the Grunewald and let rip, occasionally with fatal result. There is the Berlin argot: a roll, *Brötchen* elsewhere in Germany, is a *Schrippe*; a five-pfennig piece is a *Sechser*. Many terms that arrived with French Huguenot immigrants are still in use, such as *Trottoir* for sidewalk, and *Parterre* for a ground floor. Berliners often say *"Pardon"* instead of *"Entschuldigen Sie."*

Not all Berliners have got used to being encircled. Even those who frequently use the autobahn to get to West Germany say that they feel a slight tightening of the nerves as they go through the checkpoints. And yet none would say they are depressed by being surrounded. Some claim to live in the city without ever setting eyes on the wall.

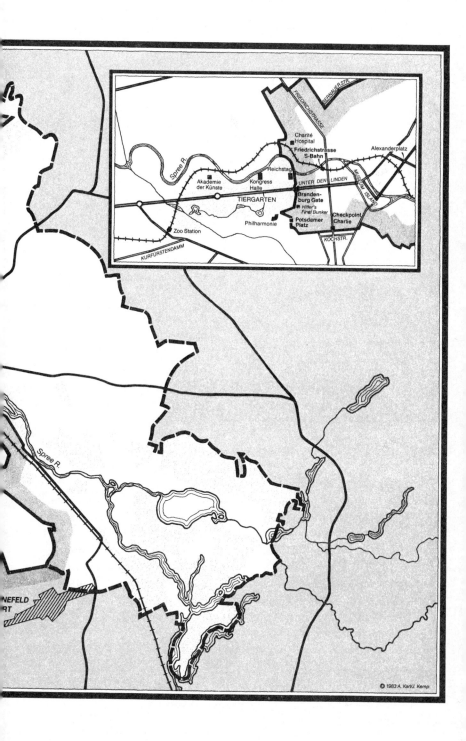

Charité
Hospital

Friedrichstrasse
S-Bahn

Alexanderplatz

Spree R.

Reichstag

Akademie
der Künste

Kongress
Halle

UNTER DEN LINDEN

TIERGARTEN

Brandenburg Gate

Hitler's
Final Bunker

Potsdamer
Platz

Checkpoint
Charlie

Philharmonie

Zoo Station

KOCHSTR.

KURFÜRSTENDAMM

Spree R.

NEFELD
RT

© 1983 A. Karl/J. Kemp

9. WALLED IN, WALLED OUT

In the days that I spent in Berlin I made numerous journeys to the wall. I walked along sections of it, drove along parts of it, flew over it, and finally went through it and looked at it from the other side. As at the border, I felt a whole range of emotions, from rage through curiosity to resignation (though never disinterest). It seemed to me in its perverse way one of the wonders of the modern world. Its construction is almost entirely up to date, though in several places one can see old sections of wall that have been subsumed in it, as in the Müllerstrasse, where long brown concrete blocks have been piled on top of one another. *Die Mauer* it is called—a feminine word perhaps because, as I remember Frau Cole saying, all words in German that have to do with work are feminine, and the wall was hard work. It is for the most part 3.5 meters high, topped with cylindrical concrete pipe, its western side cemented smooth and painted white. For 46 kilometers it forms a boundary between East and West Berlin. The 120 kilometers of boundary between West Berlin and East Germany are about 85 percent solid abutment, 15 percent fence (as at Frötinau, in the north of the city). There are the same patrolways, anti-vehicle trenches and barriers, watchtowers and dog runs that one sees on the IGB—but no longer any mines. In most places West Berliners can walk right up to it; but in others, East German–owned ground lies in front of the wall (which may at those points be taking a shortcut across, say, a projection of land into West Berlin), and although the nonchalant or daring may plant vegetables on such ground or hold a barbecue on it, there remains a chance of East German border troops appearing to arrest the trespassers.

When the wall started to go up in August 1961, it was only a few months after Walter Ulbricht had declared at a press conference, "No one intends to erect a wall." Two months later the wall—though always thereafter in process of being improved—was more or less complete. Almost all East Germans and East Berliners were sealed off from the Western city, and the flow of people leaving for the West was summarily staunched. (Between 1949 and 1961 roughly a fifth of the DDR population fled their country; the exodus reached its peak at the end, when, in the month before the wall went up, 140,000 left.)

At the time, the DDR regime offered the explanation that the wall was to protect its citizenry from the Western threat. A recent DDR publication that Mr. Steiner gave me, "DDR: 100 Questions, 100 Answers," says: "The men and officers of the workers' militia, together with other armed organizations, stood their most exacting test in August 1961 when they sealed off the DDR's state border with West Berlin. The DDR, acting in full agreement with its Warsaw Treaty allies, thus preserved peace in Europe, reminding the aggressive imperialist forces of the limits they could not overstep." In the DDR (says the same publication), freedom of the individual's is guaranteed. "People are free in a state which is their own and which they run themselves." Article 13 of the UN Declaration of Human Rights (1948) declares that everyone has the right to emigrate from his country. The DDR constitution of 1949 provided for such a right; that of 1968 confines the citizen's freedom of movement to the area "within the state frontiers of the German Democratic Republic." Since the building of the wall some seventy people have been killed attempting to get into West Berlin, and at least three thousand arrests have been made of people who were presumably about to attempt an escape.

I made a tour of the Western city one day with a young Berlin journalist, Lothar Nass, who did a few errands of his own in the course of showing me around. He visited a police station to get a new identity card (a necessity Bismarck first introduced to Germany) which Nass needed because he had recently changed his address. He also went to a travel agency to order tickets for a holiday he was optimistically planning to take in Poland in a few months' time. (It is easy to be in Berlin without realizing that one is only fifty miles (eighty kilometers) from the Polish border—which in December 1944 the Russians insisted on moving from its previous position to the Oder-Neisse line. This westward adjustment of some two hundred miles was agreed to by Roosevelt and Churchill a few months later at Yalta.) We then drove out through the leafy suburb of Dahlem with its fine museums and large houses—Joseph Goebbels and other Nazi leaders lived in Dahlem, but it is one thing one doesn't blame them for. We passed through Grunewald to reach the lakes. Berlin is twenty miles across, as large as London with half the number of people, and it sits at the southern end of an extensive lake district with interconnecting rivers. Seagulls fly south from the Baltic, following the water, and can be seen on the Spree, the river that comes from the east and roughly bisects the city. Beyond Grunewald are the Havel River and Wannsee. These bodies of water seemed spacious, but Nass said that on sunny weekends and holidays they were crowded; half of all registered West German pleasure boats are moored in West Berlin. Obviously they form a kind of escape from the island.

We got out of the car at Glienicke Bridge, which Nass told me has two somewhat-at-variance nicknames: Unity Bridge (because it joins Berlin and Potsdam, across the Havel), and Spy Bridge (because here, in February 1962, Colonel Rudolf Abel, the Russian spymaster in the United States, and Francis Gary Powers, the captured U-2 pilot, were exchanged). The far side of the bridge lands in the DDR; the East German flag was flying over a checkpoint, with a watchtower, barbed wire and the wall on each side. The bridge itself was deserted. From our end of it, where a few anglers sat, there was a view across the Havel to the entrance of a canal which leads west, to the Elbe and Hamburg. There is a checkpoint at the first lock. The breeze that blew over the Wannsee felt warm, at odds with such things as walls and checkpoints. I wondered about man's need to "pick up sides," to square off in opposing forces, to apportion ideas, ways of life, the world. To have an enemy or opposition imposes a uniformity (and a means of imposing discipline) on each side that neither really might have in its heart. Are we in fact preserving ourselves by these means, or encasing ourselves in suits of armor which prevent movement and which will be no protection from the dangers such inflexibility brings in its train?

We drove back into the city to the Bernauerstrasse. This once famous working-class street became part of the dividing line in 1945, with the houses on one side falling within East Berlin and those on the other within the West. In the days immediately following August 13, 1961, the ground-floor windows and doors on the east side were bricked up from within by the so-called Workers' Militia; and from upstairs windows people jumped or clambered down into the Bernauerstrasse. The houses were soon cleared of all their occupants by the East German authorities, and the façades completely sealed up. Now the houses on that side of the street have gone, and the wall runs along it in their place, gleaming white. Nass said an East German maintenance crew had recently repainted it. It needs frequent repainting because it is the best free blackboard a city could have. In various places along it one sees inscriptions and drawings. Representations of doors are painted on it. Graffiti that I saw included: "Class of '80"; German phrases for "Your Freedom Is Our Duty"; "To the Victims of the Red Dictatorship"; "The Wall Must Go"; "East Berlin Is under the Direction of Saxons"; and "East German High Jump Training Area." "DDR = der doofe Rest" meant DDR = the dopey dregs. There are slogans of West Berlin political parties, cartoon figures and—particularly in the Kreuzberg area—protests about city housing policy and expressions of support for squatters in abandoned buildings owned by the city government. Some sections of the wall are painted and overpainted, color on color, statement on statement, as on New York subway trains. Some remarks are obscene; some are obscure. The cost of maintenance is obviously hefty for the East Germans; the cost of building it is reckoned to be roughly that of building the modern highway from East Berlin to Rostock on the Baltic; an unquantified cost is that of the houses and other buildings demolished to create space for it.

Life goes on beside the wall in the West. Young mothers push their baby carriages; people walk their dogs. Sometimes one sees people, presumably strangers to the city, touching the wall, as if the act of running their fingers along it or laying an open palm against it might transfer to them out of the solid concrete whatever its meaning is. How else can it be understood? It provokes some of the feelings one has against concrete as a building material. In some areas it runs through old neighborhoods and in others past the great surviving monuments of Berlin: it runs just east of the Reichstag, the old parliament, and just west of the Brandenburg Gate. It forms the eastern boundary of the Tiergarten, the Central Park or Hyde Park of Berlin. Later, someone told me of an East German mother who takes her little boy to the Brandenburg Gate, where East Berliners can look out over the wall to the west. The child sees the trees of the Tiergarten. He says, "Mother—is there nothing but woods on the other side?"

In the Reichstag while I was in Berlin an exhibition was on view of events in German history up to and including Hitler's war. Near the Reichstag a little memorial of half a dozen plain crosses marked the spot where people have died trying to get across—the most recent a young woman, killed here in November 1980. South of the Tiergarten the land close to the west side of the wall is sparsely or not at all developed. The wall runs through that part of the city that held the chief offices and chancelleries of the Third Reich—the ground has parted and swallowed them up and closed over them for all time. Just beyond the wall here, closed off from the east as well, is some vacant East Berlin ground raised into what looks like an ancient mound or barrow—Hitler's final bunker.

Some of the undeveloped land on the west side of the wall is that way because it is owned by the East Germans. The DDR government may have taken possession of it without ever having compensated its owners. West Berlin recently bought some land from East Berlin in order to straighten a street and was promptly sued by a family in South America, heirs to the former owners of the land, who had never got anywhere when pressing their case against the East Germans. In one area of waste ground near the wall, where the bustling Potsdamer Platz used to be, there is a flea market, a little circus, a refreshment kiosk and an observation stand for looking over into East Berlin. These stands have been set up by local city councils at intervals along the wall. That in the Bernauerstrasse is painted a jaunty red and blue and is somewhat bigger and more permanent-looking than others. When Lothar Nass and I climbed up to its viewing platform we encountered a man, in civilian clothes, keeping an eye through binoculars on the East German border guards in their watchtower just beyond the wall. It was apparently a self-appointed task or hobby. He spent part of every day here, observing what was going on in this section of the wall. He watched where the guards telephoned from and noted what time the gray-brown motorcycle and sidecar arrived with a new pair of guards for duty. "They're two minutes late," he said authoritatively, then switched his attention to a kennel from which a savage-looking German shepherd had just loped forth on the end of a long chain. Nass said, "They also have observers detailed to watch for people approaching the neighborhood of the wall who might be thinking of making a dash for it. If they can apprehend such persons, they may avoid the bad publicity that comes from shooting them as they try to get across."

On the far side of the strip was a smaller wall, and over that, one had a prospect of gray streets. At the corner of two streets stood a drab four-story apartment building; above one of its ground-floor doorways was a sign: KLUB DER VOLKSSOLIDARITÄT. (Perhaps, after a year in which the Poles have injected new life into the word "solidarity," the name may have changed.) It was as though one were looking into a haze and could make out dimly the 1950s or even the 1930s.

The prewar center of Berlin lay between Unter den Linden and the Leipziger Strasse. The Tiergarten provided a large green space between this and the best residential area in the west of the city, along the Kurfürstendamm—which in the depressed 1920s began to become commercial. In postwar West Berlin the planners worked for a long time on the assumption that the city would be reunited. Many projects seemed placed to bring the city together again, like the new Philharmonic Hall, new Library, and new National Gallery, which have all been built on the waste ground south of the Tiergarten, not far from the wall. But the Cold War has proved unkind; none of these great structures has the population of East Berlin to help support it. West Berlin has had to lay on fleets of special buses to get concertgoers to and from the Philharmonic way out in no man's land.

A building that has been set up not far from there by private enterprise and with slightly different motives is the headquarters of the Axel Springer publishing organization—a glass and gold-metallic tower block that rises on the Kochstrasse, the prewar newspaper row of Berlin. Here, where newspaper offices and printing plants were once crowded together, the landscape is like that of the South Bronx or London dockland: empty buildings and vacant lots. Half a block away is the wall, which here for a mile or so runs in an east-west direction, casting its own spell of desolation. Springer bought the moribund Ullstein publishing firm in the late 1960s and moved his headquarters from Hamburg, choosing this site next to the wall because of its press connections and because—presumably—the land was cheap, but also as a gesture of confidence in West Berlin. Until the East Berlin authorities blocked the way with a set of tall neo-Corbusian apartment buildings, Springer informed the East Berlin citizenry by means of a Times Square–type illuminated news-message board at the top of his building. (A feature of the building which has survived—and which also might be regarded as symbolic of Springer's brash and whole-hearted commitment to capitalism—is continuously moving, doorless paternoster elevators, which one jumps on and off at the appropriate floor; any time-wasting or dithering, one is led to feel, may result in an almost Islamic automatic punishment.)

The Springer building continues to provide West Berlin's best view of East Berlin. From the press club on the seventeenth floor there is a direct prospect of East Berlin's own landmark set up not long ago in the Eiffel Tower tradition: an immensely tall radio and TV tower just off the Alexanderplatz. Two thirds of the way up it is a large orb-shaped observation chamber. The spike of the antenna above makes it look a little like a mace. To some it seems like the DDR watchtower par excellence. In the late afternoon the declining sun from the west causes the glass windows of the orb to reflect in the pattern of a giant glowing cross,

which West Berliners call the Pope's Revenge. After the war West German Christians made generous donations to help East German churches,
and some say that much of the money somehow made possible this official propaganda weapon of the Communist state. Further rumor has it
that the East Germans are considering the installation of nonreflecting
glass to get rid of the telltale stigmata.

Several ravaged blocks west of the Axel Springer Verlag is the Friedrichstrasse, a street that runs into and across East Berlin from south to north.
Where it passes through the wall is Checkpoint Charlie, one of seven
crossing places between East and West Berlin, and the one through
which non-Germans must pass when going to and from East Berlin. Although it has been in use for twenty years, the checkpoint still has an
impermanent look, like jerry-built sheds at the edge of a building site. It
is a great tourist attraction. A constant stream of sightseers climbs a wall-
high viewing stand to watch the occasional car pass through the gap in
the wall, beneath a watchtower, and enter a maze of concrete bollards,
chains, cables and barriers which causes the driver to follow a route that
gives him no opportunity to build up speed for crashing through any of
the restraints. Forming a sort of bastion of the inner wall to the right of
the checkpoint is a red brick industrial building, the printing plant of the
Neue Zeit newspaper, from a back window of which one night in 1980
two printers, who had allowed themselves to be locked in after work,
managed to climb down, get across the strip, and throwing grappling hooks
over the wall, haul themselves over it. The guards in the watchtower
must have been dozing or taking a protracted look the other way.

The last building on the right in the Friedrichstrasse on the West
Berlin side of the checkpoint is a museum called Haus am Checkpoint
Charlie. It is a decrepit, scruffy place, but judging from the crowds of
visitors who move through its cramped rooms, it seems to serve its purpose
of reminding people of the history of the wall. On the Sunday morning
that I first went there it was packed with families, couples, individuals
and tour groups. Various escape devices were displayed: a tiny Isetta
bubble-shaped car, with a hidden compartment where a person was able to
curl around the engine (nine people, on nine trips, had come out this
way); a makeshift balloon basket and hot-air heating burner, with which
two families, whom I was to meet later on the border, had sailed out of
the DDR; an underwater motor used for an escape in the Baltic; a
breeches-buoy–type harness and pulley, used to slide down a rope over
the wall from a house; and many sorts of tunneling gear. Photographs recorded various incidents at the wall. One now historic shot shows a young
East German border guard jumping over barbed wire, which at that point

formed the main obstacle to his freedom. Another showed Peter Fechter, one of the first victims of the wall, an eighteen-year-old East Berlin lad who was shot as he tried to get over the wall in August 1962 and fell at the foot of the wall, still in East Berlin. West Berlin policemen threw first-aid kits to him but he was too weak to help himself. The East German guards looked on as he bled to death. (More recently, a young Turkish boy, resident in West Berlin, fell into one of the stretches of water along the boundary between the two halves of the city and drowned while the East German guards looked on.) The sadness induced by these exhibits of what is almost civil war—or of an uncivil, murderous peace—was slightly alleviated by photographs showing a very low-slung sports car, leased from a Kurfürstendamm rental agency, in which, on two separate occasions, first a young Austrian and then a young Argentinean had sped under checkpoint barriers, their East German fiancées crouched beside them. After those successes, vertical bars were fitted to the main horizontal bar used to block the exit.

In the house next door an extension to the wall museum was being built, and an exhibition had been mounted of entries for a competition for the design of a mural, to go on the outside end-wall of the building. Most of the entries demonstrated how difficult it is to express the feelings that the wall and the divided city call forth. Some were surreal, some sardonic, some nearly obscene. Several showed natural forces damaging the wall—for example, tree roots splitting it. A few countered the wall's power to separate and desolate with representations of human ability to overcome such adversity. Possibly the least symbolic, most direct and successful showed two workmen climbing up from either side of a demolished wall with hands outstretched toward each other. The artist: Matthias Koeppel, born in 1935, living in West Berlin.

I returned to the Haus am Checkpoint Charlie a few days after this to talk to Dr. Rainer Hildebrandt, director of the museum and of Working Group August 13th, an organization devoted to keeping track of escapes from the DDR and the state of human rights in that country. Several West Berliners whom I'd talked to had given me the impression that Dr. Hildebrandt and his assistants were "cold warriors," interested in not letting the Cold War die away—and certainly in not letting the East German regime relax with its self-crowned laurels. But at Checkpoint Charlie such criticism seems a little detached, when there are manifestations of the Cold War visible right there in the middle of the Friedrichstrasse.

Dr. Hildebrandt was a large, fleshy man in what looked like his early sixties, with silver-blond hair and a small gray mustache. His left arm rested in a sling made from a purple silk scarf—the result, he said, of a skiing accident. He laughed as he said this, and I couldn't tell whether he meant to make light of the incident or to show that he said it tongue-in-cheek; perhaps—did he mean to suggest?—there was a more sinister explanation. The main part of Haus am Checkpoint Charlie had been a café before the war, and this new extension had been a brothel. Patrons had gone back and forth between the two. His own training had been as a psychologist; his experiences living in Hitler's Germany, including the loss of many friends, had led him into the fight for civil liberties, particularly for those who lived in the DDR. In warm weather the wall museum attracted roughly a thousand paying visitors a day. The Working Group received a grant from the West Berlin Senate, but the Federal government —which had once given funds to the Group—had ceased to do so, Dr. Hildebrandt said, at the time it decided to improve relations with East Germany and send a permanent representative to East Berlin.

Two young Turks were painting a wall of the adjacent room, and Dr. Hildebrandt fished some coins out of a pocket with his working hand and sent one of them off around the corner for coffee. He continued to talk about his feeling that the Federal authorities had deserted his cause. "It is unbelievable that we have a government that has done nothing at the United Nations or the Madrid Conference on the Helsinki Agreement about the installation of the SM-70s along the border." He also felt deserted by the West German people, who weren't sufficiently active in condemning repression in the DDR. This was because they hadn't learned how to live with their own past, their complicity in Nazi crimes; and also because they were interested in doing business with East Germany.

I said that I thought East-West commerce could be defended: trade and business contacts might well create an interdependence that was preferable to mutual isolation, in which each side stood back and went on arming itself to the teeth.

We drank coffee from Styrofoam cups that the young Turk brought back. Dr. Hildebrandt was saying that telling the truth was no longer enough; one had to learn the right methods for gaining human rights without provoking governments to arbitrary and counterproductive action. I watched through the window two cars proceeding slowly toward the checkpoint. "Like the Polish workers," Dr. Hildebrandt continued, "who have chosen their ground for their stand in their own factories . . ." He planned to mount an exhibition soon, to be called "From Gandhi to Walesa." "Ah, you must meet Manfred." Manfred Milde, the permanent exhibition manager, came in and shook hands with me. He had escaped in 1966 while serving as an NCO with the DDR border forces; he gave me a brief account of it. "Sometime before my escape, I talked it over with a friend I was serving with. We knew that we would never be allowed to go out on patrol together. However, as platoon leader, I could approach the various pairs of men who were posted as guards. On the night we decided to go, my pal was on duty with a private in a watchtower. He managed to sneak the bolt from the private's rifle and put it in his own pocket, and then climb down from the tower. When I saw him reach the ground, I cocked my weapon and pointed it at the man who was with me. I made him drop his gun and said, 'Just take it easy and climb the tower. But don't turn on the spotlight or we'll shoot it out.' He had no choice; he did as I said. He couldn't give the alarm because only noncoms had flare pistols and field telephones. My pal gave me cover until I'd climbed over the outer fence and then I covered him."

Border guards still have a greater chance of getting across than civilians. In November 1980 one shot and killed his noncom colleague before climbing over the wall in Berlin. A few weeks later a young man, a civilian, was killed by border guards as he tried to get over the wall into Staaken, a district of West Berlin. According to figures published in one newspaper (Birmingham *Post*, February 19, 1980), there were thirty-six successful escapes from East Berlin in 1979. Dr. Hildebrandt told me that the wall was not the best way out; in the past many have left East Berlin as passengers in diplomats' cars, which aren't searched. In the early 1960s the Chinese were very helpful, said Dr. Hildebrandt. "They hated the DDR in those days." Diplomats of other countries, no names mentioned, did it for money; DM 60,000 or DM 70,000—say, $15,000—was a common price. In October 1979 the East German chauffeur of the United States ambassador to East Germany took out his family a few at a time hidden in the ambassador's car, and on his final trip went out alone. A West Berlin printer and his assistants were tried not long ago in a West Berlin court for forging East German diplomatic passports containing permission to leave the DDR. Dr. Hildebrandt said that eight hundred people had got out using such passports.

By now there are numerous escape legends. I heard of one East Berliner who a few years ago arrived at a checkpoint hoping to sneak through unseen in the shadow of a car. But there were more guards than he'd expected. One of the guards stopped him and he said, "Sorry, I'm Austrian. I didn't understand the procedure. My papers are there in the office with my friend, the driver, being checked."

The guards were in the process of being changed. A new one turned up at that moment, and the guard who was going off duty said, without any other explanation, "Keep an eye on this man. I'll look for his papers." He went off.

The "Austrian" turned to the new guard. He said, "To tell you the truth, I don't have any papers. My mother is dying in East Berlin. Do you think they'll let me through?"

"Without papers! Of course not."

"Then I'd better go back. Thanks."

The guard opened the gate, and the man walked into West Berlin.

This story doesn't quite pass muster if you've experienced the checks and double-checks, the numerous guards and one-way systems at the crossing points; but it is a nice example of the quick thinking that West Berliners hope will outsmart the enemy.

There was a time when helping people escape from East Berlin was a courageous occupation for some in West Berlin, and for others a way of making money. In the late sixties, $2,000 or $3,000 was said to be a price often asked for helping with an escape, like providing a false West German passport; generally West German friends had to pay in advance; sometimes the East German could pay in installments after reaching the West. Some escape helpers did so out of a spirit of adventure; some just wanted expense money to cover their costs. A confusion sometimes remains about which motive predominated. Dr. Hildebrandt told me of "a well-known university teacher in West Berlin" who had been an escape helper from 1961 to 1970, when he gave up because of the ungrateful attitude of the West German government and the public—which was apparently given the impression by newspaper reports that the teacher was helping people to escape for money, for vanity or for purposes of espionage. Among his friends this helper was known as the Scarlet Pimpernel; he was reputed to have assisted a thousand people to escape by various means from East Germany. "Many women worked for him," said Dr. Hildebrandt with an approving smile. "Perhaps you should talk to him about his escape-helping activities, which are not properly known."

Good idea, I thought. An intermediary was proposed—but things at once began to get complicated. The escape helper would have to remain anonymous, and not just in anything that was written about him; not even I would know his name. I was asked, moreover, if I would be willing to make a small payment of perhaps a hundred dollars for the interview. It would mollify the man for having to tell his story again. This question startled me. I said, "Yes, I suppose so." An evening meeting was arranged. But before it occurred I thought a little more about it. If the man's activities were not properly known, why was there a suggestion that he had to be mollified into talking about them? Although I didn't mind keeping his identity a secret, I wasn't sure I could altogether trust what might be said by someone who wouldn't let me know who he was. I had never paid money for information before, and even if the sum was reduced, as my reluctance became known, to a more token figure, I felt it might warp the way in which I thought about and wrote about escapes—as perhaps it has. I explained all this to the person who had arranged the meeting, when I told him that I had decided it would be best not to talk to the former Pimpernel. Later I wondered whether I had failed to fall in with a scheme that seemed to the intermediary a straightforward matter of covering incidental expenses, like charging for a photograph one might use, or for admission to a museum—to the Haus am Checkpoint Charlie, for instance.

10. PROTECTING POWERS

Sovereignty in West Berlin still resides in an Allied military government, though that government lies low, a "protecting power." There are 2,800 French troops in the city, 3,600 British soldiers and RAF personnel, and 7,000 U.S. servicemen, all backed by necessary headquarters, civilian services, housing agencies, commissaries, schools and recreation facilities. The West German government pays all the costs of the Allied military presence in the city, except for basic wages. Although no West German military forces are allowed in West Berlin, the East German government does not recognize any constraints on its right to deploy DDR troops in East Berlin, which is the declared capital of the East German state. The Western Allies continue to exercise their right to make "flag tours" by military vehicle in East Berlin, and the Russians do the same in West Berlin—though they use less conspicuously military-looking cars, possibly to avoid being pelted with rubbish in certain parts of the city, after being identified as Russian. The Western Allied forces patrol the wall and boundary fence in their own sectors of the city and preserve a keen state of readiness with constant training at fighting in built-up areas. The other side has, in a ring some thirty kilometers wide around Berlin, 95,000 Soviet and East German troops, 1,300 tanks, 300 heavy guns, and tactical nuclear weapons. These forces include 14,000 DDR Border Command troops, whose job it is to guard the immediate perimeter of West Berlin, and are armed like a light infantry division, with anti-aircraft and anti-tank weapons. The Russians also have an independent motor rifle brigade and tank battalion stationed within East Berlin. Armed forces stationed in the DDR number more than half a million (400,000 Soviet, 150,000 East German), which is a lot for a country with a population of 17 million. The five Soviet ground armies and air army in East Germany are considered by military experts to be the best Soviet forces outside the USSR. Soviet soldiers are to be seen in West Berlin standing ceremonial guard at the Soviet War Memorial, which is on the edge of the Tiergarten, in the British sector, across the wall from the Brandenburg Gate. There they stand immobile in their long coats, in their turn guarded by West Berlin police and British army patrols, with spectators kept at a great distance to ensure that the Russian guards don't have things, or abuse, hurled at them.

Early one morning I took a #29 bus from the Kurfürstendamm, off which, in a quiet side street, I had rooms in a small turn-of-the-century hotel of great charm. The 29 took me to the junction of the Kochstrasse and Friedrichstrasse, and I walked up to Checkpoint Charlie to join a U.S. military patrol for a trip along the wall. Three drab-green jeeps were waiting there, and in each were three soldiers in baggy olive-green combat uniforms, big lace-up boots, many pouches and bits of webbing, and with deep steel helmets and chin straps surrounding their faces. A tall flexible radio antenna stood up from the back of each jeep, while in front was an upright steel bar meant to catch any wires that—with the windshields down—might hit, and decapitate, the jeep's driver and passengers. M-60 machine guns were mounted in two of the vehicles; there was room for me in the jeep that didn't have one. I introduced myself to the patrol leader, Sergeant John Kiene, a young man with buckteeth and sandy mustache; to his assistant, Sergeant Michael Gonzales; and the driver, Specialist/4 Nicholas Kalaplostos. They belonged to a platoon of Combat Support Company, Third Battalion, Sixth Infantry, U.S. Army, scions of huddled masses and products of the melting pot—cheerful, gum-chewing, slightly baffled-looking young men.

Sergeant Kiene said as we set off that he wasn't allowed to tell me exactly how many patrols went out or at what times, but their job was to keep an eye on what was happening along the wall by day and night, note any new construction or changes in DDR operating procedure, and demonstrate the U.S. presence. (This was not the last time I heard the phrase "demonstrating a presence" on this journey. One wonders what "the other side" would do or think if a presence went undemonstrated.) We drove beside the wall toward the Springer building, in the sunlight a burnished beacon. We turned in onto the ordinary city streets for a few blocks to another checkpoint at the Heinrich Heine Strasse, where Kiene and I walked up to the six-inch-wide border line painted on the road, and a man in a civilian raincoat came out on the platform of a watchtower and took our photograph. We drove on. Sometimes, along the wall, the jeeps had to squeeze through gaps between parked cars and the wall itself, wheels up on its sloped base or bumping over curbs. Postmen were delivering mail to apartment houses on our side; chimes sounded from an ice cream van making its rounds; and the driver of a bread truck was having a quiet smoke by the bank of the Spree, the wall visible on the far side across the brown water. We drove through the yard of a construction business and pulled up for a moment on a wharf where an East German barge was unloading sand. A West Berlin police car was parked there too, keeping an eye on things. The mutual dependence was plain; West Berlin needed their materials; they needed West Berlin's custom. I had read somewhere that dead bodies are part of this commerce. East German state-owned hearses drive every day through the checkpoints, bringing bodies in coffins for burial in family plots in West Berlin; others are collected for burial in East Berlin. (The coffins, needless to say, are closely examined to make sure no life lurks within.)

On the river, two fast-looking DDR patrol boats were pacing watchfully up and down. We were near the Oberbaum Bridge, fenced off at our end. "There used to be a lot of escapes here," said Kiene, who didn't look old enough to have such a historical point of view. He gazed at the patrol boats. "You should see those babies—they just pick up and move."

We drove along the edge of the Kreuzberg district, where many of the derelict old apartment houses, bought by the city for eventual restoration, were occupied by squatters. Defiant banners proclaiming their presence were strung across the streets or draped from windows. There have been confrontations, riots, arrests in Kreuzberg, but on this morning all was calm. Not a policeman was to be seen in the run-down streets. Kiene halted the patrol by an observation platform. Swans drifted on the nearby canal, and several seagulls were perched on the pipe-section top of the wall. A guard in a DDR watchtower was looking at us through binoculars. Another was talking on the telephone at the base of the tower, presumably telling the next post we were making our rounds. A third was taking a pee at the side of a little shed.

"We often see them pretty relaxed, chatting, smoking," Kiene said. "They're about our age. Sometimes we catch them dozing off, having pretend punch-ups, or kicking a ball around. Not long ago one of them saw me looking at him through the binoculars and he held out the cord around his neck, which they have knotted in a way that shows how much time they've got left to serve. They sometimes give us a wave, though they're not supposed to. Neither are we, in case they photograph us doing so. I guess they're doing a job, same as us."

One East Berlin apartment house near the Bouchéstrasse abutted the strip at right angles, the balconies on its end wall overhanging the plowed ground. A bed of spikes had been planted under the balconies, and then surrounded, like a strange garden, by an electrified fence. In most places in the urban world one can jump from an apartment balcony without the state actively assisting in one's death.

As for Berlin—Kalaplostos said, "It's a bit like being stationed in New York. The Berliners are more friendly than the West Germans. They seem to know why we're here."

The U.S. Army invited me on another excursion. I rode the U-Bahn out to Dahlem, past the university and museums, and got off at the Oscar Hellene Heim stop, where U.S. headquarters is located, complete with A & P supermarket and football field. There I sat in the empty wooden stands for a while and waited; the day had darkened; it began to rain. Shortly I heard the sound of a big helicopter approaching. It circled the football grounds once and then came in, rotors flailing, name painted on the side: FREEDOM CITY. I was strapped in and plugged in. The major up front at the controls introduced himself through my headset as we lifted off in what seemed to be the closing moments of that particular shower of rain. The major gave forth picturesque info as we flew over the U.S. military air base at Tempelhof, the prewar airport buildings shaped like a giant Germanic eagle, wings and talons outstretched, and headed toward the Brandenburg Gate. "At two o'clock now you'll see a cemetery in East Berlin, just north of the Reichstag. That's where Baron von Richthofen was buried, but his family got permission to move him to the West." I noted on the pediment of the huge neoclassical Reichstag the inscription DEM DEUTSCHEN VOLKE. From what I recalled from the Goethe Institute classes, this was in the dative, and meant therefore "To the German people."

We flew over many massive hills of coal, piled up in case of another blockade. We passed above the new International Conference Center,

"Like *Battlestar Galactica*," the major said accurately, and the Berlin Congress Hall, which Berliners call "the pregnant oyster." The "Battlestar" conference center looked ruggedly immovable, but the cantilevered roof of the Congress Hall had not long before collapsed; it looked like an oyster that a truck had run over. (Faulty steel reinforcing rods were being blamed, and not the design by American architect Hugh Stubbins.) We flew on, over Spandau Prison, a large nineteenth-century brick pile with just one prisoner, the aged Rudolf Hess—still there, it seemed, because providing their share of guards for the prisoner afforded the Russians another opportunity to appear in West Berlin. When flying over water— the lakes, canals and rivers that here and there form the border—we could see nets and underwater barriers placed to prevent the passage of swimmers. One moment we were looking at what the major called "the death strip"; the next, he was drawing my attention to "U.S. recreational facilities." From helicopter height it was possible to see that the wall sometimes took sudden jogs, went out, say, to incorporate or exclude an outlying field or village. In the Wüstemark district, one field, belonging to West Berlin, forms a small island apart from the city; the man who farms it has special permission from the DDR to go back and forth. When Berlin was expanding rapidly in the 1920s, some villages on the outskirts had to decide whether or not to be incorporated into the city; some opted for independence and thus are now in the DDR, outside the wall. Not far from Checkpoint Bravo, where the transit autobahn from Helmstedt arrives at the edge of West Berlin, is the village of Steinstücken, which did join Berlin. It was cut off by the DDR authorities for some years, with trips to or from it taking place only with special permission. But now it has a road with free access from West Berlin—a road lined by a concrete wall, and watchtowers, on either side.

The chopper flew down and around this hamlet, and as we came back the major said, "We have just left East Germany." I was thinking that the bright orange-red roofs of the small houses in Kleinmachow, in the DDR, were indistinguishable from the roofs of the cottages in Kohlhasenbrück, in West Berlin.

On the U-Bahn to Dahlem again—I read a copy of the London *Sunday Times*, and an article by the English historian and proponent of unilateral disarmament, E. P. Thompson. He wrote: "The Cold War, by dividing [the] world into two opposed parts, each of which sees itself threatened by the other, has become necessary to provide both bonding and means of regulation within each part. But this is an immensely dangerous condition . . ."

I spent the morning talking to a man at the U.S. mission about the wall and the border, about Germany and Europe. The official, whose title was political adviser, was a stocky man in his mid-thirties who moved and talked with the confident, muscular energy of an American football player. The immediate history, as he saw it, was that Germany had destroyed itself in two world wars. In 1945 the exhausted country lay at the mercy of the two superpowers, neither of which knew really what it wanted. The present situation in Germany was a reflection of the competition that continued between the superpowers as they tried to consolidate their positions; both felt insecure. Berlin happened to be the place where the effects of all this tended to rise and be most evident. But Berlin also served as a safety valve; world problems assumed a less unmanageable size here; and the pressure that was generated by the process of the two power blocks consolidating could be let off.

Moments when the Berlin valve had let off such pressure included the time of the postwar currency reform; the blockade and airlift; the foundation of the DDR; and the building of the wall. The political adviser said that the East German regime had had to build the wall to stop the outward flow of its people. "The wall is ugly—it's still a shattering thing to see—but you have to admit that it has allowed the DDR to consolidate itself into a relatively stable and prosperous state. I don't mean to ignore the inhumanities of it, but the wall has helped establish a situation that both sides can live with, and in that sense has helped make for détente between the United States and the USSR, and between the two German states."

There was a map of Europe on the wall. I let my gaze or interest blur so that the national boundaries became indistinct; rivers and mountain ranges managed to remain. I said that I was planning to go to Regensburg on my journey south; it had been on the border of the Roman Empire.

The political adviser said, "Well, that was as far as the Romans could get, or where they decided it was best to draw a line with the barbarians. The wall and the *Grenze* are there for similar reasons, because that's where a balance was finally found. It's not a condition that was freely chosen, but it's one we live with—just as the Romans did, with their *limes*, for some three hundred years."

I said, "Of course, the barbarians finally reached Rome, but presumably they were different by then—and the Romans had changed too."

"Things that look very stable can change overnight," said the P.A. "We

—that is, the United States—see ourselves as tending a very delicate balance, not simply defending freedom but ensuring that a balance is kept so that change is not violent."

We talked about nonviolent but genuine change in Hungary since the uprising of 1956. The DDR had evolved, so that it was a less spartan state. And now there was Poland, in ferment, with potential for dramatic change, dramatic repression. The political adviser said, "Poland can tip over the whole applecart."

One trouble, I thought later, was that it is people who tip over the applecart—and it is governments that react to the tipping over. Governments have a fondness for the status quo, for manageable situations, for a neat package, for conflict and competition properly organized into two sides playing by understandable rules. And what people mostly want—which is peace and an ever improving standard of life—is somehow framed by governments into this rivalry that requires terrifying weapons with which to threaten the other side. Governments somehow gather in all our individual ambitions to be allowed to live happily, comfortably, without being pushed around, and turn this into a need to be more powerful than the other side. They then justify this with a constant reiteration of the black-and-white refrain: We are right; they are wrong. Our ideas of what constitutes a good society are packaged by governments who consequently demand from us, for defending these ideological packages, certain powers, constraints on our freedom, and vast sums and sacrifices to pay for the weapons that will protect the package. Governments, being made up of human beings as well, seem to represent the more bullying, adversarial aspects of our nature. How do we get them to be ambassadors of the comradeship that we feel with fellow-men inhabiting the same earth?

One American I met in Berlin said that the place sometimes made him think of Pittsburgh: a not very old city that is rough-and-ready, gritty, on the make. Goethe (a quotation from Goethe is statutory in any book dealing with Germany) said: "I see in everything that this is a city filled with such an impertinent species of mankind that one doesn't get far using delicacy with them: to keep above water in Berlin, one must be somewhat coarse oneself." Wolf Biermann, the contemporary German poet and singer, writes (in Steve Gooch's translation):

> Berlin, you oh so German lass
> I court you with desire

> But oh, your hands are rough, alas
> from cold winds and from fire.

I had lunch one day in a gritty corner bar-and-grill in Schöneberg, which is the Flatbush or Stratford East of Berlin. The bar was crowded with locals having a lunchtime drink, but the welcome for a complete stranger was much like that I'd received in Brome. The lady of the house was delighted by the fact that—unlike most of her regular patrons at the bar—I wanted to eat there. She brought me a large plate of goulash and a big beer. One of the people sitting drinking at the bar was a small gray-haired woman, who now and then broke into song—"*Ich bin eine junge Frau.*" Twice, as if to demonstrate to her companions that this assertion wasn't just nostalgic, she came over and tried to engage me in conversation. Whether from drink or the Schöneberg patois she spoke, she was hard to comprehend. My vocabulary remained limited. I said, "*Es tut mir leid, ich habe kaum Deutsch.*" She patted me on the cheek. She spoke again, and I caught a phrase that sounded like "a thousand marks . . ." For what? One of the men at the bar was making signals to me that she was a bit crazy. The lady of the house came and shooed her away and stayed to talk about the goulash and the weather and whether I was in Berlin on holiday or business. I got conversationally a bit out of my depth and once again made my apologies that my understanding of German wasn't all that good. The lady of the house said (I think), with a gesture of reference to the "*junge Frau*" at the bar, "Just as well." When I left, there was a cheerful chorus from the bar: "*Auf Wiedersehen!*"

That afternoon a man was shot climbing over the wall—only he was going from West to East. He climbed over the outer wall and was running across the strip when the East German border guards fired a warning shot, then two more, and he fell to the ground. Next morning's papers knew only that he was about forty and that his first name was Hermann; they were uncertain whether he had been killed. Others occasionally try to get into East Berlin over the wall, as a result of a bet or because they are drunk or otherwise deranged. The East Germans generally arrest them, imprison them for a while and eventually send them back. In June 1981 an ape called Charlie climbed over into East Berlin and the authorities there charged its owner the equivalent of $250 for its return. The previous summer a young American student, hitchhiking to Sweden, came to the wall and climbed over it; he, too, was arrested but delivered to the U.S. embassy in East Berlin. Some who have crossed the border into East Germany have been fleeing debts, the West German police, paternity suits or an unhappy home life and are almost invariably sent back by the DDR authorities.

I went one evening to a reception and prize giving at the Akademie der Künste, a cultural center designed by the Berlin architect Werner Düttmann, and built in 1960 as part of the Hansa Quarter. This is a housing district just north of the Tiergarten, designed by architects from fifteen countries as a practical International Building Exhibition in 1957, and still wearing well. A throng of artists, writers, architects, musicians and filmmakers was there to listen to speeches, applaud the prize winners, drink wine and participate in the at once sparkling yet somewhat narcissistic goings-on, common to this sort of event in any great city. I talked to Tina Bauermeister, a young woman whose beautiful black hair framed her face as tightly as a cloche hat. She worked, she told me, for the West Berlin Festival, which is held every year in the autumn. She had the job of acquiring artists and performers for the festival, and she flew constantly to New York, San Francisco and Moscow—Russian artists were her big thing. She generally went to Moscow the cheapest way, via Schönefeld, the East Berlin airport. Tina introduced me to Anthony Ingrassia, a large and hirsute Brooklyn-born playwright who now lives in Berlin and had just won the Akademie prize for radio plays. Ingrassia said, "It's okay here. You feel the same sort of energy on the Kurfürstendamm that you feel in the streets of New York." I talked to Werner Düttman, who explained cheerfully the reason why the roof of the Congress Hall (on which he had been the local consulting architect to Hugh Stubbins) was thought to have collapsed. He thought that sooner or later all the undeveloped land in West Berlin near the wall would be built on; there is no stopping architects. Someone I talked to said that a number of West Berliners had not gone into East Berlin since the building of the wall. They were afraid to.

Back at my hotel I read a piece by Ingrassia in the Akademie prize catalogue. It was about the Berlin mood and meeting on the Kudamm a girl called Lucy, who seemed very like Tina. He tells her that he finds life easy in Berlin. She replies:

"That is true. It is easy in Berlin. Sometimes too easy. As you said, there is sex in every doorway, if you want. In Berlin there is everything in every doorway. There is everything. Much food and drink, there is art everywhere. It is New Year's all year round. And it is all tied up in a nice little package by the wall."

"Lucy."

"*Ja*—we Berliners forget there is a real world out there."

"But it is so gray on the outside."

"Yes, it is gray, and boring, and sad, and we have everything here, and when one is here one forgets everything and time just goes by, and we forget that we are an island here. Like a glittering spaceship floating through space."

"Lucy, why are you like this today?"

"I don't know. Perhaps it has to . . . Someone was killed coming across the wall today. I don't know if it was a man or a woman. I just heard that someone was killed."

11. TO THE EAST

One thing for which Berlin is celebrated is the *Berliner Luft*—the Berlin air. There are good meteorological reasons for it being heady and exhilarating, so one is told, which have to do with the city being located at a point where continental and Atlantic air masses converge. But since I came to Berlin the weather had been damp and dull— the collective zip of the citizenry surely came from a psychic or biological reserve rather than from any properties in the local atmosphere. Then a morning came when the overcast proceeded to break. By ten the sun was shining, the *Luft* was uplifting. I stood at a bus stop in the Kudamm waiting for a #29 and took deep breaths, unbothered by traffic fumes. It was a day I had earmarked for going into East Berlin. The weather was conspiring to put the DDR in a good light.

I grew up in the neighborhood of a castle, with Roman walls and a Norman keep. I used to play in and around it, putting myself and my friends in the roles of attackers and defenders. But until this morning, walking once more up the Friedrichstrasse, I had never imagined what it was like to approach a castle as a peaceful stranger—the walls and towers apparently unmanned, though you knew there were watchful people within; the drawbridge raised; the feeling of hidden arrows aimed or oil being brought to the boil, for pouring down on attacking forces. I passed the little Allied checkpoint hut in the middle of the road and followed the sidewalk toward where the road passes through a gap in the wall. There was a slight blur of movement within the observation slit of the watchtower, as if eyes were moving deep within the shadow of a visor. I stepped over the line that marked the border. The path, inside the wall, took a sudden turn. It was a sort of maze, with the direction signs so small that you knew where to go next only when you had reached the intended point—it seemed that you weren't allowed to do any pre-thinking or pre-planning. The shabby sheds were joined by what looked like cattle-run enclosures. I came abruptly to the end of one of these and to a gate, which was firmly shut. A uniformed guard said "Pass?" and I handed over my passport. A middle-aged couple was standing there too, and shortly we were joined by a tall young Japanese. But we didn't really look at or acknowledge one another. It was as if we wanted to indicate that we weren't attached to any of the others, just in case they were handed back their passports with a shake of the head, denied permission to enter. The guard had delivered our passports to a slot in a window behind, and there they were presumably being scrutinized. I wondered if the photos of me taken by DDR border troops had been fed into a system that would now cause a red light to flash as they tapped out my name. Out in the open air, a car—pointed toward West Berlin—was being thoroughly searched; everything that could be lifted up or opened was. I had been told that flower boxes had been installed by the East Germans at some of these checkpoints, to brighten things up, but nothing drew attention to itself by blooming here.

My passport was returned—but the guard first opened it and studied the photograph inside and compared it to my face. He looked at me, at the passport photo, and at me again; then he handed it over. "Thank you," I said, grateful to have passed this test. He pushed the button of an electric switch and the gate clicked open so that I could go through; there was no handle or knob on my side of it. I followed an arrow that directed me into the building and further inspections. Altogether there were three separate passport checks on the way through; there was the question "Any books, papers, magazines?" (I had none); and there was a payment of DM 5 for a day's visa, and the compulsory exchange of the minimum of DM 25 into DDR marks, on a one-to-one basis (the unofficial but realistic rate, quoted in some West German banks, varies from four to five DDR marks to one West German mark. But under DDR law it is illegal to take East German marks from West Germany into the DDR.) I was handed a plastic packet of East German money—rather weightless coins adding up to 5 marks, and a 20-mark note with a picture of happy schoolchildren on one side and of Goethe on the other. I doubt if he would have regarded this as an elective affinity. The visa charge of marks is in the case of West Germans paid for by the West German government—as it is for West Germans and foreigners in transit across East Germany. A list of names of those given visas is presented by the DDR to the Bonn government once a year to provide evidence for payment.

Within the building the feeling of a maze continued. There were no windows, only fluorescent lights. I reached a small booth with a sill and a slot at which evidently I had to hand in my passport again. At one point I met the young Japanese going the wrong way, and steered him in what I took to be the right direction.

And then I was out in the air and on the Friedrichstrasse in East Berlin; the street remained as shabby as before. Along here Martin Bormann was seen—was it for the last time?—dodging behind a German tank as it lumbered down the Friedrichstrasse. I passed a woman who was entering a warehouse, and it was curious to think that although she had just stepped off the same sidewalk I was using, she had no possibility of going through the checkpoint I had come through a hundred yards away. Nothing like a Communist state for reinforcing a sense of privilege!

The other sense that was immediately assailed was that of smell. The air of East Berlin was grittier, dirtier, heavy with the gray smoke of diesel and two-cycle, or two-stroke, engine exhaust, and with the smoke from lignite— the sort of brown coal mined near Helmstedt. It was also, just here, a few blocks from Unter den Linden, full of black smoke puffing forth from the third floor of a building that was on fire. The fire brigade was on hand, helmeted, in high rubber boots, and a small crowd had gathered. Having felt special a few moments before, I now stood and shared a universal interest in anything that looked like becoming a conflagration—for another few moments, anyway, until it was clear the brigade had it well in hand.

Unter den Linden was the governing heart of prewar Berlin; despite the presence now of several travel agencies, record stores and restaurants, it remains a boulevard or mall lined with great institutions—libraries, university, opera, government offices, the Soviet embassy—as it proceeds eastward from the Brandenburg Gate. This triumphal arch sets the neoclassical tone for the wide street—and perhaps the authoritarian tone, too, for those whom Greek columns remind not only of Athenian democracy but of the slaves. Here and in adjacent streets massive buildings are slowly being restored, some still bearing the marks of World War II shrapnel. Many of these buildings are the work of Karl Friedrich Schinkel (1781–1841), architect, painter, stage and furniture designer, who not only built and rebuilt much of early-nineteenth-century Berlin but for ten years made a living as a designer of stoves, vases, medals (an Iron Cross) and as a painter of dramatic, picturesque landscapes. Like Turner, he was an admirer of Claude Lorraine; in dreamlike countryside classical ruins were suffused with romantic light. In both sides of Berlin there was agreement to honor Schinkel now. Exhibitions of his work had recently been displayed in several places in West Berlin and in the Altes Museum (regarded by many as Schinkel's masterpiece) in East Berlin. Both sides also seemed ready to hail Schinkel as a great Prussian. A separation felt in both parts of Germany is that which divides present-day Germans from their past: Hitler comes between. Germans, looking for their roots, are deciding that not everything Prussian was bad; and Prussia should not be blamed for all of German's sins. Prussia may have provided under Bismarck the unifying force that made Germany a world power, but there were many other scarcely rational elements of racism and nationalism—just as common in Bavaria and Austria—that helped turn Nazi Germany into such a staggeringly effective and horrific death machine. Frederick the Great, Prussia's founder, glorified in the form of a huge equestrian statue, has recently been brought out of isolation in Potsdam and restored to a central plinth in Unter den Linden.

Another Schinkel building—a small one—in Unter den Linden is the Neue Wache. It was built as a war memorial after the Napoleonic Wars, a windowless mausoleum with the portico and pediment of a little Greek temple forming its entryway two smartly dressed young soldiers on guard outside. I arrived in front of it at the same time as a wedding party—a young woman in a white bridal dress carried her bouquet of flowers into the Neue Wache and placed it by the eternal flame. Photos were taken of bride and groom and relations. Then the guard was changed. Although it refuses to acknowledge any line of descent between itself and the Third Reich, the DDR seems to have taken over the Wehrmacht uniform: long flared gray greatcoat, a deep steel helmet with outturned edges on back and sides, and tall black jackboots; and it has also adopted the goose step—the *Stechschritt*—to which guards have marched here since Kaiser Wilhelm's time.

Half a dozen pale-eyed blond lads were marched forth in single file, kicking their legs high, by a young lieutenant. Then, stamping their feet in unison, moving their weapons sharply, two of their number changed places with the two who had been guarding the memorial. *Achtung!* They goose-stepped back from where they had come, and as they passed, the young lieutenant's wary eyes met mine. There was an unspoken exchange—

slightly challenging but not completely hostile on his part, perhaps warding off the anger he saw in mine. I am aware of the fact that the goose step is in use in the armies of various countries, but for anyone who is old enough to remember World War II it must be pretty closely connected with Hitler's armies. The sight of it is enough to raise the question, What was that war fought for? One youngster who was with a group of spectators walked off pretending to goose-step, but no one was laughing. It is an action which seems to animate the German past like a nightmarish cartoon.

Inside the Neue Wache there was an inscription on one wall: *Den Opfern des Faschismus und Militarismus* (To the victims of facism and militarism). Indeed, to us all.

On this and another visit to East Berlin I talked to various people whom I shall leave anonymous but who might be called informed and interested citizens. I got the impression that most people in the DDR are proud of their social services; they are glad not to be threatened by widespread unemployment; and what they object to most about their regime is that it doesn't give them the opportunity to come and go, or more precisely, to go and to return. There is no way of being sure how many are deeply disaffected. A person who recently fled the DDR told me she believed 90 percent of young people would quit the country if they could. One ex-DDR soldier said that a third of those serving wanted to get out of the DDR. I suspect from what others in East Berlin told me that perhaps one in ten would leave for good if they were allowed to, but that most would come back from any trip abroad—they simply wanted what they saw to be the basic human right to leave their country for a vacation or even a long stay elsewhere and then to return to it. There are also some who think the wall can be justified on economic grounds: that the East German standard of living has risen a great deal since it was built. How could the state educate people and then let them take their knowledge and skills to other countries? There is a worker shortage, and a population crunch; the DDR has the second lowest birthrate in the world. (The Federal Republic of Germany has the lowest, but in the past has made up for a lack of workers by importing them from southern Europe.) Most East Germans seem fairly stoical about their lack of political choice; most have never known any other condition. But they resent having money with little to spend it on; long waits for new cars; a shortage of fruit or quality cigarettes; dull clothes. Their money piles up in savings accounts. Their children's lives are affected by whatever their parents do, or don't do, in relation to the party.

There are numerous crèches and kindergartens in which mothers can leave their children from the age of six months, and although many women are thereby "freed" to work, many children grow up in an institutional atmosphere, trapped in the system from the start and possibly driven to seek ways out, such as drink, later on. On the one hand, many watch a lot of West German TV, and the young tape-record music from Western radio stations. On the other, there is a good deal of excellent music and opera in East Berlin—attended by West Berliners, too. *Don Giovanni* was being performed in both parts of the city while I was there. I saw the production in West Berlin, and it was so soporifically awful, I took it for granted that the East Berlin production was superior. East Berlin comedians can get away with criticism. One cabaret artist's joke: "Question: What's the difference between the theater and real life? Answer: In the theater there's always an emergency exit."

And yet the East Germans are weary of being preached at. A Swedish journalist, Hans Axel Holm, recorded some years ago an exasperated East German remark: "Our newspapers are written as if they suspected every reader of being an unbeliever."

There are, nonetheless, still believers—people who like the early Puritans feel that some pleasures have to be spurned, some rights curtailed, for the making of a better man in a better society. It may be envy with some East Germans but an honest observation with others when they say that most people in West Germany live too well.

Some West Germans agree. Some feel that the DDR provides a necessary whiff of close-at-hand astringency. One fairly important West German who worked in East Berlin for six and a half years found that it was a worthwhile experience, that it made him more aware of "the German nation." Günter Gauss was editor of *Der Spiegel* before becoming the Federal Republic's Permanent Representative in East Berlin. Now back in the West, Gauss caused a stir early in 1981 when, in an interview in the weekly *Die Zeit*, he said he favored legalizing the division and recognizing the DDR as truly separate. He thought West Germans should try to stop seeing the DDR as unfriendly; they should try to see East Germans as individuals. As for Germany, perhaps it would be best to think of it, for want of any better way, as a "cultural nation," including Austrians, German-speaking Swiss, and East Germans. Gauss said that he'd found a lot to admire in the DDR: more was preserved there of the German past, partly because industrialization was less advanced. There was much conscious attention to history (such as restoring the statue of Frederick the Great) and folklore was fostered. There was, moreover, a toughness about the East Germans, a self-reliance—they had only themselves to fall back on. Their intellectuals were more down-to-earth. East Germany, in a few words, was more truly German.

One could—as some did—see in this enthusiasm of Gauss's a Germanic desire to be part of a greater community, a *Gemeinschaft*—a sort of collective, linking-arms-together-and-singing experience in which the individual is dissolved. Other readers thought that Gauss's position as special envoy to East Germany—with which he had negotiated among other things road tolls, veterinary agreements, autobahn routes and the rights in the DDR of West German reporters—had been one of special privilege. It had hardly served to bring him in touch with the realities of daily life. Many of his observations were more nostalgic than accurate. The self-reliant and down-to-earth characteristics Gauss saw in East Germans could also be seen in prisoners in jail.

East Berlin is a good place for impromptu encounters. I was dithering by a bridge that leads to the large island around which the Spree bends its arms, wondering whether to walk across the vast Marx-Engels Platz (where the ruins of the old royal palace had been cleared to make a parade ground, rimmed by bland party buildings) or to head first for the Pergamon Museum, when an elderly man with a scarred face and a hand-rolled cigarette stopped and proceeded to tell me about the different museum buildings on the island, which was which and what was in them. In the toilet of the Pergamon Museum a girl with a funny high-pitched accent cheerfully told me which DDR coin I should give her as a payment for the use of the facilities; but I was abashed to find her stationed at an open door that connected *Damen* and *Herren,* and gave her two of them. One of the curiosities of the East—Eastern Europe, that is—is that the so-called workers' states are labor-intensive, with such holdovers from the capitalist era as cloakroom attendants and hotel concierges, in generous quantities, too.

After looking at some of the antiquities in the Pergamon—Trajan's Temple, the Pergamon altar, a processional way from Babylon—I headed across the Marx-Engels Platz (which is not going to provide any particularly interesting relics of exquisite masonry for museums in three thousand years' time). I walked to the south end of the island and across the river. I'd bought an architectural guide to the buildings of East Berlin and was standing on a street corner looking around for an allegedly distinguished 1920s office building, said to be in the immediate neighborhood, when someone began to speak to me. This time my interlocutor was a man in his thirties, wearing a turtleneck sweater and trench coat—a journalist, radio producer, architect? He looked at my guidebook and at the street. We agreed that the building didn't seem to be there anymore. And whether this made him reflect on the various causes of the destruction of Berlin buildings or not, I don't know, but he said suddenly, "*Nie wieder Krieg.*" Never again war. He added that he was sorry he couldn't help, and with a smile and "*Auf Wiedersehen,*" walked away. I had, I have to admit, a moment of doubt. Was he a DDR agent sent out to soften up foreign tourists? But I quickly put aside this as an unworthy thought. He was obviously a man of our time, horrified by the prospect of a nuclear holocaust that could be unleashed by Reagan or Brezhnev, by levels of government that seem to operate somehow unaffected by people. That "*Nie wieder Krieg*" stayed with me in the days and weeks to come.

I had lunch in the Ermelerhaus restaurant—a Huguenot merchant's mansion done in rich rococo, with sub-Watteau paintings on walls and ceilings. Soup, an omelette and a glass of wine, served by formally dressed waiters who seemed a touch offended that I wasn't going more whole hog. Another wedding party was there. Leather coats were apparently the fashionable thing. The restaurant windows were hung with georgette net curtains, more reminiscent of the 1950s or 1930s than of the early eighteenth century. Most tables were unoccupied, a condition that seemed to match the city itself. As I resumed my walk, East Berlin was half empty. There weren't the people one usually sees in cities out shopping, walking from office to office, bustling about on all sorts of errands. When I reached the Alexanderplatz, another vast, windy space of concrete, rimmed by tower blocks, I paused at the edge of a sidewalk as I prepared to cross an immensely wide street. I turned to look for traffic. I could see in the distance a thin phalanx of Wartburgs, Ladas and Trabants waiting for a light to change, so I set off across the road. There were no other pedestrians doing the same. I had proceeded a few paces when a horn began to honk in a road-repair truck parked nearby, and a man in it gave me a friendly enough but negative shake of the head. I walked on a few more paces and heard the shrill blasts of a whistle. On the far side of the square a police car had drawn up. Uniformed men jumped out of it. It was their whistles I could hear. Now they were waving, shouting, *at me.* I got the message. I retreated. (The traffic was still nowhere near.) I returned to the sidewalk and found an underground passageway that you had to use to get to the other side of the street. And I walked through slowly, hoping that the police had gone on or forgotten what I looked like by the time I reached the other side. I had no desire to expand my East Berlin visit to include the local Stalag or Gulag for jaywalkers.

Having seen the Vopos, I saw them everywhere. And soldiers, too. Some seemed to be driving through in vans and trucks. Many were off duty, with shopping bags or women on their arms. One way to avoid an uprising against the state seems to be to put a large number of the state's citizenry in uniform, armed and trained to uphold it.

In the late afternoon I walked around a district north of the Spree, which bends and heads westward paralled with Unter den Linden. The wall in this area also runs from west to east for a while, before going north again. Away from the neoclassical grandeur of Unter den Linden and the tawdry modernity of the two big squares, the city is grubby, with shopfronts of unwashed glass, chipped masonry, woodwork long overdue for putty and paint. Coal dust lies in the streets and is embedded in the rough pebble-dash stucco of apartment buildings. Dust rises from the tracks as the trams rattle by. In shops the merchandise is simply labeled, presented in a take-it-or-leave-it way: here are not the much cajoled and flattered consumers of the West.

I walked past a wired enclosure that surrounded a U-Bahn stop, no longer open to the public. Both the overhead S-Bahn and the mostly underground U-Bahn have lines that run into both parts of the city. One U-Bahn line crosses under this section of East Berlin on its way from one part of West Berlin to another. The station entrances are sealed, the platforms guarded, and the trains do not stop. At the Friedrichstrasse Bahnhof, three blocks north of Unter den Linden, visitors from West Berlin may arrive in or depart from East Berlin by S-Bahn; there they pass through controls similar to those at Checkpoint Charlie. East Berliners are, needless to say, not allowed to reach those trains that pull out for the West. (East Berlin continues to own the entire S-Bahn system, but the rolling stock is old and less comfortable to ride in than the U-Bahn's, and West Berliners show some of their hostility for the East by using the system in their own part of the city as little as they can, with the result that it is running at a huge loss, and the East Berlin management would like to sell the western network to West Berlin; but nothing has been concluded.) Here at the Friedrichstrasse Bahnhof the station extends over the Spree on a bridge. As I walked under it, I looked up at girders festooned with barbed wire and barricades of sheet metal designed to prevent East Berliners from climbing aboard west-bound trains.

Overhead, beyond the bridge, planes from the West swept round over East Berlin in a loop that would bring them down, head to wind, at Tegel.

I walked on. I was looking for the wall. It proved hard to reach, because much of this area was taken up by the grounds of the Charité Hospital, and many of the side streets that headed west were blocked off under the S-Bahn. I walked north, then northeast. Eventually, after forty minutes or so, I found a way to approach it, across the broad Invaliden-strasse and up a similar street called Gartenstrasse. I didn't realize it just then, but I was close to the Bernauerstrasse, where I'd been standing the other day looking out in this direction. (My East Berlin map showed the wall but didn't show the West Berlin streets beyond it.) Garten-strasse was empty of people. It was bordered on one side by what looked like an old railway yard, and on the other side by shabby three- and four-story apartment houses. At the end of the street I saw a bumpy, unfinished-looking wall—the inner wall, on which no cosmetic decoration had been wasted. Barbed wire. And a watchtower, within which binoculars swiveled and fastened on me. I was about a hundred yards from the wall, alone in the empty street. I came to a halt. I had—I assumed—every right to walk on. I was a foreign tourist. How was I to know that you had to have special permission to come within one hundred meters of the wall? I saw no signs. But in that moment I felt like someone who lived there, and the will to walk closer drained out of me. I stood there for a little while, as if in prayer, then turned away. I could feel the binoculars at the back of my neck as I walked off.

I waited at a tram, or streetcar, stop in Invalidentrasse and read a short history of Berlin that was connected to the map; it was in German, Russian, English and French. It said that Berlin began as twin towns, Berlin and Cölln, that grew up around 1200 as market settlements on each side of the Spree. Karl Marx, Friedrich Engels and V. I. Lenin all worked and studied in Berlin. It did not mention the wall or the present division of the city. It referred to "Berlin," to "the capital of the DDR" and to numer-ous monuments that bore witness to the struggles, sacrifices and victories of the proletariat, all of which laid the foundations for a democratic de-velopment in Berlin after the Soviet army had liberated it from the fascists. Use of the term "the fascists"—not "the German army"—clearly helped to put the past at a hygenic distance.

A tram came, and I climbed aboard. In West Berlin you pay the driver DM 1,50 (roughly seventy-five cents or forty pence) per ride, or allow him to stamp one of a book of tickets that can be purchased at a slight dis-count. The driver of this tram was up front; there was no conductor; but when I reached the driver I saw that he was in an inaccessible booth. Looking further for some way of paying, I saw a machine, something like a primitive potato peeler, which presumably dispensed tickets. But it had no instructions on it. I didn't know that one of the better boasts of the East German state is that public transportation fares have been kept to what they were in 1945—twenty pfennigs (about ten cents or five pence). I turned for help to the nearest passenger: How much did it cost to ride the tram? I asked in my best Goethe Institute German. I had addressed a young man and he replied forthrightly and so gutturally that I didn't understand a word. I reached into a pocket and held out all my East German change in my open palm. He pointed to a twenty-pfennig piece and said, again, "Zwo Groschen." Ah—light dawned. Two groschen was two ten-pfennig coins; two tens equaled twenty. Another case of East German conservatism, preserving an old usage which went with an old tramfare.

I put the zwo-Groschen piece in the machine and cranked the handle. A small piece of thick gray paper, evidently the result of many recyclings, came forth. I held it up like a trophy as I turned and gave the dozen passengers a big and only slightly embarrassed smile. I said "Danke" to the young man. Everyone in the tram was smiling back at me.

I had been feeling by turns conspicuous and invisible in East Berlin. At one moment like a creature from another world or another time who has intruded into a society where his dress and manners are wryly wrong and provoke curious looks. And at other moments like someone whom people were looking right through, perhaps deliberately, because they didn't want to see me, because it hurt to see me—or see anyone who reminded them of a world outside that they couldn't get to.

But here in the tram rattling along the tracks of this run-down street there was a different feeling, and I felt accepted by these East Berliners, whose smiles seemed to say "You may be an ignorant foreigner but we are grateful to you for being here and riding this tram with us." For a minute or two I experienced a hint of that intensity Bernhardt Fischer had talked about.

Back in the city center I spent most of my remaining East marks on a Mozart record and then went to the American embassy to visit an attaché whose name I'd been given. Unlike the embassies of the USSR, Poland and Hungary, which are at the Brandenburg Gate end of Unter den Linden, the U.S. embassy is in a side street several blocks away. Opposite the front entrance I saw a small concrete box of a building with one window glazed with a single pane of—from the outside, at least—nontransparent glass. Perhaps the building in a way looked like a reflex camera; it made me think of a camera; and it was placed there, I was told, to house DDR officials photographing people who went in and out of the embassy. Also posted by the embassy entrance were two policemen, both of whom gave me a nosy stare. I waited for a little while in the ground-floor library, to which people have access without having to pass the embassy's U.S. Marine guards. The DDR government had objected to any signs publicizing the library (I also learned later on), and when the embassy went ahead and put up such signs in the library windows, the authorities retaliated by posting two DDR policemen in front where one had been. DDR law says that no citizen may enter a foreign embassy, which gives it some excuse for stopping people who intend to use the library, and demanding to see their identification papers. Despite the threat of such inquisition, several young people were in the library: one young man was reading *Scientific American,* another was doing what appeared to be some math homework, and a girl was standing by the fiction bookshelves browsing through a novel by John Cheever.

The attaché I had come to see—whom I'll call Jack Getty—was having a standup conference with a colleague when I arrived. It seems to be one of the characteristics of American official life that such discussions are generally going on when a visitor comes on the scene; there is no attempt to be found sitting formally behind a desk; you're flattered by feeling part of what's happening, allowed to enter and participate in the talk. The other person is introduced, the conversation continues for a minute with what appears to be no perceptible change of subject, and then the other person goes off and you are left with the person you have come to see. Or was this, I suddenly wondered, a clever vetting process? Afterward they might compare notes. "Well, he said he was a writer. . . ."

Getty himself fitted in with this mood. One got the feeling that his models were Dashiell Hammett and Raymond Chandler rather than Châteaubriand and Harold Nicolson, and that he was—like the narrator of Chandler's *Trouble Is My Business*—"tough enough to swap punches with a power shovel." I asked him about countries he had served in, and after listing several African and Middle Eastern states, he said, "This is the most repressive place I've ever been." And yet Berlin itself was less of a problem than it had been. "Up to 1971, the Soviets used Berlin to squeeze our balls whenever they felt like it. They've given up on that for the time being. And in some ways you've got to admire these guys in the DDR. They did without Marshall aid. They were stripped bare by the Russkies. They've worked themselves stiff to improve their standard of living. They've got a lot of life's real problems licked, a cocoon of security, schools, hospitals, full employment, a fairer distribution of income than in many Western countries. Okay—and then the other hand. You can drive from one end of the country to the other in four hours—California's big compared to this place—and you've got to be privileged to get out of it. If you look at that map on the wall you'll see large zones colored

yellow where the citizens of this country can't travel freely. Those areas
are restricted because they're near the West German border or the Baltic
coast, or are used for Soviet and DDR military training. You didn't think
they were going to let you in any of those, did you? To get out you need
to be someone like one of their pet TV commentators, or a composer like
Günter Fischer—he wrote the music for the film *Night Kill*. He earns
Western money, which is good for the regime, and he gets to keep some
so he can buy wine and cheese in West Berlin."

The afternoon was ending. Getty suggested that I come back to his
house for a drink. As we went downstairs he said that his driver was East
German, provided by *them*, and probably a state security man. We climbed
into the back seat of a waiting car and exchanged smiles with the driver.
Getty went on, "He says he only speaks German, but who knows? Anyway, Honecker and company are just a bunch of apes. It won't do them
any harm to know what we think about them."

The Gettys' house was fairly modern, set in a suburban district of large,
older houses—though like the buildings in the city center, most looked as
if they could do with a coat of paint. Mrs. Getty was Italian; she showed
me the kitchen, full of up-to-date appliances. "Getting them fixed when
they go wrong is difficult," she said. "You can wait for a month for a man
to come."

"Yeh," said Getty, who was mixing a jug of martinis. "There's a maintenance crew that comes over regularly from West Berlin to service the
General Electric and Hotpoint kitchens of the party brass. Honecker and
his buddies have a well-protected enclave of houses out of town, and a lot
of the other influentials live in districts like this. But we haven't got to
know much about our neighbors here. One of them told one of our kids
that they'd been warned not to socialize with the Americans, or to let their
kids play with ours."

Mrs. Getty said that it wasn't just the repair of modern domestic machinery that was hard to arrange; getting shoes mended was a real problem,
too. *Eulenspiegel*, an East German humor magazine, had recently published a cartoon showing a road sign: "Next shoe repair shop—50 kilometers." The choice of meat in butcher shops was very poor. The Gettys
bought their meat in West Berlin, and so did many of the East Berliners
who worked for the American embassy. The embassy paid such local members of the staff as drivers in East German marks, and had found it impossible to get them to work overtime. Now that it pays for overtime in
West German marks, there are volunteers for overtime, and chauffeurs
who drive their employers into West Berlin have the currency to buy
fruit and meat there for their families.

"One of the best presents you can give people over here is flowers—bought in West Berlin, grown in East Germany," said Getty.

Although the Gettys gave the impression of having borne up under the strains of an artificial and unbalanced life in East Berlin, their children have not found it so easy. One of their sons, now at college in America, felt absolutely choked by the DDR; he wanted to tell everyone he met what he thought about the regime. Most of the time he kept silent about it. Getty said, "And yet he was also affected by the contrast between life in West Berlin and here. He came back from West Berlin one afternoon and said that he'd been up on the sixth floor of Ka-De-We, the big department store, where they have their huge food section. He said he'd never seen anything so gross, so obscene."

Getty's driver, whether a security man or not, still gave me a friendly smile as I climbed into the car. He drove me back into town, across Unter den Linden, and down the Friedrichstrasse, where he dropped me at Checkpoint Charlie. It was much the same procedure going back—three or four passport checks—a question about how much DDR money I had. I had a return of that strange, slightly grubby sense of privilege, of being unfairly favored, as I went through the last gate and it clanged shut behind me. The stars were out in a clear sky. I walked fast through the gap in the wall, trying hard not to run, and in the Kochstrasse was relieved to reach the bus stop at the same time as a 29, which took me home.

12. BRASCH AND OTHER WRITERS

t was a lovely morning and I walked west along the Kudamm to meet Thomas Brasch, a writer and formerly an East German. I swung my arms and felt the sun on my face and appreciated the street-corner stalls selling flowers and the kiosks selling books and magazines, some of which were meant to arouse the flesh and some to prod the brain. Damn the West, if you like, for its wealth, stress and overindulgence, but admit its ability to provide an abundance of words and—I am thinking of the flowers—beauty.

Writers in East Germany who are accepted by the regime seem to live in pampered restraint. There is a fine, oblique picture of an East German writer in Joel Agee's recent memoir, *Twelve Years*. Agee spent much of his childhood in the DDR; his stepfather was a German Communist novelist, Bodo Uhse, who returned from exile in Mexico to a position of some comfort and influence—he was editor of *Aufbau*, a leading literary magazine, until an article he published about a Hungarian dissident caused him to fall into disfavor. Agee suggests some of the faltering in his stepfather's Communist faith after the Twentieth Party Congress in Moscow, when Khrushchev—three years after Stalin's death—let loose on the Communist world the news that Joseph Stalin, the glorious "Father of Nations," had been a mass murderer. But gradually, Agee writes, as everyone else made their adjustments, [Bodo] made his. I heard of a new kind of hero—from Bodo's lips more than from anyone else's: a victim of Stalinism, a Communist, unjustly imprisoned for years, is reprieved, returns to society, and humbly, without bitterness or recrimination, devotes himself to the Party work he was forced to abandon long ago. These weren't just inspirational tales (though they did serve that purpose); there really were such saints, and not just in the Soviet Union but in our neighborhood. I regarded them with a respect approaching awe.

In my mobile library I had Heinrich Böll's *Group Portrait with Lady* and *The Search for Christa T.*, by the East German writer Christa Wolf. Both novels have as a main character a woman who is conjured up out of reports of her impact on other characters, out of a series of memories and interviews, as it were. And yet they are very different books. Böll's is both moving and humorous, truthful—one feels—about how it was to be a civilian in Germany during World War II, and successful in presenting its heroine, Leni, as a well-rounded person. Wolf's book is not at all humorous; it is deeply in earnest, puzzling, truthful in a depressing way, and steadfastly inquisitive about recent history. While it doesn't create a full-blooded person (and perhaps that wasn't the author's intent), it clearly renders certain facets of character that create a sort of prism in which a person can be glimpsed. And the fact that the reader remains unsure whether Christa T. is Christa Wolf, whether the "I" of the book will be revealed as the other Christa she was trying to conjure up, makes for suspense.

A West German woman I met later told me that she thought many people in the DDR found points of identification in Christa Wolf's book. "It is a sort of code book for them," she said. "Christa Wolf has created a way of escape in her prose—her readers can join her in that lyrical escape without political consequences. I have heard her lecture here. She comes over about once a year to West Germany. I sometimes wonder why no one asks her how it is that she can come here but their friends and relatives cannot. Is it because they know she would have no answer and decide to spare her? Or maybe she would attempt an answer. She is convinced—like many intellectuals in the DDR—that they are in the more advanced part of history, and that after various privations the world of the future will be theirs."

I had also been reading Christa Wolf's earlier novel, *Divided Heaven*, which seems to reflect the almost religious enthusiasm or commitment felt, at least in the 1960s, by some East Germans. In that book, Manfred arrives in West Berlin and feels despair at "having failed to stand up to the pressure of that harder, sterner life." Perhaps there is an element of masochism as well, which those who indulged in it didn't mind spreading around: one man's hair shirt is another man's punishment. From that puritan point of view, life in West Germany was evil. And indeed, for them as for us, there seemed to be a need for the other, to be able to say of themselves that they were good and we were bad.

In Hamburg I had talked with Joachim Seyppel, a teacher and writer, who told me that he thought division was Germany's natural state, and that neither East nor West Germany would have flourished unless they had been sundered from each other. Seyppel said that he felt the division in himself; he was very much a split man, born on the outskirts of Berlin in 1919, a resident of the United States from 1950 to 1961 when he studied at Harvard and taught at Bryn Mawr, and after that an inhabitant of both Germanys. He had lived in West Berlin for ten years; then, leaving his wife and children there, moved to East Berlin, where he started a new family. Since 1979, when he was thrown out of the DDR Writers' Union for protesting about the house arrest of the physicist and dissident Robert Havemann, he has been living in West Germany again, though he had been given an East German passport good for three years, with the right to go and return.

Seyppel was a trim, gray-haired man, with the weathered face of a sailor who has experience of tacking back and forth against fickle winds. He told me he was planning to ask for an extension of his East German passport; he hadn't made up his mind about his ultimate plans. He said, "I can picture myself living in East Germany again in five years time. I'm sixty-one now. My wife is thirty-two, my son is two. It isn't like Nazi Germany over there. There's a lot to be done—I'm idealist enough to believe that it can still be done. I feel guilty that I've run away from it. There are so many factors to consider: Which army will my son serve in when he grows up, east or west? Where will I get published? Sometimes my books have been rejected there and published here, and sometimes the other way around. Writers, once accepted, can have a more secure life there. To be frank, you occasionally get paid for what you haven't written. There's also something of a captive market—if you write for instance about Turkey, they read it, because they can't go there. As a writer, it's true, you have to live with a sense of being especially privileged, but the situation there makes for good friends, close friends. I don't get homesick in East Berlin, I'm at home. I know there is also some corruption there, and a sort of Balkan grubbiness. It is often hard work keeping two separate compartments in your mind, and needing to keep some thoughts superficial because you don't want to consider the depths. Schizophrenia is our common condition, being German. I need to speak German and live in Germany. But sometimes I would rather be something else, maybe half-French, half-English—not German."

Later I imagined a type of schizophrenia that arose from two parts of an entity, each seeking forms of perfection. That, possibly, was what caused the turmoil, for if both parts were prepared to compromise—to accept something less than the absolute best—there would be no firm division between them. The double quest for perfection created havoc. And one could extend this beyond the two Germanys, to view the Western and Eastern worlds as representing man's separate strivings for freedom (which risks inequities and unemployment) and for security (which risks inequality and totalitarianism).

Brasch lives in a third-floor walk-up apartment with large bare rooms, with a few chairs, a bookcase, and on the walls some child's drawings and a street map of Los Angeles. Thirty-six years old, dark close-cropped hair, with cheeks and chin that perhaps always look in need of a shave. A big table that serves as a desk. The apartment, though lived in for some time, has the air of a place that has not quite been moved into. Brasch smokes as he talks. He continues to call himself an East Berliner, though he has been living in West Berlin for five years. He is a British subject by right of having been born in Yorkshire in 1945; like Bodo Uhse, his parents had fled from Germany in the 1930s and in their case taken refuge in Britain. Brasch's father, a devout Communist, brought his family back to East Germany after the war, and after a while, overcoming what his son feels was official antipathy toward refugees and prisoners of war who returned from Western countries, began to work his way up in the party apparatus. He was deputy cultural minister in 1968. In that year he lost his job because his son Thomas was arrested for writing and distributing leaflets— these were in protest against the Soviet-directed invasion of Czechoslovakia by Warsaw Pact troops.

Apart from the accident of being born in Britain, Thomas Brasch is a child of the German Democratic Republic. His first thirty-one years were the first thirty-one years of state socialism in East Germany. He grew up with a huge portrait of Stalin on the living-room wall. He recalls in his first school being taunted by other children because he was the son of committed Communists, and he felt obliged to defend their cause. On one occasion a fellow pupil said to him during recess, "The Vopos are just like the SS," and Brasch was involved in his first fight. At the age of eleven, with the sons of other party officials, he was selected for military academy, where he started training to become an army officer. For four years, until the government closed the academy, he was in uniform, allowed home for four weeks a year, and given a mixed education of ordinary lessons, Marxism, tough physical exercise, and military training. After two years he had had enough. He felt it was just like prison, with a wall and guards. In order to get thrown out he poured water over an officer and fired a rifle in the air, but he wasn't expelled, only punished. When the school was closed they were told it was because officers henceforth were going to be recruited out of the regular school system, but some felt it was a gesture at the time to West Germany to indicate an interest in disarmament. Some had suggested quietly that the military academy was a successor to the National Political Education Institutes, which served the Nazis from 1933 as military boarding schools.

At fifteen Brasch was sent to a regular East Berlin high school. It was a year before the wall was built. He suddenly found himself out of the prisonlike academy and in a position where he could go and see movies in West Berlin. He was already writing a little. In West Berlin he bought books—Camus, Hemingway, Sartre. He wrote poems about death and about World War III. Like other East German youth, he listened to Brubeck and Mulligan; he made tapes from borrowed records, working in a factory on his vacations to get the money to buy a tape recorder. He and his school friends bought jeans and nylon jackets in West Berlin, and banded together when contemporaries who were members of the Free German youth, a Communist young people's organization, tried to confiscate their jackets. Brasch began to feel unsympathetic towards a regime that took on itself the duty of thinking for its people and telling them how to live. Together with other students he was asked to sign a pledge not to listen to Western radio. Brasch listened to AFN (the U.S. Armed Forces Network) every evening from five to six and refused to sign. He was denounced as a troublemaker. A workers' brigade was prompted to write to his headmaster condemning him. He already felt as if he were a member of a subculture, taping records, putting up posters and distributing leaflets against the wall, seeing the contradictions in Marx (like Marx's maxim that everything should be called into question—then why not Marxism?), and witnessing the closure of the school newspaper after a few issues because it was critical of everyday things, like the school-cafeteria food.

In 1963, when he was eighteen, Brasch spent a year working, as all students did. He began as a typesetter. Then he was asked if he would participate in pre-military training sessions, and he said no. It was decided that because he was color-blind he couldn't be a typesetter. After various other jobs he went to Leipzig to study journalism at Karl Marx University; there he lasted a year. He was asked to make a public declaration affirming his belief in socialism or to leave the university. Brasch gave vent to a few powerful comments and left. From the university's point of view, he was expelled for "existential views and slandering prominent DDR citizens."

For several years the existential heretic had odd jobs; in 1967 he enrolled in the School for Film and Television at Potsdam; the following year was that of Czechoslovakia and his arrest. He was sentenced to two years and three months, but was released early on condition that he work in a factory until 1971. The factory made transformers. After this he got a job in the Bertoldt Brecht Archive and for the first time found sympathetic conditions for getting on with the writing that had become his main preoccupation; he turned out translations from the Russian, records for children, radio-, television-, theater—and screen—plays, poems and short stories. The only work of his that was published in the DDR was a thirty-two-page book of poetry, in 1975, but other things were passed around in mimeographed or carbon-copied samizdat.

In the late autumn of 1976 the songwriter, guitar player and poet Wolf Biermann was banished from the DDR. Biermann grew up in Hamburg and emigrated to the DDR in 1953—his aim was to demonstrate sympathy for a state that was trying to put Communism into practice, and to flee the corruption that he thought would swamp him in the West. He worked as an assistant director at the Berliner Ensemble with Brecht, and he performed his own works. These expressed a commitment to Communism but also a critical and sarcastic view of life in East Germany. By 1962 he was in trouble with the authorities; for a year he was banned from performing in public. His works weren't allowed to be printed. He was in West Germany again on tour when the East German government announced that he was no longer a citizen because he had slandered DDR socialism.

In the wake of Biermann's banishment, fifteen other East German writers, publishers and artists—all presumed to be Biermann supporters—were expelled. One was Brasch. But he sees his own case as his own, as separate from the others. Brasch didn't want to be a Communist, and he doesn't want to be an anti-Communist; he simply wants to be a man who writes. Just as he didn't want to be one of the privileged East German writers who were allowed to go abroad on trips and who were cut off from ordinary life in the DDR, so he doesn't now want to be considered representative or typical of some sort of opposition. He is simply a man who grew up in East Germany. Brasch says that the main reason he was thrown out of the DDR was a manuscript—some fiction pieces he had collected under the title *The Sons Die Before the Fathers*—a title which, despite the author's desire not to be representative, might be taken as a commentary on the two generations of East Germans to date; his own generation had been forced to reject what his father's generation had brought into being. No publisher in East Berlin would accept the manuscript. Brasch therefore sent it to a West Berlin publisher, who did.

As Brasch tells it, lighting another cigarette, recalling an experience now five years old, the DDR authorities said that he had two alternatives: he could take back the manuscript or he could go to jail. But while he was mulling this over, a third proposition was made—he could leave the country. He accepted. He went to a police station where he and the woman he lives with, an actress, were given exit visas, good for one crossing of the border, in one direction, within two days. He and his companion left.

Since then he has traveled to the United States, where his play *Lovely Rita* was performed Off Broadway. He has visited other cities in West Germany. But, he says, "the only way I can live in Germany is to live in Berlin. I could live in New York except that I wouldn't have the German tongue around me. In some ways West Berlin isn't as German as East Berlin. Soviet culture hasn't influenced East Berlin as much as American culture has here. On the other hand, there are obvious advantages in not living in a state which tries to regiment every aspect of your existence, which wants to see the manuscripts beforehand when you're going to give a public reading, and where you can easily get the feeling that it's enough just to be against the government."

In West Berlin, Brasch is writing with no sense of being an exile, or of any increased difficulty from not being at home a mile or so to the east. He is working on a screenplay set in 1948 about a Berlin hangman who worked for two of the occupying powers, the United States and the USSR. He has plans for a novel about several generations of a German Jewish family. He does not feel constrained by the fact that he isn't writing about the present when material from a few years back wells up inside him, and is relevant.

I ask what the main differences are that he notices in ordinary everyday life here and there.

"On the surface, things like shops and cars of course. Here so many private shops with so many things in them. Here so many cars. And fewer police here. There more intervention by the state in everything—though as the economy here declines, there may be an increase here. The East is certainly richer than it was. People ask if one feels claustrophobia from being bottled up in West Berlin. But in East Germany claustrophobia is part of one's identity—which is to be the citizen of a country one is not allowed to leave."

And the wall?

"The wall is there. It is like nature. If you lived beside the sea, you'd accept the sea the way we accept the wall. In fact, I cannot imagine Berlin as one city. It is as if the wall has been there for a thousand years."

I ask what he thinks of the wall museum.

"It's agitation, propaganda. For me, the wall is a feeling in myself. I don't need pictures of it."

But doesn't the wall also demonstrate that most of the world does not want Germany reunited?

"Yes. It is also like an open wound, a punishment for Germans, a division of our soul."

Here is a synopsis of a story by Brasch, "Flies On My Face," that was part of the collection *The Sons Die Before the Fathers*. A young man, Robert, says goodbye to his girl friend and promises to pick her up in the morning when her factory shift is over. In fact, he is planning to try to escape to the West and thinks he may well be dead by the next morning. He has a few hours to kill before making his attempt and aimlessly rides a tram. He gets off and walks. An old man calls down from the window of an apartment that he has dropped a pillow and is unable to come down and get it. Robert takes it up to him. He realizes that the old man has lured him up for company. The old man is ill, has an attack, and Robert puts him to bed. When the old man recovers a little, he sits up and tells Robert stories about his days fighting as a Loyalist in Spain. He condemns Robert's generation. The apartment buildings out there were ruins and rubble thirty years ago. Robert thinks they are giant jailhouses—he says. "You built beautiful houses and put a wall around them." The old man replies, "I was in Spain . . . I saw the flies on the faces of the dead." Robert is conscious of being part of a game that they are both forced to play, speaking lines they both have to say. He shouts at the old man and confesses that he is planning to escape. The old man rambles on about Spain and puts on a record about the Red cause in Spain. Robert thinks, Five hours to go and I'll be at the border. They'll shoot. I'll lie there with flies on my face. He turns up the volume of the record player full blast. A woman

from a neighboring flat comes in and tells Robert the old man is a phony—
"He never got any farther away than Oranienburg in his whole life." The
old man shouts at the woman, "Get out of here, fascists, Nazi crow. . . ."

"They both stared at each other, filled with hate, face to face. Robert
pressed himself against the pillow and looked at his watch."

I asked Brasch if he ever wanted to go back.

He said that he had tried to go back on a visit not long ago to see his
father. He took his British passport and went to Checkpoint Charlie. He
waited for two hours at the barrier while officials deliberated. Finally one
of the guards came and handed his passport to him and said in slow
English, "No, Mr. Brasch, you cannot enter the German Democratic Republic. Please leave the border station at once."

In the afternoon I walked in the park behind Charlottenburg, the château-
like palace of the Prussian royal house. "The park was landscaped, with
English taste, by Friedrich-Wilhelm II," says *Michelin*, "and is an oasis of
tranquillity." English taste, perhaps, but the German sense of order was
evident, I thought, in that each one of the trees in the park was numbered.
Some of Schinkel's work was here: the Romantic fantasist and stern neo-
classicist combined in a summer pavilion built in the Pompeian style;
some of Caspar David Friedrich's paintings are hung within, and suit the
pavilion and the park extremely well. I walked on and reached a path
beside the Spree, where small weekend cottages—the pavilions of ordinary
people—sit in neat flower and vegetable gardens. I watched an East German barge and pusher tug going through a lock from the river to a canal.
Then I returned to the park and sat for a while in the sun, admiring the
ducks on the lake and the dark pollen-yellow walls of Charlottenburg. A
couple who shared my bench for a while in silence bade me a friendly
"*Auf Wiedersehen*" as they got up and walked away. The noise of city
traffic was muted to a soft whirr, over which one could hear the birds in
the trees. There was nothing on hand to suggest that one was in an enclave
deep in the Communist side of Europe, and perhaps no one in the park
at that moment except me was giving it a thought.

I flew out of Berlin the next day to Hanover. A minute after the British
Airways jet had taken off from Tegel we were over the wall, flying west at
less than ten thousand feet over the fields and woods of the DDR. As we

crossed the Elbe one of the cabin staff made an announcement and I realized that she was making it first in German; it was for the moment an internal German flight. In half an hour the border appeared, looking like a seventeenth-century fortification pattern by Vauban where it turned the corner of a big field, the plowed strip making a lighter line where it passed into some woods, and the shadow of the plane skimmed over it.

13. *HIER IST DEUTSCHLAND NICHT ZU ENDE!*

I resumed my southward course in Helmstedt on a Saturday morning, when the market was in full swing. Fresh vegetables, work clothes and hardware were being sold from stalls in the ancient Marktplatz, and so were Japanese cars—an enterprising salesman had set up a booth and had a sample model parked close-by. Old houses surrounded the market-place, except for a few spots where buildings had fallen down or been demolished, leaving a view of inner walls constructed from various materials: interwoven wattles, rubble, bricks and stones. Apart from a street or two with fine houses that were once part of the former university, there isn't much in Helmstedt to suggest that it was once a center of learning comparable to Heidelberg or Göttingen. Out in the country again the morning mist persisted—though how much was mist and how much was smoke, smog and steam from two rival power plants, one West, one East, is hard to say. Here were the open-cast coal pits, lying on either side of the minor road I took close to the border. The border ran through the easternmost of the pits I could see, but the DDR fence was at the far side of it—I could see it running along the skyline, with intermittent watchtowers. Klaus Lüders had said that in the pits the East Germans forgo some of their security measures for the sake of getting out the brown coal. The guards in the East German workings wear an industrial sort of uniform, and patrol with dogs but without guns. West German and East German mining equipment is allowed to transgress on rival territory for greater mining efficiency, and the ground of the border—re-marked from time to time with stakes—is actually sinking as coal is excavated.

Every other town or village in this area seemed to have a name that ended in *-leben*, which has to do with life. Most are just within the DDR: Uhrsleben, Wefensleben, Eimersleben, Erxleben, Bartensleben, Eilsleben, Ausleben, Hötensleben, Ohrsleben, Wackersleben, Ottleben, Warsleben, Altbrandsleben and Hamersleben. West of the border are Grasleben, Ingeleben, Gevensleben, Sambleben and Offleben. Such a concentration of lives or commitment to living prompted questions that perhaps Klaus Lüders could have answered—a Leben river would have been one solution, but I couldn't find a stream of that name on the map. Offleben is right on the border, a village that it took about two minutes to drive through. I parked at the far end of it. Although this was where Offleben halted, a black, red and yellow sign by the roadside said firmly: HIER IST DEUTSCH-LAND NICHT ZU ENDE! AUCH DRÜBEN IST VATERLAND! (This is not where Germany comes to an end. That over there is also the fatherland.) On the other side of the road was a restaurant that had capitalized on its involuntary position and taken the name Restaurant Grenzblick, which is to say, Borderview Restaurant. Ahead was the fence, the plowed strip and a watchtower planted athwart what had once been the road to Barneberg and Ausleben. Fastened to the red-and-white-striped barrier was an information board, put up by the local district council, which addressed the visitor to this spot and gave details of the land that had been lost because of the border and what had happened on the familiar dates in 1945 and 1952.

As I stood there, aware that one of the reflecting glass windows of the watchtower was being slightly moved, presumably to allow a guard with binoculars a better view of me, an elderly man pedaled up on a bicycle. We exchanged "Guten Tags" and then remarks about the lovely weather. He said that he came down there every morning—it was part of his morning ride around the village. He began to tell me about the fence—the ugly, dreadful, awful fence, he called it. Had I noticed that they had put up an additional section on top of the fence right there, sloping inward toward the DDR, to make it more difficult to climb over? Did I know about the mines? Did I think the tower was leaning slightly? (I thought it was.) In Offleben people wondered if it would go over as far as the leaning tower of Pisa, or just fall. Did I know that some of these DDR towers had fallen down? The elderly man had relatives over there, in

Völpke. If it weren't quite so misty, I would be able to see the briquette factory there. It had become too expensive for him to go to visit his relatives in Völpke very often.

I asked him when the border fence would be removed.

"Oh, it will be there always," he said, though he didn't sound absolutely sure of this. I suspected that one reason he came down to the barrier every morning was to check on the situation. He might pedal down here one morning not looking very far in front of his bike and glance up as he reached this spot and see that, yes, by some magic, the horrible *Grenze* had gone away.

I took the road south toward the Harz Mountains. My map called it the Baltic-to-Alps tourist road; the name and upgraded state of the highway were part of a scheme to improve north–south links along the border, where most east-west links have been severed, and attract more people to regions that need as much trade as they can get. Not that the Harz have any trouble in this respect. A small range, the Catskills of West Germany, they span the border about halfway down the dividing line between the two Germanys. Very few of the mountains are over a thousand meters high. The loftiest is the Brocken (1,142 meters), which is just inside the DDR and is the chief haunt in German legend of witches. On *Walpurgisnacht*, the witches' sabbath, the eve of May 1, the witches are said to have a lively get-together on the Brocken. It is also said that the witch legend was got up in the Middle Ages by Harz people who were trying to discourage intruders. Perhaps some such spirits were in the air overhead trying to discourage me, for at the small town of Jerxheim I blundered badly—almost fatally. The road I was meant to take went right, but I followed the old main road that used to cross the border—I followed it across the junction, and a car came whizzing around the corner at just that moment, following what it correctly felt was the route that gave it the right of way, and missed my stern by inches. I drove with extra attention to the road for a while thereafter.

The countryside began to lift, calm giving way to a heavy swell. The Harz appeared, a dark-green elevation of the horizon. It was good to see mountains after a long spell in flat country. I remembered my first sight of the Rockies as I drove across the Nebraska plain and an afternoon spent with an uranium prospector near Steamboat Springs. The Harz hold mineral wealth too; they were famous once for their gold and silver mines, and now for zinc, lead and barium. Goslar, which sits on the north side of the range, has been a mining town since medieval times; it looks less like Steamboat Springs or Deadwood Gulch than the sort of place where Snow White and the Seven Dwarfs would feel at home. In fact, it is hard to see how Günter Gauss can claim that East Germans have a greater concern with historic preservation when towns like Goslar, by their very existence, proclaim West German attachment to the architecture of the fourteenth and fifteenth centuries and various remains of earlier times. Goslar was a favorite spot of the early Holy Roman emperors. The Saxon dukes—in the course of pulling the Germanic tribes together under an elective kingship, within borders that roughly coincide with those of present-day West Germany, and extending its sway to western Austria, parts of Slovenia, and the Istrian peninsula—achieved the grand title that effectively bestowed the inheritance of the Roman tradition on the descendants of the barbarians. When the Salian line took over from the Saxons in the eleventh century, Goslar was one of the towns the emperor traveled to and stayed in, as he administered justice with the aid of bishops and attendant nobles, quarreled with papal autocrats in Rome, and oversaw the colonization and Christianization of the country east of the Elbe and northeast of the Danube—clearing the forests of the northern plain, draining the marshes and enslaving the Slavs.

The imperial palace in Goslar is very much a replica, built in 1879, covering the same ground as the eleventh-century palace and incorporating a few early structures like the Palatine chapel of St. Ulric, a zealous tenth-century bishop of Augsburg. (The *Dictionary of Saints* I have at hand says sparsely: "A letter against clerical celibacy ascribed to St. Ulric has been shown to be a later forgery.") I stood on the front steps for a while and admired the small park and grassy ramparts in the foreground. Then I turned into the old town, where a stream ran in a stone-walled cut with a path on one bank or the other as it rippled by medieval miners' cottages and mills. Some of the houses in town are half-timber—*Fachwerk* —with overhanging upper stories; some have façades entirely covered with slates, which makes them look as if they were encased in armored mail. In the town center, access is restricted to the vehicles of residents or those making deliveries. In the cobblestoned Marktplatz you can walk without thinking about traffic or traffic police (it would be some time before I forgot the Alexanderplatz) while admiring windows and doorways, gables and roofs.

The slate roofs of Goslar are wonderfully steep-pitched, joining one another at different heights, angles and slopes—a challenge for the craftsmen who hung the slates and arranged for hips, verges, gullies, ridges and eaves to come into a proper and watertight conjunction. Many houses have carved eaves and beams, painted to pick out the carvings and mottoes in Latin and German. One side of the Marktplatz is formed by the late-medieval town hall, whose ground floor has an arcaded gallery that once served as a covered market, and whose second-floor Great Hall is reached by an outside staircase. In the center of the square stands a fountain with two bronze basins, a larger one below to catch what overflows from the smaller basin above, and crowned by an imperial eagle with wings out-stretched.

After the pleasures of perambulation came the pleasures of contempla-tion. I sat opposite the town hall on the terrace of the Kaiserworth Hotel, which dates from 1494 and was at one point the guild hall of the Goslar merchant tailors, and carries on its upper, Gothic reaches various statues, including several emperors, a figure of Abundance, and the so-called Ducat man, who in a thoroughly gross and forthright way symbolizes the right of Goslar to mint its own coins. On the terrace, people were eating ice cream and cake. Slightly drunken men were singing snatches of traditional songs. In the square, children were splashing in the fountain. Among the people strolling past were men in lederhosen or knickerbockers and long bright-colored wool stockings. The ladies with them were attired in simi-lar costumes except for their skirts. Their outfits indicated that they were serious hikers, or wanted to be taken for such.

I spent the afternoon with a Bundesgrenzschutz border patrol. The officer in charge was Polizei Hauptkommissar Günter Sonnenschein, who reacted nobly—or stoically—to my remark in greeting, as we shook hands, that he had obvious influence with the heavens; the day continued fine. Our means of transportation was a new four-wheel-drive Mercedes-Benz, and we had with us two young BGS men who were to be taken out for a rendezvous with another patrol. Sonnenschein told me as we drove out of Goslar and up into the hills that things were fairly quiet on this section of the border. "Our biggest problem is that many tourists come to the Harz and they don't realize where the actual border is. Some are foreigners—a lot of Danes come here, looking for a change of scenery. These are the first mountains you reach coming south from Denmark. And as long as the Danes keep coming, the shopkeepers of Goslar don't do a lot of worrying about the border. But most of the people who cross the border and get into trouble are Germans. They think they can get away with it—they succumb to temptation. Sometimes a whole school class will wander over it while on a nature ramble, following a teacher who may think it's safe to do. Sometimes cross-country skiers cross it in winter, because over there is unbroken snow. Flower lovers, butterfly collectors, souvenir hunters after one of the DDR border-marker plaques—we get them all.

"I was duty officer last year when a call came in. An old man was missing—it was thought he'd gone mushroom hunting on the border. We went out and searched on foot, and a helicopter went out too. I went to the spot where he was believed to have been and with a loudspeaker called to some DDR troops in a watchtower, asking if they'd seen him. No reaction. No answer. We didn't know for three days whether he was alive or dead. Then they sent him back via Helmstedt. He said that he had known he was crossing the border, but there were many more mushrooms, which obviously no one would pick, on the other side. And just last week three men who were at a Trade Union Congress in Göttingen somehow went across near Duderstadt, just south of the Harz, while out sightseeing. They haven't been returned yet."

We reached the border at Eckertal. A brook, the Ecker, runs from south to north, and the border signs said: ACHTUNG! BACHMITTE GRENZE—that is, the border is the middle of the brook. A small wooden observation platform provided a view through trees toward the East German village of Stapelburg and a nearby DDR watchtower. A family of sightseers climbed the platform and stood alongside us, peering toward the village roofs visible over the usual length of wall and fences. Sonnenschein said that as with other such places, the residents of Stapelburg had mostly been moved farther from the border. "In the house nearest the watchtower lives the captain of their company of border troops stationed here. In places like this, they generally have directional microphones that can pick up conversations over here. And yet when I look over there, I don't feel that it's another country. Those are Germans too; it is still Germany."

The West German sightseers weren't very vocal, microphone or not. They looked stolidly at the prospect of the *Grenze* for a minute and then returned to their car. We did the same and followed a track which ran beside the river, still the border, higher into the Harz. The East German fence had disappeared from view behind some heavily forested hills, where, Sonnenschein said, it was easier for the DDR troops to survey long stretches of it. We came to a reservoir, the Eckerstausee, which has been formed in recent years by building a dam across the valley through which the Ecker flows. The project was the subject of long negotiations on the Grenzkommission. Use of the water is shared by both states, the West German portion going mostly to Wolfsburg and Salzgitter for the VW works. The dam was paid for by West Germany.

Although trade between the two Germanys is roughly in balance,

money for other things flows largely from West to East. West Germany
is contributing several hundred million Deutschmarks for the moderniza-
tion of railroad tracks in East Germany—trains running between the two
states do so more slowly than before the war because of poor DDR track.
The West German government has paid DM 1.4 billion ($700 million
or £360 million) toward the improvement of the Helmstedt–Berlin autobahn. Bonn pays DM 525 million annually to the DDR for Western
traffic to go to and from West Berlin, and another DM 50 million a year
in lieu of individual toll fees for West Germans who visit the DDR by
car. Some West Germans feel that without their government's financial
support, the East German regime would be even less popular with its
citizenry than it is. But in all this, West Germany is merely doing for its
bloodbrother what the Western world as a whole has been doing by way
of loans and export credits for most other countries of the Eastern bloc.
When I asked Günter Sonnenschein what he thought in particular about
West German subsidies for West Berlin, and were they worth the cost,
he said, speaking as a private citizen, "I think we should be prepared
to pay extra to keep them going. After all, they put up with a lot living
there, and they need us."

We drove away from the border for several kilometers and joined a
main road which brought us to an elevated viewing point called the Torfhaus. Here was the border as tourist attraction in full swing. The big
draw was a prospect of the Brocken, five kilometers to the east—a gently
rounded summit that rose above the surrounding hills, with spruce, fir,
pine and larch covering its slopes, and a Flash Gordon set of structures
on top: antennae, towers, domes. "Soviet radar station," said Sonnenschein.
On the Torfhaus, shorter by several hundred meters, were West German
radio and television transmitting devices, while on the Wurmberg, a
thousand-meter-high eminence to the south, was a U.S. military radar
tower facing across toward the Russians on the Brocken. I could hear the
wind shivering through the trees and the West German transmitting
towers, and I could imagine the ether crackling with various kinds of
radio waves as the Germans broadcast and the two great rivals probed,
listened, and tried to interfere with each other.

In the parking lot at the Torfhaus, big tourist buses were at rest amid
dozens of cars. Stalls selling beer and bratwurst were doing a spanking
trade—I added my custom, though I didn't join those at other stands
who were buying souvenir hiking sticks and toy witches. Youngsters eating ice cream jostled one another to be next looking through coin-operated
telescopes at the modern witchcraft on the Brocken. It was the wrong
time of day for the Brocken Specter to be seen. This is a phenomenon

caused by low cloud or mist lying on the western slopes of the Brocken and by the evening sun, which extends and enlarges the shadow of a person—standing, say, at the Torfhaus—onto what appears to be the white floor below the mountain. The Specter was perhaps one of the reasons why, as Samuel Coleridge noted on a visit to the Harz, the Brocken was "the seat of innumerable superstitions." This is the country where Humperdinck set his opera of Hansel and Gretel. Over there are also small resort towns where people stay for hiking and skiing. In Christa Wolf's novel *Divided Heaven*, a young couple goes to a small town in the Harz for a holiday. From a viewing platform there was a glimpse, on clear days, of a town in West Germany.

" 'You'll see,' said Manfred, '. . . the guidebooks will soon be advertising "a glimpse of West Germany" as one of the sights of the town.' "

In the nineteenth century the writer who made the Harz his own stamping ground was Heinrich Heine, poet and essayist, and people have been walking in the Harz in his footsteps even since. Although his essays remain lively, his verse, perhaps because it was often translated by Victorians whose language seems arch or quaint to us, has trouble getting through to present-day English readers. Goethe, at least with *Faust*, travels better. Mephistopheles leads us into the Harz on Walpurgis night:

> Voices in the height you hear,
> Distant now or sounding near,
> Streaming through the mountain range,
> Magic chanting, maddening, strange.

I stayed the night at a pension in Goslar where a notice in my room asked in German, English and Danish that guests please come in quietly. I ate dinner at the Kaiserworth, where the cooking—at least as far as I was concerned—didn't reach the high standards of the architecture. Too much salt had found its way into my medallion of veal, and no amount of wishing, damning the chief or asking for help from supernal powers would get it back into the Lüneburg salt caverns. My complaint produced a frosty comment that no one else had complained about it. Perhaps it would have helped if I'd been staying there.

No mist early next morning, simply sunshine. Although there were other guests at the pension, they had come in quietly the night before and were sleeping late. I had a solitary breakfast. Then I drove up into the Harz, following the valley of the Ocker, a much more powerful stream than its near-namesake the Ecker. The Ocker tumbled down through rocky gorges, splashing and booming, a melodramatic torrent. I had the car radio tuned to the Deutschlandfunk, which was broadcasting appropriate music, Beethoven's *Fidelio*. I stopped here and there for short hikes. In midmorning I climbed the Sonnenberg—or at least the last hundred meters or so of its 853 meters that the road didn't climb. From its summit there was a good prospect of the Harz interior—some hills severely tonsured, and some with sturdy clumps of growth on top. The deforested areas were a light green-brown, the treed parts a darker BGS green fading into a green-gray in the distance. Here on the Sonnenberg the hilltop resembled a piece of World War I no man's land: trees had been cut and fields were left full of dried, bleached gray stumps, with dead boughs sticking forth from hunks of cut but abandoned timber. I stepped cautiously over and around these obstacles. Near the summit was the disused machinery of an old ski lift. The long grass was dry and crackled underfoot, but even so a few small pools of purplish water lay in depressions next to some of the stumps. Heather, bracken and ferns flourished, and so, I imagined, did rabbits, though it wasn't the time of day to see them. There were no human beings in sight. The air was clear and warm, and I filled my lungs with it. I took advantage of the solitude to express my hill-walker's elation by shouting all the German superlatives I could remember: "*Wunderbar! Prima! Fantastisch! Super!*"

By noon I was in Braunlage, a resort and spa town deep in the Harz and a bare kilometer from the border. I expressed my attachment to the split city on the Spree by halting at the Hotel Berliner Hof and acquiring there a *Zimmer mit Dusche*. As I stood at the reception desk a young man, who looked Greek or Turkish, came in and asked the proprietor, "*Haben Sie Arbeit?*" "*Nein*," said the proprietor, "unfortunately not." The golden days of plentiful work for the *Gastarbeiter* are over, as the miracle recedes and unemployment begins to affect even the West German economy. I had a beer with the proprietor, who was nevertheless sanguine about the fortunes of Braunlage and the Berliner Hof—plenty of Danes, plenty of Berliners, plenty of elderly people wanting to take a cure or take the air. "And now even the border is interesting." he said, with some astonishment as I gave him a brief idea of my journey.

With sweater, plastic raincoat and map stuffed into my nylon knapsack I walked through Braunlage, which had something of New England about its houses—vertical siding, wooden shingles, even asbestos shingles. I walked past other hotels and big sanatoriums in parklike grounds and out of town, northward in the direction of the Wurmberg. In the woods, the wind in the pines sounded like the sea; occasionally there was a little shower of pine needles, and the smell of pine was strong. The ascent was steady and not oversteep. I was about two thirds of the way up before I saw the border—a watchtower to the east and an expanse of grass before the pine forest in the DDR began. Birds and butterflies flew across my line of sight.

The path veered around behind the Wurmberg. I climbed under a cable-car way, the cars gliding eerily overhead. And when I got to the top, puffing, twenty minutes later, I found what I now began to realize was an essential part of most of these lofty *Grenzblicke*—a Gasthaus with terraced beer garden, and quite a lot of people who were today enjoying a Sunday out. There was also a small detachment of West German conscript soldiery.* Their vehicles were parked nearby, with a temporary radio antenna, a generator and a camouflage net thrown over most of the equipment. A tall wooden tower provided rather rickety-looking access to a ski jump, from which a master of the sport could soar, so it seemed, into the DDR. Next to the Gasthaus terrace was a circle of rough stones, like a ring of large, gray misshapen loaves. This (a sign said) was prehistoric, the remains of people who had lived and no doubt kept watch up here, though no exact date could be put on them.

I sat on the terrace with a beer and munched a cheese sandwich I'd made from things served to me at breakfast. Emmenthal on pumpernickel is delicious at 1 P.M., as far as I'm concerned, but not first thing in the morning. Sundays are when you don't get fresh rolls for breakfast but have to put up with bread from the day before. (My everyday *Frühstück* problem was the lack of orange marmalade, without which I find it very hard to begin the day—what the Germans call *Marmelade* is in fact any kind of jam.) Quite a number of people on the terrace were also trying to outsmart the management by ordering a soft drink or beer and then eating their own food. Most had arrived by cable car, young people in jeans and old ladies in flowered print dresses; but there were also some hikers in either modern hiking gear (nylon anoraks, corduroy trousers) or the traditional *Wanderungen* get-up, whose healthy-looking faces suggested that they had reached the summit on their own feet.

The German fondness for hiking—or for going out dressed to look as if they had a passion for long-distance walking—has been stimulated in the last few years by the Federal Republic's President, Karl Carstens. He and his wife have hiked, in short stages and generally at weekends, the

---

* Conscripts from about half of the 495,000-strong West German Bundeswehr. They serve fifteen months. East German conscripts serve eighteen months, plus another twenty-four months in the reserve. Both armies are facing a shortage of recruits because of low birth rates.

seven hundred miles from Hohwacht, on the Baltic coast a little north of Lübeck, to Garmisch in the Bavarian Alps, for the first part of the way paralleling the border but gradually bearing off in a southwesterly direction. The President intended to encourage Germans to get out of their cars and walk—"Less Mercedes, more *per pedes*" was his somewhat pedantic suggestion—while at the same time seeing his own country and countrymen. Much of the way he was accompanied by local officials, schoolchildren and hikers; he learned about various regional problems, ate all sorts of local *Wurst* and *Kuchen,* and was given umpteen souvenir walking sticks. He also collected 100,000 marks for a multiple sclerosis charity and helped hiking associations increase their membership fivefold, to 600,000, mostly as a result of newspaper attention given to his hike.

I walked away from the heavily peopled part of the Wurmberg summit and into the woods. Half a mile from the ski lift I came upon the other large structure on the mountain—the early-warning radar tower I'd seen from the Torfhaus the previous afternoon. Close up, it looked like something out of the inside of a television set or a giant eggbeater within which concrete had solidified, standing above the trees, its handle stuck in the ground. There was no security apparatus around it of the sort that I'd been told surrounded the Soviet installation on the Brocken. Here merely a single though effective fence girdled the tower, enclosing a small parking lot with a few cars and a basketball net on a post. There was a faint rumble in the air, though I couldn't tell if it came from here or the more distant cable-car workings. To the fence were fastened signs in English and German ordering the reader not to make sketches, photographs or notes, "by order of the commanding officer"—a rather old-fashioned turn of phrase—on pain of confiscation. So I walked on a few hundred meters downhill toward the border before hiding behind a tree (which I thought might prevent my image showing up on radar, pen in hand), and there communicating a few words to my notebook ("eggwhisk . . . parking lot . . . basketball").

I walked along the border southeastward. The DDR fence was about fifty paces away, and I was briefly in view of two watchtowers about a mile apart. No one else was in sight. I walked along a little track next to the BGS warning signs, the border posts and occasional concrete markers. The Wurmberg rose on my right hand, and on my left, across a shallow valley, a hill nearly as high called Gross Winterberg, in the DDR. The path became a deep rut, where a small stream perhaps made its way in spring. The shrubbery thickened, and trees bent out of the hillside over the path. I felt excessively lonely. I wondered where the *Aufklärer* were. What if they just popped out and grabbed me? I was in a small wood, which felt old, full of old spirits. I felt the need to assert myself, to buck myself up a bit—what if I did walk on the other side of the marker posts for a little way, just so I could say I'd walked in East Germany? What if . . . I went to the left of a marker pole and took a few quick paces before stepping back onto the proper path again. That wasn't difficult. I swerved left again at the next marker and walked along a meter or so inside the DDR, swinging my arms. I stepped around a bush and stopped dead still. There they were. They saw me at the same moment I saw them, two of them in their drab-green uniform, about six meters away, squatting on the grass while they smoked cigarettes. They were about six long paces inside West Germany. The astonishment was mutual, but they moved faster than I. They were up and running onto their own ground, Kalashnikovs swinging, clutching binoculars and cameras, before I'd thought about what do next. And having thought, I took a sudden jump sideways, nearly fell over and kept walking fast, once again on the path on the right side of the border. Had they noticed? As I passed them, standing at least as far back on their own territory as they had been on that of West Germany, I didn't look at them in case I prompted them to cover their tracks by taking me prisoner—two against one; their word against mine. I had made my rash gesture of the day and hastened on, and as soon as I knew they couldn't see me anymore I left the path and went farther up the Wurmberg slopes, just in case they changed their minds and came after me. After five minutes I felt relatively safe, sat down and stayed there until my heart stopped pounding. Just as well they'd been in the wrong, too, at that moment. I could hear Sonnenschein's voice as he talked to the next visitor to the border he was asked to guide, adding someone else to his list of conference-delegates, skiers, schoolchildren and mushroom collectors.

In the next hour I saw a small shed in the woods with chalked graffiti: BRITS RUSKIS AMS OUT; a young couple, sitting on a log, hands interlocked, with their feet just inside the border, oblivious—so it seemed—to a DDR watchtower a hundred yards away; a little brook, the Bremke, running south; and a road, the former Elenderstrasse, intersected by the border. There were the remains of a bridge that had once carried the road across the Bremke and on to Elend, now in the DDR. Over there, *drüben*, the road was narrow and deserted. On the West German side it was wider but equally without traffic; it had become a lane on which people could take a Sunday-afternoon stroll out from Braunlage without the exertion of climbing the Wurmberg. Naturally, there were watchtowers here, too— an older type, apparently empty; a newer one, apparently manned. Beyond the fences, outer and inner, two German shepherds were attached by leashes to long wire runs. A man and a woman came walking from Braun-lage, guiding a toddler who was pushing his own carriage. They arrived at the striped barrier that ended the road and stood looking at the ruins of the bridge. I had recovered my nerve and felt annoyed that this small family couldn't keep walking. *Hier ist Deutschland nicht zu Ende!* Here, however, was a dividing line between two views of the state—on one side, where the state was still seen as the creation of and servant of the people; and on the other, where people were considered to exist for the benefit of the state. And these concepts could be, as I'd seen, a mere quick and sudden jump apart.

14. EICHSFELD AND ESCAPES

South of the Harz the border turns west and then southwest for a way before bending south again. Down from the hills the country is undulating farmland. It was another fine day. I drove to Göttingen, which is only twelve kilometers in from the border but doesn't seem at all preoccupied with this fact. Rather, as befits an old university town, full of enthusiasm and aspiration, it has the feeling of being concerned with things at once higher and lower, such as student housing or the nature of the universe. Bicycles thronged the streets. Pedestrians packed the extensive pedestrian zones where chairs and tables outside cafés were solidly taken up by students who apparently didn't have a lecture or a tutorial to attend. The university was founded in 1737 by George II, Elector of Hanover and King of Great Britain and Ireland. A statue of William IV, last of the Hanoverians to be both king and elector, stands in a little square, the Wilhelmplatz, opposite the Academy of Science. (Under Salic law, which was then honored in Germany, women of nobility could not succeed to the titles and offices of their family; therefore William's heir, Victoria, was unable to become Electress of Hanover when she became Queen of Great Britain and Ireland, Empress of India, etc.) In its early days Göttingen University was considered a fine place for young aristocrats interested in improving their riding skills.

However, in the nineteenth and twentieth centuries Göttingen gained a reputation for scientific learning from the work of such men as Karl-Friedrich Gauss, mathematician and astronomer, and Max Planck, author of the quantum theory. The Brothers Grimm lived in Göttingen for ten years, obviously enjoying it more than another literary resident, Heinrich Heine, who said, "Göttingen looks its best when you have turned your back on it."

Göttingen is full of posters advertising meetings against nuclear power, for disarmament and for ecological causes. In one street of half-timbered buildings I stopped to ask the way of some young men who were sitting at a trestle table, collecting signatures for a petition against the sale of dried milk to Third World countries. (I had, coincidentally, Günter Grass's novel *The Flounder* under my arm. In it, in the course of dealing with various aspects of the age-old cold and hot war between men and women, Grass discusses ways of feeding babies and writes: ". . . it is known that our vitamin-enriched powdered milk is positively fatal to many infants in the less industrialized countries, so that the advertising of a leading concern that is trying to develop a market for powdered milk in Africa can only be termed criminal.") In one bookshop with much radical and anarchist stock I bought a magazine called *Atom Express*, published in Göttingen, that gave news of demonstrations and protests against nuclear power projects, including the nuclear waste disposal site near Gorleben. I browsed through a pamphlet illustrating first-aid procedures to perform if one was on hand when someone was injured at a demonstration. Quite a number of books and periodicals had to do with disarmament. Günter Grass, I noted in one paper, was among one hundred and fifty European writers—including twenty-four East Germans—who had recently signed an appeal for an end to the arms race, claiming that "Humanity is to be made to get used to the criminal idea that it is possible to conduct a limited nuclear war with new rockets, neutron bombs, cruise missiles, etc." The West German authors, who included Heinrich Böll, also demanded a nuclear-free Germany "as the first step to a nuclear-free Europe and a nuclear-free, peaceful world."

The next day I met someone who had a good reason for wanting the border to remain, at least for the following twelve years. That was the length of time BGS Hauptkommissar Lochner had to serve before retirement. He was stationed in Duderstadt, a border town fifteen kilometers from Göttingen, and he didn't want the reason for his being there to disappear. He loved Duderstadt. At the end of the day, as I was taking an after-dinner stroll through Duderstadt's somnolent streets, I met Kommissar Lochner and his wife doing the same—they had paused in the course of their evening walk to look in the windows of a furniture store. We chatted for a little while. I felt as if I were back at home in a village, where running into someone one knows is the occasion for a short gossip, a joke or two, a catching up on what one's been doing since the last such encounter—in this case, skating over good-humoredly a slightly disappointing visit I'd made with Kommissar Lochner that morning, and thanking him for putting me in touch with an interesting guide to Duderstadt in the afternoon. We talked easily, as people will who have an occupation or hobby in common.

With the border itself, I'd begun to realize, a certain repetition of facts and figures had to be faced when calling on the professionals who kept an eye on it: the fence system—the weaponry—the border troops—the infrequent escapes—the increasing quietness. As Kommissar Lochner gave me a briefing on the *Grenze* in this area—which is called the Eichsfeld, the oak field—I felt it was like listening to a coast guard whose section of beach has waves breaking on it, the tide rising and falling, flotsam washing up, as on beaches all the way down the coast, but to whom his section is nevertheless unique; he knows its small differences, the incidents particular to it, like the trade-union delegates nabbed in the last few days, two Australian tourists captured a year before, and an Englishman, a headwaiter who had come to Duderstadt to improve his German and was arrested by DDR border troops on his first day here. He was taken to East Berlin for questioning. Herr Lochner showed me a small section of DDR fence material, as if he were showing me a fragment of a reef that had pulled the bottom out of many ships. He told me of a family that had tried to come across in the mid-1970s; the woman had stepped on a mine and had both legs blown off. But some survived the dangers of the sea and coast—he showed me a photograph of a small DDR observation plane in which several people had escaped a few years ago. Last January, two DDR border guards had found a gate in the outer fence unlocked and plunged forth together.

We drove along the border, which had been the border between the kingdoms of Hanover and Prussia. Fields were being harvested of rape and wheat. Fruit was visible on trees in orchards. A hawk sailed above us, over the border fences. A gray civilian DDR truck moved slowly along the plowed strip, spraying defoliant, followed by two border guards on a motorcycle. A strong etherlike smell drifted over to us. Lochner pointed out a place behind some woods where dogs were kept because it seemed a likely spot for people to try to escape. We paused at a crossroads where a lane—now cut by the border—had once gone to the village of Kirchgandern. The river Leine still crossed the border, its polluted waters a problem for Göttingen farther downstream. We drove in through the gates of Friedland camp, set up just after the war to shelter refugees from the former German territories in the East and still in use.

Here I had the first serious language difficulties of the journey. I'd been lucky, managing to conduct most conversations in English, in a mixture of German and English, or in simple German. Here simple German wasn't enough; the camp director spoke no English; and the man whom Kommissar Lochner had in mind as translator, a visiting Dutch journalist, turned out to speak very little English. After I had asked the director a question, the Dutchman wrote down the answers in his notebook and seemed unable to find the English words for what had been said. I elicited the information that Friedland had also been a reception center for German servicemen released from captivity in the Soviet Union. (The last ten thousand had returned in 1955, after Chancellor Adenauer visited Moscow and negotiated their release. Heine, in his essay "The Emperor and the Drummer," writes that many of Napoleon's soldiers captured in Russia were "Dragged to Siberia as prisoners and held there for several long years although there was peace.") Some 300,000 people of German origin have left East European countries, particularly Poland, the USSR and Rumania, since 1970, when the Federal Republic embarked on its *Ostpolitik* and various treaties were signed making relations easier. (The number of ethnic Germans who have been allowed to leave Poland increased considerably following an agreement signed in 1975 on the mutual payment of pensions and social-insurance contributions, and on the provision of a West German loan to Poland.) Friedland houses roughly a thousand refugees at any one time; they stay, on the average, four days while being processed, as it were, into the West German system and given the various papers and documents they need as citizens. Here they are questioned by intelligence officers, partly for information, so I gathered, but mostly to establish their *bona fides*. Then they are sent on to other centers in the parts of Germany where they hope to settle and find jobs.

Within the camp compound, people were sitting outside huts. Some had their faces turned to the sun; others were clutching file folders in which they had papers ready for an interview. I asked if I could talk to some people who had just arrived. The director wasn't keen on this, but eventually agreed to a short meeting with a family. We met around the staff dining table: the director, the Dutchman, me and the new arrivals—

an older couple and a younger couple, consisting of father, mother, daughter and son-in-law. The older pair were in their Sunday best; she had blond hair freshly permed. The younger couple was less formally dressed; she was very pretty, and he was about six and a half feet tall. The problem here was not so much one of language—the young man spoke some English, and I could understand a lot of the German his parents-in-law spoke —but the director would not allow them to answer my questions. Whether for diplomatic reasons, to make sure that they didn't tell me things I wasn't supposed to know or simply out of his directorial nature, he answered them himself. But one way or another I established that the family came from Upper Silesia, in Poland. They were descended from ethnic Germans, who had been there for some generations; the older couple had stayed at the end of the war when most German Poles fled or were expelled by force. The older man said they had driven from Poland via Berlin in their Polish Fiat; they had Polish passports good for visiting West Germany, but they weren't going back. They had made a similar trip the previous year but had decided to return because of his mother; now she was dead.

The young man told me, over and around statements from the director, that they were not leaving because conditions were worse for them, ethnic Germans, than for ordinary Poles—things were equally bad for everyone right now. He was twenty-seven. He had taught basic engineering in a high school. His wife was a dental technician. They had left everything except what was in a couple of suitcases. They were looking for a better life for the children they wanted to have, but hadn't ventured to have in Silesia. They had relatives in Düsseldorf who might be able to help them find work. He knew there was growing unemployment in West Germany, but anything was an improvement on what they had left. The young man pointed to the large photograph of President Carstens that hung on the wall. He said, "He has a true look on his face. I think everything will turn out for the good."

Herr Vincenz Gerlach is the tourist director of the town of Duderstadt and the editor of the monthly journal *Eichsfelder Heimatstimmen*— literally, "home voices of the Eichsfeld"—which covers events in the entire Eichsfeld region; the Eichsfeld spans the border, an area containing three to four large towns and a score of villages in West and East Germany. Herr Gerlach was a robust, boisterous man in his late fifties, brimming over with local patriotism and its corollary, local indignation. A large map of the Eichsfeld hung on his office wall in Duderstadt's town hall (which dates from 1229). The map had no indication of the intra-German border on it. We had for translator a young woman, short and blond, named Sabine. Herr Gerlach said, "I come from over there—ten kilometers from here. I left in 1949. I go back once a year, which is all I can afford since Honecker raised the fees. My nephew there is in the army—he is forbidden to have contact with West Germans, so when I come he must leave the house. Apartheid, isn't that what it is? My sister, over sixty, now lives here and has a West German pension. For my twenty-fifth wedding anniversary last year, my brother, who is fifty, was allowed to come for a week, but he had to leave his wife and children behind—they were hostages for his return! If he had been single, they wouldn't have allowed him to come. I know a single man over there whose sister was dying here—they wouldn't let him come. If a married man is known to be on bad terms with his wife, they won't let him out—he might not come home."

Herr Gerlach had several East German newspapers on his desk. One was *Neues Deutschland*, the national Communist Party paper, whose title made him angry—"*Deutschland!* They do not have the right to that name!" The other was *Das Volk*, a provincial paper from Worbis, the nearest East German town to Duderstadt. I glanced at the classified ads for used cars. A four-year-old Russian Lada was offered for 19,000 marks (a new one could be bought in West Germany for roughly DM 10,000); a 1971 Wartburg was for sale for 20,000 marks. "Color-television sets are twice the price over there," Herr Gerlach said. "A man's shirt—if you can find one you want to wear—costs half as much again as it does here. Have you heard the story about the two East German neighbors? One is calling on the other when a coffin is delivered. 'Oh, I'm sorry,' says the first, 'I didn't know there had been a death in your family.' 'There hasn't,' says the second man, 'but you have to buy what you can when you can.'"

Herr Gerlach became a little evasive when I asked him how he had got the Worbis paper, which was four days old. His own magazine is not officially allowed in the DDR, but is full of news of small-town events, of births, deaths and anniversaries, in the Eichsfeld over there, to which it makes its way. "We are the free part of Germany," said Herr Gerlach. "We must speak for those who cannot." He fished in a drawer of his desk, found a coin and handed it to me. "Look at their new ten-mark coin! See, on one side, a military aircraft, a naval ship and a panzer tank. The peace-loving DDR! Do you know what the differences are between elections in the United States, West Germany and the DDR?"

"No."

"In the United States, people can choose between Carter and Reagan.

Here they can choose between Schmidt and Strauss. In the DDR they can choose between going to vote early in the day or later on."

Herr Gerlach, Sabine and I went for a walk. We strolled up the broad main street of Duderstadt, which has a Catholic cathedral of St. Cyriakus at one end and a large Evangelical church of St. Servatius at the other. Near the former, Herr Gerlach pointed out statues of Wenceslas II, King of Bohemia and Holy Roman Emperor, and of St. Johannes Nepomuc, a Bohemian saint who is patron of those who have been unjustly slandered. The Eichsfeld is a mostly Catholic region; during the Reformation and the wars that followed, a Catholic prince-bishop kept the area safe for Rome on the principle that was then followed, *cuius regio, huius religio.* Religion still has a hold, particularly in the DDR. Herr Gerlach said that in the last ten years, three Catholic priests had been ordained in Duderstadt, fifty-five new priests in Worbis.

Duderstadt has city gates and ramparts that provide a path on which you can circumambulate the town, on a grassy bank fringed with old trees. It has some five hundred half-timbered houses with bright-red roofs and painted friezes. Herr Gerlach now and then stopped in mid-street and boomed out the ages of nearby houses—five hundred years old; four hundred and fifty years old. He pointed out post-Renaissance emblems; grotesque Gothic figures; obscure mottoes. Sabine translated gamely, in a lower voice, "This is the seal of the city of Brandenburg . . . There are eight thousand people in Duderstadt itself . . . The people of the town were not allowed to piss in the river Bremke on the day water was drawn off to make beer . . . Once there were fifty brewers, now there are none. There are still eight bakers. As long as there are bakers the town lives."

I thought Duderstadt for all its proximity to the border and consequent loss of hinterland was alive, all right. Herr Gerlach said that it was trying to build up its tourist trade. The nearest railroad station was in Göttingen, but Duderstadt was on the Baltic-to-Alps tourist route. Although there was no big industry, one factory prospered making artificial limbs. As we walked down one narrow street and church bells rang the hour, Sabine said, "Do you like apples?" She whizzed into a shop, throwing over her shoulder, "—my mother works here." She came out with three crunchy green apples, which we ate as we walked on.

Back at the town hall, Herr Gerlach showed me the dungeons and torture chamber. Old seals, old documents. "One man came here from America and traced his ancestors back to Charlemagne," he said. In a cupboard were various town trophies, none quite that old; one had been won by a team from Duderstadt in a TV competition called "It's a Knockout," in which various European towns compete in contests that are a bizarre mixture of athletics and slapstick. Duderstadt, trained by Kommissar Lochner, had beaten Cheltenham in the finals in England in 1967.

The Hotel zur Tanne, where the ubiquitous Goethe once stayed, was now an empty shell. I stayed a few doors away at the Hotel zum Löwen. There were several French guests. Perhaps Herr Gerlach's campaign to encourage tourism was bearing fruit. Spanish music from the bar next door flooded my room but ceased abruptly at ten-thirty. I read in Herr Gerlach's magazine, among the local jottings which bravely assumed that the Eichsfeld was one region still, a poem called "protest" by Gerda Kraus-Bohner. (Since the last lines depend on a repetition of the letter g, I've translated those lines word for word.)

> I write now
> everything small
> and without punctuation
> particularly small
> do I write the words
> that begin with g
> *gehorsam* [obedient] *gesellschaft* [society] *geduld* [patience]
> *gerechtigkeit* [justice] *gewissen* [conscience]
> *gesetz* [law] *gedankenfreiheit* [freedom of thought]
> *geheimdienst* [secret service] *genossenschaft* [cooperative association]
> particularly small
> would I like to write *grenze*
> but then
> no one could read it.

In the early morning I drove south from Lower Saxony into Hesse. Children were biking to school. There were few cars, but I was on my guard against farmers shooting out on tractors from farmyards into the road, obviously regarding the chances as small that a car like mine would be coming along at that moment, swerving or braking fiercely without time to blow the horn. Villages: Etzenborn, Weissenborn, Bischhausen, Bremke, Ischenrode, Ellershausen . . . At Ellershausen the road to Eschwege ran right next to the border for a few kilometers or so, with the river Werra between road and fence. The East Germans had their own road inside the fence and a working party: two cars, a truck, a motorcycle, workers, guards. A hundred meters up the forest hillside behind the road I could see with my binoculars an observation post, most of it below ground, and probably invisible from their road.

In Eschwege I sat for a while in the market square, had a cup of coffee and watched people shopping. At the next table on the café terrace sat a young couple; a German shepherd lay at their feet, quiet and happy, since he had just been fed a raw sausage. I thought, Maybe I will take to Germany to such an extent that I even come to like German shepherds. At eleven a bell rang in a nearby clocktower and I took this as a signal to get going again. The local bookshop had a window full of the works of the German-Swiss author Max Frisch—whose books I admire, but which I will not yet attempt in German. From a market stall I bought instead some English apples, Laxtons, and from a bakery shop a *Berliner Pfannkuchen*—a glazed doughnut.

In Bebra I visited the railway station, the last stop for trains on this line going into the DDR, including the Paris–Warsaw and Paris–Berlin expresses, and from Cologne to Leipzig. Staff at the station told me that roughly a million people a year cross in each direction, mostly old people, and mostly in summer. I had missed two special trains by an hour that were taking East German football fans to Düsseldorf for a European Cup tie between Jena of the DDR and Tiflis of the USSR, being played that evening on neutral ground. A number had got off the train at Bebra to stretch their legs but no one had left the station. Stalwart supporters of team and/or state are presumably the only ones allowed out for such occasions. However, later that evening I watched on television at my hotel some West German reporters questioning some of the East German fans in what seemed to me a pretty belligerent manner ("Why were *you* allowed to come?") and I felt sorry for the East Germans. What if they were just plain interested in football? What if it was one permitted outlet, which they enjoyed? How, in any case, could they be expected to give a frank answer and not get into trouble at home? I was on their side, briefly.

A train came in from the East, from Frankfurt on the Oder, its destination München-Gladbach in the Ruhr. Faces were pressed to the windows, and as I walked along the platform an elderly lady leaned out of an open window and caught my eye. For a moment I thought she was one of my companions on the train journey to Berlin.

"Is this the *Bundesrepublik*?" she asked.

"Yes," I said.

"It doesn't look very different from home." Then she looked at me, as if she had just woken up. "But you aren't German."

"No. English."

"Well, that's different." Then, perhaps unsure about the legality or correctness of talking to foreigners in this way, she gave me an abrupt "Auf Wiedersehen" and returned to her seat.

The Werra dodges in and out along the border in this area. An old section of prewar autobahn heading toward the DDR border at Herleshausen is cut off by a bulge of DDR territory, and traffic is forced to detour by country roads. Just inside the DDR between Herleshausen and Wartha a new section of autobahn is being built with West German funds. At the Herleshausen Übergang, BGS chief warrant officer Hans-Werner Wiegand showed me the computer terminal on which he could tap out names and car details, and which enabled the BGS to nab the occasional thief or youth reported missing from home. "This is how it works," he said, typing the name Bailey, A. Within a few seconds the particulars of several A. Baileys with criminal records appeared on the screen—one American, two English. I was not among them. Close at hand was one of his red emergency telephones, now and then used here for announcements from the East Germans of dangerously high water in the river. Wiegand had used it the day before to help the driver of a bus coming from West Berlin. A message had come from the bus garage, saying that it was believed the nuts of one wheel were not properly tightened. Wiegand called his East German counterpart, who called the autobahn police, who stopped the bus, and the driver tightened the nuts.

I asked whether there had been any escapes recently in this area.

"The last civilian was about three years ago," Wiegand said. "He came through a minefield—he was drunk and had fought with his wife after finding her with another man. Last year five DDR soldiers came over. This year we've only had one so far. One of their border troops got across near Heldra, southeast of Eschwege, where they don't seem to have either mines or SM-70s at the moment. He disarmed and tied up his colleague, then stuck his Kalashnikov into the ground next to the fence, stepped up on the butt and climbed over."

Finding out about escapes from the DDR is not simple. Statistics given out by the West German government, by state governments, and by private groups such as the Working Group August 13th in West Berlin, don't always agree and don't make clear the ways in which people have managed to get out of East Germany. From various press reports for 1979, published in Britain, one gets various figures. The London Daily Telegraph, on April 11, 1980, quoting a Bonn government source, said that only eighty East German refugees had succeeded in crossing the border in 1979. The Birmingham Post said on February 19, 1980: "Last year, 170 East Germans fled to West Germany, most of them border guard patrols who walked across. In Berlin itself, 36 attempts were successful." The *Times* of August 13, 1980, quoted the Working Group August 13th figure of 161 escapes for the first half of 1979. The *Financial Times* of July 2, 1980, reported that 463 East Germans made it to the West in 1979, and that roughly 400 came out via the transit routes, smuggled through in Western cars.

Some of this confusion may arise from failure to distinguish between civilian refugees and fleeing border guards, some from the ways escapes take place and are announced. Part of the obscurity, on the other hand, is deliberate. Some years ago people realized in West Germany that reporting full details of where and how an escape had been made was helpful to the East German authorities, who immediately plugged the loophole, and even sometimes caught others trying to get out in the same place. A Bavarian border policeman told me later that opportunities exist from time to time for people to get across if they have up-to-the-minute knowledge, for example as to where fences are being repaired, or mines removed, or where guards have developed habits that may permit an escape. In the past the DDR authorities may have had no idea how an escape was made—or even that one was made—until it was reported in the West German press. Now papers usually mention only the state—for instance, Schleswig-Holstein—to which the person escaped, or the town where the BGS have announced the escape. (On the other side, many are caught—it is assumed—trying to escape, often as they make their way through the five-kilometer zone; and this goes unreported in the West.)

I shall be cagy too and not reveal the real name of a man who told me how he got out of East Germany, very close to this crossing point at Herleshausen; nor shall I mention the large West German city where he now lives. I'll call him Dieter. He is a successful industrialist in his late thirties, dark-haired, stocky, immensely fit-looking. He was born and grew up in Leipzig. At school he became a keen member of the Communist Young Pioneer organization. Doubt set in when he was nearly fifteen, influenced by programs from West German television and West German visitors he'd talked to.

"There was a great difference between what I was taught at school and what I saw and heard on these occasions," Dieter said. "I remember opening an atlas one day, finding countries like France and Switzerland and thinking, Will I ever be able to go to them? For the first time the thought came to me: I will have to get out of this cage."

These feelings intensified as he found out that he would have to be a party member to get a good job and sure promotion—and he refused to join the party. The building of the Berlin Wall closed the cage door. In the mid-1960s Dieter and a friend, Wilhelm, began to have long talks about how to escape. Wilhelm had done his military service as a border soldier, and after much consideration and poring over maps, Dieter and he picked a place Wilhelm knew, near Wartha, just across the border from Herleshausen.

"On the thirteenth of January we took a train to Eisenach," Dieter told me. "There was snow all day. We stayed overnight in Eisenach and the next morning we caught a bus to the edge of the five-kilometer zone. Of course we didn't have the special pass needed to get inside it. It was just after midday and we walked along the edge of a field that got us around a checkpoint. But it wasn't just checkpoints—in that zone the whole population are vetted for their reliability. They're one hundred percent Communists, or supposed to be. And if they see strangers, they're supposed to telephone the authorities straight away.

"We could see the low hills of the Thüringerwald to the south. We went through a village, trying to look as if we had a purpose there. It was a question of walking through the main street or skulking through gardens and around the backs of houses, which would have been more conspicuous. I had my gear in a sports bag and Wilhelm carried an attaché case. The village was nearly empty; it was like a ghost town. On several corners military band music was coming from loudspeakers hung from lampposts. Snow began to fall lightly. One or two people moved past but they didn't seem to see us. I wondered if we were invisible. Then we were in open country again, heading toward Wartha. We broke boughs from trees and tried to brush the snow behind us over our footsteps. But it didn't help much.

"At two P.M. we were nearly at the *Grenze*—the spot where we wanted to cross was a bit more than a kilometer away. We had reached the Werra. We could see Wartha on a hill on the other side of the river to the north, on our right. To the south, there was an old ruin of a castle on a hill. It looked like a watchtower. We knew that if we went on in broad daylight, we'd be spotted. So we went along the hillside below the castle and found a little hollow. We stayed there waiting for darkness. Those were the worst couple of hours of my life. Once we heard a series of detonations—maybe it was animals setting off mines. I wanted to quit, and I think Wilhelm did too. But there was no going back. We both had to prove to each other that we could go on.

"At six P.M. the church clock chimed in Wartha. It was a moonless night. We went slowly down to the river to see how we would get across. There was a bridge, but when we got close to it we saw that it was well guarded and brightly lit. So we went back along the riverbank a little way and wondered what to do. Then Wilhelm stood up, walked a few paces forward and stepped in. He didn't say a word to me. None of this was in the plan we'd made. I jumped in, waded out and started swimming. We both had our winter coats on, and our bags, and somehow we managed to swim. The Werra there was about two hundred meters wide. The current was fierce. The water was icy. Wilhelm crawled out on a flat bit of the far shore. I got swept farther downriver, and where I landed the bank was steep—but Wilhelm had run along and pulled me up. We took off our coats, which now weighed a ton, and left them on a cattle fence. It was pitch-dark, though to the west we could see a single light. Wilhelm whispered to me that it was beyond the border, the checkpoint of the West German side of the road crossing. We walked in that direction. We had to be on the watch for wire—for barbed wire, and for signal wires. If we set off an alarm, the flares would go up. But Wilhelm thought he remembered where the trip wires would be. We got down and crawled, feeling ahead. We crawled for nearly a kilometer. Then we saw the first fence. We'd reached *die Grenze*.

"There were two fences, each a bit taller than me, in those days made of strands of barbed wire about ten centimeters—four inches—apart. Between the fences was the mined strip, fifteen meters across. We couldn't see a watchtower, though we knew one was nearby. Well, this was it. In the next minute or so I tapped all the energy in my body, pulling two strands of wire apart, so that Wilhelm could get through. He did the same for me. The next bit was Russian roulette. Wilhelm had no idea where the mines were. He went first—he threw his attaché case as far forward as he could jump—he threw it hard on the ground ahead. Then he jumped onto it. No detonation. He put one foot on the ground just next to the case and lifted up the case and threw it again. I jumped behind him, trying to land on exactly the same spot where he had been. So we reached the outer fence, which was just like the first. We helped each other through. Our hands were bleeding.

"We went on toward the light. It was about two hundred meters away, where the road and the railway from Bebra cross the border. We reached the road. As we stood on the edge of it a car went by westward but didn't stop. We dashed along the road. There were two painted white lines across it and we rushed across them. That was the actual border.

"Then: 'Guten Abend!' Two BGS men stepped forward to greet us. They had binoculars, and said they'd been watching us since we reached the outer fence. We went to their control post, where they gave us some brandy. Our body temperatures were pretty low, believe me.

"Not long after that the pastor came from the village of Herleshausen with some dry clothes. The BGS drove us to Eschwege, and we were put up for the night in the jail. We didn't have any West German money. Next day we went to the reception center at Giessen. U.S. military intelligence and the Federal police interrogated us to make sure we weren't spies. How I made good in the Federal Republic is another story."

15. THE SERGEANT AND THE LIEUTENANT

Water was a dominant element the next day. While waiting for a dinner table at the Hotel zum Stern in Bad Hersfeld, I went to the cellar to use the men's room. I could hear rushing water; the cellar was several inches deep in water. I reported to the reception desk that the hotel was being flooded. They thanked me, but my table came no sooner. Bad Hersfeld is, as the *Bad* part of its name suggests, a spa. The town was pushing the attractions of its thermo-mineral baths to make up for its lack of industry and its position near the border; but I didn't try them. Outside the town I saw a nomadic shepherd, tending his flock as it grazed on the broad grassy verge of an autobahn access road, near the bridge over the Fulda River. I was driving to the Werra again, to the spot where on its more or less northward course it first enters from East Germany at the small West German town of Phillipsthal, population 6,000. Roughly 1,500 of Phillipsthal's men work in a potash processing plant and mine, whose machinery and great heaps of potash dominate the place.

"Without the mine, Phillipsthal would be dead," the town's Bürgermeister, Herr Schaefer, told me as we walked through the town, accompanied by an elderly gentleman, Herr Billing, who kindly acted as our translator. Herr Schaefer was a vigorous-looking man in his early forties;

Herr Billing was of slighter build, speaking a precise and cultured English—he had been in the import-export business in Hanover, he said, until coming to Phillipsthal in the mid-fifties to run the town's haberdashery store with his wife, whose family came from Vacha, the town just across the Werra in the DDR. *Kali* is the German word for potash; it made me think of one of those many-armed Indian goddesses. Herr Schaefer said, "We hope there is enough potash to last another thirty years."

What used to be the main road east from Phillipsthal comes to a halt just outside the town at a red sandstone bridge that crosses the Werra to Vacha. Herr Billing told me that Napoleon's army had marched across the Werra here in 1812 on the way to Austerlitz and Russia. The bridge was now protected by various East German devices: fencing, walls, watchtowers, weapons. "Half of Phillipsthal have relatives in Vacha," said Herr Schaefer. "Most people used to do their main shopping there, and many worked there. In the last few days before the border was sealed in 1952, a number of people from Vacha packed up and moved over here."

The Werra was a chocolate-brown color; it is one of the filthiest rivers in Europe. "The DDR dump their potash waste in it," said Herr Schaefer. "Over a thousand railroad wagons a day. The waste is basically salt, and the result is that the Werra is biologically dead. We have stopped doing that. Our potash waste is sunk in caves in the hills—not a perfect solution but better than theirs." On the other side of the river the fence was partly down, the result of recent flood waters which had washed the ground away, causing posts and wire to collapse and SM-70s to go off. In Vacha, a factory chimney sent up a tall plume of light brown smoke, and though the wind was blowing the other way, I imagined the smell of lignite and East Berlin traffic exhaust. The great potash heaps were a darkish gray. Herr Billing said that this meant it was going to rain; humidity changed the color of the heaps. They were white in fine, dry weather.

We visited the gatehouse to the former *Schloss*, which had once been a monastery, then a semifortified mansion, and was now about to be converted into a private school, with old peoples' apartments in one wing. The gatehouse contains a border information post run by the Zoll. Films are shown to parties of visitors; a graph indicates the declining number of people escaping from the DDR; and glass-fronted cabinets display devices used by both sides in the early border days to deliver propaganda: leaflet-carrying rockets, and footballs stuffed with Cold War literature that were kicked over *die Grenze*. Among the escape devices on show were some that looked like spurs but were meant for the toe rather than the heel of a boot, intended to pierce and obtain a grip on the fence as one climbed over it; also some boots fitted with thin metal angle-plates under toe and heel, to raise the wearer off the ground and lessen his chances of setting off a mine. Although these made smaller the area of ground one stepped on, they increased the depth of soil disturbed and the pressure one imposed on it. Herr Schaefer thought the wearer would have been better employed looking for and trying to follow the tracks of game. But he had, it seemed, made it; the boots were there.

We stopped in the small Hotel Rhönblick for a beer. The waitress who served us was English, from Liverpool; she had come to Phillipsthal because a friend of hers had married the proprietor of the hotel. She said, "I was a bit bothered about how close the border was when I first got here, but it doesn't bother me now."

Herr Schaefer said, "It is so peaceful here in Phillipsthal that it is easy to forget how close we are to people who are not free."

Herr Schaefer went back to the Rathaus and Herr Billing asked me to come back to meet his wife at his shop. It was crowded with customers buying sheets, socks and underwear, but Frau Billing left things in charge of her two young assistants and led me upstairs to the Billings' apartment for coffee and a chat. From the windows of their living room was a view of the potash works and the Rhön hills beyond. A print of Rembrandt's "Staalmeisters" hung over a well-stocked bookcase. Herr Billing said that he was currently rereading Somerset Maugham's short stories in English. "He is peculiar, I think, but wonderful," Herr Billing said. The previous night they had watched a television program on Egypt, narrated by Lawrence Durrell. "Wonderful," said Frau Billing—but she didn't add, "but peculiar." They traveled once a year to a small town in the French Pyrenees —a town that was "twinned" with Phillipsthal. Their only son was an officer on a merchant ship but now had a steady girl friend and was getting fed up with the sea. Where was I heading for next? Ah, Bavaria.

"Very rough, the Bavarians," said Herr Billing. "Very crude. But very likable. Things are also cheaper there." Frau Billing told me of an English couple who had appeared on a German TV show and said how much they liked Bavaria, with the result that they were deluged with invitations from Bavarian families to come and stay with them for free.

The rain, foretold by the gray potash heaps, arrived. Bavaria-bound, I drove back past Bad Hersfeld, windshield wipers wiping busily. The border begins to veer southeast here, preparatory to its eastward stint along the top of Bavaria, tucked in under the DDR. My destination was Bad Kissingen, another spa town. The dome-shaped hills got higher now and the valleys deeper, the earth was red and the trees more darkly evergreen.

This was the Rhön, a range of hills that is the remains of an extinct volcano. In this region the sport of gliding was born, but I saw only a U.S. military helicopter in the air. On the ground, too, the American sector of continued military interest was made evident in the form of many civilian cars with green USA license plates. On the radio I had temporarily deserted the Deutschlandfunk for AFN, the Armed Forces Network. I learned that the USO was holding an anniversary celebration in Heidelberg. A marathon was to be run in Frankfurt. Herman and the Hermits were followed by the Parker Sisters, or was it the Pointer Sisters? Outside the Bavarian villages were roadside calvaries.

Bad Kissingen reminded me of the English south-coast resort of Bournemouth. It was hard not to see it as a Hockney painting: immaculate parks; slightly faded grand hotels; and the *Kuranstalt*, a stately pleasure palace where the waters can be taken and string orchestras play to audiences composed mostly of elderly women, sitting among palms and rubber plants. King Maximilian of Bavaria came in 1815 and popularized the medicinal use of the town's mineral springs. King Ludwig I spent much time in Bad Kissingen from 1833 until, fifteen years later, he abdicated, infatuated with Lola Montez. In large secluded gardens off the quiet streets stand immense houses on whose gateposts are discreet plaques saying, for example, SANATORIUM DR. DIETZ or SANATORIUM DR. RAINER. Here the stresses of capitalist society, as felt by its survivors, are relaxed, massaged and washed away.

Bad Kissingen also houses an important U.S. Army base, and so among the gray-haired Germans strolling to and from the cure one sees bunches of off-duty Americans, black and white, chewing gum, plugged into transistor radios. The prewar German army's Manteuffel Kaserne is now called Daley Barracks and houses roughly a thousand members of the Second Squadron of the Eleventh Armored Cavalry Regiment and its supporting units. They form a small part of the 276,000 U.S. military personnel in Europe, most of whom are in West Germany. The Eleventh Armored Cavalry Regiment fought in Germany during the closing stages of the war, served with the occupation forces until 1948, was stationed in Germany from 1957 to 1964, and after periods in Vietnam and the United States, returned to Germany in 1972. In some ways the Americans seem to be in Germany—despite this history—as unassimilated visitors. There is a barber shop, a post exchange, a bowling center, nursery and grade school. And yet many of the men have ties with Germany. Lieutenant Colonel Louis Sturbois, the commanding officer of the squadron, served first in Germany in 1964. Major Keith Skidmore, one of his aides, told me that an uncle of his had served with the U.S. occupation forces in Germany in 1947. Sergeant Albert Tatrai told me that his wife was half-

German—her mother was German and had married an American soldier just after the war; the sergeant and his wife often spoke German at home.

The colonel and the major briefed me on the role of the Armored Cavalry in Germany. Their mission was to be prepared to go to war "in minutes, and to win"—I assumed in a conflict where Pershing and SS-20 missiles had remained in their launch areas—and to conduct surveillance of 140 kilometers of the IGB.

"The two parts of the mission are compatible," said the colonel. "While patrolling the border, we examine ground that we might have to occupy. Furthermore, the border is a motivator. The troops see why we're here. The border is evidence of a system which incarcerates its people behind bars. Our men feel the malignant power behind the fence."

I drove up to the border in a jeep with Sergeant Tatrai—long face, shaggy mustache, born in Pittsburgh, Hungarian descent, thinking of becoming a police officer in a small town in Oregon when he retires from the Army. The jeep was elderly, and when it reached its maximum 45 mph there was a teeth-grinding noise from the gearbox.

"It sounds a bit shaky, but it's really okay," shouted the sergeant. He had the heat on full, and great blasts of hot air hit my knees. It was a gray morning with heavy mist; the sergeant said that he thought it would burn off. Several civilian cars overtook us, their drivers casting us rather impatient looks.

"They're not discourteous usually," said the sergeant. "They're just in a hurry. Up along the border, though, people are real friendly. I got stuck in a ditch the other day and a farmer who came by on his tractor pulled me out. Cross country maneuvers generally take place in winter, and on one occasion last winter one of our tanks threw a final drive at three A.M. While we were working on it in the middle of the street of a border village, an elderly lady brought us out a pot of coffee. When it was empty we put it back on her steps. Half an hour later it was there full again. I enjoy duty here. It's better for training than anywhere else I know, including the U.S.A."

I asked if he saw Russian soldiers on the border.

"We occasionally see Soviet officers, but when they catch sight of us they tend to disappear. We're also on the lookout for them over here. Their military liaison missions are allowed in certain areas of West Germany. Now and then they drive into restricted areas and we spot them. Trouble is, they're generally in big civilian cars, and we haven't a prayer of catching them in a jeep."

We arrived at Camp Lee, a forward base in the woods near Wollbach, about ten kilometers from the *Grenze*—which Sergeant Tatrai pronounced to rhyme with "fence." Here one troop of the Second Squadron was always on duty. Under the trees sat their tanks, nine big dark-olive-green M-60 A3s, together with some armored personnel carriers, a pair of huge towing vehicles, and several jeeps. I walked around the camp with a young lieutenant named Ferguson who was in love with his job and with army jargon. "This vehicle must be able to move within a ten-minute time frame," he said as we halted momentarily beside a personnel carrier before going on to where a young mechanic, covered in black oil and grease, was tackling a tank engine that hung from a gantry. "We have to be fully equipped to pull a pack out of one of these," said the lieutenant, referring— I gathered—to the science of engine removal. He patted the flank of the M-60 A3, which was clearly unable to move within a ten-minute time frame. "I'd go to war in this baby and feel safe," he said.

I asked the lieutenant how much peacetime activity there was on the squadron's sector of the border.

"Well, it's been pretty lively recently. Quite a few IBCs—illegal border crossers. Last week a thirty-one-year-old man and a one-and-a-half-year-old child made it across near Ermeshausen in the southern part of our sector. They came over at four A.M. and were picked up by the Zoll on a country road. Two months ago a DDR sergeant and a private who were driving a truck parked next to the outer fence, climbed on top of the truck and jumped over. They told us they were disgusted with army conditions and especially the lousy food they got. But not everyone gets to stay—one individual who came over recently was sent back when it was discovered he was a bank robber. One of their soldiers got sent back, too, not long ago. He must have said something to military intelligence that made them suspicious, made them think he'd found it just a bit too easy to get across."

The Americans stay at Camp Lee for the thirty-day period. They maintain their vehicles, train in various combat procedures and go out on border patrols, "covering the trace," as Lieutenant Ferguson put it. The camp has an indoor gym and an open-air basketball court. I saw a game of horseshoes being played by two black and four white soldiers. A truckload of Coke and Fanta arrived while I was there. In the cafeteria, which was remarkably like a school dining room, I had an early lunch: Salisbury steak, kidney beans, salad, chocolate cake, and a glass of milk.

By noon, when we set off in three jeeps on what Sergeant Tatrai called a wheel patrol—apparently distinguishing it from a patrol of the trace conducted by an Air Cavalry helicopter—the morning mist was lifting. Villages appeared in the folds of hills, each with a different type of spire or tower on its church—some covered with charcoal-gray slates; some the shape of witches' hats. The houses were generally less fancy than those farther north. Usually two jeeps went out on patrol, but Sergeant Tatrai was making use of my visit, which required an extra vehicle, to monitor the performance of the patrol leader, a newly arrived lieutenant named Doherty, who was being "border qualified." Tatrai had to ensure that the patrol was done according to SOP—standard operating procedure.

"This is really going to seem significant to *them*," said the sergeant, with a flick of his head toward the East. "They don't usually see three jeeps on a patrol."

A case of Mountain Dew soda bounced around on the back floor. We drove through Bad Königshofen, Herbstadt and Breitensee, where we arrived at the border. Sergeant Tatrai showed me where we were on his military map—a spot marked "Primary Vantage Point 142." Across the East German fences, pasture land rolled into a distance delimited by fairly high hills, the Grosser Gleichberg, festooned with cloud. On the map, the border was indicated by a line of symbols—looking like a child's drawing of a bed: I———I. We had arrived at the border by a lane, but now turned northwestward and jounced across a plowed field; I could feel the discs in my spine compress. The second jeep was following right behind the lieutenant in the first.

"The second vehicle's covering the lead vehicle from too close behind," said Sergeant Tatrai, in his role as tutor/inspector.

We drove through the edge of a field of winter wheat.

"These farmers complain about us," said the sergeant, "and yet they plant right up to the border markers. They don't leave a track or even a path—they really make it difficult."

The lieutenant and his team came to a halt on a small grassy bluff overlooking the border. Sergeant Tatrai took a quick look at where the lieutenant had stopped and drove farther on around the bluff, where our jeep lay hull down.

"He's got a lot to learn. There's a much better view from here. Listen."

The radio was crackling. The lieutenant was making contact with Camp Lee and starting his border report. I watched an old-fashioned cream-colored bus running along a road in the DDR. It reminded me of a model car—a Schuco—my godfather sent me when he was American consul in Munich in 1939, resembling a toy version of the Chrysler Airflow sedan. Over the radio the lieutenant was talking about the trace. He reported the sighting of two "Bravo Tangos"—two DDR border troops—standing guard near a dog run, with two dogs, "German shepherd type." Also, one truck, a Robar, heading south on the patrol road.

Sergeant Tatrai chuckled. He gave me a meaningful look, which I answered with a nod. The lieutenant really ought to have got out of the front seat of his jeep.

Sergeant Tatrai pushed the call button of his radio and began to send a message to the lieutenant. He said that from this position four dogs could be seen, two German shepherds, two black Labradors.

A few minutes of silence followed. Then the lieutenant sent out across the air waves to Camp Lee an amendment about the number and breed of the dogs.

"The object of the exercise is to see that all the information is obtained and that it is accurately reported," said the sergeant.

We set off again. We heard the lieutenant tell the second jeep to drop back to a better covering distance. The lieutenant was sharpening up. But the sergeant proceeded to demonstrate who had the sharper eyes. We pulled up by several pieces of paper that had blown into a hedge. The sergeant retrieved them. They were U.S. Army vehicle-condition reports, and judging from their slightly damp and muddy state, had been dropped by a previous day's patrol. The sergeant shook his head. "You can learn a lot from that sort of report," he said. Later he gave them to the lieutenant to hand in at the camp and earn some kudos.

We pass through a thin strip of woods; under the trees are bluebells, cow parsley, old-man's-beard—and a light-brown VW van belonging to the Zoll. We exchange waves of the hand as we pass. A hundred meters on, another Zoll van, almost invisible in the trees.

"They must be up here for a reason," says the sergeant. "Maybe they've got word of someone trying to come over. They'll sit up here for hours waiting for an IBC."

We cross a stream. Here, the sergeant says, he sometimes comes in off-duty hours with his fishing rod. There are trout in the stream. We stop for a few minutes to allow some foresters to finish cutting down a tree next to the track. We pause to receive some abuse from an elderly German farmer, sitting on a tractor, who feels strongly about U.S. military vehicles ripping up his fields. Sergeant Tatrai hears him out, nods understandingly, and wishes him a nice day, in German. "Sometimes you want to ask them if they'd rather have a Russian tank division going through their crop," he says. "But you don't."

After maneuvers the American troops scrape mud off the roads left by tanks; they pay compensation for any damage done to crops. When small children wave at them in the border villages, they wave back, glad of the greetings. They are aware of the fact that although Americans have been here for a long time, the West Germans are beginning to wonder if the

American troops are really necessary—if their presence doesn't suggest too close a West German tie to United States foreign policy—and whether or not Americans really understand European interests. The Americans are now viewed with slightly less taken-for-granted expressions. Some calculating glances seem to say, "Do we really need you here?" (And one or two perhaps follow this up with worries about Europe's ability to arm itself—as perhaps the best deterrent—for a conventional, defensive war.)

The lieutenant has got far ahead. He has missed a feature that the sergeant says should be looked at, and when we reach it, Sergeant Tatrai radios the other jeeps our position and tells them how to reach us. We are near the village of Irmelshausen. A stream comes through the border here and the East Germans have just finished a new concrete structure carrying an extra high section of fence over the stream, with a sort of portcullis reaching the stream bed and blocking the way of anyone hoping to swim through. A BMW is parked on our side, and Sergeant Tatrai gets into conversation with the driver, who says he is an insurance inspector visiting the area and interested in the border. When the lieutenant's party turns up, the lieutenant takes photographs of the structure and reports back to Camp Lee on the radio, describing it in detail. The sergeant tells me that two DDR border guards escaped here while on duty clearing the stream-bed not long ago. Obviously the new structure is meant to put a stop to that sort of thing; a rough guess at the cost is DM 100,000. The lieutenant meanwhile has got into conversation with the insurance inspector. The lieutenant's German is remarkably fluent, and the conversation develops into a bit of an interrogation. The sergeant is impressed; he says, "I didn't know the lieutenant could speak German that good."

Leaving the lieutenant and his men to follow the trace, the sergeant and I take a shortcut to go scouting a little farther ahead. The sergeant has heard from a previous patrol that something may be happening near the DDR village of Mendhausen, and when we get there the sergeant has a quick look and picks up the radio to the lieutenant. He says, "Keep coming up the trace till you reach us and you'll see some real fine activity."

There are three West German civilian cars here; several of the passengers have binoculars. What they are watching is an East German mine-clearing detail.

The sergeant parks twenty meters from the border-marking posts where only a small clump of bushes is between us and the outer fence. Inside the fence are three military trucks, one with a Red Cross painted on the side, and eight men, all quite young. They wear white helmets and clear plastic shields over their faces. Most are probing the ground with long rods, but one, moving ahead of the rest, wields a metal mine detector.

The scene resembles a ballet. The soldiers step lightly, in a precise pattern dictated by where the ground has been tested. Tapes are unraveled, markers placed. "They'll blow the mines when they've found enough," says Sergeant Tatrai. "They may replace them with fresh ones, but I except they'll put SM-70s on the fence instead." Obviously a mine may blow if it's found accidentally, and this is what the spectators are unable to stop hoping for.

Beyond the inner fence, on a rise of ground, is another party of DDR troops, some standing, some lying on the grass, talking, smoking. It is unclear whether they are a guard detachment or waiting to replace the mine-clearing party. The lieutenant and his two jeeps arrive in a flurry of dust, brakes squealing. The lieutenant stands up in his jeep and puts his binoculars to his eyes, though everything is clear to ordinary sight. He says, "What vehicle is that in the middle? A Robar? A Whiskey Fifty?"

"No, sir," says a black enlisted man. "That's a Ural Two-seven-five."

Soon the lieutenant starts his report to Camp Lee. He describes the mine-clearing operation. He explains that a section of the inner fence is down so that a T-54 mine-blowing machine—a large bulldozer with a sort of anteater attachment on the front—can be brought into the strip between the fences. He gives the details firmly and clearly, really doing his job and sounding pleased—this is a better-than-usual border occurrence to be reporting.

I think it only right, when he pauses, to draw his attention to something I've just noticed in the clump of bushes beyond the border markers, perhaps ten paces away. It is almost a drawing or etching by Rembrandt, except that instead of two lovers in the bush, camouflaged and nearly hidden by branches and leaves, are two *Aufklärer* in their green uniforms. They are smiling broadly—to have been noticed only now, ten minutes after our arrival! But now that they have been seen, one proceeds to start taking photographs of us. If this had been a real encounter between cavalry and Indians, the Indians would have won. The lieutenant, however, in no way acknowledging any connection with General Custer, coolly works the *Aufklärer* into a continuation of his report to Camp Lee.

We travel on, leaving the young East Germans and their mines. Good luck, lads, I say silently. The countryside is somewhat like the Yorkshire wolds or northwestern Connecticut, low hills and extensive meadows of long grass, dandelions and clock thistles. The sergeant and I part company with the lieutenant's party and proceed directly toward the *Grenzübergang* at Eussenhausen. Here not a car is to be seen going to or coming from the DDR. We take a lane up a nearby hillside and into some woods where the U.S. Army has an observation post. Hundreds of birds, disturbed by the jeep, rise out of the trees. At a rustic corral type gate a young black soldier, basketball-player height, stands with his carbine at the ready. We pull up. Sergeant Tatrai gives the password, Honey Bear, to which the guard is meant to respond with a counterword. The guard looks blank.

Sergeant Tatrai repeats the password, and the guard consults the back of his left hand—he has written something on it in felt-tip.

"That's not the password, Sergeant," says the guard slowly, as if wondering what sort of trickery is being played on him. "Give the password."

"What do you think the password is, soldier?"

The guard is silent. Then he says, "Blue Moon."

"That's the password for *tonight*. I gave you the daytime password."

"Oh. Yes, Sergeant."

We are let in through the gate. Sergeant Tatrai gives a shrug, and I try to console him by telling him about a British television program I'd seen dealing with the Soviet army: its problems with vodka; problems with mechanical breakdowns; problems with weaponry—like inside their tank turrets, where the ejected shell cartridge apparently has a way of flying back and ricocheting around, in all likelihood decapitating some of the crew.

Inside the compound is a dugout, with grass on the roof and observation slits facing out across the *Grenze*. Two men are stationed within it; they share the space with a large device on a tripod, and one of them tells me it works with the help of a gyroscope and sensitivity to infrared light. Looking into its eyepiece, I see the bright-red roofs of the small East German town of Henneberg, eerily close—I can almost see how one tile overlaps another; the church clock gives the time of 4:45; two girls are walking along the main street with the air of going somewhere, perhaps to catch a bus. Adjusting the device, I see the road from Henneberg dip toward the *Übergang*, a solitary car on it now.

"This post is here because of that highway," says Sergeant Tatrai. "The road could be a high-speed avenue of approach for their forces. We practice evacuation of the O.P. once a week. At night, or on days when the visibility is bad, we often send out a radar team onto the hillside to keep lookout. The main problem is that it's generally very quiet up here. Some evenings you hear shots—hunters out for boar and deer. Not far from here we saw one of their helicopters one night, with a searchlight directed at the ground. We had heard an explosion. When we finally made out what they were up to, we saw they were cutting up a cow, which had somehow hit a mine. But mostly it's a matter of staying alert even if nothing happens."

When we got back to Daley Barracks in Bad Kissingen, I thanked

Sergeant Tatrai for the day with the border patrol. I got the impression he was going to give the lieutenant a good report for his border qualification.

But the sergeant was feeling critical about himself. "You know what I should have done?" he said. "I should have got the name of that man who said he was an insurance inspector."

16. THE FRONT LINE

My dreams that night were not sweet. I dreamt of war. I believe it was World War III and Soviet tanks were coming up through the woods around an observation post, and wild boar and deer were scattering ahead of them. I had trouble getting away. Perhaps the password was the wrong one, or I couldn't remember it at all. The neutron shells were going to go off overhead at any minute. The jeep I found wouldn't start. I woke up, and it was five o'clock, and I couldn't get to sleep again. After an hour I got up and took a walk through the deserted stately streets of Bad Kissingen, which at dawn looked more than ever like a surrealist stageset painted by de Chirico.

It was a Saturday. After breakfast I drove southeast toward the border, to pick up with it again just beyond the point where the patrol had started the day before. The road, empty of traffic, looped gently over the Hassberge hills; the sun shone; I felt a pleasure in driving that is rare these days. Ten kilometers west of Coburg the road ran for a way next to the border, and when it turned away from it I found a country lane that returned to it near the village of Autenhausen. I no longer felt curious about the border system; it was more of an obsession. Here the meadows full of succulent grass and tall buttercups fell away through a gap in the woods on our side; on theirs, beyond what appeared to be only a single fence, plowed strip and patrolway, there was a low, forested hillside. The West German border-marking posts were in the Bavarian colors, white and blue. The lane halted at the border, and an elderly black Mercedes was parked there, with a plump woman and a plump little girl nearby picking wild flowers. I offered them the use of my binoculars to look at a DDR scout car which rolled up just then.

"No, thanks," said the lady. "I see them every day."

Despite this, she sat in her car for several minutes watching the activity on the other side of the fence, as two men got out of the scout car, observed us through their binoculars, took some photographs and then lit cigarettes, apparently satisfied that we weren't going to launch a surprise attack on the workers' state. Behind them in the woods I could make out a handsome but deserted-looking farmhouse. On our side stood a small Zoll hut, unoccupied too, with a poster on the wall advertising the dangers of rabies.

The Saxe-Coburg family established itself in Coburg in the sixteenth century, and within three hundred years, through well-arranged marriages, was connected with many of the ruling houses of Europe, among them the English, Belgian, Portuguese and Bulgarian. The town, one of the largest on this part of the border, has two castles: Schloss Ehrenburg, where Prince Albert, consort to Queen Victoria, spent his childhood, built in the style of a Renaissance palace; and Feste Coburg, a fortress that sits on a hill overlooking the town, visible from afar, looking like a fairy-tale castle. Coburg itself is full of old buildings, scruffy when compared to, say, Goslar or Bad Kissingen, and quite appealing. Since it was a Saturday that was not the first Saturday in the month, shops were closed, but various vendors hawked their wares in the marketplace, and clouds of smoke and steam rose from bratwurst and currywurst stalls. The Schlossplatz, several hundred yards away, contains a statue of Prince Albert's elder brother, Duke Ernst II, and is flanked by the Landestheater, the Ehrenburg Castle and the porticoed terrace at the foot of the Hofgarten, through which I walked up to the Feste. The day was now warm and close, but despite a crack of thunder in the distance, no sign of an impending storm. Halfway up the Hofgarten —a meadowy park with large shade trees—I came on another statue of Ernst II, this time on horseback. Nearby was a 1914–1918 war memorial, with three stone figures carved in an Aryan—which is to say, Hitlerian— style, their arms holding aloft a single sword, and on the plinth the inscription VATERLAND. The word perhaps has no more meaning than "*Pour la patrie*" or "For King and Country," seen on similar French and British war memorials; but it did provoke the thought that the Germans considered that their involvement in World War I had been to defend the Fatherland. Perhaps for many it was. And the peaceful, productive and cooperative behavior of West Germans in the past thirty-five years certainly inclines one to listen more sympathetically to scholars who may be called revisionist, and who see the Germans as less innately "bad" and less to blame for imperialism, expansionism and totalitarianism than many —even German historians—have claimed them to be. The American historian David Calleo writes: "Even Germany's Nazi episode may be seen less as the consequence of some inherent flaw in German civilization, some autonomous national cancer developing according to its own inner rhythm, than of the intense pressure put upon Germany from the outside."

The battlements of the Feste are capped with a narrow red-tiled roof. Castle buildings rise from the walls, with tall roofs dotted with tiny turrets. It must have been reassuring to be able to command a truly defensible dwelling place, safe save for sickness or a long siege. No one's home is his castle anymore. Unfortunately, the visitor can't wander around freely inside. An entry fee entitles him to join a conducted tour, which means moving at the speed ordained by the guide and listening to his historical digest of Saxe-Coburg doings. I would have been happy to move swiftly on my own through the ducal collection of ivory-decorated crossbows, and linger with the Dürer engravings. But it was not to be. I managed to hang on for a while in a room which contained a Cranach portrait of Martin Luther, but the guide signaled me to follow the rest of the party to see armor and four-poster beds elsewhere. Luther had stayed at Feste Coburg for half a year. Cranach made him look like a mixture of Willy Brandt and Franz-Josef Strauss—a German face, tugged both ways. The DDR has plans to make a big thing of the 500th anniversary of Luther's birth in November 1983. Erich Honecker has announced that he is personally overseeing preparations for the event.

From the battlements of the castle I looked out over forested countryside to the east and saw the DDR. Several gliders were circling overhead. After I left the Feste I walked along the hilltop to a little airfield. I lay on the grass at the field's edge and watched the gliders being towed up one after another by a small plane. This sport has been banned from time to time in the DDR, after gliders have been used in escapes, but as far as I know, is permitted at the moment, presumably because it is felt that the sport can be controlled by strict monitoring of the membership of glider clubs. Hang-gliding in the DDR was outlawed in October 1980 and remains so. Before now I had never been close enough to gliders to notice what noise they make. I could hear the rush of air over their wings as they circled overhead, preparing to land, a vigorous, shushing sound, annoyingly interrupted by a motorcycle that racketed past along the hill-top road.

On weekends in these towns the young lads get out on their motorbikes or in their first cars, and snarl and squeal through the streets. But it was fairly quiet at the Golden Anchor, the hotel where I put up. I had trout—*Forelle*—for dinner, and several *Schopens* of dry white *Frankenwein*. I was sufficiently far south in Germany to be within the ambit of the *Süddeutsche Zeitung*, the excellent Munich newspaper, and in its weekend edition, among news stories, thoughtful pieces of analysis, and criticism, I came across a full page and a half of lonely-hearts advertisements. Many of the men sought women five to ten years younger than themselves; some of the women wanted to meet older men. Height seemed to be the most important criterion. Classical music, skiing and books were much noted interests—though one man more specifically declared that he was keen on hiking, Woody Allen, Kurt Valentin and *Erotik*. An American businessman from Lafayette, Indiana, touring Europe in a new Mercedes 380 SL said he was looking for fun and possibly a permanent relationship with a nonsmoking woman who had a model's figure and was a good conversationalist in English.

I began to feel a bit lonely too. There was a jolly party at a nearby table—three middle-aged men; five younger women. But they were not speaking German; it sounded to me like Czech. According to the local paper, a troupe of Czech actors would in the next few days be performing some of the works of the Czech playwright Pavel Kohout at the Landes-theater. Kohout himself, an exile living in Vienna, whose work is not allowed to be published in his homeland, was going to read a chapter from his latest novel, *Die Einfalle der heiligen Klara*. Kohout was reported in the *Coburger Tageblatt* as saying that he didn't feel like an emigrant. The important thing about emigration was this—to be able to decide freely whether to go. I sat there for a while wondering whether I should try to strike up a conversation with them, but my Czech is nonexistent; German was not what they were speaking and I felt I would need some fairly in-gratiating or sophisticated expression to make the jump and not seem to be rudely barging in. For that matter, I have moments in the course of a day when my curiosity and need to make contact with people are backed by the requisite nerve and energy, and periods when a greater concern is my own fragile self, its coherence and competence and—maybe—esteem, which may be shaken by the effort to meet strangers.

I called some friends in Munich and let them know I was making progress in their direction, and then retired to my room, high under the roof, to read. Outside, rain from the overdue thunderstorm teemed down and bounced high off the tiles.

I had begun to note various uses of the word *Grenze*, derivatives and compounds of it. It seemed to crop up frequently in spoken and written German, perhaps no more so than "border" or "frontier" in English, but striking me because of my interest ("keen on Thoreau, borders, beautiful women . . ."). On weather maps and in weather forecasts a *Grenze* occurs between a high-pressure area and a depression. *Ein Grenzfall* is a "borderline case." *Ein Grenzgänger* is someone who works or lives in the *Grenzland*, or who comes and goes across a border, or even, perhaps, as I was doing, travels along a border. *Grenzsituation* is a philosophical term, a concept of Karl Jaspers': "*Situationen, die an den Grenzen unseres Daseins gefühlt, erfahren, gedacht werden.*" On the borders of our existence . . .

In the telephone directory of the area of the Bavarian town of Hof there were a surprising number of people whose surname was Grenz.

"*Grüss Gott!*"—Greet God!—is what they say, instead of "Good day," in this southern part of Germany. The calvaries on country roads and approaches to villages suggest a more demonstrative religious temperament in Bavaria and also in Austria. In Coburg the Lord's Day came gray and wet. Possibly I should have gone to mass in answer to the church bells and my Catholic upbringing, but I drove instead to the border near Neustadt. What little traffic there was on the border road was moving fast, heading for Sunday lunch with inlaws, and apparently not concerned about the fence or the Bravo Tangos in their damp watchtower, its gray concrete darkened by rain. I parked for a moment by the roadside and looked through a slightly rolled-down window at the forms of two or three East German soldiers up there; they didn't bother to open a window to look at me. Good weather, I thought, for attempting a crossing, if one was so compelled.

The rain continued. I decided it was no day for going far. In the village of Furth-am-Berg I stopped in a pub near the crossroads where the talk was partly about *Arbeit* and *Häuser*, but mostly about *Geld*—so many hundreds or thousands of marks, so much percent. I was asked if I was a Hollander and replied, "*Nein, ich bin Engländer.*" For a place to stay I followed the directions of a gnome-faced man who was wearing a small pointed hat, leather breeches and rubber boots, and drove out of the village center with its church, parish hall, calvary and mill across a small stream, the Steinach, and down a road that had once crossed the border. It was unusual for this sort of road in that it was lined with modern houses and a new agricultural machinery depot. Near the end was a recently built Gasthaus—indeed, the Grenzgasthof Fürth-am-Berg—with a twin establishment under construction across the road.

Here, at twelve thirty, people were rolling up in cars and a pair of buses. It seemed that having tracked down a border village to stay in, I'd found one that many others were going to spend part of the day in, too. From the balcony of my room I could see the border a hundred meters away. Prosperous farmland on both sides, and on both sides, farther back, low wooded hills, with mist rising like smoke from them. And the first revelation I had in Fürth-am-Berg was that on a Sunday in this part of the world, life went on absolutely normally right up to the fence. In the jammed restaurant of the Gasthof I lunched off *Rinderroulade* (braised beef roll), beer, and vanilla ice cream with hot cherries. Afterward, with the rain clearing, I took a Sunday-afternoon stroll. On the Gasthof steps a wedding party stood to be photographed, the bride crying as her mother kissed her goodbye. I first surveyed the neighborhood of the Gasthof, where a single railway line, which had once gone through to the town of Sonneberg, now in the DDR, came to a halt. Two newish houses had been built where the lane reached the border. The garden of one had a border-marking pole next to a post that held up a line of wet laundry. The back wall of the other house had no windows facing on the DDR; a row of thick pines had been planted in the narrow strip between house and border. I wondered if the houses had been built here because the land was cheap or because the owners felt that they were protected, in property-owning terms, from a development on one side at least.

From here I walked along a narrow road that ran parallel to the fence for a kilometer or so but finally converged with it; once it had gone through to the village of Mupperg, whose church tower rose out of a belt of trees, tempting one still in that direction. The thought occurred to me: to walk up the lane to the border was to walk as far as you could go. There was no choice; the decision was imposed on you. There, at the striped barrier and Bavarian state sign saying LANDESGRENZE, having looked around and brooded on the situation, you had to turn around and go back the way you had come. So I saw a couple returning whom I'd seen setting off from the Gasthof some twenty minutes before me.

In the evening the road to Mupperg becomes a useful cul-de-sac for lovers; young bloods speed their cars down to the barrier and there park, to hold hands or whatever, while the low beams of the sun hit the Mupperg church tower. From it at six o'clock a somewhat out-of-tune bell could be heard throughout Fürth-am-Berg. In the Grenzgasthof the proprietor told me that the border had been good for his business. People from Coburg and Neustadt found Fürth-am-Berg peaceful, remote and yet near enough for a day's excursion. He was less interested in the *Grenze* than in what was going on in London and at the EEC Commission in Brussels. What about Mrs. Thatcher? What about the Common Agricultural Policy?

Mist hid the border the next morning. Monday morning sounds included blackbirds singing and a cement mixer at the new Gasthof across the way. School buses picked up children waiting at the border markers. I drove east for a few kilometers and then followed the border north along a minor road called the Frankenwald Hochstrasse. The road was high in its fashion; the hills, not lofty, were steep and forested. I stopped in one hamlet, which had a Scottish or Vermont feeling, and watched an old man digging a garden plot that abutted the border. The DDR watchtowers were generally of the old type. A Zoll hut had for its sole piece of furniture the back seat from a car. In one lonely area, without watchtowers, it took me several minutes with the binoculars to find a bunker under distant trees, buried almost up to its eye slits in the East German ground.

And so to Hof: a town where one still sees chimney sweeps in their top hats and the *Wörschtlamann*, vendor of local sausages, standing on a street corner with a miniature copper oven; and also a number of South European *Gastarbeiter* hanging around on street corners—slow times in the textile industry. Hof used to be near the center line of Germany; it's now on the edge of the Federal Republic, in the Bavarian boondocks. Apart from the textile industry, breweries are Hof's thing—there were ten and are now six. Ninety percent of Hof's pre-border trade with the area around the town of Plauen, now in the DDR, has been lost. The railway has gone from two tracks to one; young people go elsewhere for higher education; the town's population is declining by a thousand a year. For all that, in one newspaper shop the *International Herald Tribune*, the *Times* of London and *Figaro* (from Paris) were on sale. On the edge of town, some of the other interests of the Western world are represented in what looks like a giant piece of sculpture by Noguchi: one of the three largest U.S. radar stations in Europe.

One of Hof's contemporary problems is that, like a place in the American West that didn't have a railroad stop, it is by-passed by the autobahn that comes from Nuremberg to cross the border at Rudolphstein/Hirschberg on the way to Berlin, about four hours away. Rudolphstein is a village of

280 people that was doing its best to come to terms with its position. A small complex of services had sprung up as at a superhighway intersection to take care of people as they crossed the border. A family named Vogel was in the forefront of this, owning a Rasthof Berlin (with a provision store, bar and lodgings); the Gasthof Vogel, with rooms and restaurant; and the Hotel Vogel. I booked into the latter, which sat on the slopes of a hillside within view and earshot of the autobahn. Because the traffic to and from the East is channeled through few places, there seemed to be a never-ending stream of it. The big trucks made a collective roar as they passed into the *Übergang*. From the terrace outside my room, at the back of the hotel, there was a long and beautiful prospect southwestward up a valley, with pasture land in the bottom, woods on either side and in the distance. The license plates of most of the cars of people staying at the Hotel Vogel began with B, for "Berlin."

I walked up to the *Übergang* in the afternoon. The warrant officer in charge at the temporary-looking checkpoint buildings told me that the DDR checkpoint, across the bridge that spans the river Saale, had a more permanent appearance, and twenty-four separate ramps where trucks were inspected. Four remote-controlled East German TV cameras monitored approaches to the bridge (which had been built by the East Germans with West German funds). If I wanted any men's magazines, the places to look were the litter baskets at the filling station and restaurant just before the West German checkpoint, where East German drivers dumped copies of *Playboy*, *Penthouse* and local equivalents, which would be confiscated at the East German checkpoint. I talked to a West German driver of a truck carrying compressed air who was doing some repair work on a radiator pipe before heading into the DDR. He said that if you broke down over there, autobahn officials were helpful but everything cost a lot. An East German truck driver walking past from passport inspection gave us a cheerful "*Grüss Gott.*" A year ago a Russian truck driver had come across with a false driver's license and stayed. In 1977 a DDR truck trying to break through at the *Übergang* hit an emergency roadblock and both men in it were struck by bullets and dragged away. Each of these crossing places has its own litany of victims. Here at Rudolphstein people particularly remember an Italian truck driver, Benito Corghi. In August 1976 Corghi drove through from the East German checkpoint with a load of pork and had just crossed the bridge into West Germany when he pulled up. He had forgotten some of his papers at the checkpoint. Rather than turn around and drive back and get involved in the difficulties of having to pass in to pass out again, he started to walk back. He was shot as he crossed the bridge. He was the first non-German Western person to die on the border; he was a member of the Italian Communist Party; and he had a wife and two children.

"They may have yelled at him to stop," said the warrant officer, "but he was Italian, and perhaps didn't understand." At the time, the Italian embassy in East Berlin lodged an energetic protest and an East German deputy foreign minister expressed regret.

In the car I drove a little way east to Untertiefengrün, a village on the steep hillside sloping down to the Saale. On the other side of the river is Hirschberg, a town where many work in a large leather factory that makes boots for the East German army. That's what an elderly man said who joined me as I stood at a railing where a low bridge had once spanned the Saale. We talked over the noise of the river's gray-brown waters falling over a weir, and, farther away, the noise of the factory from behind a Berlin type wall that ran along the far riverbank.

"I come from Berlin," said the elderly man. "No one understands a wall like Berliners. I have a summer house here, and I come here as often as I can."

On the other side of the river, a street ran to one side of the factory, and a few people were leaning from the upper windows of tired apartment buildings, receiving the afternoon sun and watching the river over the wall. What looked at first like streetlights were powerful floodlights, to illuminate the wall at night.

The old Berliner looked at the scene and said, "If we had a key, we'd unlock the doors."

I walked along the river for a way, feeling that I was being watched by the people in the buildings opposite, who had no riverside walk. The Saale's bitter-chocolate waters eddied around unseen snags. A sign warned people who launched their boats in the river not to stray from the central channel unless absolutely necessary. Back in Untertiefengrün by the former bridge I looked at the old mill, on a wall of which was the declaration:

> *Sechshundertfünfzig Jahre stand*
> *die Mühle hier in kühlem Grund.*
> *Gott half in Sonnenschein und Not,*
> *Er gab auch weiter Korn und Brot.*
> (Six hundred and fifty years this mill's been found
> Standing here on chilly ground.
> God helped in sunshine and in need,
> He gave continually in grain and bread.)

From a spot on the hillside, where a footpath went to the villages of Lamitz and Joditz, I looked out on Hirschberg. Stone-colored and faded yellow stucco houses with gray slate roofs were packed in between the factory and a *Schloss* on a hill on the far side of town. At 3:25 P.M. a siren sounded in the factory as if for the end of a shift. On what I assumed to be the Rathaus a red banner was draped across the façade, proclaiming unshakable proletarian brotherhood and the victories of socialist achievement.

Farther up the hill, in the larger village of Tiefengrün, I called on Herr Sacher, the Bürgermeister, who the old gentleman from Berlin said was the best person to talk to in these parts. Outside, the modern house had a touch of Alpine chalet about it. Inside, it was stuffed with hunting trophies. Herr Sacher, a prosperous-looking man in his late fifties, led me into a living room with antlers everywhere. Shotguns were in a glass-fronted cupboard. He said that although the border had preserved a long strip through Germany from extensive development, it had also had a disturbing effect: it had put a stop to much natural movement of wildlife and the natural exchange that had gone on before the fence system, the strip, mines and SM-70s, and armed patrols. Frau Sacher brought in coffee and a strawberry *Torte*.

"Before the war, men in this place were farmers, quarry workers or employed in the leather factory in Hirschberg," Herr Sacher said, "Now the quarry is closed and there's no way to Hirschberg—which is also where we went to catch the train, to shop or go to the movies. Boys and girls from both sides of the Saale met there. Workers from there would come here to drink the cheaper Bavarian beer. It isn't just Germans being divided from Germans, it's Bavarians from Thuringians. It's like being in a cell here—people don't visit us much. We have to drive a long way to go to museums and see films. Of course, there are also advantages in being in a backwater. There's no urban terrorism, no crime to speak of. Maybe someone's rabbits are stolen. Some dirty words are written on a wall. But not much stress."

I asked if he thought much about the border.

"One thing I think about is that *they* think about us; they keep an eye on us. I'm sure that everyone living in the border area of West Germany is listed in DDR records. When my wife went to visit her sister in Berlin two years ago she was detained at the border for two hours while they verified that she lived in Tiefengrün, as she had stated on her form. First of all, the official said she was lying. Then they said finally that it was all right—she could enter—they'd found she did live in Tiefengrün."

Herr Sacher told me that he was an officer in the army reserve, and I asked if this felt like the front line.

"A lot of people around here complain about the U.S. Armored Cavalry," he said. "Some of their tanks broke a water main here recently. Well, I like them here. I think they should drive right up to the ruined bridge at Hirschberg now and then and look as if they mean business. It would be their job to try to stop a Soviet invasion—though I think they would do so only after the Soviets had got some way in. I expect to wake up one morning and hear on the radio about traffic jams in Bayreuth—it will be from people fleeing from the border, fifty kilometers away, ahead of the Russians. I think they'll go right through here, hardly stopping. We'll probably be safer than in Hof, where there will be real fighting. Of course, then there's the matter of what happens on their way back."

He didn't think the bomb had made a conventional war unlikely. He seemed to expect one to take place in the not too distant future, and for the Russians to lose it. The only army allied to them they could count on, he said, was that of the DDR.

As I left I saw a medal hanging in a small case on one wall, under a pair of tremendous antlers: the Iron Cross. I didn't ask Herr Sacher how he had won it. The sides had been picked differently now, and the medal was almost reassuring.

I had dinner at the Gasthof Vogel, half mile down the lane from the Hotel Vogel. On the wall of the Gasthof dining room was a painting of the valley, showing a previous bridge across the Saale. The painting was a gift, one of the staff told me, of a farmer who had owned land just the other side of the border. In the early days of the division, before 1952 and the fence, the farmer had a horse that used to carry refugees from the Soviet zone across the Saale into the American zone and then return by itself, walking back to its own stall. The farmer was eventually arrested and sent for a spell in Siberia. Now, retired, he lives near Hof.

In the Vogel restaurant one could tell when Berliners arrived. They were pushy and noisy, like New Yorkers. They talked more loudly than the other people there, who were conversing in tones that seemed right for keeping what was being said a private matter. The Berliners charged around the dining room, looking for menus and calling for the waitress. Perhaps they were still in a way driving. In a few minutes, with food and drink before them, they had somewhat quieted down.

After dinner I walked out of the village, along a farm track, toward the setting sun. I had a sudden feeling of strange independence and self-realization. Fields and meadows led away to pine woods on the higher hillsides. The edge of Germany—was it a way of assuming the worries of the world while forgetting one's personal concerns of family and fortune—like a knight errant, riding south, testing oneself in chance encounters . . . My romantic train of thought broke off sharply at this point. Where precisely was I? There, straight ahead at the bottom of a dip, following a small stream, was the border fence. For a brief weird moment I thought: I am on the wrong side of it. How did I get here? How did it get behind me? It was like an act of evil enchantment. I pulled out my map of the Rudolphstein area, which I had failed to consult closely as yet. The problem was soon clear. Rudolphstein is in a small finger of land poking north-westward into East Germany. The view down the beautiful valley that I had admired earlier was a view into the other Germany.

I stood for a while, getting properly oriented. In the valley bottom the stream could be heard. The hills and fields were deep-shadowed green. The sky was a ferocious pink. And overhead, as if it were midday, a lark cartwheeled and sang.

The earth seemed round and feminine, ready to enfold man. The plowed field to one side of the track was brown and furrowed. In the east, almost directly opposite where the sun had just sunk, rose the pale pink moon.

17. A BUSY DAY

The following morning I still had a feeling of being unsure about which side I was on, or where exactly I was. I knew for certain that I was now near the end of what I thought of as stage one of my journey, the last part of the intra-German border, and many things that should finally have become clear had instead become more confusing. I sat during breakfast trying to list some aspects of the border in order to get rid of this puzzlement. In one way, the border was something that made everything artificially clear: it divided everything into one side or another, between us and them, right and wrong, with no middle ground. *Die Grenze* was an emblem of institutionalized conflict—the visible manifestation of the entire apparatus of political, industrial, scientific and military machinery on both sides, confronting one another. In another way, the division was like that of substances in a chemistry experiment—substances that should not mix, that create a barrier between one another so as to avoid combustion or explosion—or was that to look at it from a peace-and-quiet-at-all-costs point of view? Many people still regarded the Iron Curtain as an edge, the edge of our own world, off which one might fall forever, as off the edge of the flat earth. But perhaps this fear was as falsely based as that of mariners and geographers before Columbus. Despite the emblems, the chemical analogy, the actual, tangible barrier of fences, walls and weaponry, the world was not as distinctly divided as we allowed ourselves to believe.

Abgrenzung is another *Grenz* word; it means ideological demarcation, at least in the DDR. In West Germany it has an everyday meaning of marking off, fencing off something from something else. One aspect of the marking off of West Germany from East Germany is language: some people suggest that German, spoken and written, is no longer quite the same, East and West. There are some simple differences: orange juice in West Germany is *Orangensaft*; in East Germany *Orangenjus*. Young people in West Germany tend to use a word like *super* when they mean "great"; in East Germany a more likely term would be *fetzig*. One effect of two different governments trying to fulfill two different ideologies is that many seemingly identical political terms have different meanings in each German state—"democracy" is a good example. Seen from the West, many words seem to be used by the DDR government to put its all-pervasive power in a good light: "free" and "people" are frequently so used. East Germany calls itself a *Volksrepublik* (people's republic), West Germany calls itself a *Bundesrepublik* (federal republic). A state-owned organization in the DDR is *volkseigen* ("owned by the people"), and the state youth organization is the *Freie Deutsche Jugend*.

The code or jargon of Marxism-Leninism is now and then attacked in West Germany as linguistically degenerate, "the language of the Fourth Reich," and as demonstrative of the gradual Sovietization of East Germany. The influence of Russian words with similar pronunciation has warped some German words into meanings that are not the same in the DDR as in the Federal Republic; some Russian words have been directly incorporated into DDR official vocabulary—for example, *Kader, Kombinat, Kollektiv, Traktorist, Kursant*. While West Germany inevitably has borrowed a number of English and American words, East Germany has adopted others—particularly American words—that seem to have come to it the long but orthodox way around, via Russia, like *Broiler* for roast chicken (the West Germans still say *Hähnchen*); other examples of this are *Pioneer, Dispatcher, Combine* and *Meeting*—a word that is generally used to describe a daily assembly of the party. *Akademiker* in West Germany means someone who is involved in academic study; in East Germany it means a member of the Academy of Sciences. Emotion—and propaganda—naturally enter different epithets applied to well-known features of the intra-German landscape: the Berlin Wall is occasionally referred to in the West as *die Schandemauer* (the shameful wall), and in the East, officially, as *der antifaschistische Schutzwall*. If you used the word *Arbeitslosen* in the DDR, people would know you were from the West—there

are no unemployed in East Germany, or at least there is no word to
describe a condition which, the party line has it, is only to be found in
capitalist countries.

Christa Wolf writes in an essay, "Plain German" (1966), touching on
what she calls "nonrecognition": "This is something that spreads and becomes a way of thinking, forcing people to venture into curious linguistic
constructions; if their words were bridges, no one would care to cross them.
The mass of facts not spoken about increases; the number of taboos increases; a language of the initiated has to be invented. Augurs' language,
accomplices' language. And, for the general public, a language that says
as little as possible in as many blurred phrases as possible, so that one can't
be pinned down."

She speaks to both East and West.

Of course there have been different dialects of German spoken long
before the present East/West division—a horizontal division can be
drawn perhaps more definitely between Low and High German, between
the German spoken in Schleswig-Holstein and in Bavaria, and between
that spoken generally in West Germany and in the German-speaking part
of Switzerland.

And it might be said that the German language—for all the contemporary
differences of usage and nuance—is the greatest bond holding the two German states together.

Bavaria is the one *Land* of the Federal Republic that has its own police
patrolling its borders with East Germany, Czechoslovakia and Austria.
In consequence, you see fewer members of the Bundesgrenzschutz, though
the Zoll is still present in strength. Bavaria has a somewhat Texan pride in
its semiautonomy; its border-marker posts are not red-and-white as they are
elsewhere, but blue-and-white; other signs indicate that this is not just
the border of the Federal Republic but the border of the state of Bavaria.
The Bavarian Frontier Police, for that matter, have a slightly more home-
spun quality than the BGS. Their headquarters in Hof, running the section
that looks after eighty kilometers of the East German and Czechoslovak
borders, looks very much like a private house on a quiet side street; they
drive VW Beetles still, finding them more suitable for their more rugged
border terrain; and members of the force are all Bavarians and usually local
men.

I spent the day with two officers of the Bavarian Frontier Police, Hans
Jacob and Alfred Eiber, both in their middle years, and with Tim Mueller,
a young U.S. military intelligence officer. Jacob and Eiber were based in

Hof. Jacob told me that his family had lived until the end of World War II just inside Czechoslovakia, where they ran a Gasthof not far from the place where the borders of the three states now meet. Mueller, six-foot-two and a native of Rochester, New York, was stationed for several years in Hof, which, coincidentally, was the town his paternal grandfather had come from. We set off driving along the Saale a little way west of Rudolphstein, where the river twists through a green gorge, and two large paper plants stand on the East German bank; this was near Blankenburg and Blankenstein. We stopped to watch a party of East Germans rebuilding a length of fence. Eight men, with guns and dogs, were guarding the four men who were working. A red tape had been stretched on the ground as a warning line a meter or so outside the fence, not to be stepped beyond. One could have jumped over it in a second and dived into the Saale.

Mueller was having similar thoughts; he said, "I feel sorry for those guys. They must be tempted to make a dash for it. They'd probably make it—but what would happen to their families?"

Hans Jacob said that there had been several escapes, successful and attempted, near here. In 1974 a man drove a truck down the hillside, through the fence, and into the Saale, and climbing out, swam to the Bavarian shore. In 1978 an East German glider landed just on the East German side of the river—it was assumed the pilot was trying to get across. Jacob said that he made model gliders as a hobby, and that one problem with trying to escape in a full-size one was that you had to go up to a great height to achieve real distance, and there was no way of doing that without attracting attention. Over this stretch of the river the home-made balloon had floated in which two East German families, the Strelzyks and the Wetzels, escaped in September 1979, landing near Naila, eight kilometers south of the border.

Near the downstream paper factory many trees were dead, presumably because of pollution. Eiber said that of the thousand workers in the plant, roughly three hundred were Polish. The DDR had a labor shortage and needed its own *Gastarbeiter*. But despite the pollution, there were ducks on the river. I watched the binoculars of an East German guard in a watchtower swivel as his gaze followed three men who rode by on our side on big Honda motorcycles.

We drove east again to the village of Mödlareuth, which is the Zicherie of Bavaria. Since 1524 the village had spanned the Thuringian-Bavarian border; in 1945 the interzonal border was drawn through it, and in 1952 was made impassable. Most of the village now is in the DDR. Three houses were demolished for the concrete wall, 700 meters long, that the

East German authorities erected to divide Mödlareuth. The village school is now in the DDR. In Bavaria are half a dozen houses, a farm and a duck pond. Cows were wandering across the border, past the markers, and drinking from a brook, the Tannen, which here ran alongside the wall. Behind the wall was a fence, with an alarm wire running along its top, and red bulbs on a post that lit up if anyone triggered the wire; a blackbird had made its nest on top of the post, and was perched on the edge of it. Where the wall ended, on the edge of the village, and the normal fence began, SM-70s were in place.

In the farmyard we found two old ladies sorting potatoes just inside the doorway of a barn. One wore slippers, the other rubber boots. They both had white headscarves and pale, blotchy skin. The lady in slippers, the farmer's wife, said that this farm had lost forty hectares "over there" and had not received any compensation. In fact, the DDR authorities had recently cut down some trees on the confiscated land and sent a bill for timber clearance to her husband. Both the ladies had relatives in the other part of Mödlareuth, and despite the lack of direct contact, seemed to know a lot about what was going on in the DDR part of the village. A frequent complaint of people over there was that they couldn't pass on their houses to members of their families when they retired or died; their houses were then often pulled down. The DDR Mödlareuth had a good bus service, but strict controls over everyone going in and out of it. One male resident had had special problems a few years before, when he became engaged to a woman who lived in a town ten kilometers away. She wasn't allowed to move to Mödlareuth. She could visit him during the day but had to leave every night. This restriction lasted, said the old lady, even after they were married and had a child.

Tim Mueller asked, smartly, "How did they get the child, then?"

"Ah," she said, "*die Mittagspause*"—the midday break.

Now the man has been allowed to move to join his wife and child in the town.

On this side a bread man still delivers, but the few children are bused away to school. As we climbed back into our car Mueller said, "What I still don't understand, even after being here a year and seeing the border frequently, is why people accept it the way they do. I mean, if this wall went through a small town in the U.S.A., the kids would heave rocks over it. They'd try to demolish it, set fire to it, blow it up. At the very least they'd play practical jokes on the East German border guards. It's this unhesitating acceptance that bothers me."

Jacob said, "It may be the real deadliness of it has got through to them, even the youngsters—they know those men can kill. That, and also the fact that we have conditioned ourselves to accept it, just as the people over there have. Maybe it is the German attitude toward authority, following the rules that are laid down for us."

East of Hof, just beyond the small town of Regnitzlosau, the two Germanys and Czechoslovakia meet. There is no particular physical reason for a border to be there. Rolling farmland continues from Bavaria into Czech territory, although at the apex of a fifteen-kilometer-long finger of land that Czechoslovakia pushes between West Germany and East Germany there is a little hill and a small grove of trees, and within the grove three stone markers, one from each of the three states, that stand about six strides apart, like three people who don't know each other very well. This finger of land is an area where many Germans once lived, as they did in much of the northern area of Czechoslovakia known as the Sudetenland, and the names of most of the towns and villages in it sound no different from those in Bavaria and Thuringia.

Here, on the last stretch of intra-German border, I talked to several farmers. One, whose rather run-down establishment near the hamlet of Mittelhammer faced directly on the fence, with small unkempt fields divided by the wire from a large field of maize in the DDR, told me that his wife's family had lost two thirds of their land in the DDR; they had been compensated for the loss of their crops but not for the land itself—which the West German government considered as still belonging to the family. The farmer, a beer-bellied middle-aged man, said, "They've changed everything over there—bigger fields, big machines, men working as if they were in a factory." He knew about factories, it seemed, since he worked a shift in a plastics factory; his farm was part-time. I asked him if he expected the situation to change.

"A war will change it fast enough," he said.

A white Mercedes sat in the yard, and chickens walked around it. Some of the houses of Mittelhammer have collapsed or been demolished, after standing empty a long time; most of those that remain belong to Berliners.

Near the next village, Hinderprex, was the point where the three countries meet, the Dreiländereck. From here the DDR fence headed away east along the northern border of Czechoslovakia—Jacob said it continued for another five kilometers, to discourage East Germans who might try slipping across the narrow neck of Czech land into West Germany. (Even so, some East Germans manage to escape via Czechoslovakia. "Czech trains have deep seats," I was told.) As we walked in the little grove of trees by the three markers, which also represented the borders of the old provinces of Saxony, Bohemia and Bavaria, Jacob pointed out two oaks that had been planted by one of the Hapsburgs. In 1813 Napoleon's army came back this way from Russia. Two French soldiers had died here and were buried up in the woods; local people had always tended their graves, despite world wars. Another grave is visible, with pansies growing on it, marked by a cross of silver birch topped by a World War II German army helmet: the grave of an unknown German soldier, one of many killed in these parts in the spring of 1945 as they tried to escape through the Soviet lines.

Hans Jacob grew up half a mile away in the hamlet of Kaiserhammer. The Gasthof his family ran had stood there until 1946 when it and all the houses in the hamlet were dynamited by the Czechs. His parents had been expelled, together with most Sudeten Germans, with some violence the year before, as the Czechs took out the pent-up hostility of the war years on their ethnic German citizens. Hans Jacob, while describing how his father was beaten up as he tried to protect his homestead, didn't seem to feel the Czechs were to be blamed; perhaps he didn't need to be reminded of German massacres in Czech villages like Lidice. In any event, German-Czech relations along the border were soon friendly again, he said. He had a friend who remembered riding a bike out of Hinderprex and up the lane into Kaiserhammer in 1948, and drinking beer there, a month or so before the Communist takeover of the Czech government. And in 1949, when Jacob had returned from being a prisoner of war in Russia, he had played in a soccer match between two teams of Czech border guards, one team being a man short. After that there was a long frosty spell until the time of Dubcek. Then, in 1968, Bavarian and Czech border guards drank beer, and collected firewood together while patrolling. After the Soviet-directed Warsaw Pact invasion of Czechoslovakia in August 1968 the Czech border guards, who had been regular soldiers, were replaced by a force directed by the Ministry of Internal Security, and the beer drinking stopped. Even so, relations with them remained more amicable than with the DDR border troops. Jacob said that not long ago near the Dreiländereck he had greeted and shaken hands with some Czech guards while DDR troops looked on, in some surprise.

Near Kirchbrunnlein, the next settlement, we stopped at another small farm. An old mill, an old farmhouse, a stream, small fields, the border, a low forested hillside that was Czechoslovakia, a view of the rather tatty single Czech fence with two rows of rusty barbed wire on top, vehicle blocks that didn't look as if they would stop a modern tank, and a watchtower that looked like something used for spotting forest fires, with a platform open to the elements, protected only by a camouflage net on top. It seemed unmanned, and the elderly farmer, whose name was Höllerung, said the Czech guards were probably all in their hut at ground level. Herr Höllerung was working in his garden with his wife and her father, who was ninety-three. Herr Höllerung was wearing shorts and black galoshes; his wife wore a print dress. He told me that he had grown up over there; he had served in the Czech army. It was his wife's family who had owned the mill here, first founded in the fourteenth century. Her father, the former miller, was splitting logs, moving very slowly, as a man his age had every right to; his face was like bark, his bones thin—a frail old tree himself, he paid not a jot of attention to the visitors who had descended on the place. Herr Höllerung said a small amount of compensation had been paid to them in 1952 for the land they had lost to the Czechs; his nephew now farmed the land they continued to own here on Bavarian soil—he grew mostly potatoes. They had no contact at all with the Czech land workers, who were brought out when needed from a central agricultural depot to plow the big field that could be seen through the trees up the hillside. But he sometimes talked Czech with the Czech border guards. Last winter he had shot a deer which fell just inside the Czech border— and two Czech guards carried it over to him.

I asked him if he expected the barbed wire to remain forever.

He said, "It will stay as long as the Soviets make this their border with the West. The next war will determine that."

Another Bavarian talking about the next war.

Mueller, Eiber, Jacob and I had lunch in Regnitzlosau in the Gasthof Grüner Baum, whose proprietor was the village butcher. The special of the day was goulash and it was good. We talked a little about the last war. Jacob said that he had been called up in 1943 at the age of seventeen. He had trained in the Luftwaffe to fly Focke-Wulf 190s, but by the time he got his wings there were few planes to fly and a shortage of fuel to power them. He was transferred to gliders, but with the German armies everywhere on the retreat, what was needed most were men on the ground. He was sent off to join a unit of paratroops fighting the Russians near Brno in Czechoslovakia. His company was reduced from a hundred men to sixteen in a week's combat. Jacob's sergeant had both legs blown off and died shortly after Jacob had carried him three kilometers to the rear.

"War stinks," said Jacob, borrowing a potato dumpling Eiber had left, and using it to mop up the last of the goulash. There had never been enough to eat—and the diet was largely potatoes—in the Soviet POW camp he had been held in for several years after the war. He was, he said, one of the lucky ones: the last German prisoners of war in the USSR weren't released until 1955, when Chancellor Adenauer visited Moscow and negotiated the release. Now Jacob lives in Regnitzlosau, the town he was baptized in, and in his spare time flies his model gliders, trying to ensure through radio controls that they don't come down in Czechoslovakia. After lunch he took us to the local Evangelical Lutheran church, which had recently been restored at great cost and was the pride of the community. It had a large, barnlike nave and huge tower, painted a custard yellow; the tower was crowned by a slate-covered onion dome, out of which sprouted another, smaller onion dome. The Baroque interior contained richly paneled pews, galleries and ceiling, with florid carvings and highly colored figures of saints and angels. The Baroque period approved of rosy cheeks.

We drove into the woods near Trogenau, between Regnitzlosau and the border. Here a television team from the Norddeutsche Rundfunk in Hamburg was making a semidocumentary to be called *Die Grenze*. Although the actual DDR fence was barely a kilometer away, the company of half a dozen actors and a small production crew had preferred to work with a replica fence and slightly less than full-scale observation tower—the latter had recently been used in a film called *Night Crossing*, based on the Strelzyk-Wetzel balloon escape. The scene now being shot for *Die Grenze* involved two surveyors, one East and one West German, at work defining the border between the two states—here assumed to be running through a small quarry. The director sat in a director's chair. The camera trundled forward on a length of track and the two actors spoke their lines. As surveyors, they were apparently getting on with their job in a friendly fashion.

The actor playing the East German surveyor said, "Which is the longest river in the world?"

The West German replied, "The Amazon, of course."

"No."

"The Mississippi?"

"No."

"Well—which?" asked the West German, smiling as he realizes it must be a joke—

"The Elbe."

"Why?"

"Because it takes sixty-five years to get from Dresden to Hamburg."

—a joke perhaps best appreciated by Norddeutsche Rundfunk's East

German viewers, who at retirement age of sixty-five are allowed to leave for West Germany if they want to.

The Wetzels live now in the small town of Schauenstein, close to where they landed two years before at the end of what is still the most original escape from the DDR. They have a spacious apartment in a modern building facing on the market square. The flat has a sparse amount of furniture, though what there is of it looked solid and expensive. There were flowers in a vase and what sounded like film music coming from stereo speakers. The Wetzels are living more prosperously than they did in Pössnech, a mere sixty kilometers north of here, partly because of income they are receiving from the *Night Crossing* production and partly because of the generally high standard of living in West Germany; but they hasten to say that in Pössnech, by East German standards, they weren't badly off. They left for other reasons. But here they are also living quietly, almost lying low. Günter Wetzel, in his late twenties, was a building worker, bricklayer and mechanic when he lived in the DDR; he now works as a truck mechanic. He has soft, benevolent features, a droopy, unassertive mustache and thick-fingered hands. His wife Petra is a chirpy redhead, willing on most occasions to do most of the talking. Their two small boys, Peter, seven, and Andreas, four, ran in and out of the room, wearing sheriff's badges and firing cap pistols.

A little more than three years before this, Günter Wetzel had begun to have conversations about leaving the DDR with Peter Strelzyk, then thirty-seven, an electrician who had served in the East German air force as a ground mechanic. Strelzyk had just seen a television program about hot-air ballooning; he began to read up on the subject. When the Strelzyks and the Wetzels had exchanged opinions about life in the DDR, and how caged they felt, they decided to build a balloon as a way of getting out. Their first model would not rise from the ground. Their second didn't have enough lift for four adults and four children, and the Wetzels staunchly told the Strelzyks to try on their own. The Strelzyks did, but ran out of gas and came down just inside the border—a mere two hundred meters from the fence. Fortunately it was dark. They crept away, managed to get out of the five-kilometer restricted zone without being seen, and after some hours of hiking cross-country, got back to where they had left their car hidden in a remote place. They returned to Pössnech, and together with the Wetzels set about making a third balloon.

From the previous attempt a certain amount of launch gear had been salvaged, but the balloon itself had been left where they came down. What the DDR authorities thought when it was found is of course unknown; it was not the sort of item that appears in East German papers; it is possible that they thought the balloon had come across from Bavaria—but in that case, where was the crew? Acquiring materials for a new balloon involved a great deal of risk, especially as it was likely that word had been spread to keep an eye open for people buying quantities of fabric. The Strelzyks and Wetzels traveled to many places to buy many rolls of nylon sheeting and curtain stuff from haberdashers and department stores. Stitching the long narrow panels together took fifteen days' work on a sewing machine. A new gas burner had to be constructed, and propane gas tanks bought. The gondola was a simple wooden platform about four and a half feet square, with a post in each corner and five lengths of rope running around it to hold the passengers in; it looked like a tiny boxing ring. The balloon itself was to be approximately twenty-four meters high, twenty meters in diameter, particolored in thin stripes of browns, beiges, blues, reds, oranges, greens, blacks and yellows. It must have made a sudden dent in East German sheet and curtain stocks. Wetzel and Strelzyk tested their machinery and checked their calculations; this time they hoped the balloon and equipment were right.

On September 15, 1979, a Saturday, the weather forecast was promising: a cold front coming in from the north and a light-to-moderate northerly wind. At 11 p.m. Strelzyk and Wetzel drove out into the countryside to take a closer look at wind and weather; things seemed all right. They returned to Pössnech and got their departure under way. They loaded the balloon and its gear into a small trailer, to be pulled behind Strelzyk's ten-year-old Wartburg. Young Andreas Wetzel, who was two, was given some drops of a tranquilizer by his mother to keep him quiet. Everyone else had quick cups of coffee or tea. Then they bade a hurried farewell to their homes, in which they left all their possessions, such as TV sets, washing machines, and clothing, apart from what they had on. The two women and three of the children squeezed into Strelzyk's car with him. Wetzel took the fifteen-year-old Strelzyk boy Frank behind him on his moped. They drove slowly south, scared of being stopped by the Volkspolizei.

Just before 1 a.m. they reached the place they had chosen for the ascent— a clearing in the woods near Oberlemnitz, about fifteen kilometers due north of the border. For some time they sat in the car and remained with the moped, until they were sure that all was quiet in the area and that the DDR border troops from the barracks at Wurzach three kilometers away weren't out on night maneuvers. Then they got to work. The balloon was unrolled; the gondola or basket pegged down to short guy ropes; a home-made fan, powered by a motorcycle engine, started up; and a homemade portable burner, rather like a flamethrower, lit. Two of them held up the open mouth of the balloon while the heated air was driven into it by the fan. Slowly the huge length of nylon began to swell and rise. When it was over the gondola, the balloon hot-air burner, standing like a fireworks rocket between four propane tanks on the gondola platform floor, was lit. The balloon filled; it began to lift the rickety gondola. They all scrambled aboard and waited for the balloon's lift to overcome their weight. It did. The ropes, straining, were released—except for one, which wouldn't come undone. The basket tilted suddenly and the burner looked for an instant as if it was going to burn the balloon fabric, but Wetzel managed to cut the rope with his knife. They were loose, and rising.

They went up at roughly two hundred meters a minute. The wind moved them south at nearly thirty knots—fifty kilometers an hour. They rose to an altitude of 2,000 meters, as indicated on their simple altimeter, and Strelzyk turned down the burner flame. But the flame still illuminated them, crammed on the platform with the children on the inside up against the propane tanks, and the four adults trying hard not to lean heavily against the surrounding ropework. All they could hear was the hiss of the burner. The huge, tall bag of the balloon blotted out most of the sky above them, though it was a night full of stars. They reached 2,600 meters. It was freezing cold—eight degrees below zero centigrade. Andreas' drops began to wear off; he got restless and fretful, and Petra Wetzel hugged him and sang a song about a teddy bear that she made up as she went along. Down below, all was dark, until suddenly a bright light appeared— a beam panned the sky, a searchlight, which moved their way, caught the balloon for an instant and moved on. Would the shooting start? But nothing happened.

They had been on their way for twenty-three minutes when the burner flame began to die down; the gas was running out. They dropped slowly to 2,000 meters, the balloon revolving. The flame spluttered on the last of the propane. Their descent became rapid. They didn't know whether or not they were still over the DDR. Looking down, Petra saw many lights, red and amber, which didn't seem to her like the DDR. The earth was rushing to meet them: hills, woods, fields, roofs of houses came into view. They were coming down over a pine wood. It slipped past—here was the ground—and they landed with a sharp jolt in a thicket of blackberry bushes. Another 150 meters would have taken them into a high-tension power line. The flight had lasted twenty-eight minutes. Where were they?

The small size of the fields gave them hope that they were in West Germany. The two men, Wetzel hobbling with a leg injured from the landing, moved off to the edge of the meadow, as it seemed to be. There was a road, and a car coming along it. Now they would know: was it a Trabant, Lada, Wartburg or Moskowitsch? Günter Wetzel let out a happy cry and shouted to the women and children: they were in the West. The car was an Audi. And it was the police from the nearby town of Naila, alerted by an insomniac lady who had called them to say she had seen a balloon coming down.

Within a day the Strelyzks and the Wetzels were the sensation of West Germany—and probably of East Germany, too, as most of the citizenry there heard of the flight on West German TV and radio. The DDR authorities were assumed to be miffed that their radar system hadn't picked up the balloon (West German experts said that perhaps it had been moving too slowly for devices intended to spot missiles and planes). In any event, since the balloon flight only small quantities of nylon material may be bought in the DDR by private citizens. The West German press made immediate heroes of the Strelzyks and Wetzels. *Stern* magazine bought the rights to their story, and within two weeks had started to run a multipart series on their adventure. The balloon was filled again with hot air for TV films and press photographs. One German journalist described the balloon the morning after the landing, lying draped over bushes and young fir trees, as looking like a work by Christo, the artist who wraps parts of a landscape. Film offers were made (and agreement reached with Walt Disney Productions). The initial excitement wore off, but the public interest and publicity continued, and took some getting used to.

"Yet we've never regretted making the flight," Petra Wetzel said, topping up a glass of beer her husband had brought me. "We live here in a smaller town than we did in the DDR. Günter has a good job in a truck repair workshop. He finds there is less regimentation and more incentive to get things done. I have a part-time job as a mail-order saleswoman for a Nuremberg department store. We don't give interviews to German papers anymore. We didn't want to become prominent people."

Despite this, they have had to be prominent—to be introduced to notable people like Franz-Josef Strauss, the Bavarian politician, and to fly to America, to be guests of their film producers in California for ten days. They were impressed by American hospitality and American waste—Petra was particularly aggravated by the way people in Beverly Hills left lights burning day and night. Günter has been made a member of a Nuremberg balloon club, and is also learning how to pilot a small plane. But it hasn't all been easy sailing. For reasons they didn't want to go into, but which apparently had to do with feeling on one side or other that fame and royalties weren't being fairly shared-out, the Wetzels are no longer in touch with the Strelzyks—who are living in Bad Kissingen. They don't feel quite such close links with the acquaintances they have so far made here. They are effectively cut off from their relatives in East Germany. Günter Wetzel's father, who at the age of eighty should be able to leave the DDR without trouble, went to the authorities to get a permit to go to West Germany but was ejected from the office abruptly once they realized that he was Günter's father. The Wetzels believe that some of their friends were suspected of helping them acquire materials and gas, and are now suffering from special constraints. The Wetzels have heard that since their flight, a number of people—perhaps a dozen—have been caught attempting to build balloons.

I thought it curious that the Wetzels had stayed so close to the border, almost as if they had been imprinted with it or were still in its magnetic field. They said that their impression of the area had been good from the start—people were friendly—though there was a nervous strain in West German life that took some getting used to—the greater amount of free time you had to make use of; the greater choice of everything, as with the vast numbers of items for sale in shops. Perhaps they were here because it was as close to their old home as they could get while living in West Germany. They were living in the same region still, almost as if the border weren't there. "Our life there wasn't bad in material terms," Günter Wetzel said. "But it was a prison. If I'd been free to come over here, I probably wouldn't have come for good."

I thought an interesting thing about the Wetzels was that they demonstrated how extraordinary "ordinary" people can be—in other words, how extraordinary anyone can be. Neither intellectuals nor active dissidents, they were representatives of plain and energetic discontent.

Petra said that she wanted to go to California again, but Günter seemed happy enough to be here.

18. CROSSING IN THE WOODS

The Iron Curtain, once it has become the West German–Czechoslovak border, heads more directly south. I was glad to see the last of the DDR's fence system and of the dividing line between the two Germanys. The road I took from Hof was known first as the Porcelain Way and then as the Bavarian Ostmarkstrasse; the hilly country on the German side of the border was the Oberpfalzer Wald, and the Ceskyles Sumava, or Böhmer Wald, on the Czechoslovak side. Michelin told me that this range of hills was formed of "crystalline massifs . . . The region, whose highest point, 1456 m./4777 feet, is at the Grosser Arber, attracts visitors with simple tastes who enjoy solitude. The frontier, being part of the Iron Curtain, should be approached circumspectly, or, better still, avoided until excursions to Czechoslovakia are again possible." "Excursions" has a nice, old-fashioned ring to it. The fields here had the appearance of clearings in the woods, and the woods in the distance once again gave the impression of being a continuous fir and spruce forest. After finishing *The Flounder* I had begun to dip into the *Nibelungenlied*, the weird, inconsequential but gripping early-medieval German epic of retribution and revenge; it is thought to have been written in southern Germany or western Austria, making use of various Norse and German material. The old forest is where some of the action happens. In the Norse lay *Atlakvioa*, of the ninth century, a messenger is sent across "the gloomy forest," which the modern scholar A. T. Hatto believes may be "a memory of the great forest known as Hercynia Silva or Firgund, north of the Roman road from the Rhineland to the Danube."

The sun slowly burned through the low morning haze. Men and women worked on the small farms, sometimes with children who for one reason or another hadn't set off for school. Women rode on plows, worked cement mixers and set milk churns out at the roadside. The church spires had a simple shape. Some of the place names began to sound less Germanic, more Slavic or Eastern: Estlarn, Herzogau, Cham. The Deutschlandfunk kept in step with me, broadcasting the death of Siegfried from Wagner's *Götterdämmerung* as I drove through the mist-shrouded woods. The most tragic occurrence now in these forests is the death of trees. Thousands are being poisoned by sulfur dioxide, the by-product of urban, industrial civilization. All over Germany, not only in the Ruhr, it is falling as dust or as acid rain, which then releases metal deposits in the soil, damaging tree roots so that they can't absorb enough water. Particularly the less resistant coniferous trees of these old forests are ailing, going thin and gray on top, needles and branches beginning to fall, while the experts consider how to control the output of sulfur dioxide before the forests die altogether.

I had lunch in the village of Leuchtenberg, whose castle can be seen from afar on its hilltop; the castle was closed, but I ate at a *Gaststätte* that was well patronized by local repair and delivery men engaged in games of cards or dice. Then I drove on, through more and more rugged country, to the town of Furth-im-Wald, which is roughly halfway down the West German–Czech border. Furth-im-Wald means "the crossing in the woods." A fair-sized market town with road and railway connections to Czechoslovakia, it still has something of the village about it: some barns in town and a glass-fronted display case opposite the station in which was noted the recent birthday celebrations (from fifty-ninth to eighty-first) of members of the local army old-comrades association. The peace and quiet that Furth-im-Wald offers has encouraged the establishment of many rest homes and guesthouses. I stayed at the Hotel Hohen Bogen, across from the station, where I had an excellent room for about a third of the price one would pay in a more centrally located, large West German town.

I walked round Furth-im-Wald with Joseph Andes, an immensely friendly man in his early fifties, the local border commissioner of the Bavarian Frontier Police, a man whose air was that of someone who taught school or ran a store—but by no means authoritarian. We visited the church, the town hall, the marketplace and a large lot full of Czech Skoda cars. "They aren't selling very well. You can get one very cheap," said

Andres. "The kids here have found out that the ignition keys are taped behind the left rear wheel, so occasionally the cars disappear on joy rides at night." We called in at what looked like a fire station to look at the town's collective symbol and toy: a giant mechanical dragon. For more than five hundred years Furth-im-Wald has had an annual dragon festival called the *Drachenstich*—"spearing the dragon." It is a parade and pageant every August, which culminates in the ceremonial slaying of the beast by a knight on horseback. The dragon, Andres told me, represents "the forces of evil from the East, which have always endangered this border." Furth's previous dragon was taken away by the Czechs in the end-of-war chaos in 1945; the current dragon is a monster about sixty feet long, and some fifty thousand people turn up to see it in action at the festival, when it rumbles through the streets belching fire.

The doors of the dragon garage were rolled up and there it was, larger than myth. Herr Walter Pfauntsch, the town's tourism director and dragon curator, gave me the facts while the mayor's chauffeur (who doubles as dragon-driver) got inside the beast to take the controls. The dragon weighs nine tons; it cost DM 370,000; it is built around a bulldozer, steel-frame covered with canvas, papier-mâché and rubberized paint. When started up—the roar of the bulldozer's diesel engine exaggerated by the confines of the garage—its wings move, its front paws lift and fall, and its huge jaw goes up and down, revealing a red cavern of a mouth lined with sharp white teeth, while flames shoot forth from the nostrils and a terrifying bellow comes from somewhere in its interior.

"The flames are gas, lit by spark plugs," said Herr Pfauntsch. I could see the reason for the blackened asbestos panels on the ceiling. A small child who happened by with his parents began to cry. I suggested that Furth loan it to the BGS for occasional patrols along the intra-German border.

At the Furth-im-Wald railroad station the big daily event is the arrival and departure of the *Donau Kurier*, which comes in from Prague just before noon and leaves for that city in the late afternoon. From the west it arrives with carriages from Dortmund and Munich, generally with a hundred and fifty passengers. The stationmaster said that the train stops in Furth for twenty minutes for passport and customs control; it then halts for another hour just inside Czechoslovakia for similar controls. (An agreement between the two countries for officials to conduct their business on the train while it is motion would seemed to be called for.) While on its return journey to Prague, the train is searched thoroughly by the Czechs, panels opened in the tops of carriages, battery boxes examined, and dogs used to sniff freight and parcels. On their way through the train the Czech officials remove all German newspapers from the seats and take away from passengers any periodicals regarded as offensive to the Czech regime—those of sexual or religious interest are most likely to be confiscated. Despite this, the old lady running the kiosk at the Furth-im-Wald station had a good selection of girlie magazines for sale, possibly for local or west-bound customers. On this particular afternoon the "Danube Courier" was nearly empty, with only twenty through passengers for Prague. The attendant in the Czech dining car sat resignedly totting up his meager accounts. I had a sudden desire to go to Prague, only a few hours away; but I didn't have a visa and no way of getting one at such short notice.

After dinner Herr Andres and his wife took me to Cham, a larger town about twenty kilometers away, to attend the opening of an exhibition dealing with *Wälderhäuser*, old Bavarian forest houses. These are the traditional buildings of the back woods, the sort of log-cabin architecture one finds where the most plentiful building material comes from trees. Herr Andres said, "Most other Germans think of Bavarians as hillbillies." (The German nickname for Bavarians is *Seppels*, which is derived from the name Joseph—husband of Mary, and obviously regarded as an unsophisticated character. Despite having the same Christian name, often shortened to Sep, Herr Andres didn't seem to have a chip on his shoulder about this.) The *Wälderhaus* is now considered in some circles to be a fine, primitive sort of indigenous construction, a view which comes about at a time of their increasing rarity. The farmers who own most of them generally don't want to live in them. They build modern houses nearby. But they also don't want strangers living close at hand and therefore don't sell the old houses; they prefer to let them decay and fall down. I enjoyed the detailed drawings and photographs of the *Wälderhäuser*. I endured a thirty-five-minute speech by an architect who had helped mount the exhibition, and which had not only me, half comprehending, but the other sixty or so people there, from local society, nodding on our feet. However, I had a good time helping them drink a big barrel of Cham beer, brewed in the Hofmark brewery and donated by the brewery's owner, Paul Häring. Herr Häring told me that he was in the midst of negotiating a deal by which, he hoped, Hofmark beer would soon be on sale in Columbus, Ohio.

The Bavarian-Bohemian border is 375 kilometers long; it is the old border established between the Kingdom of Bavaria and the Austro-Hungarian Empire in Maria Theresa's time, resurveyed and re-marked in 1932–1934. There are now five road crossings and two rail crossings. The Czechs have fenced in their side of it, but their fence is not always right at the border;

in some places it is as much as five kilometers back. There are no mines, no automatic firing devices and fewer watchtowers. Czechs who make it over the fence may think they've escaped but they may still have several kilometers to cover before getting out of Czechoslovakia. Since the fence generally is fitted with an alarm wire, to alert the guards, Czech patrols usually manage to pick up would-be border crossers between the fence and the border. (It makes sense, therefore, to attempt such a crossing where the fence is close to the border.) In 1980 only eight people got across the Czech–West German border, and five were Czechoslovak border guards; in fact, the border guards tend to be Slovak rather than Czech, conscripts from Slovakia with less of a tie with the local population. As is the case with getting out of East Germany, greater success is believed to attend those who hide in cars, trucks and trains. Several years ago a boxcar filled with chicken feathers, in a train from Rumania, was opened for inspection in Furth-im-Wald and two Rumanians climbed out, delighted, asking for asylum.

I spent the following day looking at several sections of the Bavarian-Bohemian border with Bavarian Frontier Police officer Eberhart Pilz, a tall man in his thirties with a friendly, casual manner which seemed to suit the border here. We drove north toward Waldmünchen and along a small road that had once crossed the border at Höll. The hills are some seven hundred meters above sea level, with wide meadows on the Bavarian side of the border and thin woods on the other—pine, chestnut and birch. There was a striped barrier gate where the road reached the border, along with the usual signs and one of the old men who seem to make it part of their morning routine to come up to the border and have a look at things. This old man had binoculars with which he was inspecting the Czech woods; we exchanged "Grüss Gotts" with him. A small path lined with ragged robin and forget-me-nots ran on the Bavarian side of the border-marker posts. Another small path, identical, but worn into the grass by Czech boots, ran on the other side of the posts. We reached a little stream, and there was a single plank bridge for us, and another slightly less solid looking plank for them, a meter away. Through the trees I could see a Czech watchtower with two men in it. Down below, six meters in from the border, were two Czech border guards with two German shepherds.

"Dobryden!" called Pilz.

"Dobryden!" said one of the Czechs, returning the "Good day" greeting with a wave. The dogs were even more friendly. Neither of them was on a leash, and they came bounding in our direction. I retained until the last moment the conviction that they would halt on their side of the markers—but they didn't. They ran around us, tongues hanging out, tails swinging. It was funny, and almost embarrassing; I felt sorry for the Czech guards, who looked quite taken aback. Then one began to whistle for the dogs. The other called out what sounded like the Czechoslovak for "Here! Here!" The dogs, apparently defecting, took these signals as indications to run farther into the Bavarian meadow, dashing through the long grass. One of the guards now came running toward the border, his gun slapping against his side. I thought he was going to chase the dogs across the meadow, but he came to a stop at the line of the posts, looking red in the face and thoroughly flustered, like any dog handler shown up in public by a dog that won't answer to commands.

He called again, and then again, more sharply, anger getting the better of self-consciousness. The dogs slowed down. Their course changed; they turned and came trotting back, looking (I thought) fairly pleased with themselves. The two guards gave relieved smiles, and Pilz and I made encouraging noises ("Well done!" and "Nice work!") as the dogs were patted, and leashes snapped on, perhaps to receive a good tongue-lashing when off the scene. The guards walked their charges back into the trees, where I now saw that a patrol vehicle had turned up. We watched some-one, clearly an officer, get out. He began to shout at the two guards; he went in shouting. The Good Soldier Schweik lives on!

"You did the right thing," Pilz said to me.

"Oh—what was that?"

"You stood still. Always stand still when a dog runs toward you." He lifted a trouser leg and showed scars in his calf, where a Bavarian police dog had bitten him. "If we hadn't been here," he went on, "the guards would have chased the dogs over on this side. We know they come over here sometimes—we've found one of their hats and a signal pistol in these fields."

I asked if the Bavarian dogs ever ran over there.

"I don't know about the dogs, but last year a local farmer lost a mare. He'd bought it not long before. We let the Czech border command know it was lost. Four months passed and then we heard that a Czech wood-cutter had it. They asked a thousand marks because he had been looking after it all that time. So we talked with them—a few bottles were pre-sented—we discovered that the woodcutter had been working the mare, and we made some deductions for that—and we finally offered five hundred marks, which was accepted. The farmer got his mare back. Not long after-ward she had a foal—worth at least five hundred marks."

We stopped by at the Furth-im-Wald *Übergang*, which in 1980 had seen the passage in both directions of 150,000 people. Three hundred and forty trucks had gone through the day before. Unlike the DDR, Czechoslovakia permits people to ride a bike or even walk into the country with the proper visa. Official relations are also more relaxed. Pilz said that Commissioner Andres had gone over a few days before to congratulate the commander of the Czech border station on his birthday; Andres had been asked to stay for a cup of coffee. The Czechs presented two faces, Pilz said —an official face that was correct; an unofficial face that was fairly human. "But they're under great political pressure, and they don't trust one another. It isn't a good atmosphere."

There has been no serious incident on this part of the border for ten years. In 1972 a Bavarian customs man was killed at the Furth-im-Wald crossing point; the bullet case found nearby was from a Czech AKM weapon. It was thought a Czech patrol followed a refugee across the border and was spotted by the Zoll man. The Czech patrol overreacted and shot him when they were challenged; but this was never proved. More recently a Czech farm worker got drunk, climbed the fence and walked into Furth-im-Wald. When he had sobered up, he wanted to go home, and was handed back at the *Übergang*. "I doubt if he's still working near the border," said Pilz.

We drove southeast of Furth-im-Wald for twenty kilometers. The day, gray from the start, had turned wet: a heavy drizzle fell. Pilz told me that the Bavarian-Czech border from here to its junction with Austria, another sixty kilometers away, was almost entirely high forested hills. It was twelve days since I had climbed the Wurmberg in the Harz and I reacted heartily to Pilz's suggestion—made a little reluctantly as he looked at the weather— that climbing one of the peaks of this range, the Osser, 1,293 meters high, would give me a good idea of the border landscape. We stopped at a border-police station in the village of Lam to pick up a local policeman and a German shepherd, to be our guides up the Osser. It was a young dog, I was told, named Husain, and still being trained. Husain wore two patches, strapped to each shoulder, saying POLIZEI. We drove to where a road ended, about a third of the way up the Osser, and set off up a rock-strewn track. The drizzle got thicker; it was hard to see very far through it. Ledges of rock stuck out of the hillside like balconies; on thin patches of soil, berries and a sort of heather were growing. The dog suddenly dashed off through the trees, perhaps on the scent of an animal. "Husain!" yelled his keeper. "Husain! Husain!" It was clearly a day for dogs.

Husain did not return. Possibly it was time for him to visit Czechoslovakia and he would be returned in four months, for a suitable payment. Pilz and I walked upward, leaving the local policeman to try and retrieve the dog. The path corkscrewed around to the north flank of the Osser, a hill which I was beginning to think of as a mountain. I had got ahead of

Pilz somehow. Suddenly the border appeared—the blue-and-white posts. The ground looked a little less rocky and rain-soaked on the other side, so I walked in Czechoslovakia part of the time, and when the rain came down heavily, I stopped and stood with Pilz for several minutes under a Czech pine tree, as good as any umbrella, though we should have had visas. I could hear Husain's policeman still calling for him. Then, the rain thinning out a little, we set out for the summit, which Pilz said was traversed by the border, knowing that what, on a clear day, is a superb view of the hills, forests and distant villages of Bohemia would be absolutely blotted out by wet cloud when we got there.

19. *LIMES*

The river Regen rises on the border near the Osser and flows west and southwestward to Regensburg through open country. I followed much the same route. At Regensburg, an ancient university town, the Regen joins the Danube, and the old riverside brick warehouses and wide bridges indicate a waterway that is now large enough to carry big barges, which can go from here to the Black Sea. Here was an old border, the *limes*, the limit of the Roman Empire. Regensburg, then called Ratisbon, guarded the imperial frontier at its northernmost point, and some Roman remains can still be seen, like the huge stones of the Praetorian Gate, built into a wall in a narrow street called Unter den Schwibbögen. The Romans, to prevent raids on their provinces, insisted that the German tribes beyond the frontier leave several miles of territory without crops or settlement. Nor were the Germans allowed to use boats on the Danube. Trade had to be conducted at specific places on the frontier. E. A. Thompson writes in his short book *The Early Germans*:

The aim of Roman diplomacy . . . was to keep in office or even to put in office chieftains who would carry out a policy friendly to Rome, men on whose "loyalty" the Imperial authorities could rely. And this they sometimes succeeded in doing, according to Tacitus, even in cases where their nominees were men who had so little support from their followers that "their power and their ascendancy were derived from Roman authority" and from that alone.

The Romans now and then assassinated or kidnapped German military leaders, a practice (Mr. Thompson says) that usually ended by damaging the Romans more than those peoples whose leaders they removed. Some chieftains were carried off to Rome as hostages, educated and trained there, and then sent back—often with subsidies—to run things in an approved manner. The historical parallels, of course, are not clear-cut. We in the West may feel that in some sense we are the civilized ones, the inheritors of Roman culture; but in other respects we are more like the less organized tribes faced with a powerful empire which manipulates its subjects.

I had met Suzanne Kurz in London, a young Bavarian woman who had been a student at the University of Regensburg and was now training as a teacher there. I had lunch with her and her friend, Günter Lugert, a twenty-nine-year-old research physicist whose family were what he called "rucksack Germans," who had left the Sudetenland in Czechoslovakia with little more than they could carry. (History revenges itself in strange and not always very fair ways. The Sudetenland has had an evil ring to it since the late 1930s, when Hitler made it an excuse for enlarging the Third Reich; and now the Sudeten Germans are a somewhat displaced people.) Günter talked while we sat in the cobbled courtyard of the Bischofshof, once a seminary, eating at a table under the chestnut trees, while the waters of an old fountain splashed. Günter and his parents left Czechoslovakia in 1967, when he was fifteen; it was, he thinks, just about the last moment for getting out of that country without great trouble— nowadays German Czechs have to wait years for permission to leave and pay considerable sums for exit permits. In Czechoslovakia, among his Czech contemporaries, Günter had felt compelled to act like a German because that was the more difficult thing to be. He knew that he would have difficulty getting a higher education there because his parents weren't Communist Party members. He was allowed to attend a German class once a week, at the intentionally awkward hour of 7 to 8 A.M. Then there was the wrench of coming to Germany, where he and his parents stayed in a Bavarian camp for two years. An uncle, living here, got him into a good school where, speaking with a different accent, he was nicknamed "the Czech." In Czechoslovakia, for no good reason, he had been taunted as a capitalist; in Bavaria he was taunted as a Communist. For a while he was deeply homesick for Czechoslovakia. With his parents the home-sickness has lasted longer.

They get together four or five times a year with old friends from the Sudetenland. They belong to a Sudeten German association, which has its own journal and holds meetings at which traditional costumes are worn and Sudeten songs and dances are performed. In this the Sudeten Germans are little different from transplanted communities of German Hungarians, German Poles or German Rumanians. But the younger generation have got over the need for these nostalgic organizations, even if they continue to feel a bit different.

"Many young West Germans of my age either take things for granted or reject everything altogether," Günter said. "I couldn't do either of those things. I'm grateful for many of the benefits and opportunities here. In Czechoslovakia it would have been almost impossible at my age to own a car. Here, as a not very well-off research student, I own a car, and I also have immense possibilities. In fact, that's the real difference. The possibilities, not the material possessions, are the richness of the West."

Günter and Suzanne walked with me around the old city, more Romanesque than Roman. We visited the old town hall, which contains the medieval *Reichsaal*, the chamber where the Diet of the Holy Roman Empire occasionally held its meetings to attempt to govern the strange assortment of states federated within the empire. Here in 1156 was solemnized the founding of the Duchy of Austria. Here, from 1663, a perpetual Diet—the beginning of a German parliament—began to sit. And here, in 1803, the Diet agreed to Napoleon's demands for territorial reorganization by which many of the tiny German states would be amalgamated into larger units. We were given a tour of the dungeons, here—as in Duderstadt—an integral part of the municipal headquarters. After this, needing the air that those who were held in dungeons must have craved, we walked to the Gallery of East German Art, situated outside the old city in a small park. In the gallery are works by Otto Dix, Schmidt-Rotloff, Oscar Moll, Max Beckmann, among others, all born in German territory east of the present intra-German border. Not all the work was of exceptional quality, but the general effect was of world pain and individual sadness—for me most forcefully concentrated in one piece by Käthe Kollwitz, a sculpted self-portrait that brought tears to the eyes.

Apart from escaping, reaching retirement age and being able to join close family members who have already left, many East Germans manage to leave the DDR by first going to prison and being ransomed out by the West German government. I met a businessman in Regensburg who has acted as a go-between in several of such cases and has helped resettle some ransomed East Germans. The facts of the matter are not publicized in detail in West Germany, where the government seems to feel that the less said the better about what has been called a trade in human beings. But it is believed that roughly a thousand people a year are bought out in this way. (The *Guardian*, on October 5, 1981, reported that between 1964 and 1978 nearly 14,000 East German prisoners were ransomed at a cost of more than $500 million/£300 million.) The Ministry of All-German Affairs is understood to have set aside for this purpose an annual budget of DM 30 million to DM 40 million. My informant, who wished to remain unnamed, said that the cost of getting someone out was reckoned to be between DM 50,000 and DM 80,000, though a well-educated person like a surgeon could cost from DM 100,000 to DM 150,000. The East German authorities justify the ransom demands as repayments for the state's investment in the upbringing and education of the person concerned.

The ransoms are of course a useful source of hard currency for the DDR. The price involves not only status and education but the length of prison term a person may be serving. The highest prices have often been asked for those convicted of helping others escape to the West—for one person of aristocratic descent imprisoned for such a "crime," the East Germans demanded a ransom of DM 200,000. And not all who are sold in this way are necessarily the sort of people the West Germans want to encourage to come to the Federal Republic: some are criminals whom the East Germans are trying to get rid of; some are spies who are thus neatly introduced into West Germany while the East German regime makes some upfront profit on the deal. Most, however, are genuine prisoners of conscience, whose main offense has been the political one of applying to leave the DDR—a right inscribed in the Helsinki Agreements but regarded by the East German authorities as a provocation against the state. Party Secretary Erich Honecker said in an interview published in February 1981 by the *Berliner Zeitung*, a DDR paper, that since 1979 there had been no political prisoners in the DDR.

For a period, repugnance at this trade in West Germany caused the government to shift to payments in goods—fruit, fertilizer, coffee, radios and drugs were bartered for individuals. Although cash payments are now believed to have been resumed, the West German government continues to try to avoid publicity for the scheme, believing that it hinders efforts to buy out the prisoners. Others, including members of human rights groups such as Amnesty International, believe that publicity is needed to throw light on violations of human rights in the DDR and that publicity has no adverse effect on prisoners; moreover, prisoners of conscience should be released without financial conditions of this kind.

For East Germany there are obvious advantages—not just financial—in getting rid of opponents to the regime without making martyrs of them. In East Berlin the kingpin of the operation is a now fairly well-known fifty-six-year-old lawyer, Wolfgang Vogel. He is one of the dozen or so private lawyers allowed to operate in the DDR. He designs his own well-tailored suits, drives a Mercedes, and appears to have the freedom to come and go through the Berlin Wall. Vogel has been at this business for some time—he helped negotiate the exchange in 1962 of the American U-2 pilot Francis Gary Powers, held in Russia, and the American student Frederic Pryor, imprisoned for spying in East Germany, for Colonel Rudolf Abel, the Soviet spy who had been captured in New York. Vogel traveled to London to work out a transaction whereby British subjects imprisoned for espionage in the USSR were released in return for Soviet spies held in Britain. West German money has been passed to him by way of Western lawyers and a German Lutheran bishop. He set up meetings for then Chancellor Schmidt and Party Secretary Honecker, and he is to be seen at official dinners given by the U.S. Ambassador in East Berlin. A few years ago he was reported as saying that he thought the ransom arrangements brought "a tangible result, freedom, to people moldering in jail," but that the East German government might put an end to the arrangements if the Western press continued to write about it as if it were trade in human flesh.

But the trade goes on, and the discovery in the West of East German spies gives West Germany an additional bargaining counter. According to the West German counterintelligence service, the East Germans are particularly interested in electronics, energy and chemical firms. Industrialists and scientists are approached not only in West Germany but at Black Sea resorts and at the Leipzig trade fairs. Seventeen East German agents who had worked in these fields were arrested as a result of the defection to West Germany in 1979 of Werner Stiller, a lieutenant colonel in the East German Ministry of State Security. In September 1981 a West German engineer and his wife were charged with passing on to an East German agent details about the Tornado, the joint British–West German–Italian combat aircraft. An East German general, Heinz Bernhard Zorn, was arrested in Lille, France, in August 1980 and imprisoned for espionage, while two NATO secretaries in the last few years have defected to East Germany, having had access to NATO plans. It is necessary for the East Germans to arrest West Germans on spying charges to give themselves

pieces to trade with. In October 1981 Günter Guillaume, former aide to
Willy Brandt (whose downfall Guillaume's uncovering as a spy helped
to bring about), was one of six East German agents exchanged for a
mixed bag from the DDR, including nine West German intelligence
agents, thirty political prisoners and three thousand East Germans who
wanted to join their relatives in the West. Herr Guillaume was sped
across the border at Herleshausen, near Eschwege, on the night of October 1. People coming through the *Übergang* from the east said that
Wolfgang Vogel, the lawyer, was there on the East German side, presumably waiting to meet him.

My informant in Regensburg told me that the problems of the Germans who thus make a sudden passage from East to West do not necessarily stop when they arrive in the Federal Republic. In most cases, in
an attempt by the West German authorities to weed out spies or common criminals, a two-day interrogation awaits the newcomers at the state
security bureau in Bonn. A stay in a transit camp gives officials a chance
to brief the arrivals from East Germany on problems they are likely to
meet; but most don't seem terribly receptive at this point—something akin
to a state of shock has them in its grip. They are not officially recognized
as refugees for six months, and whether financial help will be forthcoming
depends very much on such recognition. Jobs are now hard to find. Even
if one is found, West German life doesn't always come up to expectations:
it is noisier, faster, more lonely. There isn't the tight cocoon of security
that hugs every citizen of the DDR. In the vacuum which "freedom"
suddenly seems to be, some turn to drugs or crime. Perhaps the time
served in an East German prison doesn't make for an easy adjustment—
as it apparently didn't in the case of Michael Gartenschläger.

Of course others were possibly maladjusted to everyday life in East
Germany for reasons that would pertain anywhere; idle or unhappy there,
they would be here, too. The man who talked to me in Regensburg knew
of one young East German who found a good job with a Hamburg publishing firm but fell apart and started using drugs. He knew others who
complained that West Germans seemed ignorant or insensitive about
East Germany and who found nothing to commit themselves to here.
Some have given up and gone back to the DDR. One jazz musican came
to the West for money and success, and he hasn't found them; he is out
of work much of the time; there's too much competition in West Germany, he thinks; he is considering going back to what now seems like a
life of more regular pay and gigs in East Germany.

Many are eventually assimilated into West German life—a few do well,
and one or two become more West German than the West Germans—

but the proportion of those who make the transition in every way is thought to be higher among those who escape under their own steam rather than being ransomed out. Perhaps they are naturally more adventurous and attuned to the ups and downs of Western society. My informant knew of one East German couple who had escaped by going on vacation to Hungary and plunging into the Danube where it crosses the Hungarian-Yugoslav border. They had met some West Germans, who lent them wet suits and arranged to wait for them just inside Yugoslavia. But the East Germans were swept too far downstream, and when they came out, were taken to a police station. However, the Yugoslavs released them after a week and allowed them to travel to West Germany. They are now here, prepared to put up with a long period of looking for work, not much money, a tiny flat and no car—all worth it, they say.

That evening I met several fairly recent arrivals from the DDR. The occasion was a barbecue, held by members of the physics department of Regensburg University. Suzanne and Günter brought me along. It took place in the terraced courtyard of the modern physics building—four or five families with children, three or four couples, a few single people. The grill was being prepared—physicists seem to have the same difficulties with charcoal fires as ordinary mortals. Children played in the shrubbery; dark fell and the stars appeared. Some of the adults had spent time at British and American universities, and there was chat, for instance, about the pros and cons of life in California. After a while I got into conversation with a young couple who had just been in the DDR visiting relatives and were incensed by what they saw as petty officialdom there. One cloakroom attendant wouldn't return their coats when they couldn't find their stubs, so they had gone behind the counter to shouts and screams, and seized their own coats. Their elderly East German uncle had come over to visit them a year before, but refused to be taken to see the border. They didn't give a thought to the prospect of German reunification. "Anyway," said the woman, "the Americans would be terrified of us if the two Germanys were reunited."

Günter introduced me to a young colleague, Wolfgang Mars, who was, like himself, a solid-state physicist. A genial, bearded man in his late twenties, Mars said he had left the DDR nearly three years before. His parents had come to West Germany several years before that, on reaching retirement age. He had then applied to join them here under the provision of the Helsinki Agreements allowing for the reunion of families. "In the two years or so that I waited," Mars said, "my friends would congratulate me on my success. For what they regarded as success was not the fact of being able to leave but that I had decided to leave, and applied to do so." After making his application to emigrate, he was twice called in by the police, who checked to see if he had a job. It is illegal to be unemployed in the DDR, and he could have been jailed. Fortunately he was able to show them his stamped work card—for he had a temporary job as a film extra.

Mars was a preacher's son. He learned Latin at school. He went to Wolf Bierman concerts, which were sometimes held in Lutheran churches when no other auditorium could be obtained. He said that the first time he read Orwell's 1984 he thought it was exaggerated, but as he grew a bit older he realized that it was not. Knowledge of the East German border system spread without being put in writing, he said, with the help of West German radio and television, and also by information passed on from one good friend to another.

I asked him what he had found most difficult to adjust to here.

"Ways of thinking. For a long time after you get here, you go on thinking as if you were still there. You go on reading between the lines, though you don't need to in most cases. You read something that is perfectly straightforward and you can't help asking yourself, 'Now, what does this *really* mean?' "

20. AIRWAVES

Two hundred thousand foreigners live in Munich, roughly a sixth of the city's population. Despite being in the heart of Bavaria—despite its centrality in tourist Germania as the place where overflowing steins of beer are quaffed, and its notoriety as the spot where Hitler, head of the relatively unknown Nazi Party, came to public notice when he staged his unsuccessful beer-hall putsch on November 8, 1923, in an attempt to seize power in Bavaria—Munich does not feel overwhelmingly German. Perhaps I was prompted in this feeling by several walks I took in the Englischer Garten, the lovely park that Count Rumford (1753–1814), formerly Benjamin Thompson, the Anglo-American entrepreneur and adventurer, planned for the city when he lived here in the late 1780s on the lines of landscaped parkland surrounding an English country house, and a forerunner of Olmsted and Vaux's Central Park in New York. I stayed with friends, the Jablonskis, in the Schwabing neighborhood, and walked through the Englischer Garten on the way to Radio Free Europe. The radio station, where nearly a thousand foreigners work, is housed in a long, low building of domestic scale but fortresslike security on the edge of the garden. Funded directly by the United States Congress (an arrangement that in 1971 superseded covert financing by the CIA), RFE and its sister station Radio Liberty represent parts of a communications effort that effectively vaults over the Iron Curtain and brings information about events in the world to millions of people in the Eastern bloc. In this, RFE and RL are joined by the Voice of America, the BBC, the Deutschlandfunk and its subsidiary Deutsche Welle, and such stations as RIAS in West Berlin, Radio Luxembourg, Radio Vienna and the U.S. Armed Forces Network.

Radio Liberty broadcasts to the Soviet Union in Russian and fifteen other languages spoken in the USSR. Radio Free Europe broadcasts to Poland, Rumania, Bulgaria, Hungary and Czechoslovakia. The Deutschlandfunk broadcasts to most of the East European countries, and its German-language programs are listened to in the DDR—where almost the entire country, about 80 percent of the population, can also receive West German television. (In Dresden, where reception is more difficult, soccer fanatics have been known to take portable TV sets onto the tops of nearby hills to pick up televised West German matches.) In West Berlin I had called at RIAS (which stands for Radio in the American Sector) to talk with Patrick Nieburg, a United Press correspondent in Berlin in 1939–1941 and now a U.S. Foreign Service officer and one of two American directors of RIAS. Mr. Nieburg, speaking with a slight German intonation, told me that RIAS had been set up by the American occupation forces in the first postwar days to advise Berliners where and when water, coal and food would be available; it played music to keep people's spirits up. During the Berlin airlift the station sent out radio signals to guide in Allied planes. After the erection of the wall in August 1961, RIAS redirected some of its programing, thinking that it no longer needed to entertain and cheer up prosperous West Berliners so much as to sustain and inform those in the East. It now has a staff of 650, almost all German; the West German government provides most of its financial backing.

"Our schedule is designed to suit East Germans," said Mr. Nieburg, a trim-looking man with gray hair and a gray mustache. "They have a different life rhythm—the day starts an hour earlier there. They go to bed earlier. When we review a book, we assume they can't go out and buy it— we quote large chunks of it so that they know what it's about. In our early days people escaped from East Berlin and wanted us to broadcast messages to their families that they were okay. We still have a weekly Red Cross program for people to contact one another across the wall and the border. We've slowly evolved away from a sock-it-to-'em approach, and East Germany has evolved too—they don't all have horns over there. We try to give them an accurate day-to-day picture of our society, warts and all."

RIAS receives some five hundred letters a month from DDR listeners, mostly about singers and music, but a few asking for more news and news analysis—the demand for which the station is recognizing by giving more airtime to such programs. RIAS has reporters in Warsaw and Moscow, and sends special correspondents to the DDR. The station tries to discuss problems common to both German states, such as conscription. The night before the new West German representative to the DDR, Klaus Bölling, took over from Günter Gauss, he was interviewed on RIAS. At the ceremony the next day in East Berlin when he presented his credentials, Erich Honecker referred to a remark Bölling had made during the interview.

"So we know we're getting to them," said Nieburg with a quiet smile. "In fact, what with RIAS, five other German radio stations in West Berlin, three West Berlin TV stations, three Allied TV stations, and their own East German broadcasting, the people of the DDR are probably better informed about what's going on in the world than those elsewhere."

One effect of Western broadcasting has been to cause East German television to face competition and produce spectacular entertainment programs—bizarre contests of the "It's a Knockout" variety; even nude dancers. Another effect, suggested by Brasch in *New German Critique* (No. 2, 1977), is that Western television programs and radio broadcasts "serve the function of formulating a counter position to the DDR government. And in doing this, they diminish the force of any potential opposition. . . . At one time the opposition was actually thinking about suggesting to the government that it block reception of Western TV in the DDR. Only then, they thought, would a true need arise in the DDR for different sorts of programming and other information." Brasch thinks that the DDR leadership is aware of this, and knows that people can relieve their frustrations by coming home at night and watching Western television.

At Radio Free Europe there is a sense of being at a main crossing point of émigré and refugee fly paths. In 1981 the station was hit by a bomb attack and an editor of its Rumanian services was nearly murdered by (he thinks) men working for the Rumanian secret service. Most of the East European and Soviet languages are to be heard in RFE's corridors and canteen, and quite a few American accents, too. The station's director, however, is English: a former historian, James F. Brown, who came to RFE from a journal called *Historical Abstracts*. Before becoming director, Brown ran the RFE research and analysis department—the largest private research center in the world devoted to Eastern-bloc affairs—which engorges hundreds of East European newspapers and periodicals, wire-service reports, *samizdat* literature, monitored broadcasts and academic papers, and then collates, précises and catalogues them, for quick retrieval from the archives and for the use of RFE weekly situation reports and background reports on each of the five East European countries (Radio Liberty has its own research department on Soviet affairs). Munich has the advantage of excellent bookshops and periodical distributors who manage to get hold of all sorts of East European and Soviet journals, papers and magazines for RFE and RL. The station's programs are sent out from transmitters in West Germany, Spain and Portugal. They reach a weekly audience of twenty-five million people (according to surveys of East European travelers in the west), nearly half of whom listen every day.

Except in Hungary and Rumania, listeners often have to put up with jamming. RFE reckons that the Soviet Union spends twice as much on trying to make RFE and RL programs inaudible as it costs to produce and transmit them. The jamming results from the sending out of a loud signal on the same wavelengths that RFE and RL are using, but it isn't completely effective; it works best in the big cities, and it is sometimes only a minor irritation when the RFE or RL signal—bouncing the news, for example, off the ionosphere, from Portugal into Poland—is strong. In Prague, a few days after this, I was told that during a cold snap the previous winter, one of the pleasant effects of power shortages was that jamming had been suspended and Radio Free Europe came in loud and clear.

James Brown, an affable man with little sign of scholarly hesitation in his manner, told me that RFE had changed considerably since it was set up in 1948. Its funding through the Central Intelligence Agency came to an end in June 1971, and there was a two-year period of consideration and debate—and a moment of crisis when Senator Fulbright, prepared to sacrifice the station for détente's sake, refused to sign the RFE/RL appropriations and the staff was on the verge of being laid off, at which point President Nixon stepped in to the rescue. The U.S. government then set up a Board for International Broadcasting to oversee and finance the station, with the lofty aim of encouraging "a constructive dialogue with the peoples of Eastern Europe and the Soviet Union by enhancing their knowledge of developments in the world at large and in their own countries." RFE and RL have become less polemical, less stridently propagandist. Possibly, since they are supported by yearly appropriations from Congress, they feel less secure than they did in days of covert CIA funding.

"A lot of people say we've become too polite," said Brown. "We are less aggressively critical, more careful in checking our sources. We see the nuances in situations. We discuss our difficulties in the West, as with widespread unemployment. We operate within the idea that Communism has been imposed in the five East European countries, and that people in those countries have to make an accommodation with the system to stay alive. We realize more than we used to that the people of those societies have received some advantages—in social welfare, education, upward mobility. We're also more scientific in our methods of collecting and appraising information. We stretch our net farther. We try to find out, for instance, how the worldwide tendency toward urbanization is affecting them too. We have an important task in supplying those countries with information, and we need to be aware of the frightening everyday problems and inconveniences people in those countries face. But our job springs from the belief that the two halves of Europe are essentially one, historically and culturally—and we believe our audience feels this as well, despite thirty-odd years of Communist rule."

Brown believes that the period to come will be difficult, as agricultural and industrial production difficulties mount in the Eastern bloc and the Soviet Union faces the problems (also facing the West) of paying for constant rearmament. Other crises, like those in Poland, will pose questions to the West: What do we mean by détente? What do we want to happen in the East? How much are we prepared to pay or risk?

The Polish desk at RFE had been working a ten-hour day for more than a year at the time of my visit—more than a year in the Polish struggle to form, for the time being, trade unions independent of the Communist state apparatus; more than a year of strikes, protests, resignations, plans for recovery, party congresses, meetings and appeals, with the Solidarity movement making dramatic gains but the enclosing predicament of Soviet pressure and domestic economic chaos making those gains seem increasingly Sisyphean—and indeed, as time was to show, soon to be given up. The world's attention was focused on Poland not only by the cliff-hanging nature of the political drama but by such events as the Warsaw Pact military exercises in and around Poland in March and April 1981 and by the long last illness of Stefan Cardinal Wyszczynski, whose refusal to die symbolized for a period the tenacity of the Poles.

I sat in the RFE canteen over a cup of coffee with André Krzeczunowicz, an editor on the Polish desk, while he took a break from helping to put out that day's nineteen hours of broadcasting to Poland. "We emphasize Polish news," said Krzeczunowicz, who has lived in Munich for twenty years, and was wearing a Solidarity button on his sports jacket. "Today we're discussing the new wave of criminality in Poland—a big upsurge in petty crime—while the police force is highly discredited. We also have a roundup of the week's events in Poland—student marches, agricultural troubles, and we discuss the claim that West German funds to compensate concentration camp victims haven't got to the victims, or their heirs, but have been diverted along the way. We review some Polish books, some published there and one that has been banned there. Plus world news."

I asked where RFE got its Polish news from.

"Well, we subscribe to all the major news agencies, each of which has at least one correspondent in Poland. We read all the European papers and most of the Polish ones. We monitor all the Polish radio programs and then read between the lines, the way people try to there—of course, they monitor us, too. We know that what we decide at our morning editorial meeting will have an effect on their party meeting next day, when they discuss what has been on our news. We get some news smuggled out to us, like Solidarity bulletins, and we get reports from people who've just visited Poland. We get attacked by the more reactionary papers there, such as the army daily, and that shows they're listening to us. It is said to be a common question even at party meetings there: 'Why do we have to listen to Radio Free Europe to find out what's happening in Cracow?'"

The Polish desk, busy with Poland, has been further exercised by the fact of a Polish pope: several RFE men accompanied Pope John Paul II on his travels to America. Their reports were heard in Poland. Polish scholars have discussed Polish history and thought on a twice-weekly program. The men on the Polish desk meanwhile discuss among themselves the chances of the Polish "renewal"—as they call it—lasting, and spreading. They have hopes, but they are not optimists. They know their own history too well.

Zygmunt Jablonski, my host in Munich, also works as an editor on RFE's Polish desk. I have known Zygmunt and his vivacious German wife Hildegard for several years. Zygmunt, who is in his early sixties, left Poland in 1939 and has not been back; like most of his colleagues he has had long Odyssean periods in his life. He still feels that he is a Pole, though not as a citizen of present-day Poland: "I belong to a Poland that doesn't exist anymore." Zygmunt has acquired American citizenship by working for RFE. He and Hildegard have brought up two children; they have a pleasant modern apartment in Schwabing and a cottage outside Munich where Zygmunt feels more at home, and where he goes as often as the Polish desk will allow, to read, write and look after his fruit trees, and to surmount with the help of rural chores the particular melancholy that the Iron Curtain imposes on exiles.

Walking in the Englischer Garten, Zygmunt recalls for me parts of his past. When he left his country for the last time, World War II had not yet begun. He was nineteen; his father—a colonel in the Polish army—had presented him with a trip to the United States for doing well in his final school exams. He went to the World's Fair in New York and saw something of the country. He was on his way back when the Germans invaded Poland, and Britain and France declared war on Germany. His ship went to England; the passengers disembarked in Newcastle. And there began Zygmunt's war. He traveled to London and joined the Polish merchant marine. He served as a deck boy for five months on a Polish cargo ship, until one spring day in 1940, as his ship docked in La Rochelle in northwestern France, Zygmunt told the captain that he wanted to join the Polish army fighting in France. His captain said, "If you must, you must." Zygmunt was captured in the great German onslaught that overwhelmed the French army and the British Expeditionary Force. He was put in a prisoner-of-war camp near Trier, in the Mosel area of Germany close to the Luxembourg border. Early in 1941, when out on a farm labor detail, Zygmunt and a friend escaped. They had very little idea of where to head for. German police picked them up as they were approaching a bridge near Metz, and they gave their story: they were Frenchmen looking for work in Germany; naturally they had no papers to prove this. A local court gave them ninety-day sentences as illegal border crossers—quite a crime to commit in 1941—but the German police put them on a train to France and told them to go home and get their papers. The need for workers in Germany was great.

Zygmunt and his friend believed they deserved this sort of wild good fortune, but they didn't count on more of it; they got off the train as soon as they could in occupied France. They made their way south, hiding by day, walking by night, hungry and wet, sleeping in hedges and thickets. At last they made contact with a village priest, who put them in touch with the local helper for a resistance escape corridor. On this route they went from one friendly home to another and across the border into southern and as yet unoccupied France. The authorities there sent them to Pau, near the Pyrenees, where there was a reception center for Poles. From there Zygmunt tried to get into Spain, so that he could reach Gibraltar and then Britain; but the Spanish turned him back. So he and his fellow ex-prisoner sailed to Oran and joined the French Foreign Legion. Zygmunt enjoyed his legion service. After the Allied invasion of North Africa his unit helped the U.S. Army capture Tunis. "How wonderful it was to be with an army that was moving forward rather than back," says Zygmunt. Then, despite his good times as a legionnaire, he absconded and made his way to London. He was kept for several months at a repatriation center while British and Polish intelligence officers questioned him. No one believed his story about being captured and sent into France to get his papers. Obviously he was a German plant. But when things were beginning to look black, his companion in that escape also turned up from North Africa and told exactly the same absurd story.

Zygmunt went to the naval base at Plymouth to be trained as a radio telegraphist. He served on the Polish cruiser *Conrad* and then on a Polish motor torpedo boat, operating from Channel ports. The Poles had eight MTBs; two were sunk. Zygmunt came through the war unscathed and went up to Oxford University on a grant from the Polish government-in-exile. On one occasion, hitchhiking up to London, he was given a ride by an elderly lady in a huge Daimler limousine. It was only when they pulled up in front of some gates in London, and the old lady said imperiously, 'Young man, you must get out now—this is where I live,' and Zygmunt recognized Buckingham Palace, that he realized that this was Queen Mary. He received a master of laws degree from Oxford. He failed his final exam at the London School of Economics, which he attended next. The only job he could find was in a restaurant in Park Lane. He became a waiter, and in his spare time wrote short stories in Polish. After a dreadful year or so he heard of a temporary job with RFE in Munich, and got it. In Munich he met Hildegard, daughter of a distinguished Bavarian civil servant. When the RFE job ended, he and Hildegard, now married, went to London; he was a waiter again, and Hildegard taught German to private students. They lived in East Dulwich with their two small children. But once again RFE called, and they have been in Munich ever since.

"I feel fortunate to have escaped the worst," Zygmunt says, "to be here now—to have *not* been in Poland during the German occupation—to have *not* died in a concentration camp or the Katyn Forest—to be able to say that the worst moments of my life were in the Fifty-Five Restaurant in Park Lane, Mayfair—that is to have been lucky, at my age, as a Pole, living through these years."

Zygmunt's mother had died in 1936. His father remarried after Zygmunt left Poland, but Zygmunt never met his stepmother. His father died during the war. A few years ago Zygmunt had a letter from a lady named Jablonski, living in Gdansk. She had heard Zygmunt on Radio Free Europe—was he her stepson? Since then they have met; she has come on short visits to stay with Zygmunt and Hildegard. Zygmunt sends her parcels of food and occasional gifts of money. She has one room in a small flat in Gdansk, which she doesn't want to leave. All her friends are there.

Most of Zygmunt's friends in Munich are Poles. Zygmunt says that there are probably a hundred thousand Poles in West Germany as visitors but working on the black economy. Many arrived and asked for political asylum—the acts of making the application gave them three months' grace, during which time they could work, earn 10,000 marks or so, buy an old car and then fill it with food and clothing and drive back to Poland, where they could sell the car for ten times what they paid for it. With the proceeds they could buy a house. (Needless to say, this conversation and the circumstances it deals with occurred before the crackdown on Solidarity and military takeover of the government in December 1981.)

"What Poland proves," said Zygmunt, "is that the Communist system of distribution and production does not work. Although I am fearful that the Russians will invade Poland, I think two things are against it—first, the Poles have a keen sense of what is ultimately possible. Second, the Russians may actually recognize what the Polish situation means, and know in their hearts that they have to change their system."

Zygmunt regrets the short stories he has not written during his years at Radio Free Europe, but he is grateful for the occasional acknowledgment of what he has been doing instead. On the plane with the Pope coming back from America, he was greeted by John Paul II, Karol Wojtyla, who paused in the aisle and said to Zygmunt, "Thank all your colleagues at Radio Free Europe for their work in keeping Poland informed."

prolonged my break in Munich. I put the car in a garage for a much needed service, and when a Czechoslovak visitor's visa came through, flew to Prague. Clouds covered the forested hills on the Bavarian border. Down there were the blue-and-white marker posts, the patrols, the errant dogs—worth a smile except for the fact that the Czechoslovak guards would attempt to seize and possibly shoot anyone trying to get out of Czechoslovakia that way. Emigrating Poles were still finding it simple just then to drive or take the train across Czechoslovakia on their way to Austria, but this was brought to a halt by the Czech government in December 1981 so as to prevent any spread of the Polish disease. Most Czechs had nothing but admiration for the Poles, and kept their fingers crossed that the Poles wouldn't get what they got in 1968, after a similar period of dissent and reform that appeared to threaten the Soviet system. "If only the government would prohibit the East Germans' coming here," said one of the people I knew in Prague—a friend of Czech friends I have in London. "They act as if everything here belonged to them." The Czechs call the East Germans *Dederones*, which is a pun on both the initials DDR and the Czech word for nylon, and indicates their feeling that the East Germans—to be recognized by their plastic raincoats and artificial-leather shoes—are synthetic people. It seems we all need an enemy—the West

Germans and Czechs have the East Germans; some Bavarian farmers feel that way about the Czechs. And yet some of those East German tourists in plastic coats one sneers at in Prague may be the same people who seemed at once depressed and friendly on the trams in East Berlin—or people like the Wetzels.

I took a bus, which was free, in from the airport. The hotel where I had a room for a week was fairly small, furnished in modern Scandinavian style. There was a telephone in my room but I had been told before that my conversations might be monitored, so I used public phones instead. None of the people I was hoping to see were directly connected with any of the main dissident groups, and so it was unlikely that their telephones were tapped. But a crackdown was on against dissenters from the ultra-orthodoxy of Gustav Husak's regime—eight had recently been detained (and at the year's end were still in detention, among some sixty political prisoners, awaiting trial on a charge of "subversion of the republic"). I thought therefore that my movements might be watched, and not wanting to involve any of my acquaintances with the security police, was for the first time in my life careful in these respects. Apprehension made me suitably nervous, so that I hung up if I heard any clicks or static on the telephone line, kept looking behind to see if I was being followed, and wouldn't have taken the first cab if I had thought that a second cab would ever appear (as in most East European cities, public transport in Prague is cheap and efficient, but taxis are hard to come by).

I was in Prague as a tourist. In my passport, where for occupation it said "Writer," the visa authorities had inserted a mimeographed slip of paper: "Notice for Journalists—Tourist visas do not authorize the holder to journalistic activities." I decided to regard this warning as a prohibition against sending dispatches from Prague, and not as anything that would stop me from jotting down odds and ends of information in a stiff-backed black notebook I carried everywhere. This notebook was regarded with horror by a number of people in Prague—they were sure I would be detained because of it. With one of them I spent a funny afternoon clipping items—news snippets, jokes, cartoons, photographs and drawings—from brochures, programs and periodicals, to stick into it and make it look like a souvenir scrapbook, if it was examined, say, by the police at the airport as I left. "They have a machine now that can read a letter without opening an envelope," said one of my Prague friends, who keeps a copy of Orwell's *1984* openly displayed on a bookshelf, like a badge of opposition. Whether or not "they" have such a machine, it is perhaps enough that people believe they do. "You wait to get to know someone before telling them your real opinions on anything," I was told. The sort of outspoken conversation you might have with a stranger in a pub in London or at a party in New York was clearly something to avoid here.

In Prague, red banners and placards proclaimed the socialist development, dear to Mr. Steiner. Every house and apartment had a metal flagpole holder affixed to wall or window sill for flying the red flag on days of party celebration. Stars, hammers and sickles, *Socialismus*; loudspeakers attached to lampposts, through which martial music blares on occasions like the First of May. The party seemed ubiquitous, inescapable. " 'Napoleon is always right,' " said someone, quoting a character from another Orwell book, *Animal Farm*. Kafka, Prague's own writer, is regarded as insufficiently suggestive of totalitarianism: "Everything here has far surpassed what he imagined," I was told. Communist indoctrination begins in nursery school at three. There are party representatives in factories, offices, schools, newspapers, apartment buildings, neighborhoods. The party duplicates all forms of management and government from the top down, matching Prime Minister with Party Secretary. About one in fifteen of the population belongs to the party, the self-proclaimed "vanguard." Generally a person is asked to join, as with a club. People do so for profit, promotion or from belief—though the latter is rare except with some of the older generation. Being a member helps in the everyday troubles of life like getting a decent flat, a car, better health care, and better education for one's children. Tatra limousines and executive cars ferry around the privileged elite. Not being a party member means putting up with second best, with envy, with a sense of disenfranchisement, with a submerged sort of life.

I had been in Prague a few years before and now found little changed as I walked around the city. Prague, unlike East Berlin, is beautiful. Despite dirt from the exhaust fumes, the lack of paint on houses, the wooden scaffolding masking many buildings, one is impressed by the solidity and scale of architecture several centuries old. The skyline of the city center is formed from Gothic towers, Renaissance spires and Baroque cupolas, interrupted by few modern tower blocks. Many of the streets are cobbled, the footpaths made with tiny stone blocks. The Vltava River (the Czech name for the Moldau), dividing the city, is spanned by ten bridges, the most ancient and lovely being the narrow Charles Bridge, over which one can stroll from the old town to the old district around Hradcany Castle. There are still monuments to former kings, such as that of Charles IV at one end of his bridge, and the splendid equestrian statue of St. Vaclav, better known by the name of King Wenceslas, in Wenceslas Square. However, the huge statue of a smiling Stalin that used to stand on the hillside overlooking the river and the old town was pulled down in the mid-sixties. It was backed by companion statues. People in Prague used to ask visitors,

"Do you know why Stalin is smiling?" The answer was, "Because he is first in line."

There are still plenty of lines, or queues, in Prague. Women know that for some necessities they must be up at dawn; for other things they must slip out from their jobs. Certain vegetables will be unobtainable, certain cuts of meat only to be had on certain days. (Distribution problems are generally blamed for these shortages.) In my hotel restaurant, despite a long list of vegetables on the menu, only a skimpy salad could be obtained. The last time I was here I was told that half the taps in Prague were dripping for lack of washers. People often buy things they don't really need simply because they are available—and who knows if they will be when you do need them; this is a reflex common throughout the Eastern bloc. Twenty crowns (roughly a dollar) to a salesperson, plus one's phone number, is the best way of ensuring that one finds out quickly when an item has arrived that's been desperately awaited.

Much of what I learned about the pinpricks and pains of life on the other side of the curtain here came from a family whose surname I will keep to myself, and whose Christian names I will change. Milan, as I will call the father, is a former film director in his early fifties; he hasn't had much work since an avant-garde movie he made some years ago won plaudits abroad and annoyed the regime. His wife Elena is a dentist and the main breadwinner of the family. They have two sons, one a biochemist in Czechoslovakia, the other a teacher in West Germany, and a daughter, Margareta, who is twenty-one and wants to be a writer.

I arranged to meet Margareta at the Wenceslas statue, which is where many people in Prague meet when they aren't sure what they're going to do next. The tenth-century warrior prince sits erect on his pacing charger, the ruler who first bound his country to Christianity and the West. Trams stop on either side of the statue, heading up and down the square, which is really a broad avenue in the heart of the city. Here in 1968 and 1969 demonstrations took place against the occupying Soviet forces. Here Czech flags and anti-Russian posters were hung. And nearby, the twenty-one-year-old Prague university student Jan Palach set himself on fire on January 6, 1969, as an act of protest and in the hope of arousing the Czech people. Five hundred thousand lined the streets a few days later as a procession followed his body through the city. Tributes and flowers are still left in the cemetery where he was buried, though his body has been moved away. As a meeting place, the statue of St. Vaclav holds a high charge of association and emotion.

Margareta is tall, with straight reddish-brown hair and round hazel eyes. Slightly broad cheekbones hint at something from east of the Urals in her ancestry. With her, in the next few days, I met people—her friends, her parents' friends—and saw aspects of the city. We went to the place in Letenske Sady Park, where, on Sunday mornings, youngsters in blue jeans trade Western pop records—and Margareta added to her collection of Jethro Tull. We went to mass in a church that seemed fairly full for a weekday service, not only with women and old people, as in some Western countries, but with quite a lot of young people, too. We walked through department stores and museums, rode the trams and the excellent new Metro with its futuristic stations and slightly old-fashioned Russian rolling stock, and rowed in a rented boat on the Vltava. We sat in coffeeshops talking about life, its possibilities and limitations. We browsed in Tuzex shops, which sell for coupons purchased dearly with Czech money or, more reasonably, for hard, foreign currency, which the state desperately needs, all sorts of hard-to-get and luxury items. Although Margareta's parents did not suggest it, I exchanged money with them. They wanted to give me the black-market rate for my pounds and dollars—a rate roughly five times the official exchange and nearly three times the special tourist rate; but we compromised on a rate halfway between the black market and tourist rates, which was pleasing to both of us. Margareta's mother was saving for a visit to her son in West Germany, for which she hoped to get permission, but for which the necessary Western currency would be hard to come by.

Perhaps at this point I should mention some of Margareta's personal history. She graduated nearly at the top of her class but had not been accepted at the university. She had been offered a scholarship by a university in California, and for the last three years had unsuccessfully been seeking permission to take it up. In 1980 she had asked for an exit permit to go to France for four days, to visit a young Frenchman she'd met in Prague, but this had also been turned down as "not in the interests of the state." She believed that she had several black marks in her file. Her father was not a party member; indeed he was *persona non grata* as a result of his avant-garde filmmaking. Her brother in Germany had left the country on a so-called visit, and stayed abroad; he had not yet regularized his position by paying the Czech government roughly $5,000 for an emigration permit (a sum based on a notional cost of his education), which would enable him to return home on visits. Presumably one reason Margareta had not been allowed her French trip was that the authorities would have been suspicious of anyone asking for a trip as short as four days. In fact, she told me, she'd been hard at work trying to finish a science-fiction story; she only had time for four days in France. Her problems have been increased by reason of her failure to be admitted to the Writers' Union. It is hard for her, with her father's name, to find publishers and editors willing to give her commissions or publish her fiction; she has written her most recent stories under a pseudonym.

The Iron Curtain assumes an iron reality when a Czech wants to travel to the West. (Traveling east, going to Bulgarian Black Sea resorts or on Russian cruise ships, is less difficult, except that such tours are often sold out long in advance.) As in East Germany, those who are past retirement age and those with close relatives in the West are generally given permission to go abroad—and others with a clean record in the eyes of the regime were allowed one trip to the West every three to five years. (However, new restrictions imposed in February 1982 are likely to reduce these.) Margareta's mother told me what she had to do in order to visit her son in Düsseldorf.

First, she had to get a written invitation from him. This had to be endorsed by the Düsseldorf police because without the endorsement the Czech officials wouldn't believe it was genuine.

Second, she had to go to her local district legal department which gave her—after a two-week wait and a payment of 6 crowns—a certificate saying that she had never been to prison.

Third, she had to queue up at her local police station for an exit-permit application form. This generally required further standing in line on two days, once to leave the forms with the right official at the permit department and then to pick it up.

Next with all the papers she returned to the police. Here there was another line, whose length depended on the season. She handed in the papers and was told to return in two or three weeks for the exit permit. If when she returned it wasn't waiting for her, she knew that refusal was on the way to her. Even if the permit had been granted, she had to pay a 300-crown "exit tax" at the state bank before leaving. She was allowed to exchange only a small amount of Czech money for hard currency, and at a punitive rate of exchange. Yet she felt fortunate—she was one of the lucky Czechs allowed to leave for the West once a year. It remained a mystery why she was given permission and Margareta wasn't.

There are disadvantages for some who go abroad: they may not be able to get back in again even though they want to. Pavel Kohout, the playwright whose works were being performed in Coburg, was permitted to go to Vienna with his wife in the fall of 1978 to work for a year at the Burg Theater. In the course of that year he refused to make any public political statements, despite the arrest of several friends in Czechoslovakia and their conviction. But when he tried to return to his country on October 8, 1979, he was not let in. A day or so later he was told by the Czechoslovak embassy in Vienna that he had been deprived of his nationality because of his "subversive activities abroad." When his appeal against this decision was rejected, the embassy told him that his wife Elena was also being deprived of her citizenship. The reason given was that she was continuing to live with him!

The system that punishes dissenters in this way does a good job of looking after the faithful. Party members have special hotels and hospitals—though Margareta's mother told me, sardonically, that the medical staff members are chosen for their party loyalty rather than their medical skills. Children of party members are favored for entrance to higher education, and some are sent to "finishing school" in the USSR—which they don't always regard as a favor (a friend of Margareta's commited suicide while studying in Russia). Nonparty members have less chance of taking up grants and fellowships abroad. Party members generally get higher pay, better housing and better prospects of promotion. Writers and actors who are party members do not run into savage criticism from reviewers. Yet it is said to be more of a Mafia than a Freemasonry; mistrust rather than mutual protection is rife among the membership. Even party members, discussing a particular mistake of policy, will speak of "they" ("They insisted on doing such and such . . .") in just the same way that the rest of the nation does.

Some people dread being asked to join the party; it will be a mark against them if they say no; it will foul up their lives altogether to be taken in and later thrown out during a purge. While you are in, the anxieties are considerable: on joining the party, you may lose a number of your friends; in positions of eminence someone is always keeping an eye on you. You are no longer free in many jobs to meet foreigners without reporting whom you met and what was discussed. For the parades in early May you are expected to volunteer for the quota of personnel who have to attend from your place of work—though in exchange for a bottle of wine or a favor owed, you might manage to get out of carrying a flag or banner.

Being a party member has particular advantages in housing matters. Despite the gradual construction of new apartment buildings around Prague, there is a great shortage of places to live in. Almost all housing is in state ownership or under state control. There is no security of tenure. Each person has a space allowance: a family of three would be entitled to between 36 and 48 square meters, plus a 6-meter family bonus—say, three 12-foot-square rooms. However, if the family drops below that number, some of the space is supposed to be relinquished, a lodger or a co-tenant taken in, or the flat exchanged for a smaller one (generally with an under-the-table cash adjustment with the family moving in). Most people would rather keep their flat, which in all likelihood is not large enough as it is. They therefore practice various deceits, and if necessary bribe housing officials. Margareta, who lives at home, can scarcely envisage a time when she will cease to do so. Until recently, when her second brother left, she had never known the luxury of having a room of her own. She does, however, have a chance of inheriting her grandmother's small flat because she is registered as living with her (a fairly well-known dodge in Prague). And when the grandmother dies Margareta should be able to inherit it as co-resident.

A thirty-year-old photographer friend of hers, Josef, whom she introduced me to, has paid a deposit for a state co-op flat. He has been on the waiting list for eight years; because he is single he is low on the priority list; and because the co-op is building flats fifteen kilometers from Prague, he isn't sure he will ever want to live there. He thought of joining a self-build scheme, putting in two or three years of evenings and weekends with a group constructing a small apartment building, but eventually found and bought rights to an empty attic, which he started to convert. Unfortunately, the people down below, through whose apartment new pipework would run, complained to the authorities and work stopped. Josef then advertised the attic—or use of it—for sale, "with special circumstances." What this meant was that anyone with good connections, particularly party members, would be able to get around the red tape and the impediment caused by the people below; he had several sizable offers and soon sold it. Josef is still living at home and feels now and then that he is going out of his mind. According to Margareta, he spends more and more of his time in a local bar.

A lot of talent is obviously wasted in Prague; a lot of energy goes into various schemes and stratagems for getting around the system. Although, with an officious and ubiquitous police, there is said to be little street crime, there is also said to be a great deal of larceny and fraud. Most people regard it as all right to rip off whatever state organization they work for. Margareta's brother, the biochemist, has a still at work where he makes splendid liqueurs. The saying is, "The person who doesn't steal deprives his children." And yet a number of people are constantly in trouble with the authorities for honorable work: for writing a book, making a film. There is no unemployment compensation in Czechoslovakia, and following one's vocation often means depending on the charity of friends and relatives— or taking a menial job if it can be found. Margareta's mother gets a fair salary as a dentist; she also gets various "presents" from patients who want special treatment. Since her husband hasn't made a film for ten years, she can't afford to refuse these gifts. Many of their friends who signed Charter

77, which demands the restoration of civil and human rights in Czechoslovakia, lost their jobs, their driving licenses, their telephones. One friend, a lawyer, is now working as a gardener. For a while the philosopher Julius Tomin was a night watchman at the Prague Zoo, and conducted private seminars at his apartment. In 1980 he was dragged down three flights of stairs by the police, bundled into a car, questioned at the police station for several hours, and then, having refused to cooperate, dumped in a coal yard some way from home. Some of his subsequent seminars were broken up by the police. Tomin and his family have now been expelled from the country.

Writers can be arrested for "publishing" their own books in carbon-copied typescripts which are then passed from hand to hand. Plays may be rehearsed but are often closed before opening night as "not in the interests of the people." Margareta's father told me that most writers, editors and directors learn to work according to unwritten guidelines: productions should be optimistic; there shouldn't be any unresolved problems; no Jewish heroes—for the regime is anti-Zionist. "Associations" can be troublesome—a script that purports to be set in the past and be against the Austro-Hungarian Empire may be read as anti-Russian; historical plots and allegorical themes may be too relevant and get the producers into hot water. (One Flew Over the Cuckoo's Nest, the film of Ken Kesey's book about life in a mental hospital for the sane and insane, has been shown in East Germany and Hungary, but not in Czechoslovakia—perhaps it isn't the theme of the film but the fact that Milos Forman, its director, is an expatriate Czech is the reason it isn't shown.) Another difficulty is that there is little censorship in advance, which makes things easier from the government's point of view. People don't know where they stand; they censor themselves out of anxiety and keep a sharp eye on what happens to someone who tries something different. Many have to make compromises in order to make a living—artists who are refused an artist's registration card are unable to buy materials from art-supply shops.

In this sort of situation some make out. Many moonlight—plumbers, electricians, car mechanics thrive. Bribes are given to get things done or prevent things from being done. In Margareta's aunt's apartment building, plumbers sent by the housing authority were bribed by the residents not to start a pipe-repair project that everyone knew would result in no running water for six months. A "tip" of 60 crowns can get you a certificate saying your dog is a hunter or retriever or watchdog, with a smaller license fee in consequence; a similar sum can get you a single room at a spa if you don't want to share a double with a stranger. "The worst thing about this regime is that it brings out the cheat in people," Margareta said to me one day. Everyone has some guilty secrets is the assumption—and a self-confident person can get away with a lot by suggesting to those in authority that he or she knows something about what they're up to. Going out to lunch on one occasion with Margareta's mother, we were told there was no room for us in the restaurant because of the expected arrival of an East German tour party. Margareta's mother asked to see the manager. She had a short conversation with him, which—I gathered—contained a few hints of knowledge about how the restaurant got its meat supplies, and we soon had a table and immediate service.

"You grow up very shrewd here, a bit bent, not trusting people," said Margareta. "We have a double life from the start, learning in school about Marxism and Communism, and then coming home and having our parents tell us it's all nonsense." Most teachers don't believe what they have to teach in this area; a few of the braver ones, supposed to be lecturing, say, on Marx, talk about anything else, from Aristotle to Diana Ross—but try to make sure their students have a good idea before the exams of what the questions on Marx will be.

The system also creates a separation between a person's inner life and the life he is forced to lead for the state. Most people don't try too hard in their working lives. There are constant efforts to improve efficiency in management, and plans for worker participation, but top jobs remain reserved for party members, who often duplicate the executive functions of directors and managers. The rigid system makes for constant failures in production, distribution and servicing—though not on quite the grand scale that brought on the Polish debacle. A lot of shops are closed part of the time because they can't get enough help. Because a manager would rather obtain two hours' work a day from an idle worker than fire him and have no work done at all because there is no replacement, labor discipline is slack and morale is low. Margareta's mother said, "It's a system that suits the second-rate—those who don't have great aspirations or don't want to try too hard." Everything runs at half speed—in research institutes, in assembly plants, on the land. A forester told me that he felt immensely thwarted—he liked doing his job well, but "the self-perpetuating mediocrities" in charge of his forest region blocked his efforts. They were the sort of people in every sphere, he thought, who were slowing the nation down.

I drove out into the country on Friday evening with Margareta and her parents. The family has a small cottage about an hour's drive south of Prague toward the Bavarian border. Margareta's father built a lot of it with his own hands—"I've had the time," he said. Just about everyone in

Prague seems to have such a cottage, or hopes of one, even if it is only a fixed-up garden shed on a vegetable allotment not far from town. Many of the Charter 77 dissidents have moved out to country cottages and are attempting to lead Thoreau-like existences. The system will not let them participate; they have withdrawn themselves as much as they can from the system. Unlike city flats, cottages are a form of property for which one can still buy land (at some difficulty and expense), build the structure, and either pass it on to one's heirs or sell it. Cottages are not only a means of getting away from the cramped conditions of city apartment life, and the day-to-day difficulties imposed by the totalitarian regime, but also an agency for expressing one's personality in architecture and carpentry, for expending skill and hard work, and for spending money for which there aren't enough outlets. There is insulation to be put in the roof, grass to mow, shutters to hang. The government appears to tolerate the cottages because of their value as a safety value. Disagreeable economic announcements—like a rise in the price of coffee—are made in the afternoon before people set off for a weekend or vacation at their cottages. Most traffic accidents seem to take place on Friday evenings, when people are dashing off for a weekend of relative freedom. "Our real life is led down here," Margareta's mother said when we arrived at their cottage, which is built on a hillside with a view over treetops at a distant river. "Here we breathe deeply and think—well, almost freely."

I had the impression that Czechs of fifty years of age and older had a double nostalgia—for the Republic, which lasted from 1919 to 1939, the one period in modern times when Czechoslovakia was a free and independent nation; and for 1968, when there seemed for a while a chance of introducing open dissent, doubt and debate—the basic factors of democracy—into the arid Communist state. This nostalgia might be thought debilitating, but it co-exists with two up-to-date feelings: a total hatred of the Soviet Union, and a widespread sense that the West is not to be relied on. Czechs are on their own. This disenchantment with the West goes back to Munich in 1938, when England and France abandoned Czechoslovakia to Hitler; and it was reinforced by events in 1968. Most people, rightly or wrongly, are convinced that the United States knew that the Soviet Union would send in the Warsaw Pact troops on August 21 that year and effectively, over the following year, introduce the hard-line Husak regime. Seventy thousand Soviet troops are now stationed in Czechoslovakia. Sometimes small parties of them are to be seen, wearing their distinctive wide-peaked khaki hats, visiting historic sites. (My hotel, like others in Prague, had menus printed in both Czech and Russian, catering to Russian tourists and advisers.) But most Russians who come to Prague are apparently aware of their unpopularity, and, for example, when asking directions, will go through linguistic or semaphoric gymnastics to avoid letting on where they come from. (Yugoslavs have some words that sound similar to Russian, and are inclined to introduce themselves in Czech shops and cafés with the statement "I am from Yugoslavia," which ensures that they get served.) In fact, though things are bad in the CSSR, Czechoslovaks take comfort in the thought that shortages, restrictions and censorship are worse in the USSR. Czechoslovakia does not have a Gulag archipelago. The Soviet empire is one where most of the colonies are in most ways better off than the imperial country.

On Saturday night I suggested a visit to the inn in the nearby village, but Margareta's father didn't think it advisable. Although the village people were friendly to them, and probably of liberal sympathies (the last time he'd been in the inn some men had sung a prewar song about Thomas Masaryk, President of the First Republic), it was quite possible that someone would note and pass on the information that a foreigner was staying in the area. Questions might be asked why he hadn't registered at the police station. It could be used as an excuse for further investigation. So we drank some wine at home. The wood stove was fired up, and Mozart's Clarinet Concerto came from the record player. We talked about "other things"—about plays, books, films in London, small-town life in the United States. But talk came gradually back to how one lived on this side of the Curtain. I was particularly interested in how one put up with the fact that there was little hope of change. In the West, whatever the difficulties arising from the remoteness of those who lead from those who are led in large democracies, one always had the feeling that things could be altered for the better with one's own effort: another party might come to power at the next election; one's votes and energies, however small, might make a difference. But here?

"It is like living in a year without seasons," said Margareta's father. "It will go on and on like this. We would be deluding ourselves to think otherwise. As long as the present balance of power exists in the world, nothing will alter in Czechoslovakia. Maybe, in twenty or in fifty years, China will make a difference. Maybe something will happen that will affect the Soviet Union so that it loosens its grip slightly—the energy crisis, the Muslim expansion, natural catastrophe." But most people don't believe there will ever be a return to Western-style capitalism here, and they find it hard to envisage, in any future "liberalization," the Communist party allowing any genuine democratic party system, with a real opposition, which might result in the Communists being turned out of office. (Of course, since that conversation, everything that has happened in Poland has shown the justification for such pessimism.)

"Now and then we imagine that we can see small signs of improvement," said Margareta's mother. "Someone we know may be given a job after eight years of not being able to work at his profession. When an official retires, there is a chance his replacement will change things a little." You hear gossip—an actress I know told me that she understood the top men would like to ease conditions a bit, but they don't know how. You read an article or see a play on TV and think it means something, an indication of movement in the ice that surrounds us. But if you talk about this to a friend with a hopeful note in your voice, he is liable to say, 'Oh, you're suffering from an attack of normal thinking.' "

"It is a matter of sheer survival with some," said her husband. "If you have been in prison several times, had various successes and reverses, you get to feel like an animal that has been hurt and doesn't want to lose its life altogether. You develop a shell, you reduce your area of consciousness, of perception, of sensation. You make a very small space in which you live, where you can cut yourself off and not let the propaganda penetrate."

He went out to split some logs for the stove, though the warmth was not yet diminished.

Margareta's mother said, "Who knows, if we can just go on, survive physically, it may be different for future generations. Margareta may see it."

Margareta met me again on my last day in Prague. As I waited by King Wenceslas on his horse, I noticed a new forged chain, with links like manacles, that had been hung around the plinth to keep people off— though it seemed almost as much to keep the good king in. When Margareta arrived, we walked first of all to the old Jewish cemetery, where the confined ground over the centuries has grown higher within the high walls, pressed up, so it seems, by the crush of bodies within. Here are twenty thousand graves and several thousand headstones leaning together, their Hebraic inscriptions worn away—mounds and barrows, graves upon graves, a forest of stones holding up one another. I had been reading Kafka, son of Prague, whose books haven't been on sale there since 1968. In a story called "Resolutions" he writes:

So perhaps the best resource is to meet everything passively, to make yourself an inert mass, and, if you feel that you are being carried away, not to let yourself be lured into taking a single unnecessary step, to stare at others with the eyes of an animal, to feel no compunction, in short, with your own hand to throttle down whatever ghostly life remains in you, that is, to enlarge the final peace of the graveyard and let nothing survive save that.

A prescription for living in a totalitarian state.

An old man looked out of a third-floor window overlooking the cemetery. Music—more Mozart—came from another window; it sounded like a string quartet being rehearsed, at once more slow-moving and more spacious than it probably would be when later performed. Mozart was another, though temporary, resident of Prague. His music seemed like the purest exhalation of freedom—a balance for Kafka.

We had lunch in the Slavia café, whose shabby thirties elegance provided a suitable home for numerous quiet conversations, suggesting that intellectual and romantic activity were by no means absent. Margareta said in a whisper, when I mentioned this, "Yes, there are many things you don't say too loudly. You don't know who is sitting at the next table."

We saved some talk for a little park, not far from Wenceslas Square. It had begun to rain, a sort of English drizzle. We took shelter in a stone grotto with a bench. An old lady came in from the rain and sat down beside Margareta; she obviously wanted to talk. She told Margareta about a film she'd seen the day before, about the Russian liberation of Prague in 1945. She talked about the trees in the park, which didn't look very healthy. It was the pollution from industrial fumes that was killing them, she said. She added to the local pollution by lighting a foul-smelling cigarette. But she didn't mind Margareta going on talking in English to me. We had been watching the sparrows—one flew in and found a crumb under the bench and flew out again. Big drops of water fell off the overhanging lip of the grotto roof and splashed at our feet. I had been wondering in the past few days what I could do to help Margareta. Would she leave Czechoslovakia? I had heard that it was possible to do so if one married a foreigner. I wasn't putting myself forward as a husband, even a temporary, bigamous one, but I knew at least one man in London who would have volunteered. I asked her. But she said she couldn't leave—didn't want to leave. Her family needed her. It would remain difficult there; life would be easier if she went to America, Britain or France. But she felt that she had got used to living with a minimum of possessions. She said, "It's best not to want anything too much—once you do, you're in the grip of a corrupt system, having to bribe or sign things you don't believe in, or even to join the party. I want to know as much as I can about what's going on. I don't want to turn my back on the problems of living here. Some of my friends have married and have children and have such a struggle to make ends meet that they have no time to worry about their real rights and freedoms. I don't want to be like that."

At the airport the customs and passport officials looked at me intently. I had had an uneasy night—nightmares with sea monsters. Would I be searched? What did I say when they opened my notebook? But I wasn't searched. The notebook with its pasted-in tram tickets and comic strips stayed in my raincoat pocket. I walked up the steps to the Lufthansa plane past the Czechoslovak soldier with his machine pistol, and gave the stewardess a big smile as she looked at my boarding pass and handed me the *Süddeutsche Zeitung*. At Frankfurt airport, where I changed planes and the Bundesgrenzschutz and Zoll were on the lookout for terrorists, my raincoat and suitcase were thoroughly searched, but I didn't mind in the least.

22. ANOTHER COUNTRY

I drove from Munich to Passau, where the Inn joins the Danube. Austria's proximity was advertised by many cars with Austrian license plates and the clear radio reception of Österreich Eins, broadcasting Bach and Braun. The news mentioned a Soviet ultimatum to the Poles—which may have been the first of many that year—telling them to set their house in proper Communist order. The road came out of the relatively flat land around Munich into long valleys between wooded hills, with mist rising out of the woods. And then Passau, which the guidebooks call a border town, full of splendid Baroque churches and houses, for the most part on a peninsula between the converging rivers. Young Adolf Hitler lived in Passau from 1892 to 1895, from the ages of three to six. It occurred to me that I hadn't seen any signs of neo-Nazism in my journey through West Germany. I hadn't looked for it; it hadn't flung itself at me. The DDR authorities are inclined to suggest that it is rampant in the Federal Republic (one of the East German magazines Herr Steiner had given me made a big thing of it). A copy of the news magazine *Der Spiegel* from March 1981 which I came across in Munich discussed two recent surveys into right-wing attitudes among West Germans. One survey found that one in three Germans harbored strong anti-Semitic prejudices, while one in eight believed that foreign workers were a threat to the German race and that West Germany needed a Führer or strong single party. The second survey found that extreme-right-wing people blamed the Western Allies and particularly the Americans for the collapse of the country's values and moral fiber. However, these attitudes seem to be more common among older people and in rural areas, and actual voting figures cast some doubt on whether the right wing in West Germany could be as large as these surveys suggested. Some political analysts believe that in fact it is about 5 percent, half what it was ten years before. The neo-Nazi National Democratic Party polled less than 1 percent in the elections of October 1980.

I stayed in a hotel near the tip of the peninsula and before nightfall walked down to the stone-embanked point where the Inn adds its green-gray waters to the browner Danube. A smaller river, the Ilz, also adds its contribution from the north, as the great stream pours eastward through Austria toward the Balkans and the Black Sea. In July it had flooded the ground floors of most of the buildings in this part of the old town. At dinner it seemed that my German had got rusty from a week in Prague—it was at any rate incomprehensible to the waiter who served me. I asked for *Apfelstrudel* and got instead a bottle of *Sprudel*, which was soda water. I drank the *Sprudel* and ordered a different dessert, a *Bayernbecher* of cherries, strawberries, cream and ice cream, over which there was no confusion.

From Passau it is twenty-five kilometers to the mountainous place where the German, Czech and Austrian borders come together. Nearby is the Dreisessel (the three chairs), where a rock formation at the top of a granite ridge resembles three seats, which local tradition believes represent Bohemia, Bavaria and Austria. On the way there I passed prosperous-looking dairy farms with Alpine-style houses. In the small town of Wald-kirchen, bells were summoning people to church, the men in local costume, the women in dirndl dresses. Then the hills became steep-sided, round-topped and thickly forested. On a bend of the road going up the Dreisessel a sign warned Allied military personnel: "Attention—50 meters to the Border." I got out and walked up the slope to the blue-and-white border posts and a LANDESGRENZE sign. There was nothing to be seen in Czecho-slovakia except trees.

From a parking lot I climbed a tarmac path to a little hostelry, built next to a point of railed-off land that is Czech. The only access for vehicles bringing supplies to the inn is across this point of land, for which purpose barriers in the fence are raised, presumably with Czech permission, and despite signs erected by the Bavarian Border Police, intended for the general public, saying: "Do Not Enter." When I got there, children were running across the triangle, giggling with the excitement of doing something forbidden. The three seats are to be found on a spur of rock next to the inn but I didn't sit in any of them, since the amount of mist billowing through the air at that height was equal to rain and formed a pool in each of the three shallow basins of rock. For pre-lunch exercise I walked along a path to the next outcrop, the Hochstein, the highest point on this part of the border. The wind had been strong before, but here it blew like a gale at sea. A young couple in navy-blue sweaters arrived and asked me in English how far it was to the Dreisessel. We had a short conversation about the weather and the border. They were English tourists and had been walking around in the mist, somewhat in circles, and had apparently managed not to walk into Czechoslovakia. A coin-operated telescope placed here was of little use in the mist, which hid everything beyond the treetops fifty meters away. A grid next to it gave directions to and the names of places in Bohemian Sudetenland and the distance—106 kilometers—to Prague, to Margareta and her family. In the inn I had a celebratory last lunch in Germany of beer, bratwurst, sauerkraut and potatoes, and cheese cake.

I drove that afternoon along a country road toward Schwartzenberg in Austria. The same hills, meadowed below, rising to higher, forested ground along the Czech border; the same chalets; same onion-domed churches. At the Bavarian-Austrian border the West German control post was an ordinary house built next to the lifting barrier. A Bavarian border official took my passport and car documents into the house. I could see him through the window on the phone, as presumably he checked to see that I wasn't a terrorist or car thief. When he returned, handing me passport and papers, he said in English, "Thank you, Mr. Bailey." The Austrian border officials were sitting on kitchen chairs by the roadside two hundred yards farther on. One of them got up, glanced at my passport and waved me through. Hitler's father, Alois, was a customs officer on the Bavarian-Austrian border at Braunau, on the Inn—where Hitler was born—before he was posted to Passau and then Linz.

This part of Austria is called the Mühlviertel (the mill quarter) and I had arrived at it more than halfway east along the northern border of the country. From here I intended to travel around the bulge that Austria makes to the east—a horseshoe route around the two upper chains of Alps, then south to the Adriatic. It was a journey, I saw from the map, that also resembled the shape of a question mark, omitting the underlying dot.

But despite the fact that I was traveling as far east as one can get in non-Communist Central Europe, I felt—perhaps prematurely—that I was leaving behind in Germany some of the less tractable aspects of the journey together with the SM-70s, the mines and the *Aufklärer*. The Austrian countryside had something to do with this mood. It was pastoral: small farms, gentle fields, quietly munching cows. For the moment I had no appointments. I drove from place name to place name, prompted by words that looked pleasant on the map. Aigen was a trim little town a few kilometers from the Czech border, with winter sports when there was snow. St. Oswald, a nearby village, was a collection of farms and suburban-looking houses right on the border, with chickens wandering in the street. St. Oswald—like Wenceslas both saint and king—seems to have been venerated far from his Northumbrian homeland, saints being the stars or heroes of the Dark Ages; his name crops up in villages also in Bavaria and northern Italy. He died in battle against the heathen Penda of Mercia in A.D. 642, and the story has it that as he fell he prayed aloud for those who died with him.

A lane ran out of St. Oswald northward. A cross and memorial stone gave the names of villages just inside Czechoslovakia, including Asang, Rosenhügel, Berneck and Linden, where German-speaking people had lived before 1945. The lane petered out by what had once been the customs house and was now being converted into apartments. The lane continued as a single track for a few hundred meters through woods to the border. A red-and-white barrier, a sign saying STAATSGRENZE; a wide field beyond, then coniferous woods, at the edge of which I could just make out the Czech fence. There were numerous birds in the trees roundabout, wild flowers, wet grass, and the sun almost out.

An old lady wearing a flowered apron and rubber boots, with a permanent blink, one eye shut, came out of the woods carrying a basket of mushrooms. She told me the road had been closed since the end of the war; one rarely saw any patrols, Czech or Austrian, along here. (Austria has no special border police; its border is looked after by the usual gendarmerie. I was told in Vienna that there was little need to patrol the border: "The other side do it for us.")

I was in Haslach by midafternoon, a small market town near the border, and after a short walk around, decided to spend the night there. The sights were soon seen: the market square, surrounded by old brick houses; the church; the museum of weaving machinery in a former mill. Both museum and church displayed small blue-and-white signs saying, in English, German, French and Russian, that they were "Cultural Property," protected by the Hague Convention of 1954 in the event of armed conflict. Why does "culture" imagine itself less vulnerable than homes, offices, schools and factories in any war to come? As if age and beauty, warranted by official signs, were any protection. Haslach itself, though not the sort of town to make the guidebooks, is a fine place. Behind the church, in a little orchard on one of several sloping terraces of ground, an old man was shaking figs from a tree. The sun had come out and it was warm.

At the Pension Ortner the owner was away and two elderly ladies running the café were unable to say whether there was a room free. So I sat and drank coffee and read while the radio emitted the sounds of yodeling—a form of singing perhaps no less melodious than that current in Detroit or Liverpool but for some reason comic to the Anglo-Saxon ear. When the owner, Herr Griesser, returned from a Sunday-afternoon drive with his wife and children, he showed me a comfortable bedroom and bathroom at the back—charge for the night roughly £3.50 or $6. There were four or five other guests, and we dined in the rear room of the café while the front room filled up with regulars, mostly elderly men, with whom Herr Griesser had a drink or a hand of cards in between helping Frau Griesser wait on the dining tables.

In the morning I walked around the corner to the Rathaus, facing the market square, to talk with the mayor, Friedrich Andexlinger; the town secretary, Josef Cupak; and a secondary-school teacher, Josef Wolkerstorfer, who translated for us. Haslach was like other towns on the border with the East: it had lost its Czech hinterland; it had lost its cross-border traffic, particularly that between weavers here and in the Sudetenland. The border area on both sides had lost population. At least one person in ten in Haslach still had relatives there. Now the textile industry here mostly employed women, and the men of Haslach commuted to Linz to the huge steel works or to office jobs in the regional center of Rohrbach. Before the war the two dozen houses in the marketplace had been owned by farmers; now only one was. The farmers had built new houses outside the town. Haslach, however, still has 126 house owners who are permitted to call themselves burghers, and who have special rights to firewood in the town woods. There is no contact with Czech farmers, who all work for a state organization. Tourists are mostly West German, with many from West Berlin, and they tend to be older people seeking peace and quiet. "Not the Club Méditerranée crowd or casino addicts," said Wolkerstorfer. Haslach also sees a great number of hikers, as it is on a long-distance trail that roughly follows this section of the border and that since 1973 has been part of a European trail that goes from Roskilde on the Danish Baltic coast to Rijeka in Yugoslavia. Some bits of this trail, I now saw from a booklet Herr Cupak gave me, I had in fact walked along in

Bleckede, the Harz, Coburg, Furth-im-Wald and the Dreisessel; but I'd had to get to Haslach to find out about it.

From 1945 to 1955 Haslach was in the Soviet zone of occupied Austria. There is a graveyard in which numerous Soviet personnel were buried; many Haslach schoolchildren of that generation learned Russian. Although Austria had been annexed by Germany in 1938, the view of the Allies during the war was that Hitler's aggression had been matched by Austrian acquiescence and even (with some people) enthusiasm for incorporation in the Third Reich, and that Austria shared some responsibility for the war. At the London meetings of the European Advisory Commission, Soviet Ambassador F. T. Gusev wanted a plan for the postwar occupation of Austria put to the Allied governments at the same time as the plan for Germany, but the U.S. government, according to Lord Strang, couldn't make up its mind whether it wanted an occupation zone in Austria or not. By the time it had, the Soviet army was in Vienna and Gusev was truculent. It took strong interventions with Stalin by Churchill and Truman to secure an agreement on Austria that did not give the Soviet Union more than an equal share in occupation rights, and ensure the formation of a free Austrian government. The Communist Party failed to get more than 5 percent of the vote in the November 1945 elections. Austria, while being regarded with some ambivalence as part of the former enemy empire, was able to make most of its own decisions through a long occupation, and the democracy that emerged began to strive for a neutral position between the two power blocs. Two of the main obstacles to a final peace settlement were the question of German assets in Austria, which the Russians wanted a large share of, and the matter of Soviet rights in Austrian oil fields. But Stalin's death in 1953 seemed to speed up the treaty negotiations and caused the Soviet occupation authorities to ease various restrictions. The Austrian State Treaty was finally signed on May 15, 1955, and Austrian sovereignty was restored. The last occupying troops had left the country by October 26, when the Austrian parliament approved a law on Austrian neutrality—a day since celebrated as a national holiday.

"Things were more backward in the Soviet zone," said Herr Andexlinger. "There was much less investment in industry, because no one felt sure of the future. Until 1955 we weren't certain the Soviets were going to leave. In fact, we still consider ourselves lucky. This is the only part of Europe where they have been and then gone away."

I didn't feel I needed to cling to the border. Austria is small and its position makes all of it feel like border country, pushed out into the Eastern world. The Turks, coming northwest, got to Vienna in 1529 and 1683, and many towns still have memorials thanking God for deliverance from the Ottoman scourge. Russian armies have fought on Austrian ground in previous centuries. I drove to Linz, Austria's third largest city, a steel and chemical manufacturing place where the Danube widens to become a great waterway. The Romans were here (and now Italian words begin to appear in signs for tourists). Johannes Kepler, the great seventeenth-century astronomer and mathematician, taught in Linz. Here Mozart composed his Linz Symphony, Beethoven his Eighth Symphony, and Anton Bruckner, the Linz cathedral organist, numerous works. The first railway line on the European continent went from Linz to Budweis in southern Bohemia, following a medieval trade route north to Prague. And in Linz, Adolf Hitler went to secondary school from 1900 to 1905. He was good at drawing, excellent at gymnastics, and was considered "very satisfactory" in moral conduct. The headmaster was a German nationalist, and in a speech in 1902 assured his listeners that the idea of one nationality for all Germans would be kept in the forefront of school life. He also expressed the hope that "the German spirit which has inspired our pupils in the past shall never be allowed to die." One former pupil, sending his armies into Austria in 1938, did his best—or worst—in that respect. Young Hitler also drew up designs for the replanning of Linz.

Linz was just inside the American zone. On the bridge across the Danube, people had to show their identity card as they entered or left the city. After the Russians left, Austrians let their minds withdraw from the problems of the border; but the 1968 crisis in Czechoslovakia brought it back. A director at the radio station in Linz told me that for ten years after 1968 few people in the city went to Prague. Now, although visas for even a day's visit have to be obtained in advance from the Czechoslovak embassy in Vienna, more people are going there again. From the small town of Gallneukirchen, not far from Linz, a bus goes to Budweis every two weeks with Austrians who shop there for cheaper shoes, sheets, suitcases. Last year's annual excursion for the radio station personnel was to Prague. Out of roughly seventy who applied for visas, two were turned down— both with prior Czech connections, though neither person was given an explanation.

"We don't feel toward the Czechs the way the West Germans do toward the East Germans," the director said. "There's no antipathy. It's mostly a matter of feeling sorrow for them and pleased with our own good fortune. I go there and I see houses with no flowers in window boxes as there are here. And I think how lucky we are to live in a free country."

. . .

Perhaps to counteract this pervasive contentment, which seems to be expressed in the softer German spoken by the Austrians, I left Linz the next morning and decided to make my way to Vienna not along the border or—the fastest route—along the A1 Autobahn, but by the older road along the north bank of the Danube. This road passes through Mauthausen, a small town east of Linz that gave its name to a concentration camp of the Third Reich. In the course of my trip I had passed not far from the sites of other concentration camps—Flossenburg, on the Bavarian plateau east of Weiden, near the Czech border, and Dachau, near Munich. In the litany of Nazi terror, Mauthausen did not rank with Auschwitz and Treblinka; it was not a mass-extermination camp. But it was a slave-labor camp, a place where human beings were concentrated and compressed until they became as dry and fragmentary as powder; a place where some 100,000 people died and many more suffered dreadful torments. It was one of the artifacts by which Hitler maintained his regime. It was a working part of the system that caused the war to go on and end as it did. It led to a divided Europe, a divided Germany.

It was a morning of thick fog. I took several wrong turns and arrived by a roundabout route at the town of Mauthausen, where I asked for directions on how to reach the *Lager*, the camp. It was up another back road, several kilometers away, where the low granite hills of the Danube valley have long been quarried: the paving stones of Vienna came from here. Some of the quarries are still in use, and I could hear heavy machinery at work as I drove up the little road, following signs that said LAGER. And there at the end of the road it was. The fog hung around it—a gray fortress, built of stone quarried on the spot. The gates in the wall under a watchtower were open, but I hesitated before driving in. Even if I hadn't known what it was, I would have felt on seeing it that it was part of a nightmare—shrouded—not a human being in sight.

I parked the car outside the gates and walked in, into a fortified outer court. A plaque on a wall, first of many memorials:

> In remembrance of the members of the 11th Armored
> Division of the 3rd U.S. Army who liberated the
> concentration camps at Mauthausen, Gusen, Ebensee,
> and others located nearby in Upper Austria in May
> 1945, their deeds will never be forgotten.

I walked up some steps and along a path to the main gate, as solid as the gate of a medieval castle, with a watchtower on either side and a platform walkway across the top. The camp must have been designed by someone who had had a toy castle as a child, with outer courtyard and inner walls, lower and higher levels, keeps, gates, bastions, drawbridge and portcullis. Even the gray stone had the look of papier-mâché, but when one tapped it it was stone, sure enough. I arrived at a little office by the entrance. Since 1949 the Austrian government has kept the camp open six days a week as a historic monument. I bought a ticket for 10 schillings —roughly sixty cents or thirty-five pence. Admittance is free for groups of students with their teachers, and also for former inmates of concentration camps, their wives, widows and children. I wondered if I would have returned for a visit if I'd been there. I was the first visitor of the day, but in the course of the next hour a few others came in, drifted slowly around, at first avoiding one another's eyes, but after a while nodding to one another in a friendly way, needing to, perhaps, in this place of ghosts.

Inside the main walls is a long parade ground. To the left, several lines of faded green wooden huts, survivors of many more that were here between August 1938 and May 1945. On the right, more permanent-looking buildings. The huts are empty now—doors sagging a little on their hinges, floors swept clean—though in one hut there is a collection of wooden bunks and lockers. Information sheets have been pinned to the walls, in numerous languages, including Hebrew, Russian and Serbo-Croat. Each hut was meant for two hundred people—which would have been inhuman overcrowding; each hut often housed from three hundred to five hundred. The signs tell you the nationalities of the people who lived in the huts, what they worked at, and how they died.

Mauthausen was set up at the Mauthausen quarry in the summer of 1938 as a sub-camp of Dachau and as a so-called fieldpost. After March 1939 it developed into an independent concentration camp, with sub-camps of its own. It was the "mother camp" for all of Austria, or Öster-reich, which after the *Anschluss* with Germany was known as the Ostmark (a revival of the name which the German Emperor Otto the Great gave to the Danube district that is now Lower Austria, after the Battle of Lechfeld, in 955, where he defeated the invading Magyars). To begin with, most of Mauthausen's prisoners were criminals, who gradually became the camp functionaries, but before long, German and Austrian political prisoners were sent there. In 1940 they were followed by Poles, Spanish Republicans and Czechs. In 1941 came Dutch Jews, Yugoslavs and Soviet citizens—many of the latter were prisoners of war. In 1942 more political prisoners were brought from France, Belgium, the Netherlands, Greece, Albania, Poland, the USSR, Italy and Hungary, as well as Germany and Austria. In 1945 prisoners from other concentration camps evacuated before the Russian advance were moved to Mauthausen, together with thousands of Hungarian soldiers and Hungarian Jews. A few Allied prisoners of war somehow ended up in the camp. On May 3, 1945, among the camp's polyglot population, there were four Britons, two Chinese, one Canadian, and two Americans. There were, for comparison, 18,015 Hungarians, 15,803 Poles and 15,581 Soviet citizens. Roughly 1,700 prisoners were women.

At the very beginning, prisoners worked on building the camp and the quarters of the 6,000–9,000 SS men who guarded Mauthausen and its nearly fifty sub-camps. For several years following, most prisoners worked in the quarry, but after 1943 the majority labored in armaments factories, a number of which were constructed in underground caverns in the area. In summer the prisoners were roused at 4:45 A.M. Roll call began at 5:15, work was from 6 to 12, with an hour's midday break often partly occupied by marching to camp for another roll call and then back out to work; work again from 1 P.M. to 7 P.M., followed by another roll call. This was the routine Mondays through Saturdays; some prisoners were also made to work on Sundays. Reveille in winter was at 5:15 and work in the quarry began at dawn and ended at dusk. In the arms plants, prisoners worked "only" an eleven-hour day.

There were various ways of dying at Mauthausen. Some prisoners, particularly Russian officers, were subjected to "nutritional experiments" and starved to death. Many were gassed in the camp's small gas chamber. There were medical experiments. A stunted and crippled Dutch schoolteacher was put to death by an injection and then his body was stripped of flesh and dissected; photographs, before and after, were kept. Prisoners were often shot "on the run"—that is, ordered to run and then shot down as if they were attempting to escape. Some were whipped to death over an exercise horse in the middle of the parade ground. Some were hosed with ice-cold water until they died. Some sick and incapacitated prisoners were sent on details to pick raspberries growing outside the guarded perimeter and then shot "while attempting to escape." Other sick prisoners were sent to the so-called recreation center at Hartheim, near Linz, where they were gassed. Many committed suicide, by electrocuting themselves or more frequently by jumping from the cliff into the quarry—the SS guards called these prisoners parachutists. A number of Dutch Jews were thrown to their deaths from the cliff top by SS guards. One man, an Austrian named Bonarewitz, escaped in a crate but was discovered and brought back to the camp. He was forced to remain in the crate for ten days, then paraded behind a camp band to a gallows and hanged. Many prisoners were stood against a height-measuring board and then shot, through a hole in the board, in the back of the neck. Many hundreds died on the irregular steps leading up from the quarry, where they stumbled and fell carrying blocks of stone, or from exhaustion at the end of a working day. One mass breakout occurred, by Soviet prisoners under death sentence in Hut 20, on February 2, 1945. Thirteen got away but the rest were recaptured and slain on the spot, their bodies then brought back to the camp and burned. Records were found after the war showing that, in all, 122,767 prisoners were murdered by the Mauthausen organization; it is estimated that tens of thousands more perished in total anonymity.

I walked from one hut to another. Grass and trees could be seen through the windows; bare wooden floors, tongue-and-groove wall boarding covered with bumpy brown shellac. It was strange—here is a place, on earth, a construction of man like many others, and yet so unlike in that it was entirely evil. The evil remains so repellent that it seems to hug the dead, to wrap around and sully them. One should make the effort to consider and remember them as individual human beings, to disentangle them from the terrible fate they suffered, and thereby honor them. In one walled area, the walls still topped with barbed wire, a graveyard was made on the site of former huts for 9,800 corpses exhumed from a mass grave outside the sub-camp at Marbach. A sign says: "May they rest in peace." But to be buried behind barbed wire! Another graveyard for prisoners who died after the liberation was created in the area of a camp extension known as Camp II; now small trees and wild roses grow among the stone crosses.

The camp hospital is a museum. In its cellars were three furnaces used for cremation and a gas chamber, camouflaged as bathrooms and showers. Today it is a museum without guards. There are displays of SS photos of prisoners at work in the quarry, of the bodies of prisoners who were shot, of naked prisoners standing at attention for roll call with shaved heads, sticklike arms and legs, rib cages protruding. There are SS reports; identity discs; samples of prisoners' clothing (striped hats and uniforms, wooden clogs, slippers); metal rods used for torture; examples of letters written by prisoners (each letter to a relative had to contain the sentence "I am well and in good health"). There is a photo of SS Reichsführer Heinrich Himmler visiting the camp, looking like a math teacher or company lawyer, except for his uniform. There are samples of objects made by prisoners: cigarette lighters, chess sets, wooden goblets. One Polish prisoner carved a knight on horseback in relief on a casket lid. Some wrote poems. There are photos of living people with shrunken heads, nothing but bones, all drawn in, arms clasped as if to hold themselves together. Zyklon B gas canisters, gray pellets like stone chips. A photograph of a man who had rushed out and seized the electrified wire, his last gesture—frozen, with eyes closed, rigid hands gripping it—seems to be a desperate cry for help.

In the cellar crematorium, where the ovens have narrow trays long enough for a wasted-away human body, the walls have been turned into a place for memorials: small plaques, photos, framed testaments, bedecked plastic flowers and faded ribbons, placed by relatives, mostly to Italians who died here. One says:

> Louis Aletrino, redacteur, international journalist.
> Born 1892 Amsterdam, shot 29.8.42 Mauthausen.
> "Auch töten könnt ihr, aber nicht lebendig machen."

I walked fast through the shower room, shivering. In April 1945 the SS disconnected the pipe that had brought in the gas, as they thought removing the evidence. The room is filled with unseen presences. In the laundry room, where prisoners were put under ice-cold showers until they died, there are now national flags, national memorials. In an adjacent chapel, built since the war, one can sit and try to collect oneself, or pray.

It was still foggy outside. I walked through an area of large monuments. Here had stood the SS barracks, the SS hospital, stores and a canteen for the camp staff. There is, among monuments erected by different countries to their citizens who died at Mauthausen, a memorial to the Soviet General Karbyshev, who died with two hundred others on February 16, 1945 from being drenched with cold water and left outside in freezing temperatures. There is a Jewish monument: a welded steel construction that looks like a thicket of upraised fists—a burning bush—a defiance. The Hungarian memorial also shows figures with upraised hands and the inscription VERGESSET NIE—never forget. I didn't expect to see a German memorial there, but the DDR had erected one, and perhaps uncharitably I thought that there was once again an attempt to distance itself from responsibility for the war. It was a massive monument: a bronze woman sculpted with mannish head and features, set on a stone floor, and with a stone wall behind which had a long open space in it partly and effectively filled with wrought iron in the shape of giant barbed wire.

In the same area as these monuments and memorials are a number of apple trees.

The steps down to the quarry, which is called *das Wiener Graben* (the Vienna ditch), are known as the death stairs. It is a long and steep descent. The stone steps, now more or less uniform, were not so then. Each step was and is about half a meter high. At the end of a day of toil each prisoner had to carry up a hewn stone. Sometimes they fell, or were made to fall. The quarry itself is like a stone coffin with uneven sides cut into the earth. At the foot of the tallest side, which is a sheer cliff, is a pool of dark gray-green Wehrmacht-colored water. In it one can see minnows, reflected stone, reflected dragonflies. A plaque gives the names of men—many being Dutch, Flemish and British—who were pushed off the cliff or "shot on the run" on the days of September 6 and 7, 1944. Going up the steps again, I noticed wild flowers growing in the crevices between the stones. I wondered if they had grown there then, and whether, if one had noticed them, one would have felt they were beautiful or a mockery. I—in good shape—was puffing when I reached the top.

By the Italian memorial I picked up a windfall apple from the ground. It was by no means perfect-looking but I took a bite from it, as if to partake of something from the spot, perhaps hoping for a little knowledge to come with the sweet-sour taste. In the parking lot my car had been joined by a score of vehicles: an Australian tour bus, a Polish car, and a mixed bag of West European cars, including six from West Germany—people who will look around Mauthausen and, I imagine, never forget. I got into my car and tried to think about which road I would take next through pastoral Austria on my way to Vienna.

23. SUITCASES IN THE CORRIDOR

At a hamlet called Sarmingstein, on the north bank of the Danube, I stopped for the view. The morning fog had finally burned off. I walked out onto a little quay and breathed the warm air. Green hills formed a broad V in which the river ran. There were bright-green meadows and darker-green woods on the hillside opposite. The waters of the Danube moved powerfully. I thought, The world includes both Mauthausen and this.

At Persenbeug, where the river makes a U-bend, I crossed to the other side. It was here in the *Nibelungenlied* that the princes and knights of the court of Worms halted on their ride to Etzel's court; here they went hunting as they paused on their way to meet their doom from Kriemhild's vengeance—Kriemhild being Siegfried's widow and then the wife of Etzel, also known as Attila, King of the Huns. Along here, Frederick Barbarossa led an army in the Third Crusade. The river, flowing out of Western Europe, was once full of dangerous rapids and whirlpools in this stretch, but now forms a lake above the dam that has been built between Persenbeug and Ybbs, to furnish hydroelectric power. River shipping locks up and down. At Ybbs I joined the autobahn to Vienna, hoping to get there before the evening rush hour. Vienna is farther east than Berlin or Prague. Among the vehicles moving in that direction were a number of East

European cars with their skimpier license plates: Czech, Hungarian, Rumanian and Polish. One small Polish Fiat was parked in a rest area where I stopped briefly, and its driver and passenger, both men, busily repacked what looked like more than a small Fiat-load of belongings, stowing each item carefully as one might in a boat preparatory to a long voyage. I was now receiving Radio Vienna. Many of the lead news items had to do with Rumania and Hungary, as well as with Poland, where Solidarity and the failing economy continued to exercise the regime.

A generation has passed since Harry Lime, the Third Man, prowled the grubby postwar streets of Vienna. If there are spies in the city now, they probably have the cover of commercial attachés and are as interested in Arabian oil or Israeli arms as in the long-lasting competition between the East and West. Vienna is now a thriving city of the international bureaucracy, with branches of the United Nations and the International Atomic Energy Agency, the headquarters of OPEC, and the periodic meeting place of world statesmen. It is the historic center for culture in this part of the world but also retains the *Gemütlichkeit* of provincial Austria, where people—at least the older ones—say *"Grüss Gott"* to complete strangers they pass in the street, as if they lived in a village.

I found a room, with difficulty, in a modern hotel in a quiet sidestreet near the Prater park, a twenty-minute fast walk from the Kärntner Strasse and St. Stephen's Cathedral in the center. A warm wind blew, and hats and newspapers whirled across the streets. This, apparently, was the föhn, the warm, dry wind that comes off the north slopes of the Alps, melting snow and causing great risk of forest fires. In some parts of Austria its effects on people are said to be so severe that examinations are suspended in the schools when it is blowing, and it can be used as part of the defense in criminal trials. In Vienna the föhn didn't seem to be seriously disturbing the general equanimity. In the Foreign Ministry, off the Ballhausplatz, the porters found it amusing that a windswept-looking Englishman kept returning across the central courtyard to the front lodge, unable to find first of all the right staircase and then the right office on it in the huge rabbit warren of the Chancellery Building. I began to wonder if Room 125, which I couldn't discover on any of the long, haphazardly connected corridors off the staircase, was some kind of grail to be found only by a knight of the requisite purpose and purity, or else a goal in some Central European puzzle of the nervous-making kind we call Kafkaesque.

But when eventually I found Room 125 there was nothing sinister about it or the young diplomat, Robert Wiesner, who answered my knock. He suggested we go to a nearby café. There, among newspaper-reading gentlemen and couples having quiet assignations, we discussed Austria and the world as seen from Austria. Which is not to say that we confronted these subjects and came up with direct answers. The conversation was more oblique than that. Wiesner gave me the impression that people of his age were reasonably happy with the present Austria, a country with a stable identity—perhaps more so than either of the two Germanys. This sense of itself was something Austria didn't have between the wars, when many of its citizens seemed to follow the lead of Germany. That had been one way for Austrians to pursue their old imperial ambitions without full responsibility, vicariously participating in German aggrandizement while still being able to blame the Germans for all that went wrong or all that was wrong with it. Nowadays many Viennese and people of Lower Austria (in the northeast of the country) are sensitive to what they consider to be any Germanization of Austrian life. Many of the television programs that they see originate in West Germany. Many English-language films and TV programs are dubbed in West Germany, which annoys those who prefer the Austrian accent and often slightly different word usage. Austrian children are now beginning to say *"Tschuss,"* a colloquial North German way of saying "Goodbye" (believed to be a corruption of the French *adieu*). In western parts of Austria, on the other hand, people often make deliberate efforts to help Germans feel at home, putting menu prices in Deutschmarks and giving things German names—for example, *Sahne* instead of *Obers* or *Schlagobers*, which is what the Viennese call the whipped cream they like in coffee and on top of all pastries; they make a chauvinistic point of asking for it in the proper Austrian manner.

Out of the war and the long occupation that followed came a need for independence and realization of the special spot Austria was in. Austrians needed to deal as practically as they could with the problems of their country's position, a Western state in almost all respects except geography. There was a general feeling that Austria couldn't afford to show off anymore; the empire had gone for once and for all. Other constraints were built into the State Treaty of 1955, which forbade any union with Germany and made impossible any accession to organizations like the European Economic Community. The pressures from West and East, and the example of Switzerland, helped create an impulse toward neutrality. It was a law giving effect to this that was the first act of the Austrian parliament on the final departure of foreign troops. Permanent neutrality had been proposed by the last imperial Austrian prime minister, Heinrich Lammasch, in 1918–1919. In the mid-fifties the Soviet Union encouraged the idea of neutrality for Austria, as a way of keeping Austria unattached to Western defense alliances. However, when Khrushchev, on a state visit to Austria in 1960, said in his punchy manner that the USSR would not look on inactively if Austrian neutrality were infringed, the Austrians responded quickly that it was up to them to decide how and where their neutrality had been threatened.

Neutrality, Wiesner said, is not an act of withdrawal but a way of cooperating actively with neighboring states. Austria has a conscript army, he reminded me, which could conceivably slow down an aggressor for a few days on his way through to somewhere else, but Austria depends more on foreign policy as a means to defend the country in peaceful ways. Other means to the same end are trade and communications. The Eastern-bloc countries would lose all around if Austria ceased to be its independent self, providing an avenue for East-West commerce, a linking point for gas pipelines and the transfer of electrical power between the Comecon grouping of Eastern-bloc countries and the EEC. It forms in many ways a big gap in the Iron Curtain. And it is defended best of all by a state of mind, which is for the most part relaxed and confident.

Much of the time the Viennese feel the border only as an abstract threat. They say, "They're there—but then they've been there for thirty-five years—or for centuries." However, there are occasions when the Viennese, in their exposed outpost to the east, don't sound quite so nonchalant. At the time of the Yom Kippur Arab-Israeli war in 1973 there was a good deal of hoarding in Vienna of rice, canned goods and flour, just in case World War III ensued. In the months of Polish drama in 1981, some shopkeepers said they had noticed considerable purchases of staple foods for putting by. For that matter, Austrians do not have precisely the same relations of amicability and closeness with each of their Iron Curtain neighbors. Czechoslovakia presents the biggest problem. This is partly the result of Czechoslovakia's long democratic tradition—long in terms of this part of Central Europe—which has brought down on it a regime that is tougher than the average and means to suppress that tradition, which 1968 showed could easily be reanimated. This conflict between the Czech past and present causes repercussions on border relations with Austria. The Czechs have imposed greater restrictions than the Hungarians have on traffic with Austria. Border controls take longer, inspections are more searching. In Haslach, Herr Wolkerstorfer told me that Czech visas were sometimes a long time in coming; the Czechs could decide to investigate your whole life if they wanted to. At a border post he watched a tarpaulin being torn off a truck that was being inspected; the tarpaulin was damaged. "It is the arrogance that comes from feeling inferior, when you think that you have enemies everywhere. Hitler's Germany had it too." In

Czechoslovakia, as in East Germany, there is a minimum amount of money that must be exchanged into Czech currency for each day's stay. Along the Czech border many Austrian towns that have no crossing point into Czechoslovakia are half dead and need infusions of government aid. The Viennese, like the Berliners, buy up empty and underpriced houses in the country for use as weekend cottages. This coolness in Austro-Czech relations was demonstrated by the long postponement of a state visit to Austria that had been planned by President Husak. Dr. Bruno Kreisky, the Austrian Chancellor, said that one reason the Prague government had finally called off the visit was the angry Austrian reaction to news that a Czech intelligence agent, Joseph Hodic, had been living in Vienna for four years pretending to be an exiled member of the Charter 77 civil rights movement, all the time spying on Czech émigrés.

Austrian relations are much better with Hungary. Citizens of both countries do not need visas to visit one another. Most Hungarians find some difficulty in getting together the necessary foreign currency for private trips, but a number come on group tours, paid in advance. Many Austrians go frequently into Hungary to do their weekend shopping, to buy salami, have dinner or have their teeth capped by the cheaper Hungarian dentists. The governments of Austria and Hungary are now working on a treaty of cooperation for their border regions, but the Austrians feel it best not to make too much of such measures in case the Hungarians run into trouble with Big Brother for it. The Austrians also simply feel closer to the Hungarians than to the Czechs. In part this dates from imperial days: the Hungarians were lower-ranking partners—but still partners—in the empire. The Czechs were regarded rather as workers and servants. But the Czechs don't seem to bear any grudges against the Austrians because of this. Many of them (as the Hodic case showed) live in exile in Vienna. The best way out of Czechoslovakia for those who want to leave for good is via Austria. Many who are allowed to go on vacation to Yugoslavia stop in Austria en route and stay.

The place to which many East Europeans who are leaving their homelands for good go first in Austria is the small town of Traiskirchen, half an hour's drive south of Vienna. Here the Austrian government has set up a *Flüchtingslager*, or reception camp for refugees—the word *Lager* is all it has in common with Mauthausen. The Traiskirchen camp has been operating since the Hungarian revolution, in 1956, put the Austrians to the test, and they showed that, for them, being neutral also meant offering asylum. In 1968 Austria welcomed many Czechs, in 1972 many Ugandan Asians, and in the last few years, numbers of Vietnamese and Cambodians. Kurds, Chileans and Argentineans have been given sanctuary. (Austria also used to run a camp for Jewish emigrants from the Soviet Union, but since a terrorist attack several years ago this has been managed by the Red Cross and the Jewish Agency, under conditions of tight security and secrecy; the camp's whereabouts in Austria are not publicized.) In the twelve months before autumn 1981, most of the people arriving at Traiskirchen were from Poland, and the numbers were far higher than the previous year. In the first six months of 1981 Traiskirchen welcomed 654 Czechs, 16 Yugoslavs, 373 Rumanians, 12 citizens of the USSR, 479 Hungarians and 5,550 Poles. In August 1981, 4,047 Poles arrived in Austria, compared with 335 in August 1980. Summer is usually the time for leaving home—it is easier to pretend one is going on vacation—but this summer was being extended into autumn. While I was in Austria, Poles were coming in at the rate of nearly two hundred a day, mostly across Czechoslovakia by train but roughly a third in their own cars. The flood was finally halted a few weeks before General Wojciech Jaruzelski's crackdown, when the Czechoslovak government sealed its country's frontier with Poland on December 7, 1981.

On the day I visited Traiskirchen a number of recent arrivals were milling around the entrance gates, talking about how they had got there and what they thought might happen next. Another crowd was clustered in the anteroom of the camp offices, where half a dozen men and women were attempting to cope with the paperwork, registering new arrivals, taking down the details of people's lives and ambitions, and trying to convey to them what could be done for them right away and what they would have to be patient about. Here were people who had enough of shortages and despair and decided to make what must be one of the greatest voluntary changes a person can make in his own life; they had found a hole in the Curtain open for a while and plunged through.

I walked around the camp with Dr. Gabrielle Neugebauer, an attractive lady who works for the Ministry of the Interior, which administers Traiskirchen. The camp is very much an institution—a collection of stone barracks with huge rooms, a former Austrian army cadet school and Russian garrison in the postwar occupation years. Dr. Neugebauer introduced me to Karl Radek, the camp director, a jovial man in his late fifties, who managed to keep a conversation going while his phone rang constantly and he dealt with various camp matters. On a wall of his office was a landscape of woods and a waterfall that looked curiously Austrian *and* Chinese. Radek explained that it was a present from a Chinese Cuban refugee who had come via Spain to Traiskirchen and eventually reached the United States. A forest of rubber plants crowded the room; a bird-feeding tray sat on the window sill.

"We're in the business of trying to make the impossible possible," Radek said. "Austria has a very liberal asylum policy. We accept more people as political refugees than other countries do. There's criticism that some people come here for economic reasons, for better jobs and better living conditions, but I say their reasons are primarily political—any economy must operate inside a political framework. Bad politics produce a bad economy. The people coming here now are mostly young, in their early twenties, often with small children—though quite a lot are on their own. In fact, nearly a third are single women. They have to have a very deep reason for leaving home and country. They've had to put up with a repressive, overordered and badly organized system until they boil over. They come here, living evidence of a system that doesn't work, and we can't reject them."

Radek said that the refugees go through various phases after reaching Austria. First there is plain joy at having made it out. Then there is depression, as the future appears highly uncertain. Then, for most, a return to better spirits as possibilities become apparent. Most refugees stay at Traiskirchen for only a short period before they are farmed out, at the Austrian taxpayers' expense, to inns and boardinghouses, where they often stay for six months or so. The camp is supposed to house 1,500 but was accommodating 2,200 just then. The government provides pocket money of 240 schillings per ten days for families, 180 schillings for single people. Various charities provide a "welcome payment" of 650 schillings. Those at the camp can come and go as they please, and some help in the camp, for small wages, while others get part-time jobs in vineyards or on building sites. Some sell the cars they've used to get here in Viennese street markets, presumably at a bargain price that compensates the buyer for any ensuing complications of customs charges and registration. Some have brought their parents, mothers or mothers-in-law. One elderly lady recently arrived on her own. A few have to get over the hurdle of thinking that once they've actually reached the Golden West they can put their feet up and be looked after as victims of Communism. Most of the Poles want to get as far away from Poland as possible—anywhere in Europe seems too close to the Russians. Australia, Canada, the United States and South Africa are on top of the list of places to go. "Austria needs help," said Radek. "It needs help from friendly countries to accept these people speedily."

As I walked around the camp with Gabrielle Neugebauer I noticed lots of East European cars parked between the buildings, and a few small camping caravans, or trailers. I wondered if the Polish Fiat I'd seen on the autobahn to Vienna had come here yet. Except for the cars, this must have been very much what Ellis Island was like—hope, impatience and resignation. Standing in line for bedding and meals. Small groups of people hanging around on staircases. Suitcases in the corridors. (Most of the suitcases were brand-new; items, apparently, that aren't in short supply in East European countries.) Most people seemed well-dressed—if you leave your country, you do so in your best clothes, even your best blue jeans, as for going out on a Sunday. In some of the quarters where only men were living, a few windows were broken, the result of drunken discontent or high spirits. The floor of a hut, supposed to be the library, was jammed with mattresses to accommodate the recent influx of arrivals. We looked at several rooms used by voluntary aid organizations that help people apply to embassies for permission to settle in their countries, and the chapel, where Catholic and Orthodox services were regularly held. An impromptu barbershop had been set up outside one building: a straight-back wooden chair, no mirror, a striped towel stuck in around the collar of the seated customer, and the barber—whose skill or lack of it seemed to be reflected in a rather tight-lipped expression on his customer's face— earnestly wielding scissors and comb.

One long, high-ceilinged dormitory was crowded with bunk beds. In some cases, gray blankets had been hung from the top bunk to make a sort of tent, or curtained four-poster, out of the bottom bunk, in which privacy could be obtained. Shopping bags and suitcases stood at the foot of the beds; clothes lines were rigged between some of the top bunks; cans of food and plates sat on the window sills; several radios played quietly. Some people were asleep; some—mostly women and children— were playing cards and chatting. One red-haired young woman from Gdansk told me that she, her husband, who was a silversmith, and their small son had left Poland because there wasn't enough to eat and because they thought things were going to get worse. They wanted to be able to look ahead with some hope. They had driven across Czechoslovakia, which had taken about five hours. Friends who had come earlier had written to tell them about Traiskirchen. They wanted to go to Australia and knew they might have to wait six months to do so.

I'd been told in Vienna that no one at Traiskirchen would want to give me his name, but this was not so. Two persons out of three seemed unsecretive and indeed carefree, though they may have been those who had brought out all their immediate family. Lech Rolniczek, a twenty-nine-year-old truck driver from Kolobeck on the Baltic coast, wearing jeans and denim jacket, told me that he was divorced, without children; he'd said he was going on vacation when he came to Austria three months before this. Since he arrived he had done a lot of reading, writing, teaching himself English, and generally helping around the camp. He was going for an interview at the Australian consulate in a week's time. He was expecting a Russian invasion of Poland any minute, and thought that it might at least have the advantage of speeding up some countries' immigration procedures for Polish refugees.

All sorts of people were among those who had recently left Poland. There were university professors, engineers, taxi drivers, welders. Andreas, a plump young man in a blue track suit, told me cheerfully that he had been a patisserie maker and movie projectionist; he, too, wanted to go to Australia. One electrician, who had many family members still in Poland and didn't want to give his name, said that he had been very scared crossing the Polish-Czechoslovak border in case the guards found his electrician's diploma, which would make it clear that he was leaving. He had hidden the diploma deep inside the rolled-up tent with which, he had said, he and his wife were going camping. After four years of marriage he and his wife had still been without a home of their own, forced to live with her parents, and they couldn't stand it any longer. He didn't think Solidarity was going to last—it wouldn't be able to pull off the vast changes Poland needed without provoking a crackdown. But he hoped to go back one day when things improved.

In one large room an English lesson was in progress. The desks formed a big horseshoe, and the teachers stood in the middle, walking around to help those students who needed it. Among the students were Poles, Czechs, Albanians, Rumanians and Hungarians; children, adolescents, young, middle-aged and old; several well-groomed women; a distinguished-looking man in a gray suit. It was Lesson Four: a mimeographed sheet, with questions for which the answers had to be filled in. My name is _____ Her name is _____ He is _____ years old. Most of the people there had no English when they arrived; all were hoping to go on to live in an English-speaking country. One of the teaching assistants was a Kurd, fluent in English after being at Traiskirchen for a year. He was leaning over the desk of a pretty Polish girl saying aloud for her, "My name is Ursula." A young Pole, Jaroslav Matek, told me that he had been helping with the English classes since arriving at Traiskirchen six months before. He was twenty, an only child, a student of chemistry—and a whiz with a yo-yo, which he was twirling up and down as he talked. Matek said that he had been in trouble with the police for posting political handbills. He had paid 50,000 zlotys for a doctored passport (5,000 zloty was an average monthly wage). Anyone with a question about his past found it hard to get a passport, though the administrative confusion of the past year and a half had helped some people get passports who otherwise probably wouldn't have. Matek had said goodbye to his parents, who wished him luck, doubting that they would ever see him again; he bought a one-way plane ticket to Vienna. He was now waiting for a Canadian entry visa.

"It's a bit like the army here," he said. "Long, boring days. But I've made friends, and these classes make you feel you can help. I try to avoid listening to the news from Poland. You hear it anyway, since everyone always talks about the situation there. I am worried for my parents. I am looking forward to Canada. And we thank God for Austria."

The man in charge of the English classes was Sid Jones, an energetic American in his thirties, employed by the Intergovernmental Committee for Migration, a U.S.- and UN-funded outfit concerned with the resettlement and education of refugees. Jones, author of several books, including a biking and hiking guide to England, said that the English-speaking countries to which these refugees would go ought to invest more in teaching them English before they left so that they would be better prepared for their new lives. "After a few months here, many of them get pretty depressed. Apathy sets in. It's hard sometimes to get them to come to class, though this room is cheerful compared to the lodgings many of them are in. This may seem a happy sort of thing to be doing, but despite the efforts of the Austrians and everyone at Traiskirchen, life for anyone who gives up his country is sad at this halfway stage. All sorts of problems are intensified here, including marital difficulties, drink and depression. And just plain worry—a lot of these people, though they don't let on much, are terrified for the relatives they've left behind."

24. OUT OF THE WOODS

In the Austro-Hungarian border, in the province of Burgenland, the land rolls gently through vine fields. The Danube forges through. The country near the river is molded by the danger of flooding, with the rural roads raised on dikes above the level of the big open meadows, trees lining the roads like in the paintings of Hobbema. It was a lovely afternoon as I drove eastward, munching on a Kölnprinz apple that Gabrielle Neugebauer had plucked for me from the Traiskirchen commissariat. Just beyond the village of Petronell, in the Danube plain, I stopped and walked around a small Roman amphitheater. As excavated, it was just below field level, a simple arena made from not very large stones well cemented together. The surrounding fields gave me the feeling that a shovel stuck in at random would have a good chance of hitting more Roman masonry. This was Carnuntum, the capital of the Roman province of Pannonia, whose northern border was the Danube. Here the XIV Legion guarded the *limes* against the Quadi and Sarmatae. In the next town, Bad Deutsch Altenburg, was a small museum containing pieces from a Mithraic temple, stones with funereal inscriptions (to Lucius Plotidius Vitalis; to Aurelia, daughter of Aurealianus—people who lived then, the names in the stones conferring a touch of immortality); and such artifacts as tools, pots, glassware, jewelry, and clasps to fasten clothing. Although the Romans did not have zip fasteners or electric frying pans, many of the domestic utensils they used are remarkably like our own. The surprise one always has on rerealizing this is perhaps due to a hard to suppress belief that progress marches broadly and uniformly, like a Roman legion, rather than as scouts, in ones or twos, darting ahead of the main body. In the museum is a splendid bust of the bearded Marcus Aurelius, who died in Vindobona, now Vienna, in A.D. 180. He, too, did not look particularly antique.

I sat for a little while on the Danube embankment at the edge of a park, between river and town. Bad Deutsch Altenburg is a quiet resort. An elegant single-tower suspension bridge, painted cream, carried a road to the far shore. In the Czechoslovak distance to the east I could just make out the beginnings of the Little Carpathian Mountains, which form the northern boundary of the Hungarian plain. This was not only border country for the Romans against the Germanic tribes, but for Charlemagne against the Mongolian Avars, for the Bavarians against the Magyars, for the Hapsburgs against the Turks. The Turkish threat lasted over one hundred and fifty years, from 1529 to 1683, when the army of Karl von Lothringen defeated the Turks outside the gates of Vienna. But until 1711 there were numerous raids into this part of Austria by marauding bands from Hungary, the Kuruzzen, who were supported by the Turks as they slowly pulled back. Here and there in this part of Burgenland you can see remnants of the huge earth embankment that was built as a line of defense against the Turks and their confederates along this *Grenze*. (I hope that in a hundred years time we—meaning our descendants—can see the remains of unused missile silos, our line of defense against the hordes from the East.) On the north side of the river, the broader Danube plain witnessed many battle of the Thirty Years' War (1618–1648) and the Napoleonic Wars, including the battles of Aspern and Wagram. Most of Burgenland, south of the river, was a Hungarian province from 1648 to 1918. In 1921 much of Burgenland's population voted to confirm their union with Austria, except for the people in the area around the town of Sopron, which voted to remain in Hungary.

I stayed in Burgenland for a day and two nights. I didn't visit Kittsee, a village near the junction of the Czechoslovak-Austrian-Hungarian borders, part of which I'd been told was still known as Chicago because of connections from early in this century, when many Burgenlanders emigrated to the United States and sent money back to put into land and houses, causing a rapid, Chicago-like growth in tiny places like Kittsee. I spent my first Burgenland night in Eisenstadt, chief town of the province. The great architectural spectacle here is Schloss Esterhazy, a vast château done in neoclassical style by a succession of French and Italian architects. The Esterhazys, a princely Hungarian family, claimed to be descended from Attila the Hun, but in recent centuries have showed greater interest in the fine points of civilized life. They played a part in the making of the Hapsburgs as rulers of Hungary and will long be remembered for their services to music. This is the homeland of Franz Liszt and Joseph Haydn. Liszt was born in Raiding, thirty kilometers or so south of Eisenstadt, where his father was bailiff on one of the Esterhazy estates. Haydn was born in Rohrau, a short way north of Eisenstadt; he lived much of his working life in Eisenstadt or in one of the other Esterhazy châteaux in what is still Hungary. He was musical director to the Esterhazy court—conducted the orchestra, led the singers and composed music for them. Down the street from the main entrance to the Eisenstadt château is Haydn's small house, its flower-filled garden backing onto the wall of the *Schlosspark*, the house itself full of mementoes of the composer. In a piano from his time is a tape recorder which plays a Haydn piece as one walks through the room. For the Esterhazys or Haydn, the border was never a problem.

Eisenstadt is a rather buggy town. There were squadrons of midges and flies in the main street. I had dinner in an old coaching inn: the entrée was creamed veal, called *Eisenstadter* something-or-other, and in this dish, which was otherwise succulent, I found a small wasp, dead. I discovered the insect when I was halfway through the course, and it put me off the rest. Partly because I didn't know the German word for wasp, I pointed it out to a waiter with the phrase *"Ein klein Eisenstadter."* This description called forth a properly concerned look, and when he realized that I was taking the discovery with the aplomb of the Esterhazys, led to the hospitable question, Would I like something else instead? I said no, but I would like some Marmeladen Palaschinken for dessert. These—pancakes with orange marmalade—were without wasps, were on the house and were excellent. I also liked the red Blaufränkisch wine of the locality.

I spent the next day by the Neusiedler See, the largest lake in Austria, just east of Eisenstadt. The southern end of the lake is in Hungary. The Neusiedler See is a strange piece of warm and surprisingly salty water, an immense shallow puddle left over from some prehistoric ocean. All around it the country is relatively flat, and the actual shore of the lake is hard to pinpoint, since what surrounds the lake is a wide, marshy rim of reeds, cut into by little bays and devious channels. The villages around the lake are all set well back from it, with their beaches and small-boat harbors carved out of the marshes, and reached by causeways from which—because of the tall reed forests on either side—one can see nothing but reeds and sky until one reaches the end of the causeway, and there is the lake, and, in the distance, the flat far shore. The lake is fed by underground springs, but natural evaporation sometimes gets ahead of natural inflow, and then the Neusiedler See more or less disappears. The last time this happened, in the late nineteenth century, the property owners around the lake hastened to increase the size of their estates; but before long the lake reappeared and put an end to the aggrandizement and various squabbles that resulted from it. More frequently, after a bout of strong winds from one direction, the shallow lake waters retreat from one shore to the other. Despite these possibilities of change, the Neusiedler is favored by many thousands of birds. They enjoy the bugs and the fish. They like the reeds to nest in and wade among. There are reckoned to be several hundred types of waterfowl at home here. People in the lake villages such as Rust put cartwheels above their chimneys for the storks which come every year.

On the gentle slopes leading down to the marshes are the vine fields. In the villages many houses advertise their own wine for sale. I followed the road south from one such village, Mörbisch, a pretty place of whitewashed houses with outside stairs, bright-painted shutters, and hanging pots of flowers or bunches of dried corn. The road ended in a small parking lot, with a vineyard on the long slope toward the lake, the long hedges of vines hanging from wires suspended between low posts, and the southern edge of the vineyard formed by a rusty barbed-wire fence about two meters tall. This was the *Staatsgrenze*, the Hungarian border. Here stood several Hungarian watchtowers, more like the Czech than the East German variety, small cabins on tall, outspread legs; one was built on a marshy peninsula by the lake. In a giant field on the Hungarian side two large red-painted combine harvesters were working down the slope toward the lake, which was gray, under low gray clouds. The grapes growing in this Austrian vineyard were small and green, hanging in secretive clusters under the vine leaves.

I was standing there, wondering about picking a grape to see what it tasted like, when there was a tremendous *bang!* A border incident? World War III begins in the Balkans? I looked around for the cause of the explosion, which had sent thousands of starlings lifting off from the vineyard. A man in green overalls was standing with a slightly self-satisfied air at the wooded upper edge of the parking lot, with a cloud of smoke from a firecracker dissipating above his head. Having done his job for the moment, the bird scarer sat down on a bench, waiting for the next flock to settle on the grapes.

I walked into the woods for half a mile. I was thinking that this wasn't too disagreeable a border, when suddenly a watchtower loomed overhead. I was nearly under it, against the wire fence. There is no cleared strip on the Austrian side of the border, and no sign of any devices like SM-70s, but the Hungarian authorities obviously don't intend to allow their citizenry to walk into Austria whenever they feel like it—not that the fence, with a T-shaped top section that had a double row of barbed wire, looked as if it would be hard to negotiate at night. According to people I talked to in Eisenstadt, there is little tension on this border, and only occasional incidents. In July 1981 two young Hungarian border guards came over in this area, leaving their weapons behind, and asked for asylum (they were taken to Traiskirchen.) A year before, a Russian-built plane crashlanded at Andau, just north of the lake, where in 1956 many Hungarians came into Austria, and the Hungarian pilot asked if he could stay. There are no Soviet troops stationed near the border in this part of Hungary. The local district councils on both sides get together from time to time to discuss common problems of agriculture, drainage and tourism. Hungarians come into Austria on bus excursions; in the village of Rust, where I spent the night, the travel agent advertised day trips by bus to Budapest and Sopron. People in Burgenland watch Hungarian sports programs on television, and in some of the provincial newspapers in adjacent sections of Hungary are printed details of Austrian television programs.

Back in the parking lot a tour bus from Sonthofen, in Bavaria, had turned up. Most of the passengers stayed put, looking out through the windows, but some got out. One man took a photograph of a woman standing with the vineyards in the background, a big fat spectacular rainbow arching over the far shore of the lake, and the flat Hungarian plain, land of Bull's Blood wine if not pots of gold, stretching behind. In the vineyards between Mörbisch and Rust there were parties of grapepickers, men and women with plastic panniers on their backs and buckets in their hands, moving between the rows of vines. In Rust I stayed at the grandly named Hotel Stadt Wien, which was basically the village pub, full of friendly people. I dined on Pusztawurstzel (in honor of the Hungarian puszta, or plain); trout, in honor of the lake from which it had come; and Neuburger white wine, probably from one of the vineyards I'd seen that day.

Saturday morning and thick fog. Wet enough in the air for me to switch on the windshield wipers, but not wet enough for them not to squeak. I headed for the Hungarian border crossing at Klingenbach. While I was in Vienna I had gone to the Kärntner Strasse branch of Ibusz, the Hungarian national travel agency, and had been told that it would take only two days to get a visa to enter Hungary. Two color photos for the visa application I got from a high-priced automatic photo booth in the Kärntner Strasse—the machinery went into action, flashed and caught me by surprise in the act of bending my nose, looking strangely and floridly like Pinocchio. But the young woman at Ibusz didn't remark on it, and I hoped that the Hungarian border officials, comparing photo with person, would realize it was I.

As I approached Klingenbach, I remembered the advice of an Austrian who had told me how relatively simple it was to go into Hungary: "Only don't go on a Saturday—you'll be among crowds of Austrians doing their weekend shopping." So I found a slow-moving line of Saturday-morning cars waiting single file in the fog on the country road leading to the border. It took an hour to pass through the Hungarian checkpoint, which was undermanned for such business. The young guard who handed my passport back to me (no trouble with the photo) said, "Anthony Cowper?"—my first names, which in proper Hungarian fashion—surnames always given first—he had taken for my surname. His colleague asked me to open the car and wanted to know what was in my suitcase. I said clothes. He didn't seem interested in my traveling library, and didn't ask me to open anything. About a mile down the road there was a drop barrier, which a pair of soldiers raised for me to pass under, and a double fence running off in each direction—clearly the edge of a restricted border zone. I drove on toward Sopron.

25. A VISIT TO HUNGARY

My visa was good for a week. When I'd applied for it, I had intended to spend a day or so in the Hungarian border area and then drive out again; but as I thought about it, this seemed a poor use of the permitted time. One is inclined to forget that the telephone pierces the Curtain: one can dial direct to East Berlin and Prague from most parts of Western Europe. (It was possible to dial direct to and from the Soviet Union until mid 1982, when the Soviet authorities abolished direct dialing for "technical reasons"—the actual reasons are believed to be the increased risk of Soviet citizens being exposed to external influences, and the opportunity given to dissidents to contact exiles and Western sympathizers.) From Eisenstadt I called someone in Budapest whom I'd met several years before in New York, and with whom I'd exchanged the usual "Look me up if you ever get there" niceties. Well, George, I now said, here I am. George replied that he was going to be at his family's house in the country that weekend, about halfway between Budapest and the Austrian border; he would expect me on Saturday evening. It gave me a fresh feeling about the border, or at least about this section of it, to be able to drive into a country on the other side of it to spend the weekend with a friend.

But first, Sopron. I stopped to walk around and have lunch. Sopron is an old market town with much of the run-down, unpainted, needing-plaster look of Eastern Europe, but charming withal. On a Saturday morning it was crammed with people shopping in stores and at market stalls. The shops were full of produce, and in the market the fruit and vegetables looked particularly fresh and abundant. In Lenin Street, the main drag, a sidewalk book and newspaper kiosk had for sale Dr. Spock's *Baby and Child Care* (in a Hungarian translation) and the works of various modern Hungarian poets. However, the only foreign newspapers to be seen were an Austrian Communist Party paper and *Neues Deutschland*, from East Berlin. I had coffee in a brightly decorated espresso café—the ground floor of a very old building—where, although it was only 10:45 A.M., a young couple were drinking brandy and ginger ale, and a tape of Louis Armstrong bawled hoarsely in the background. In many of the thoroughfares, traffic police were moving on illegally parked Austrian and Hungarian cars with equal zest. Public monuments included a statue of the Virgin, crowned with stars, and a Communist Party memorial, topped with a single bronze star; on a nearby fence was a poster for the musical *Chicago*, which had been playing in Sopron several months before. In the quiet streets of the sequestered center, people were walking and biking; it was possible, as one walked by, to peek into the courtyards of the old houses through partly open gates. Old ladies were sitting at open windows, looking out, waiting for conversations that would sooner or later come.

In a district of modern apartment buildings, just outside the center, I ran into a small military parade. A sizable crowd looked on while the soldiers stood at attention, long speeches were made and a band played. I made out the words "Budapest," "Czechoslovakia," "Warsaw." The people thereabout didn't seem to be listening with much attention; many went on talking to one another while the speeches droned on. The members of the band, wearing blue uniforms that looked in need of dry cleaning, reminded me of the New England small-town bands one sees on the Fourth of July, shuffling with glazed expressions along a ritual route. The young soldiers, with pinched but not uncheerful conscript faces, wore big black boots that would have been most useful, and comfortable, in deep snow. Some of them smiled at the people lining the sidewalks, but they carried their Kalashnikovs as if they knew how to use them. There was a short display of goose-stepping by several military policemen. Some of the older, more portly officers wore white gloves and carried swords.

In the Pannonia restaurant, back in Lenin Street, I chose to eat lunch in the less fancy and more crowded of two large rooms—not the room with white linen tablecloths and wine glasses, but the room with bare wooden tables and people drinking big steins of beer. I had lamb in a paprika cream sauce, solid little noodles, tomato salad and excellent rye bread. The place was soon packed full. I shared my table with two men who also drank beer, smoked, ate stew with potato pancakes and talked intently to one another, but gave me friendly nods and smiles as they sat down and reached for the salt and pepper. The place reminded me—perhaps it was the potato pancakes—of the Bohemian National Hall, a long way east in the East Seventies in New York City, where in the late 1950s I used to eat from time to time.

It was a fine afternoon, warm and windy. The poplars were shaking their yellow leaves onto the road southeast of Sopron. Crows stalked across the stubble of the immense fields or flapped above their nesting places in occasional copses. Tractors were working, but also farm horses. I passed a wagon drawn by a pair of oxen. The wagon was carrying corn stalks for fodder and was led by two plump old men. An old lady wearing a flowered apron rode by in the other direction on a very upright bicycle. Some of the country villages looked extremely prosperous, the houses better cared for than those in Sopron. Quite a few of the cars on the roads had German license plates. On the way to Kosweg I stopped and gave a lift to a young man with a flourishing mustache; he would have fitted a part in a Ruritanian comedy such as *Arms and the Man*. We had no language in common except for a bare minimum of international terms and gestures. He was going to Kosweg for a soccer match, though I couldn't make out whether to play or watch. We traded the names of European cities and the names of soccer teams: Real Madrid, Ajax of Amsterdam, Juventus, Tottenham Hotspur. The road swung close to the Austrian border, here running roughly north-south. A double fence ran within a few meters of the road, and beyond, in Austria, was a small wooded hillside. A solitary guard sat in a sort of lifeguard chair, a gun across his lap, watching the road. A bit farther on I pointed to a no-photographing sign by the roadside (a camera with a diagonal line through it) and my passenger pointed to the fence in explanation of what was not to be photographed. I asked whether there were mines—my question took the form of making a noise, *boom!*, and adding an interrogative look. He shook his head no.

I left him near the football pitch on the outskirts of Kosweg, and drove farther into town. As I parked the car, a bunch of small boys surrounded it, talking Hungarian. When they saw that I didn't understand, one said, "*Schillings?*" Another moved his jaw in the motions of chewing gum. This was what English milords and American GIs once put up with. I handed out some chocolate I'd bought in Vienna. The boys chanted in German, "*Eins—zwei—drei!*" Then: "*Ciao.*" I taught them the word "goodbye," but when they showed little sign of actually clearing off, I left them gazing at the dusty Saab and set off to perambulate around Kosweg, which, on a Saturday afternoon, was sound asleep. The shops were all closed except for one place where I bought an ice cream cone. However, private enterprise continued in a trusting way in various doorways, where small boxes displayed vegetables, sometimes sorted into plastic bags, with a price label attached, and a can to put the money in. (Five good-sized tomatoes for five forints, roughly twenty-five cents or fifteen pence.) Flowers were growing in municipal planting boxes, in small beds in alleyways, in front gardens and on window sills. Trees grew thickly along the streets; in several places I was showered by falling chestnuts. A sign in a travel agent's window offered trips to Burgenland for 2,500 forints and a trip to Moscow and Leningrad for 6,300 forints.

In Szombathely, a larger town not far away, there was a little more life, if not exactly widespread *élan vital*. Many young soldiers were out walking with their girls. *The Muppet Movie* was playing at a cinema. Szombathely is a name that might stick in the mind when the town itself doesn't; it is briefly celebrated in modern literature as the place that James Joyce, in *Ulysses*, for some reason decided to make the prior-to-Dublin home of Leopold Bloom's father, Rudolph, who was born Rudolph Virag.

I filled up the car at a Shell garage. Shell seemed to have a monopoly on the infrequent filling stations, the infrequency being pleasant environmentally but a practical nuisance, since a long line of cars was generally waiting at each pump. Then I headed east on Route 8 in the direction of Budapest. To preserve George's identity I'll be vague about where, an hour or so later, I turned off the highway and went south onto the higher ground near Lake Balaton—a body of water that is four or five times bigger than the Neusiedler See. The house was a former farm cottage. I was not the only guest. George, a twenty-seven-year-old computer engineer whose father is a doctor, had brought his girl friend, Judit, and she had brought a friend, Kriszta. Judit, a teacher, was dark-haired with wide cheekbones. Kriszta was blond, prettily plump—one would have taken her for Dutch or Finnish. In the next day and a half we walked, sailed on the lake, ate in a local inn and sat around talking, talking. Although many of the subjects of conversation had to do with life in Hungary, a country well inside the Soviet sphere of influence and purportedly dedicated to Marxism-Leninism, what was remarkable was the sense of being free to follow the natural highs and lows of human temperament, of desires to be gregarious or on one's own—feelings one might have had on a country weekend somewhere in the West. Judit, Kriszta and I went to mass on Sunday morning, and the church was full. George talked about his ambitions and frustrations at work—it sounded like the story of a young executive enmeshed in a huge corporation anywhere in the world, though he said it was worse in Hungary. It suddenly seemed bizarre to be behind the Curtain and find that so much of life was *normal*: blackbirds sang also in Hungarian gardens; the same stars look down out of the Hungarian night sky; the same attractions and hesitations exist between men and women. But there were also preoccupations that were particularly theirs. My three companions were worried about Poland, not just for the sake of the Poles, whom they admired, but because they feared events there would have a domino effect in Hungary, causing the regime to become more strict. They were especially concerned that dents in détente might impair their rights to travel abroad.

In this, as in most areas of life, Hungarians are more fortunate than their Eastern-Bloc neighbors. In the course of three years a person is generally allowed to make one trip to the West with a small allowance of hard currency; one trip (fully paid for in Hungary) on a tour or an official visit; and one trip whose cost will be met by friends or relatives abroad. However, it is still a long way from freedom to travel. Government investigators may call at your home to check on information you've given when applying to travel. George said that he'd had his passport long delayed before a trip several years before—a fact he attributed to being stopped by a plain-clothes man as he came out of the British embassy, where he had borrowed a book from the embassy library (which is open to the public), and having his name and address taken. Judit said that she thought more people had been leaving the country for good in the last year or so because of international tension and domestic belt-tightening.

I left my car at the cottage and on Monday morning squeezed with the others into George's VW Beetle for the drive to Budapest. I got a room without trouble at an elderly hotel in Kossuth Street, in the commercial center of Pest, from which it was ten minutes' walk to the Danube bridges over to more aristocratic Buda on its bosky hills. The hotel had the reputation of having been the state security police headquarters before the 1956 rising, but now it was chiefly noted for its period décor and proximity to the street corner where touts—mostly Hungarian, but including a few Poles—tried to get foreigners to change money at black-market rates.

For a day or so the weather seemed to have broken: it rained; a raw wind blew from the east. It was twenty-five years, just about, since the Russian tanks put down the Hungarians, and it wasn't very cheering to hear rumors of the Soviet forces once again on standby on the Polish border. The gloom of the weather seemed matched by some of the tunes that the hard-to-avoid gypsy orchestras played in cafés and restaurants—

for though their repertoire ranged from the plaintive to the ecstatic, the tunes with all the care of the world in them seemed for the moment to march with the melancholy of those listening. Budapest, George reminded me, is the capital of the country that is near the top on the world lists of smoking, alcoholism, divorce and suicide. And yet another day came: the wind fell and the sun blazed. In the street stalls, bright flowers and gleaming vegetables were displayed. The streets were full of cars, the sidewalks and shops packed with people. The gypsy orchestras played their basic selection and the customers laughed and talked and sang. In one unpretentious eating place that George and I went to one evening on the Buda side, near the approach to the Arpad Bridge, everyone was singing the Hungarian words to a song that I recognized, finally, as "Roll Out the Barrel," and when they got to the line that I remembered in English as "We've got the blues on the run," I decided to add a helping burst of good cheer by singing too.

Now and then I felt that Budapest would be a good place for mental health experts anxious to study an entire city in the grip of manic depression. Ups and downs followed hard upon one another, sometimes more rapidly than changes in the weather. Perhaps being a twin city had something to do with it: Buda on its hills, Pest on the edge of the plain; the place where the Magyar tribes from east of the Urals settled a thousand years ago, faced west, and chose Christianity; a place where the skies may lower but thermal springs bubble up; a city where nearly a quarter of Hungary's ten million people has decided to live in conditions ranging from middle-class comfort to cramped slums, in a state that calls itself socialist but encourages many instincts and inclinations that are profoundly conservative. George said that the term "comrade" had never caught on in Hungary; several forms of the word "you" continue to express various pre-Communist shadings of familiarity, formality and respect.

In East Berlin someone had said that Budapest was a good place for East Germans to meet their West German relations. People in Prague had told me that Budapest was the East European city they most liked to visit. Margareta said that there were movies in Budapest you couldn't see in Prague, and she liked the old-fashioned way men bowed as they shook hands, and the way they gave up their bus seats to women. There is even advertising in Budapest (though some of it seemed pretty flat-footed, like the state-sponsored slogan "Buy your shoes in a shoe store"). To Westerners there are such benefits as a low crime rate, which has possibly less to do with old-fashioned morality than with such authoritarian rules and procedures as identity cards, registration of domicile, and no handguns. Soldiers are to be seen in great numbers, as they were in Sopron and Szombathely, being trucked about the city or working in road gangs—one practical use to which young Hungarian men are put during their two years' conscription. But the police are not very evident, and the secret police are so much in reserve that people like George and Judit feel free to sit in a coffeeshop and tell anti-Russian jokes, despite the presence of an army officer at the next table. George said—unjokingly—that the unwritten agreement that the Hungarians have with the Soviet Union gives them the right to act for the most part like free people as long as they don't rock too strenuously the Warsaw Pact boat.

What the Hungarians have managed to get away with is more than a decade of relatively successful experiment with their economy, which is no longer the totally planned and centralized system laid down by latter-day Marxist-Leninist gospel. Profit and individual initiative have been encouraged. On the land—much of it held before World War II by the owners of large estates, on which the peasants were little more than serfs—postwar collectivization was followed by grants of private plots, which collective workers were able to farm in their own time. Now nearly all of Hungary's eggs and poultry and most of its pigs come from private producers. I noticed that many people I met in Budapest would glance at the sign over a doorway, to see whether a shop or café was state- or privately owned; people say that service and sometimes prices are better in the private establishments. Yet despite encouragement for private business—and private ice cream parlors seemed to be booming—the state remains the arbiter of what is permitted. No private publishing is allowed. I met a friend of George's who wanted to open a restaurant, but was about to give up because of the red tape. A man whose large haberdashery business was taken over in the nationwide confiscations of 1949 has reopened—he now has a one-man booth selling buttons in an office-building lobby, but no expectations of being able to expand. When I mentioned this to Kriszta, she said he obviously wasn't very good at pulling strings or knowing which palms to grease. A lot of private business comes from people having second or third jobs. With state wages currently frozen at hardship levels, moonlighting is common. George said that he was all right, having a doctor for a father (private patients, private gifts), but he had colleagues at his institute who were willing to repair washing machines and record players; he knew sociologists who were driving taxis. As in most other East European countries, anyone who can do part-time plumbing, carpentry or car repair is on to a good thing; but the shortage of such help, whatever the rewards, is visible in the run-down appearance of many houses, both publicly and privately owned. An accident in a less than common car—say, a six-year-old MG—can put it off the road for months until parts or labor to improvise can be organized. You might think that such varied economic activity makes for freer political activity, but many people seemed to doubt this. One economist George introduced me to said, "Among small farmers, most are satisfied with the chance of making good money. As for others, much of their private economic activity is on the border of legality—moonlighting, earning taxfree money, and having to bribe officials to get away with it. Therefore those involved are more rather than less cautious about pushing for more political scope as well." Moreover, there is always the fear that the government may suddenly change its line and clamp down on private enterprise. This is one reason given why some private-business people, like the owners of boutiques or holiday accommodation, appeared to be making as much as they could while the going was good.

As I walked around Budapest I noticed all sorts of private trading. People were selling popcorn, sprays of flowers, and wicker baskets at Metro station entrances. Private houses can still be built, and apartments were being built to be rented out. Private-property rights are insisted on as much as in the capitalist West, whether by high hedges or the broken glass cemented to the top of a wall that I saw around one small house near the trolley line that goes out to the Kispest used-goods market.

Kriszta took me there one day. At Kispest, on the edge of town, city meets country, and country folk sell to and buy from city people. Here private enterprise rules. The market, held daily in a large walled compound, seems partly Western flea market, partly Eastern bazaar. Long sheds, divided into stalls and compartments, are separated from one another by passageways crammed with merchandise, such as books, clothes, furniture and car parts. There are a few new items for sale, such as records and jeans, and some antique things, like finely worked peasant blouses, but most is previously owned junk. At several stands, food can be bought: hot sausages; ratatouille; fried dough with sugar sprinkled on it; thick coffee with whipped cream. Among the stalls of the licensed merchants, various free agents attempt to set up shop on a packing case or suitcase. Others stroll around trying to interest the regular merchants or passers-by in their wares, like a small sheepskin, several carburetors or a bright-yellow ski jacket that was being offered for sale by a good-looking gypsy woman with a small girl at her heels. Now and then the police came through, checking licenses. I watched a policeman strolling down a passageway, holding half a dozen identity cards confiscated from nonlicensed traders. I moved to the next passageway, where, sure enough, news of the policeman's approach was being discreetly spread.

One bulky man in his early thirties was rapidly assembling all his goods in three sheets. He bundled them up like laundry, raised them as high as he could to clear the aisle lined with tables covered with goods, and dashed off, at the far end of the passageway throwing his possessions into the open trunk of a bright-red Lada, which a colleague had waiting for him.

If life of that marginal sort seems familiar to someone from the West, so do many of Hungary's problems and its citizens' complaints. Low productivity, a huge trade deficit, poor management, a housing shortage, much featherbedding in industry and the civil service, inflation (which came in a sudden rise), the need for tougher labor regulations, disgruntled youth, a privileged managerial class—it isn't just Hungary in which these exist. But Hungary has little to fall back on. It has never been rich in resources other than the talents of its people. (A random list of Hungarian achievements includes the Rubik cube, the design of the Parker 51 pen, the first Tibetan dictionary, and the first underground railway in continental Europe.) People seem depressed and thwarted in regard to their chances of exercising those talents. A computer engineer who didn't know George and worked elsewhere told me, as George did, of job frustrations, of research projects coming to a dead end, and of years of work being thrown away. "At graduation we're on a par with American graduates," George said. "But five years later we're behind. We aren't able to order spare parts for the computers we've got. My own job is frozen for at least two years. I've got nothing of interest to work on and no wage rises to expect, either."

Hungarian morale, low on this sort of score, is not necessarily improved by the tourist hordes who crowd the city much of the year, hardly seeming to know whether they are in Bucharest or Budapest. (Soviet tourists, who certainly do know where they are, are shepherded in tight groups lest they be individually contaminated by what Khrushchev called "goulash socialism.") Westerners are now allowed to buy vacation homes in Hungary. A hotel boom continues—two new Austrian-backed hotels have recently opened in Pest, near the river; a new Hilton opened a few years ago in the Buda castle district, with a fine view of Pest—underlining the fact that much Western big business gets on well with socialist state enterprises; other joint ventures include Coke, Pepsi and Levi Strauss. A sign near the reception desk in most hotels requests that guests settle their bills in "convertible" currency rather than in Hungarian forints, which they may already have got for their Deutschmarks, pounds or dollars. All sorts of souvenir shops and travel programs are designed to relieve them of further hard currency; the tourist bureau in my hotel was promoting trips to Lake Balaton, to peasant weddings on the puszta, and to the picturesque Danube bend, north of the city, where the river turns at right angles as it passes through thickly wooded hills near the Czech border. During the winter, to keep hotels busy, thermal spas and treatments are publicized; last winter balding visitors were offered a hair-cure week. Hungarians with legally acquired hard currency, earned abroad or sent in by relatives, may spend it in special stores, which as in other East European countries sell hard-to-get items such as foreign cars, French cosmetics and canned (as opposed to bottled) beer. Among Hungarians without access to hard currency these shops provoke a feeling of being second-class citizens in their own country.

Kriszta was an illustrator for a publishing company specializing in children's books. Her father was an editor in another house, and an occasional historian. We talked one day over cups of tea at their home—a rather shabby between-the-wars villa in Buda—about Hungarian anxieties. Hungarians are as scared of the prospect of war as people in the West; they are scared of being in the front line and of once again being on the wrong side. Thus they feel trapped when, as in the past year or so of Afghanistan and Poland, things go wrong with détente and they are locked into a pose by their enforced alliance with the USSR. They open their newspapers and read between the lines and wonder how this or that will affect trade, their prosperity and their ties with the West. They believe that if the Americans squeeze the Soviets, the Soviets squeeze them. Kriszta's father said, "So far we have resisted Russian attempts to get at our grain harvest, but who knows for how long?" People have also successfully resisted learning Russian—the compulsory first foreign language in schools. Kriszta said that she hardly knew it after ten years of it in school, whereas after five years of English, for which she had real enthusiasm, she was fluent. I got the impression that hatred of the Russians was not total (one man told me that he felt sympathetic to the Soviets in their situation vis-à-vis the Chinese, a sympathy he ascribed to an atavistic Magyar hostility to the Mongols and Tartars, and thereby the Chinese). But it is general. I met a physicist who *is* fluent in Russian and he told me that he feels physically sick when he speaks it. Kriszta's family is careful not to walk in front of the Center of Russian Culture but to cross Kossuth Street and pass on the other side. A Western diplomat said to me, almost gratefully, "The Russians really blew it in 1956. The impact in Hungary will last a hundred years."

I wasn't sure this was so. The happenings of 1956 may not be remembered as widely or as sharply as he hoped. (Or even as I might have hoped —I can remember being moved and upset by those bloody events; moved to write poetry and to translate a long poem by Gyulla Illyes called "One Sentence on Tyranny" for a group of Hungarian refugees in New York.) But now the last bullet and shell holes are being plastered over. For Kriszta's generation it is history, a horror for their parents, and something that people in the West go on about, as if it were the only Hungarian event they know. I detected in one or two young people an exasperation at something perhaps too often set before them as a legendary example by their elders who were there, and for whom it was traumatic. In textbooks, 1956 is discussed and taught in school as a counterrevolution, backed by Western imperialism (in the same way Solidarity is presented in the Polish press today). The students let this interpretation wash over them, sometimes exchanging knowing smiles. In families it may be mentioned in terms of members who are no longer around: "Oh—he left in '56, and is in Paris now." A successful book several years ago was *A Production Novel*, by Peter Esterhazy, a scion of the family who were Haydn's patrons; the book, I was told, treats the events of the 1950s from the point of view of the victim, and with great humor.

At the time, 1956 proved that Hungarians could go on making jokes in the midst of disaster. The Russians claimed to have intervened as friends, and in Budapest people said, "Aren't we lucky? If the Russians act like this when they come as friends, imagine how it would be if they came as enemies." Joke making continues. Just about everyone you meet says, at some point in a usually intense and wide-ranging conversation, "Have you heard the one about . . .?" The habit affects foreigners, too. A visiting Texan said recently, "In Texas if you're fed up with life, you go out and kill somebody. In Hungary if you're fed up with life, you kill yourself." That, as someone pointed out to him, was an original Hungarian joke. Many Hungarian jokes don't translate well, being dependent on subtleties of language. A number deal with parallels between the "temporary presence" of the Russians and their four divisions in Hungary and the temporary occupation by the Turks, which lasted a hundred and fifty years. There have been many Brezhnev jokes, Polish jokes and Afghan jokes— for example: There are two soldiers in Afghanistan, one short and fat, one tall and skinny. Question: Which one is Russian? Answer: They both are.

A point of view occasionally put forward is that jokes are an excellent form of political resistance—that a sense of the ridiculous deflates tyranny —and that as long as Hungarians are telling jokes, they are unconquered.

A slightly different point of view is implicit in the seriocomic notion, proposed by a few Budapest citizens, that a special section of the Party Central Committee invents jokes to keep people laughing. For there is a possibility (which most people would not want to brood on long) that joke telling is an escape from an unpleasant reality, and that the energy and imagination that go into it would be better expended in more practical forms of discussion and dissent.

Two Hungarian films that have looked at the Stalinist era leading up to 1956—a period dominated by the figure of Matyas Rakosi—are *Angi Vera* and *The Witness*. Vera Angi (to put her names in Western order) is a young nurse, furious about the poor management of her hospital, who is taken on by the local party school, and becomes a hard-liner and such a slave to party dogma that she denounces her lover, Istvan, a lecturer at the school. Gabor Pal, the film's director, has said, "It is possible to manipulate society only if there are individuals who are willing instruments for manipulation. Vera Angi is such a person." *The Witness*, quite different though it is, is also about such a person. Written and directed by Peter Bacso, it was completed in 1969 but not shown to the public until four years ago; since then it has had several long runs in Budapest to delighted audiences. I went with Kriszta, who from time to time whispered a translation in my ear. A satirical comedy set in the 1950s, *The Witness* describes the adventures of a riverbank caretaker, Mr. Pelikan, who is arrested for illegally slaughtering a pig for private consumption; he is imprisoned and pressured into giving false evidence against a government minister. Pelikan is a naïve, overweight fellow; the secret-police men are comic gangsters; and the state security boss and ruler of the country are macabre buffoons. As the security boss, popping stomach pills, entertains our hero at a sumptuous, solitary banquet in order to talk him into giving evidence, he says several times "The international situation is increasing"— an example of one of those portentous, meaningless phrases which East European newspapers go in for, and at which the audience laughed familiarly. Indeed, from the way that the audience's laughter sometimes began at the start of a line, I had the impression many had seen the film before. Near the end, at the prearranged show trial, Pelikan muffs his lines and the court has to let the minister off. Pelikan is reimprisoned and brought down for execution at dawn, but the hangman oversleeps. A reprieve is granted; Pelikan is released. A happy ending.

The Witness is funny. It makes fun of authority and the bizarre ways of the socialist state. But the case on which the plot is based, as the audiences know, is that of Laszlo Rajk, a minister framed and executed on trumped-up charges by Rakosi's regime. For all its digs at the party and the system, *The Witness* remains a Hungarian joke; no one gets executed. A woman friend of Judit's, a middle-aged teacher who talked approvingly of *Vera Angi*, told me she hadn't seen and wasn't going to see *The Witness* —"That time was a tragedy, not a farce."

Did Kriszta's father think that I, a nomadic writer, had designs on his daughter? Or did he like a good historian simply realize how much light could be shed by personal anecdote? He told me this story about the early fifties. He was at the university. He had fallen madly in love with a pretty girl, and he spent a lot of time plotting how he could get her by herself somewhere—away from the crowded flats in which his family and her family lived. At last his aunt went away for several days. He said that he would look after her flat. He talked the girl into coming there with him one afternoon; she didn't seem at all unwilling. He bought flowers and wine. He was thrilled and excited, and he got the feeling she was, too. They reached the flat; he locked the door behind him. He kissed the girl, and she returned his embrace, his caresses. They fell on the couch together. And at that moment the screaming began. It was a man's scream; it came from a building at the rear of the courtyard; and at varying intervals it was repeated for an hour. "It put a stop to everything," Kriszta's father said. "We didn't kiss after that first awful sound. Eventually we left. I saw her again several times, but it was never the same." Later his aunt told him that the building at the back was used by the security police.

26. BUDAPEST CONTINUED

I had the feeling sometimes in Budapest that people didn't quite trust their good fortune and perhaps believed that they didn't really deserve it. How had it come about that theirs was the most favored colony in the Soviet empire? Maybe my impressions would have been a little less rosy if I'd had a less vivacious guide for several days than Kristza, but it was hard not to feel that although 1956 was a revolution that failed at the time, its objectives had been partly and gradually achieved in the years since. If Hungary could do it, why not the other East European countries? Did the secret lie in the Hungarian temperament and intelligence? George Schöpflin, a lecturer at the London School of Economics whose family left Hungary in the late fifties, had said to me in London, "A failed revolution sets limits on both sides, on those who lost and those who won." The failure of 1956 led—Schöpflin believes—to a reluctant agreement to work within limits, to accept some ideas as impossible, but it also led to a climate in which police terror ceased, economic affairs were handled rationally, and the standard of living rose.

The man under whom all this happened is Janos Kadar, the party leader. "We considered him a Judas in 1956," said Kriszta's father. "He betrayed Prime Minister Nagy. He allowed the Russians to intervene. And now— in the last ten years—he has become almost a popular hero." Kadar has produced for Hungarians something of the better life while allowing no personality cult to develop around himself, unless it is one of abnegation. He lives a quiet, private life in the hilly Roszadomb section of Buda. "He drinks only spritzers of wine and soda," said a writer who knows him and approves of Kadar's puritan example compared to the life style of some other members of the party hierarchy, known for indulging their tastes for hunting parties and country-house weekends. Unlike Husak in Czechoslovakia, Kadar has managed both to keep Hungary out of trouble and to reduce the sense of antagonism between the governed and their government. One worry, Kriszta said, was who would succeed him—though he was thought to have disciples in the party's top echelons who were apparently uninspired, trustworthy and pragmatic. Kriszta's father said, "These people had to read Marx in school the way we all did, but they didn't understand it. It's far better to have *them* in power than idealists, who can lead us straight into the abyss."

For the last century or so, Hungarians have put up with being subordinate to one world power or other. They have had a succession of paternalist governments. Before the war they had the right-wing, repressive Horthy regime; then a brief illusion of freedom from 1945 to 1948, when the Communists took over. There is still a parliament, in which some seats are contested, but non-Communists have to go along with the party's general line, and the parliament meets for only two brief sessions a year in its neo-Gothic building. The center of power is a few blocks farther north on the Pest side of the Danube: the party headquarters, a drab postwar building that is nicknamed the White House, though it is off-white in color. The party's annual congress receives close attention from Hungarians hoping to spot new trends, such as whether any of the members of the Politburo have been sacked who are committed to economic reform, and whether reassuring statements are issued to the effect that socialist democracy will not be limited. As, for example, when the party monthly *Partelet* says: "The settlement of issues through discussions is particularly necessary at a time of complex problems."

Just how much discussion actually takes place within the party is difficult to estimate. Many of the 800,000 party members were recruited into the party youth organization while in school, and stay on because as in other East European countries, they know life will be made a little easier by so doing. The party membership is mostly petty-bourgeois and treats the party like a union or club, with the Marxism simply as icing on the cake. Workers may be encouraged to join, but most aren't very keen (some are too tired after working at their jobs; some simply scorn it). The membership isn't regarded as having much influence on the leadership, and for all the talk among old-line members of a dictatorship of the proletariat, or among more radical Marxists of a new class, governing Hungarian affairs, the country is in fact governed by a bureaucracy and managerial "layer" (in factories, government enterprises, and institutes) that probably isn't much different from that which governed in previous periods. Some of the workers, elevated to trade-union posts, and some of the intelligentsia, especially sociologists and economists, are flattered and—by salaries and sinecures—bought into alliance. Many of the burgherlike middle-aged men who at six in the evening stroll arm in arm with their stout wives around the ramparts of the Hapsburg castle are trusted party functionaries.

Those in Hungary who deny the existence of a continuing class structure were, I suspected, very comfortably off and well connected. George, my computer engineer friend, said, "There's still an extra touch of deference given to those with old family names, ending in double-*s* or *y*, like Esterhazy." People still frequently talk of "the workers" and "the bourgeoisie." Yet there have been definite efforts to improve the chances of working-class children to work their way up and get into college. And there is widespread restraint when it comes to showing how much wealth you have, unless at private dinner parties or weekend retreats near Lake Balaton or in Danube-side villages like Szentendre and Leanyfalu—in Budapest suburbs, it would be a brave man who built a swimming pool in his garden. This suppression of the display of difference may merely suppress class hostility and envy rather than get rid of it. In any event, despite undoubted social movement in the first decades of Communist rule, people in Hungary seem aware of definite strata in society. An old-boy net flourishes, together with a good deal of corruption and racketeering. A depiction of such events, a novella called "The Housewarming," by Ferenc Karinthy, caused a considerable stir two years ago; it has also since been successfully adapted for the stage and is to be filmed. Rumor has it that when the play opened, several provincial party bosses got in touch with Mr. Kadar to protest against the play and declare that events in "The Housewarming"— which included much lavish entertaining and a murder—had not happened in their bailiwicks. The party bosses clearly believed it to be a work of fact, not fiction.

It remains a matter of much speculation and gossip how and what gets published. Karinthy himself, son of a famous writer, possessor of an old family name, told me that he believed good work would always "come forth"—though he had had his own setbacks and delays in being published. Kriszta's father said that well-known writers can get away with more than smaller fry. In an institute, much depends on the director of your department: whether he is a party member or not, if he is a "big man," he can create freedom all around him and insulate his colleagues from nagging *apparatchiks*. Hungary has several serious journals that would do credit to larger, less hemmed-in countries, but the four main newspapers (which appear daily, except Mondays) are almost offensively dull, with column after column of indigestible Comspeak. However, one of them, *Magyar Nemzet*, has a weekend edition with good cultural coverage and a page or so of interesting classified ads, and the one Budapest evening paper takes its sprightlier style so far as having young dungareed salesmen selling it out in the middle of rush-hour traffic.

In many respects Hungarians, like East Germans, are very well-informed. When I first walked into my hotel room I turned on the radio tuned to where the previous listener had left it, and the BBC World Service came in loud and clear. Radio Free Europe is heard in Budapest unjammed. In some hotels and bookshops one can buy Western European newspapers, and some Hungarians subscribe to *Time* and *Newsweek*. Most are worldly-wise enough to know that if a story in one of their own papers from, say, Cairo is by the Magyar Press Agency, much of it may be true, but if it is a Tass story, it represents what the Kremlin wants to believe (and wants others to believe). George said that after the Soviet invasion of Afghanistan the Hungarian press preserved a shocked silence for a week or so—and then presumably pressure from Moscow was felt, and servile articles began to appear about the Soviets helping their Afghan comrades against imperialist insurgents. TV and radio have greater freedom than in other East European countries, and apart from showing such Western products as *Kojak* and *Monty Python*, attempt to deal with local consumer anxieties and generate debate if not—skeptics think—a great deal of constructive action. On one fairly frank radio call-in program, *Radio Diary*, a listener asked not long ago why the public was only informed *after* a disaster or revolt about the true nature of a regime—e.g. in Cambodia or Afghanistan—that the socialist states had been supporting. He was told, lamely, by one of the otherwise outspoken panelists, "Politicians are not only people who inform but people who try to become informed."

Freedom in these areas suddenly seems to be curtailed when the Soviet Union enters the picture. A television executive recently told a colleague (a friend of Kriszta's father) that he could not publish a new audience-research study because it showed that hardly anyone watched Soviet-made TV films and programs. Many well-known people who are forthright in private ask not to be quoted on anything to do with "foreign affairs." The limits to free expression are generally signaled by self-preservatory warning devices in the minds of anyone in or near a top job; and if those fail, the Russians sound their own claxons. The Soviet embassy in Budapest has several hundred employees, many of whom are engaged in translating and monitoring the local media, and thereafter whining and complaining. The Hungarian government does its best to comply, excusing itself to its own people by saying, "We don't want to endanger all that we've gained in the last twenty-five years." The Soviet embassy a few years ago made a great fuss about a Yugoslav novel, set in World War II, and published in Budapest, in which a character mentions "Big Brother" sending his tanks against the Finns. The Budapest publisher had to withdraw all its copies from circulation. Similarly, when Shaw's *Arms and the Man*, written in 1894, was put on at a Budapest theater a while ago, the Bulgarian embassy is said to have protested about its suggestion that Bulgarians do not wash their necks. The play, perhaps coincidentally, closed after a few performances.

I browsed happily in several bookshops. The works of Malamud and Updike, Graham Greene and J. B. Priestley, were visibly on sale, but there was no sign of John le Carré's Cold War fiction, Pasternak's *Doctor Zhivago*, Solzhenitsyn's Gulags, or Hungarian-born Arthur Koestler's *Darkness at Noon*. Judit's younger sister Maria told me that the Jamaican disco group Boney M not long ago had a song called "Rasputin" that was popular. The not entirely cogent lyrics end with the words "All those Russians— *bam bam boom!*," which is not the way a song may end in a country allied to the USSR. So, Budapest disc jockeys began to reduce the volume of "Rasputin" as it reached its close, and over the faded-out sound of the last line, announced the next number. But this didn't prevent the boys and girls listening in living rooms and discos from filling it in, singing out loud as the sound began to fade, "All those Russians—*bam bam boom!*" Some broadcasters and writers, even quite liberal ones, self-censor their material to remove items they suspect might be offensive to the Soviets. The word "Siberia" is out, they know, and they are ready to hear "Sorry, we can't do this right now—it might jeopardize the situation . . ." even if the reasons seem terribly far-fetched: for example, the fact that an American composer's name was referred to in a broadcast on Deep South folk music, might cause the program to be dropped because, on the day the program was scheduled, the composer might announce his support of Reagan's missile policy. It is almost a relief to know that some items are taboo for straightforward puritanical reasons, forbidding plays with homosexual subjects or displays of wild eroticism.

Although there is no official censorship, senior editors are expected to refer to government ministries for "guidance," which is best followed. In universities there is little direction about what may or may not be taught, but party members in the department often pass on a determining word on sensitive subjects. Now and then publication is denied. One *cause célèbre* was the seizure of a manuscript called *Piece Rates* and the trial, in 1973, of its young author Miklos Haraszti. Haraszti's work (since published in England under the title A *Worker in a Worker's State*) is a documentary account of a Budapest tractor plant, and it reads like a nineteenth-century complaint against capitalist industrialism. In Hungary it was distributed in typescript and on tape recordings. Haraszti's eight-month prison sentence was suspended, but he had to pay court costs of 9,600 forints. One effect of the case was to make many editorial people extremely cautious.

Two more recent collections of writing have not been able to find a regular publishing outlet—and have added to the work of friendly typists. (Photocopying machines are far and few between, here as in other East European states, and their use is strictly governed.) One of these collections contained pieces dealing with a Siberian labor camp, a drunken Soviet soldier, the slums of Budapest, and a student demonstration in March 1973 that went unreported in the Hungarian press. The second collection, dealing with Marxism in its fourth decade as the official ideology in Hungary, concluded that Marxism hadn't come up with a solution, either in theory or practice, that worked in Eastern Europe today. (Several contributors to these volumes lost their jobs in publishing houses and research institutes, as did the editors.) One young philosopher whom Kriszta introduced to me said, "I don't think there are any real Marxists left in Hungary. The new left, strong a decade ago, has just about withered away, apart from one or two rarified thinkers." Haraszti has said of Marxism: "It sets its absolutes at too low a level."

In what hasn't yet been officially admitted as the post-Marxist age, a certain amount of intellectual thrashing around goes on as to the nature of Hungarian society, and some of it reflects the fact that, for all their relative physical and economic freedoms, Hungarians *are* behind the Curtain: they do not have the consolation of being able to vote out the present regime and install an opposition party as the government. There is hardly an opposition in Hungary, but there are people whose activities are called "oppositional," at least by themselves. I had some names and telephone numbers. I made approaches, but people politely rebuffed me with excuses of being too busy to talk. Perhaps they were rightly nervous. Perhaps they would have had to have been offered something like front-page publicity for their views to make the risk worth the while. However, one youthful historian agreed to meet me; he was, I gathered, on the fringes of the "oppositional" group. We sat on the terrace of a hotel in Buda, drinking coffee, and he said, speaking more quietly than anyone I'd talked to so far,

"Our whole system is deformed by lack of thought and innovation. There are all sorts of caveats that inhibit useful discussion and change. Hence apathy—and political apathy makes for general apathy; people think there's no point in trying hard at anything. Well, a number of us feel bound to resist this. We think it important that some sort of plurality exists, that a minority can make itself felt, however faintly."

Although the minority is fragmented by having state-paid jobs—and by the relative comfort of Hungarian life in a state without political prisoners—various acts of dissent are made. Private, alternative lectures are given by persons who don't feel free to talk on certain subjects at institutes and universities. (Some topics—for example, the work of John Cage or the San Francisco beat poets—are discussed at university seminars without any feeling of danger, though perhaps with a feeling of luxuriance; it may be because the topics are somewhat ivory-tower.) Several public protests have been made to the regime in the form of open letters about Czechoslovak repression of the Charter 77 civil rights movement. In 1977, thirty-four well-known Hungarians signed such a protest, and four of them went, or were sent, into exile. In October 1979, 254 signed a protest against sentences imposed by a Prague court on some Charter 77 supporters. The signatories included several former high party officials, sociologists, philosophers, historians, authors, film directors, journalists—and Mrs. Julia Rajk, the widow of Laszlo Rajk. They asked the Kadar government to use its influence to obtain the pardon and release of the Czechoslovak prisoners. Although some people said to one another that Kadar himself was sympathetic, there was no official response, and almost all those who had office jobs were soon called in for informal warnings; several were fired; some didn't have their contracts renewed or were passed over for pay raises; others lost teaching assignments or failed to get research projects approved.

The young historian told me, "We protested against Czechoslovakia partly for what the Husak regime is doing and partly because the possibility exists of the same repression here. If the government were threatened, its bite could be just as sharp. Tougher times may be around the corner."

For the young, the prevailing lack of ideals seems especially disheartening. For them, the attractions that the regime presents to older people in the way of stability, prosperity and peace are not so great. State paternalism with a few Marxist trappings doesn't inspire, particularly when you see all around you with what difficulty many people make ends meet. Almost all university students live at home. Kriszta's brother Tibor told me that his tiny grant was dependent on good grades and constant academic achievement. The young feel harrassed by the police, whether for simply hanging out on the streets with transistor radios or for going, as Kriszta and Tibor did on March 15, to place a flower by the statue of Sandor Petofi, leader of the 1848 revolution, which the Russians also helped put down. And the young listen not to gypsy music but to songs like those of Janos Brody, which for one reason or another aren't always available in the shops for very long. Brody's song "If I Were a Rose" has lines I loosely translate.

> If I were a flag
> I would like to be fastened
> At all four corners
> And not blow in every wind

—in other words, as the Hungarian flag has been forced to blow, in the prevailing wind, for the last four or five centuries.

Kriszta took me on Friday evening to the Sabbath service at the Rabbinical Institute in Joszef Street. The institute has a dozen students and a small synagogue inside what might be taken for an ordinary elderly apartment building. A young rabbi was ordained not long ago, and congregations continue to meet for service not only at this synagogue but at the larger, main synagogue. Kriszta and I sat in the organ gallery; I wore an old beret as the obligatory male head covering. Down below, the men sat on one side of the central aisle, the women on the other; the men were in the forefront of the actions of worship, singing, chanting and reading. The Jewish service struck me, as it had once or twice before, as somewhat Eastern, slightly archaic, and very moving, the public expression of a people with a foothold in things eternal. After the service there was a light sitdown breakfast of bread and chocolate milk. The director of the institute made a short speech about the effects of the television series *Holocaust* in other countries (it had not been shown in Hungary); one effect had been to encourage Jews to collect memorabilia of those years. He said that he was gathering together material for the Jewish Museum in Budapest. After his talk, the director went around the room, cutting thin slices of bread from a loaf and handing them to people—a communion.

On the table at which I sat lay a copy of Bruno Bettelheim's book *Surviving and Other Essays*. I sat next to an elderly man from Zürich whose wife, sitting several places away, was Hungarian. He said that she had managed to avoid being shipped off in one of Eichmann's death trains. I overheard the name Wallenberg in someone else's conversation. The man from Zürich was saying that the chief rabbi here bowed a bit too much to pressure from the government; of course one had to be flexible, but look at the Catholic church in Poland, what it achieved . . .

Before the last war about one person in five in Budapest was Jewish; now it is more like one in seventy-five. George had told me that there was still a current of anti-Semitism in Hungary. It was partly of the traditional sort that regarded Jews as clannish, looking after each other's interests in the work place, with other loyalties from which non-Jewish Hungarians were excluded; and partly, with a few, prompted by the memory that many in the party leadership (another clan!) during the harsh Rakosi period, including Rakosi himself, were Jews—some of whom perhaps had been drawn into the party in the first place with the idealistic notion that it might put an end to all forms of sectarian and racial animosity. Still, *Holocaust* had not been shown, and the younger generation of Hungarians were not personally touched by the events of that time. Most people old enough to remember them are probably not so much ridden by guilt that a ghetto existed in Budapest and that many of its residents were killed during the war, as they are gratified by the fact that a greater proportion of Jews survived in Hungary than in other Third Reich–dominated East European countries.

I found a surprising number of people aware of the work of Raoul Wallenberg, a young Swede who personally, almost by force of personality, rescued thirty thousand Hungarian Jews in the last year or so of the war. A short street in Pest, three blocks north of the Margit Bridge, is named after him. I walked there one afternoon. On the wall of a grimy brown apartment building a plaque declared that Wallenberg "during the time of the Hungarian Fascist regime, saved the lives of tens of thousands with his brave actions and by his powerful convictions. He disappeared during the siege of Pest."

The plaque is not exactly straightforward. It doesn't mention that the "tens of thousands" were Jewish. It skates around the fact that Wallenberg, as he "disappeared," was seen for the last time by friends in Budapest getting into a car with a Soviet officer. And that though he may have been killed in some sort of shoot-out with the Germans on the ride, with conditions of banditry prevailing as the Soviet armies forced the Germans out, he may rather have been taken prisoner by the Russians and (as some think) have been kept prisoner by them ever since. Kriszta's father told me, "One suggestion is that the Russians thought the Germans were letting Wallenberg have the Jews in exchange for information about Soviet troop movements, which Wallenberg would have learned about as he went back and forth across the lines. This is what was reported by a Hungarian general who commanded forces in the area, who was himself captured by the Russians, and who returned some years later as a Red Army colonel. He was sure the Russians had it in for Wallenberg. And they probably had no sympathy for a man who saved so many Jews."

When the people of Budapest are feeling particularly under the weather, oppressed by private problems or the tragic unfairness of great events, they often take to their waters—the sparkling, medicinal, thermal baths situated in various parts of the city—in order to even out the ups and downs. Several of the most highly regarded springs rise in the Gellert Hill, near the Buda riverbank. There stands the plush Gellert Hotel, attached to which is a complex of hot and cold baths, steam chambers, saunas, and massage- and mud-treatment rooms. The first Arpad kings, who led the Magyar tribes into Hungary, made use of these naturally warm waters, and subsequently so did the Turks. The architecture of the baths is in a rich mixture of Occidental and Turkish styles; they make a forcible impression of the twin Hungarian inheritance. An instinctive knowledge of both East and West is in the blood of most Hungarians, who feel that their lives have a richer and more intense texture than those who hail from simply one area or other. For all their affinity to many Western ideals, not all Western life is self-evidently virtuous to them: they are suspicious of the more expansionist and cutthroat characteristics of American civilization, its reputedly looser family life, and the less intricate forms of Anglo-Saxon manners and conversation—though none of this prevents them from also feeling a grievance that the West often seems to be overlooking Hungary and its problems. There is a nostalgia for the East which continues to affect Hungarians: in temperament, in art, in music, in politics, and in—one might say—possibilities.

Within the Gellert bath system is a shallow, warm, semicircular pool, exotically tiled in turquoise and lilac, orange and blue, under a high, arched roof, which is decorated in the Turkish manner. Here, halfway through a weekday morning, many men of all ages can be found bathing—pink-skinned, wearing cotton loincloths. And here I finally couldn't avoid taking the waters. I asked the writer Ferenc Karinthy, who had brought me, how so many professional-looking men of working age came to be at the baths at 11 A.M. "Oh, it's always like this," he said. "A man from one ministry or institute will say that he has to go to visit a colleague at another, and he pops in here for an hour or so, to steam for a while, perhaps swim a little, or simply sit in the warm water and relax."

Here, in the rising steam and gently bubbling water, one floats, calmly.

One achieves buoyancy without effort. Pink heads rest on the surface, eyes upturned, spirits tranquil. Here seems to be the equilibrium that Hungarians have long strived for, where they can feel untouched by the winds blowing from one corner or another, the tug between the centrifugal and centripetal forces common in Central Europe, the conflicts of great powers, sudden changes in political pressure, the desire for certain freedoms and the constraints upon them. Karinthy had spent several months of the winter of 1944–1945 in a Buda cellar, nearly starving, and was imprisoned for a period after November 1956. Now he held his mouth open under a jet of thermal water for a moment, then subsided, giving a push with his feet that was just strong enough to make him float a little way out into the pool. His words seemed to drift to me through the steam: "In Hungary there have been worse times, you know."

George drove me back to the cottage and my car. Driving out of Hungary, pulling myself up from what felt like a brief but deep immersion, I was presented with several reminders of the basic authoritarian nature of the state, just in case I'd forgotten it. A few kilometers from where Route 8 reached the Austrian border near Rabatüzes, a pair of soldiers flagged me down and looked at my passport. They also waved two moped riders to a halt, but allowed through an elderly man on a motorcycle without inspection, presumably recognized as a local resident. And at the border checkpoint I got into mild trouble because I hadn't spent 50 percent of the last $40 that I had changed into forints. The young woman at the exchange counter would only change $20 worth into Austrian schillings, leaving me with a good number of unconvertible forints. "Nobody told me," I said, with the wounded air of someone who realizes he should have read the small print. In any event, my complaints didn't help. I made a gesture of eating the ninety or so forints the girl handed back to me, but she refused to smile; she had seen it all before. A young customs officer pointed out the adjacent bar as a logical place to dispose of the forints, and there I bought a bottle of wine and some chocolate. "Okay?" said the customs man, as I gave him a farewell nod, pocketing the last few forints as a souvenir. "Okay," I said. Driving out through the raised barrier, I didn't feel the same "Thank God!" of relief that I had felt leaving East Germany and Czechoslovakia.

I spent the night in Fürstenfeld, an Austrian town twenty kilometers from the point where the borders of Austria, Hungary and Yugoslavia come together. How comfortable and fixed-up Fürstenfeld seemed, compared, say, to Sopron, a town of similar size in Hungary. How much like a figure from a Vermeer or de Hooch did the young woman seem who served my breakfast and then went back to wet-mopping the sunlit floors of the pension café. It was a Sunday morning. I drove southeastward toward the Yugoslav border, pausing to inspect Riegersburg Castle. This can be seen from a long way off. The countryside was bumpy: steep little hills with meadows on the lower slopes, corn fields and small woods; terraces separated by grassy banks, and grass growing over old ridges and ancient plowings; the plowed lines of fields following the contours; clumps of whitewalled, red-roofed houses. Riegersburg Castle is on the highest hill around, posed against the skyline so that invaders could see it from a distance and be warned.

Homing in on it, I parked the car behind a roadside inn and climbed a lane that led to the town of Riegersburg, halfway up the hill, and then past the church upward to the castle. The folk of Riegersburg were going to mass. The women and girls were going into the church, while the men stood outside talking until the last minute, when they went in too. Soon the square and streets were empty. The path zig-zagged up the steep slope. I came abreast of the church bells. A little higher, and I arrived at a little terrace, still a hundred feet or so beneath the castle which rose out of the summit. On the terrace, behind a stone wall, was a memorial lawn. Here the towns and villages of this border country (*Grenzland* was the term used) had made an enclosed spot to commemorate their dead of recent wars and to record earlier events. In the center of the lawn were several slabs of granite with incised inscriptions. I read that the Illyrians, Celts, Romans, Slavs and Hungarians had been here. In 1532 the Turks had come. In 1664 the Turks had been repulsed at the crossing of St. Gotthard, near where I had come out of Hungary the day before. In 1683 the Kuruzzen bands had devastated this part of the border country. The grass was long and damp; cornflowers and clover grew in it. On the inside of the surrounding wall, plaques recorded the losses each community had suffered in the two great wars of this century—most had more deaths in World War II. Riegersburg, for example, had lost 187 in the World War I and 268 in World War II. The town and castle were the object of heavy fighting in 1945 between the Soviet and German forces (some of whom were Ukrainian); the castle was besieged, the town nearly destroyed. The Germans held out, it is said, "to the last gasp."

The castle itself, built in the thirteenth century on a site where the Celts and Romans had encamped, seems to grow out of the basalt rock of the summit. Two walls continue the vertical line of sheer cliff, and the valley floor is directly, two hundred meters, below. The views of the Styrian countryside were dizzy-making. I found the castle chiefly notable for its vast number of lightning rods, one of which was earthed by a connecting strip of metal that ran down into a well. Otherwise tours of castles have a similarity: old portraits of former occupants, weapons, instruments of torture, antlers and deer's heads. There were numerous bad paintings, including one of Salome offering up John the Baptist's head to her father the King. One of the medieval appliances was an Iron Maiden, a body-shaped, female-faced contraption whose hinged doors had sharp iron spikes fixed on the inside at breast level so that as the doors were closed on the person therein he or she was pierced through. Presumably it is only because it requires less imagination to picture one human being inside this awful thing that it seems more monstrous than modern ways of dealing out death to one's enemies, when in fact an anthrax or neutron bomb is much more so.

I stopped for lunch in Ehrenhausen, a small town south of Graz and close to the Yugoslav border. In the town square, stalls had been set up for the sale of new wine and accompanying roast chestnuts. I had goulash in one of the restaurants on the square, making up for not having had it at all in Hungary. At the next table four young men who looked like university students were talking about fascism—I overheard the names Hitler, Richard Strauss and the German Democratic Republic. The river Mur foams through the town, and on a wooded bluff is the castle of the von Eggenberg family, in whose mausoleum is the tomb of Ruprecht von Eggenberg, defender of this border against the Turks in the late sixteenth century. But I hastened on, without paying my respects there. I meant to be in Arnfels, some fifteen kilometers farther west, at the appointed hour of 2 P.M.

Here I was on the border between two neutral and uncommitted states, Austria and Yugoslavia: Austria, which is Western in spirit and feels as if it belongs on our side of the Curtain; Yugoslavia, guided by Tito to independence from Moscow, which has developed its own, idiosyncratic Communist system and is now ruled by a committee of leaders who take turns being on top, and which still feels more Eastern and remote. As for the Iron Curtain, which Churchill envisaged in those immediate postwar years running along here and down the Italian-Yugoslav border to the sea at Trieste, what had become of it?

Herman Steinwender showed me. Steinwender is the proprietor of a prosperous pharmacy and general store in Arnfels, a village with a thousand people. How I got to meet him might be of interest, since it shows how coincidence—or coinciding interests—play a part in this sort of journey. In Hamburg, on an earlier visit to Germany, I had encountered a very helpful woman, Marion Heibey, who worked for the Federal government. She asked if I'd mind taking a suitcase back to England for an English student who had stayed in her home and left it there. The student's father came to my house in London a month later to pick up the suitcase. He asked what I had been doing in Germany, and when I told him of my plans for the border trip, he said, "If you get to Arnfels in Austria, go and see the Steinwenders." He and his wife had met the Steinwenders and the Heibeys on a vacation in Africa seven years before. Herman Steinwender's grandfather had founded the Arnfels store. Steinwender himself, in his early forties, had been president of the Austrian Round Table and was currently deputy Bürgermeister of Arnfels. I had written to him, and had called from Fürstenfeld to confirm my imminent arrival. When I got there, Steinwender was still away from home visiting some relatives, but his pretty wife Karin welcomed me into their spacious and comfortable apartment above the store, and their son Christoph, a medical student in Graz, told me something about the Steiermark locality (Styrian Hügelland, as it is called), an area of wine growing and vegetable farming, known too for the dark *Kern* oil made from pumpkin seeds. The problems of Arnfels were not unusual—unemployment and the decline of local industry, in this case the recent closing of a vegetable canning factory; the Arnfels trouser factory was just hanging on. There wasn't much tourism. Most men had to drive to Graz, the provincial capital and nearest city, for jobs—even men who had been small farmers but now went off to work and left their wives and children to manage the farms. It was the Austrian region with the lowest average income. It was, despite that, a very pleasant place to live.

Herman Steinwender returned—a jovial, smiling man, dressed for Sunday in a traditional Styrian suit, with a green velvet collar on his loden jacket, and a striped ribbonlike tie, fastened in a bow. Herman Steinwender had among many interests that of leading the local Lions Club in a campaign to keep open a small country school in the area; he is also an amateur actor, who enjoys taking part in plays and summer pageants at Arnfels Castle; obviously an enthusiast. Now a Sunday-afternoon walk was called for. The Steinwenders' old black poodle, Tommy, needed a stroll. And these various demands could be met at the same time as a visit to the border. And did I drink wine? I did. Then we would get to that, too.

We drove in his Mercedes south out of Arnfels and up a narrow lane into the hills where the border runs. Vineyards on the lower slopes, then scattered woods, spacious meadows. We left the car by a solitary Gasthof and walked along a track that followed the ridge line. Tommy, who was deaf, ran ahead and through a thin hedge into what was, I gathered, Yugoslavia. Apart from infrequent white posts there was little to show that it was the border between two countries. Sometimes the hedge disappeared for ten meters or so; there were long open stretches of grass.

"Sometimes we see Yugoslav patrols, but not very often," Steinwender said. He shouted, "*Tommy!*" Tommy, on a course of his own, paralleling the border, did not seem to hear. "The countryside is more or less the same over there," Steinwender went on. "They have vineyards too. We often go over there and they often come over here. Passports are needed, but not visas. There are frequent border crossing points, every twenty kilometers or so. We occasionally drive to Maribor, about twenty-five minutes from here, to shop—sporting goods and records are cheaper there. A few years ago we used to drive over to fill up the car—gasoline was cheaper there then, now it's about the same. We go for summer holidays on the Yugoslav Adriatic coast. The Yugoslavs come here for skiing. Until the dinar was devalued a little while ago, they did a lot of shopping in Leibnitz, a big town between Arnfels and Graz—the devaluation was bad news for Leibnitz shopkeepers. There are not only the main-road crossing points every twenty kilometers but many crossing points on back roads, little more than cart tracks. There's one not far from here on the lane that goes over to the Yugoslav village of Kapla, manned by border officials three days a week. Before the war, people used to travel along it by horse and cart. It's too rough for most cars. Now a few people cross on foot. I get elderly Yugoslavs from Kapla once in a while in the store who say, 'I remember your grandfather's shop.'"

The Austrians of lower Styria take an interest in Yugoslav affairs—an affluent next-door neighbor is good for them, and they were worried now, with the Yugoslav economy apparently in not a very healthy state. (Yugoslavia's fairly democratic system of "self-management" of farms and industries makes for small-scale work units but also tends to result in poor coordination and low productivity. Moreover, many of the products that Yugoslavia depends on for export income from Western Europe are products of which the European Economic Community has more than it needs from other sources. Inflation is said to be running at nearly 40 percent. In

1982, harsh austerity measures were imposed, including gasoline rationing and curbs on foreign travel and the use of hard currency on shopping trips abroad.) Austrians are concerned that if the Yugoslav economy collapsed, like Poland's, the Russians might take the chance to push their way back in. Russia had had an ambition since Czarist days for an outlet to the Mediterranean; such ambitions were sustained rather than discarded under Soviet rule.

We passed on the brow of the hill, looking down over meadows and woods to Kapla on the far side of a little valley. Then we walked back to the car. We drove for a few kilometers along a country road, with the border on our right hand. This was now a *Weinstrasse*. By each farmhouse, wooden tables and benches had been set up. The sweet, smoky smell of roasting chestnuts was strong. A lone poplar tree usually stood by the farmhouse—a cheap lightning conductor, Steinwender said.

We stopped by such a farmhouse. A rosy-cheeked woman, the farmer's wife, wearing a flowered apron, poured us glasses of the cloudy new wine and brought us a paper bag full of hot chestnuts. The wine was a week old. We sat on a bench with the Yugoslav border a few hundred paces away, across the road to the south, and to the north, the way we faced across a trestle table, a precipitous hillside falling to more gentle slopes. In the distance, beyond Arnfels, I could just make out mountains, the eastern end of the range that lies between two greater ranges of Alps. There was stormy gray cloud overhead, and yellow light underneath. I tried some of the new Blaufrankisch red, which was still too sweet and unpulled-together; then I moved to a white, also with half of its sugar still unresolved into alcohol. It had a curious, at once fresh and fuzzy, taste. It was a good year for the grapes, Steinwender told me, but he didn't think this farm's product was remarkable. In fact, when the lady of the house asked him what he thought of the wine he was drinking, he grimaced. She seemed surprised. To make amends, I asked for another glass of white. I also asked if she saw much of her Yugoslav farming neighbors. Once in a while, she said. They didn't speak much German. Mostly it was a matter of friendly waves. They grew wine too, but the roads over there were few and far between. They didn't have a *Weinstrasse*.

Our next stop was a similar group of tables, a bit farther along, where Steinwender thought the new vintage showed more promise. Our following stop was at the establishment where he generally bought most of the wine they drank at home, the vineyard run by Franz Dworschak and his wife near the village of Leutschach. This was a step up from the previous places we had visited. Here we sat in a sort of arbor, in a garden that rose in a high bank above the lane. Here we moved back to the previous year's wine, poured out of labeled bottles. Here we exchanged conversation with two couples at a nearby table, on a Sunday outing from Graz. I recall a local Rheinriesling that tasted fine, and then a Muskateller, a little smokier and sharper. The light faded. I decided that it was important to live in a wine country, to consider the problems of blight and frost, sun and rain—the Yugoslav mountains, the Karawanken, are a help here, causing a lot of rain to fall on the Yugoslav side, and making it warmer for the Austrian grapes. Geopolitical problems faded with the light and with sobriety. We ate wurst and bread that Frau Dworschak brought to us on enameled plates, the wurst homemade, like pale salami in tough skins; the bread homemade too, rough-textured, with corn in it—the sort of bread that's good to eat when it's several days old. (I sneaked a piece of the sausage to Tommy, under the table.) As it grew dark the sound of cow bells could be heard. A small herd came ambling up the lane, urged on by young Andreas Dworschak wielding a flashlight. Against the last of the light in the west I could just see the silhouettes of hills against hills. We talked—my German suddenly seemed to come fluently—about mushrooms, and skiing, and airtight stoves.

When the night air was chilly we went inside. The two couples from Graz were in the wine cellar, testing before ordering by the case, as Franz Dworschak siphoned samples from barrels into tiny wine glasses. Dworschak was short and fair; short-necked, chin sloping down to chest; no waist. He clambered over his barrels, inserted a length of hose in the top and siphoned wine into the glasses. The barrels backed against the walls, big black barrels with green hoops; bubbling sounds came from within them. The cellar air was thick, and took some getting used to. In fact, was it air? Was there any oxygen in it? You almost drank it rather than breathed it. A few lungfulls were enough to make you giddy. The light in the cellar was dim, but gradually I made out the walls behind the barrels —walls which looked as if they were made of rough cork, or black sponge, but which, close up, I could see were covered with dark fungi. It wasn't quite crawling or heaving—not yet; it was apparently part and parcel of a properly functioning wine cellar. Steinwender and I sampled various barrels, new, not-so-new and last year's, and then some sort of liqueur, which was very old. We were all smiling, joking, though in deference to my interest in the border one of the men from Graz, who had said that he spoke no English, late in the evening said, in English, that he was a surveyor; he had worked along the border west of here. The Yugoslavs had been helpful, and the border was "No problem. No problem at all." We all repeated this, laughing, as if it were a chorus in a song. "No problem. No problem at all."

I had a head the next morning—what Herman Steinwender called a *Katzenjammer*. The Steinwenders had put me up for the night. After breakfast they sent me on my way with good wishes and good cheer. It was a miserable day, drizzling, with thick fog. I drove west, parallel with the border, slowly climbing into the Alpine foothills and higher, through a pass between two mountains, the Hühnerkogel and Dreieckkogel, both over 1,500 meters high. Now and then the fog cleared for a moment so that I could see clouds above, clouds below. Occasionally everything was blotted out by a downpour and I took the car cautiously to the edge of the road and waited for the rain to ease off. The clouds were a very pale gray with bands of darker gray behind; the wooded mountainsides a gray-green visible sometimes below and sometimes between the clouds. Without ground level, horizon or sky to refer to, it was easy to feel afloat, weightless. Then, as I went down the other side, my ears popped loudly. The road bent and shimmied.

After this inauguration in mountain driving, I stopped in St. Kanzien, a small resort just east of Klagenfurt, provincial capital of Carinthia. Eugen Freund, the Austrian vice consul in New York, had suggested that I call on his mother if I got to these parts; she ran one art gallery in Klagenfurt and a second gallery, open only in summer, in St. Kanzien. St. Kanzien is in a broad valley, with the Drau River winding through it—the river that becomes the Drava when it breaks through the mountains into Yugoslavia. The Drau joins together a series of lakes, and many tourists come in summer when this interior basin of the Alps is hot. Inge Freund, an energetic gray-haired lady, showed me around her St. Kanzien gallery, which was crammed with vivid modern works by Austrian, German and Slovene artists. Mrs. Freund was born in Germany and went to school in Hanover. "It was the time of the Nazis—modern art was forbidden. I wrote an essay about Franz Marc, which my teacher wouldn't look at— Marc was not to be mentioned. I met my husband, who was half-Jewish and became a doctor, in Vienna. I was anti-Nazi. During the war I was in a state of constant fury. The only way I could relieve it was by doing things like write 'Down with Hitler!' in telephone booths. It was silly and dangerous. My husband's father, who was Jewish, spent the war in hiding on a farm."

Mrs. Freund and her husband moved to St. Kanzien in 1951, when he set up medical practice there. Here they found that prejudice was directed mostly at the local Slovene population. The Slovenes are a Slavic people, with their own language, who have lived in this part of southern Central Europe for more than a thousand years. Present national borders cut across Slovene territory, so that there are Slovenes not only in the Yugoslav republic of Slovenia but in Austrian Carinthia, and in Friuli and Trieste in Italy. There are some 2 million Slovenes in Yugoslavia, and close to 60,000 in Carinthia, where they form about one tenth of the population. In 1918 the Yugoslavs invaded the Carinthian region, but a plebiscite was held in the border area of the Slovene-speaking population in 1920, and a majority voted to be citizens of Austria. At which point a number of German-Austrian politicians said that Slovenes who didn't want to be Austrian should leave—and many did. Those who voted yes and stayed apparently preferred their chances of prosperity and opportunity in demo-cratic—even if mostly German-speaking—Austria than in the postfeudal kingdom of Yugoslavia. In 1955 the Austrian State Treaty, whose Article 7 deals with the protection of the rights of minorities, reaffirmed the rights of Slovenes living in Austria, but the local authorities in Carinthia are regarded by many in central government in Vienna as having been slow to fulfill bilingual commitments; and many German-speaking Aus-trians applaud this slowness.

"When we moved here," said Mrs. Freund, "there were quite a lot of old Nazis living in these parts. There are also younger people who are right-wing nationalists—or simply chauvinist Carinthians—and want to send the Slovenes back to Yugoslavia, ignoring the fact that most were born in Austria, have elected to live here and feel quite Austrian. The fact that we were friendly with many local Slovene families caused a number of German-Austrians to be pretty chilly toward us."

As we walked through St. Kanzien to call on some Slovene friends of Mrs. Freund's, I thought that it was in a way a tribute to the permeability of the border here that the Slovenes bridge it. It is also in a way refresh-ing that at this late date in European history one can drive a few miles and find not a new country but a new nationality. The Slovenes have until recently managed to survive without large urban centers or any sort of overall political structure, hanging on in isolated communities—all of which has encouraged the growth of many Slovene dialects. In St. Kanzien a number of signs, in shops and banks, are in both German and Slovene.

Mrs. Freund's good friends the Grosslachers lived in a large old house in the center of the village. Mrs. Milena Grosslacher's maiden name was Mohor. She was a widow, and her son Janko, a doctor in a small town near Vienna, was visiting her with his wife and little daughter. We sat in the parlor—Mrs. Grosslacher a plump, very sweet lady; Janko, with the sort of mustache one associates with fierce Montenegrin mountain men, pouring slivovitz plum brandy; a hundred-year-old map of Slovenia, including Trieste and the Istrian peninsula, hanging on the wall.

Janko, despite having had a German-Austrian father and surname, and now a German-Austrian wife, obviously felt strong Slovene loyalties. "We have close relatives living half an hour south of here in Yugoslavia," he said. "There are no delays at the border. A quick look at our passports and we're through. We go there to buy certain sorts of food which are cheaper. When the dinar is strong they come here to buy coffee and electrical appliances."

I said that I assumed these money links were important—that even the most chauvinistic Carinthian shopkeeper realized that there was business to be had in these comings and goings. Janko said that this was sometimes true, but there was still a good deal of anti-Slovene feeling. It was partly a class thing—most Slovenes in Austria tended to be blue-collar workers and farm laborers. In the early 1970s German-Austrian nationalists defaced Slovene names on bilingual signs, many of which have never been restored. Slovenes often found it hard to get promotion, and they felt that they were the first to face dismissals and layoffs in hard times. All the Slovenes in Carinthia speak German, but few Austrians with German as their first language speak any Slovene. The Slovenes want their language used equally with German in all legal procedures. It would be better, Slovenes think, if both ethnic groups were made to learn both languages in school. As it is, Slovene is an optional subject in primary school. You have to ask to learn it, and some Slovene children—or their parents—don't; the child reaches secondary school unable to read or write Slovene. Indeed, some Slovenes keep quiet about being Slovene, to the extent of speaking German at work, so that they aren't passed over for better jobs. Some parents haven't sent their children to Slovene high schools for the same reason. But Janko thought there was a growing tendency, almost a fashion, to be proud to be Slovene. A new generation of parents was organizing kindergartens where children would learn Slovene from the start; a private Slovene kindergarten in Klagenfurt was so successful that many German-Austrian children were being sent to it, their parents felt it was such a good school. There was an increasing number of Slovene-speaking teachers. And the Slovene high school in Klagenfurt was thought by some to be achieving higher standards than the other high schools, as Slovenes, in the number two spot, felt the need to excel.

Mrs. Grosslacher said, in Slovene—which she and Janko speak in the house—that there had been no Slovene schools before the war; she had taught herself to read and write the language. The war, and Allied victory, had greatly helped their position: the Slovenes were treated as allies by the Anglo-American occupation forces in a way that the German-Austrians were not.

"The German authorities had real trouble in this part of Austria," said Janko, filling up my glass with more slivovitz. "There was a lot of Partisan activity. Although there were also German-Austrian resistance groups, we feel that Slovenes did most of the fighting. Many of the leaders came from Yugoslavia, and Partisan groups worked from the mountains, straddling the border, making raids well north of the Drau. In 1944 they freed a number of British prisoners of war who were doing forced labor in a factory here, and helped them get away through Yugoslavia into Italy."

Many Slovenes, like Janko, leave the region to better themselves. There is a large Slovene "colony" in Vienna. Cleveland, Ohio, is a city with a great number of Slovenes. Many Yugoslav Slovenes emigrated across the border into Carinthia after World War II, and nowadays young Slovenes living in Austria return on visits to Yugoslavia to look for a husband or wife, or to attend festivals celebrating Slovene culture. In Carinthia, most restaurants have Slovene dishes on their menus. Slivovitz—one of the best of hangover remedies, I decided—is to be found everywhere. There are several Slovene periodicals in Carinthia, and half a dozen hours per week of radio programs in Slovene. Yugoslav television programs, originating in Ljubljana, capital of the Yugoslav republic of Slovenia, are received, together with many American films, in undubbed form, with Slovene subtitles. In 1980, Austrian and Yugoslav television crews made a joint program on the Slovene situation in Carinthia which was shown on the same evening in both countries.

I spent the night in Klagenfurt, where I talked to Horst Ogris, the thirty-five-year-old cultural editor of the Carinthian daily paper, *Kleine Zeitung*. We met in an elegant café, which I thought might have suited the pretensions of some of the characters in the long novel *The Man without Qualities*, by Robert Musil, who was born in Klagenfurt. Ogris told me that he had grown up in a village on the edge of the mountains, not far from a border crossing on one of the roads to Ljubljana. There were five hundred people in the village, and only the policeman spoke German. Just after the war the border was closed tight, and remained so until Tito broke with Russia in 1948. Ogris said that as a child he had sensed a general feeling that the enemy might arrive any moment from the east—a feeling, indeed, that was common again in 1968, during the Czechoslovak crisis, when it was feared that the Soviet Union might invade Czechoslovakia through Austria as well as across the territories of some of its Warsaw Pact allies. In the early 1950s young Yugoslavs used to escape into Austria along this part of the border. The trouble was that while the Yugoslav side of the mountains, although steep, could be climbed without special mountaineering equipment, the Austrian side was in most places precipitous. Many of those who tried to come across the mountains into Carinthia fell to their deaths, and were buried in the graveyard of Ogris's village.

"Once, when I was seven years old, I was walking through the woods," he said. "A big black-haired man jumped out and held a knife toward me. I was terrified. But then, when nothing happened, I realized that he meant it as a gift for me. He asked me if he was in Yugoslavia or Austria. When I told him, he shouted with joy. I ran and got my grandfather, and he came and told the man where to go to make himself known to the authorities. Now it doesn't matter if you climb the mountains as long as you have an identity card or passport."

Ogris had problems when he reached secondary school because he knew very little German. However, he soon caught up. He spent a period of college studying in Ljubljana, taught primary school for a while, worked as a journalist in Vienna, and now, for *Kleine Zeitung*, goes to the openings of Slovene art exhibitions and theater productions in Ljubljana, Klagenfurt and Trieste. He feels no great strain arising from his twin nationality or identity. In fact, he believes that the Slovene contribution to Austrian culture may be all the stronger for being fueled by people who have double roots, double sources of tradition. The Slovene problem becomes less pressing with the growth of a new, less nationalistic generation of Austrians, who possibly take their own Austrianness more for granted and don't need to assert it. And in the last ten years Slovenes have come to be more confident in their own political possibilities in Carinthia, setting up a party of their own which has begun to have success in getting representatives on local councils.

It was my last night in Austria. I splurged and stayed in an excellent hotel, the Goldener Brunnen. I had my last schnitzel and walked through the old streets, which still have the feeling of being boxed between the fortified walls that the French destroyed in 1809. Before going to bed, I looked at my maps and decided that rather than take the Italian route via Tarvisio and Udine to Trieste, I would follow what looked like a shorter road through Yugoslavia. Except for a brief section spanning the Austro-Yugoslav border, the route was shown as being a highway, or *strada di grande comunicazione*. I slept a sound, dreamless sleep, in the bliss of ignorance.

28. WHERE THE BORDER ENDS

The first hint of what I had let myself in for by choosing the Wurzen-pass route was a roadside sign saying "Open." Obviously it could be changed to say "Closed." Another sign prohibited trucks, trailers or caravans, and admonished drivers of other vehicles to get into first gear. The car at that point already seemed to be standing on its back axle and to be dragging itself up and around the 180-degree bends with reluctance. A further sign declared this to be merely a 15 to 18 percent gradient, but I credited my steeply inclined senses and the fact that the glove-compartment door had just opened of its own accord, spilling registration, insurance, screwdrivers and the A to Z London street directory that were stored there. I began to glance at the temperature gauge, heart in mouth, as the grinding upward continued.

This was the steep face of the mountainous divide that the Yugoslavs had had trouble with when they crept out of their country thirty-some years ago. But the road's steep ascent ended a little over a thousand meters up—there was a narrow brown valley with the frontier posts, buffet, souvenir shop and bank for exchange transactions. I showed my passport. An inquisitive Yugoslav official looked in my briefcase, asked me in German if I was a commercial traveler (of what—used notebooks? of maps, guidebooks, pens, postcards?), and seemed satisfied with my reply, "*Nein, ich bin Schriftsteller."* I changed a small amount of Austrian currency into dinars to cover the costs of refueling car and driver in the course of the next few hours.

Yugoslavia was an impulse. I hadn't meant to come this way and had made no arrangements to meet people; I wasn't tempted to drive to Belgrade and spend a week there. I was looking forward to Trieste and the end of the voyage. The road went down for a way to the small resort town of Kranjska gora, with chalet-style hotels and parking lots full of long-distance touring buses, mostly German and Austrian, and I kept going through and up the other side. The next ascent made me glad that I'd had the Wurzenpass for training. I wouldn't—starting from scratch at this point—have believed that cars were meant to be here. I wondered if the people who had made the map, and drawn the solid red line denoting a first-class highway, had ever come this way, or were merely taking the word of some fellow in the Yugoslav Ministry of Tourist Propaganda. These were bends that involved climbing what looked like castle ramparts. They forced one to think about why bends are called hairpin—presumably not for the straight part of the pin but for the place at the end where the pin turns around and comes back again. Some of these felt like safety-pin bends, where the metal wire turns in a full circle before returning. Now there were precipices alongside the road. Great granite crags soared above. Waterfalls. Snow on peaks. The wind roaring through the thin pines. I had sometimes thought that Turner's Alpine paintings were too much—too theatrical, too melodramatic. Now I realized that they were exact. The road was only a lane wide. It ceased to have asphalt on it, was merely a rough gravel surface, deeply scarred and holed.

Was this the right road? There was no traffic at all coming in the other direction. Perhaps this was where the Western world really did have an edge, off which I was about to fall. I'd passed one other car, containing a German couple, but they could have been lost too. Now, as I stopped and cogitated and looked at the awesome scenery, they came by, tooting their horn in friendly fashion, like one seafarer to another as their ships pass on the lonely ocean. I looked at the map again and realized that this had to be the right road. There was *no other road in this part of Yugoslavia.* It said on the map: Vrsic, 1,611 meters. The peak hard on my port beam was well named: Razor, 2,601 meters.

This was the top. It was downhill from here, slowly, in second gear. The asphalt surface recommenced. Small farms appeared with the first meadows. The statue of a Partisan, set back from the road, commemorated those who had fought here against the Germans during the last war. A river formed from various mountain streams, the Soca, tumbling down a valley called the Trenta, the bubbling water an iceberg green. There were wooden racks for drying hay in the fields, and villages: Na Logu, Soca, Bovec, Srpenica, Trnovo—names with letters in the wrong places to non-Slavic eyes and ears, names that make you stick your tongue in your teeth or gargle in the back of the throat. The road swept within five kilometers of the mountainous border with Italy. The few people that I saw looked little different from Austrians. There were shrines and crucifixes by the roadside. Only in Kobarid, a small town where I stopped for lunch, was there something un-Austrian, the unpainted, slightly grubby feeling of the East, and in the one restaurant, the no-nonsense, take-it-or-leave-it attitude from the tough waitress that arises naturally in any age or state of auster-ity—as in England after the war. She would have volunteered for the Partisans, I felt. I took gratefully my ration of goulash and two slices of rough rye bread, and wouldn't have dared ask for butter even if I'd known the Slovene for it. When she said "*Bier?*" with a faint creasing of the lips that may have been a smile, I said "Yes!," "*Ja!*," and "*Sì!*," careless of whether *Bier* was Slovene for sprudel or strudel. But I was in luck—it was beer, a drinkable pilsner with a Dalmatian label on the bottle.

I have memories of Yugoslavia, filed away, as it were, with a Dalmatian label, and having partly to do with the service my wife and I received in a hotel that we stayed in, in 1959. Then it was an impulse to stay in Dubrovnik for a month. The hotel, in the center of the old town, had, as far as I can remember, no other guests. It also had no running hot water, despite taps which suggested the contrary; but after we had been there a few days, and the management took in the surprising fact that we were still around, relays of hot water in jugs and kettles came to our room at useful times. The hotel had a subsidiary purpose as a school for young waiters. They were marshaled and trained by an elderly man of some distinction who had been—he said—a maître d' in Budapest, and who accompanied squads of young white-jacketed men to our table as they brought glasses, additional cutlery, the somewhat notional menu, and carafes of syrupy wine. You had merely to turn your head and two or three of them were at the table, in a flash. Then you had to wait for the maître d' to come and translate what we needed. We were awakened in the early mornings by donkeys bringing in vegetables to market in the square outside our bedroom window. We walked in the hills and got to know a local artist, Jovan Obijan, one of whose terra-cotta pieces (of a Partisan) I bought in exchange for a supply of oil paints later sent from England. It was a place where independent life of a sort was clearly going to go on whatever the system—and the system was already allowing many variations from the Marxist-Leninist economic norm. It was a place, like

Northern Ireland, where the people seemed marvelously warm and hospitable under—the first impression—a forbidding surface, at least to strangers and outsiders, though how they could often treat one another was made clear by individuals who proudly wanted to show you where the Serbs had lined up and machine-gunned the Croats, or where the Croats had forced the Serbs to jump off the cliffs into the sea.

These passions, and partisanship, could certainly be concentrated on an invader, as the Germans found out. Although in most cases the Allied official optimism (expressed, for example, at Yalta) about the free elections the Russians would agree to in their sphere of influence was quickly shown up as self-deluding, there has been the other side of the coin, the pessimism about Tito's Yugoslavia, which Churchill and others declared to be firmly behind the Iron Curtain—and that also, more happily from the Western point of view, proved groundless. Given a little time, the Yugoslavs showed they had an intransigence if not love of liberty that the Soviets didn't dare meddle with. Partisans forever! Nevertheless, to this a Western observer has to add that there doesn't appear to be anything like a Western toleration of opposition and dissent in Yugoslavia today. Nearly six hundred people are thought to have been prosecuted for criticizing the government in 1980. People are put in jail for "hostile propaganda" and "maliciously and untruthfully representing conditions in Yugoslavia." One Serbian Orthodox priest was given a four and a half year sentence for inciting religious and racial hatred, his offense being to sing nationalist Serbian songs at his son's christening. Some members of the German Rumanian minority who tried to leave by way of Yugoslavia were arrested by Yugoslav officials and handed back to Rumania, where they were put in jail.

A portrait of Tito still hung on the wall of the restaurant in Kobarid. It is said that even Yugoslavs find it difficult to name whichever leader of the six republics and two autonomous regions is currently serving for a year as the country's President. Outside, in a small plaza off Kobarid's main street, stood a large semiabstract statue of a powerful figure which, with the restaurant waitress still in mind, I recognized as female.

In the lower reaches of the Soca valley the road, like the river, widened. Traffic built up. Homes looked more prosperous. Alongside old houses new houses were under construction, apparently by and for the same owners. The houses had wide, overhanging eaves; vines grew on trellises over back doors and terraces. Mills and factories appeared beside the Soca. Cypresses grew alongside the road. And not far from where the

Soca streams across the border into Italy and becomes the Isonzo, I came upon a midafternoon rush hour. This was in the town of Nova Gorica, which is near the border and the adjacent Italian town of Gorizia. New Gorizia is five-story concrete blocks of flats set in large open spaces. Old Gorizia, which was in the Austrian empire from 1509 to 1915, is a busy market town of faded pastel-colored houses, with the charm of peeling stucco, little squares, shops and cafés. It was the scene of much fighting in World War I, and forms the *mise-en-scène* of the early chapters of Hemingway's novel A *Farewell to Arms*:

The next year there were many victories. The mountain that was beyond the valley and the hillside where the chestnut forest grew was captured and there were victories beyond the plain on the plateau to the south and we crossed the river in August and lived in a house in Gorizia that had a fountain and many thick shady trees in a walled garden and a wistaria vine purple on the side of the house. Now the fighting was in the next mountains beyond and was not a mile away. The river ran behind us and the town had been captured very handsomely but the mountains beyond it could not be taken and I was very glad the Austrians seemed to want to come back to the town some time, if the war should end, because they did not bombard it to destroy it but only a little in a military way.

The Treaty of Paris, 1947, brought the Yugoslav frontier into the town, cutting off several suburbs, two railway stations, and the old cemetery. More rational adjustments were made to the border in 1952, and a fifteen-kilometer zone was set up in which residents on both sides could go back and forth without much trouble.

As I arrived at the border a huge amount of traffic, mostly Yugoslav, was trying to get from new to old Gorizia. It formed into two long and relatively orderly lines of cars at the checkpoint, where first Yugoslav and then Italian officials examined passports or identity cards, which are all that the border zone residents have to show. Old Gorizia may, like other border towns, have lost its hinterland, but the people of the hinterland were still coming to it. At the Italian customs the Yugoslav driver of the car in front of me was asked to open the trunk of his Fiat. It was crammed full of cabbages. He made some sort of explanation, which I interpreted as "I am taking them to a friend . . . ," and though the *douanier* clearly didn't believe this age-old excuse, he waved the man and his cabbages through. An elderly lady on an old black bicycle overtook the cars at the head of the line and didn't show any identity document, though the Italian official, who recognized her, pretended to examine the tires of her bike closely as she pushed it through.

I was in Italy. Faces were less cautious. I drove south, following the last of the border. The sun had been going in and out all afternoon, and at four o'clock when I reached the junction with the coast road between Monfalcone and Trieste, the sky was overcast where I was but ahead it was full of sunlight—and the sun lit the sea. On my left hand the coast curved around to the southeast toward Trieste. The Adriatic stretched away under a faint cloud of smog hanging over the shipyards of Monfalcone. I got out of the car and raised my arms in the air and felt a surge of what must be a common-to-all-men, atavistic, thallassic enthusiasm. The sea!

Trieste lies at the end of an appendix of Italy, a thin coastal strip thirty kilometers long, squeezed between the Adriatic and a high plateau of eroded limestone called the Carso or Karst. The border in this area is largely the result of where in early 1945 the Allied troops, British and New Zealanders, came in on the Germans from one side and met the Yugoslavs, supported by the Russians, coming in on the other. In many places the Yugoslav and Soviet forces pushed the border westward from its prewar location. But the area itself has for several thousand years been one of mixed race. The Goths and Lombards, Germanic peoples, came down into this part of Italy as the Roman and Byzantine empires lost their grip. The Slavs had entered the Friuli plain by A.D. 900. This was, for a while, the seacoast of the kingdom of Bohemia (under Ottokar II, in the late thirteenth century), and later of the Austro-Hungarian Empire. The Italians, in recent times, moved into the Istrian peninsula, now in Yugoslavia, beyond Trieste. At the present time there are many German-speaking people in the Italian town of Tarvisio; Italian villages like Lusevera, near Cividale, where many speak Slovene; and in Istria still enough Italian-speaking people to support a special school system, which Italian school inspectors are allowed to visit. Trieste is the hub of this ethnic confusion. Here the Yugoslavs and the Western Allies glared at one another, and while Slovenes and Italians rioted there was Cold War disagreement between the great powers about who should control postwar Trieste. The city was returned to Italian administrative authority in 1954, and Capodistria given to Yugoslavia. The final disposition of the area was fixed by a treaty at Osimo, near Ancona, signed by Italy and Yugoslavia in 1976.

I got to Trieste a little after five. The traffic was thick, its behavior largely Italian. Horns were being blown on all sides. Cars were double- and triple-parked. I followed local custom, found a Saab-length spot at a taxi stand in a narrow street otherwise jammed with parked private vehicles, and parked the car with two wheels on the sidewalk. The streets were wet from recently fallen rain. I found a down-at-the-heels but friendly hotel nearby, opposite the old municipal theater, an ornate building that forms part of one of the three sides enclosing the great square, the Piazza Unità d'Italia—the fourth, open side is the waterfront boulevard running along the quay, the Riva. In the offing lay several cargo ships; closer at hand, alongside a stone pier, was moored a dark-gray cruiser, looking top-heavy with electronic gear, flying the American flag.

It is part of the tradition for writers to say that Trieste is *triste*—the pun is trite, and despite several other French words in the local dialect left over from the Napoleonic occupation, not very apt. At least I didn't think so. I was glad to be by the sea again. I sat for long periods by the harborside. I took long walks, and ate and drank in small trattorie. Trieste feels like Vienna by the sea; it has a lot of the same heavy neoclassical architecture dating from Maria Theresa's time, and some of the same rooftop statuary, but also a lightness in the air that comes from the sea— a lightness which occasionally becomes a briskness when the bora blows from the northeast, down over the Carso, and ropes are stretched along the sidewalks to keep pedestrians from being blown away. Trieste was the third city of the Austro-Hungarian Empire: Vienna the administration; Prague the industry; Trieste the shipping. It was the home port of the Lloyd Triestino Line, and the great Italian liners used to dock alongside the Riva. Now it is looking for a revived role for itself as the chief port to the south for Central Europe and the Common Market.

I was told something about this by Manlio Cecovini—a lawyer, writer, leader of the political party Movimento di Trieste, member of the European Parliament, and mayor of Trieste. Signor Cecovini received me in his spacious and elegant office overlooking the Piazza Unità d'Italia, an immaculately groomed man with firm jaw, gray hair, bushy eyebrows and a positive approach to Trieste's problems—which I recognized as similar, though on a grander scale, to those of other border places. Trieste didn't feel it got enough attention or aid from the government in Rome. It wanted regional autonomy, help in restoring the fortunes of the port, and a better chance to compete with Yugoslavia. Trieste had once had trade rivalry with Venice; now it was with the Yugoslav ports of Capodistria and Rijeka, which had much lower tariffs. The Yugoslavs were cleverly building a modern expressway to tie in with an Austrian autobahn linking Passau, Linz, Graz and Sentilli. Trieste needed new autostrada connections to bring road traffic more directly from Munich across Austria to this limb of Italy. With Greece and its huge merchant fleet now part of the European Economic Community, there was a greater part for the Adriatic to play in the transport network of Europe. Already oil pipelines ran from Trieste to Ingolstadt, near Munich, and Schwechtat, near Vienna. It was possible for coal to be unloaded in Trieste as well and piped north in powdered form. Cecovini wanted Trieste to be a free port through which goods could move with the least possible hindrance. It looked to Brussels, headquarter city of the EEC, rather than Rome as the capital of the political and commercial world it now belonged to.

If Trieste's future is, in broad brush strokes, European, its present is something a little closer and more intense. Many people in Trieste still hunger for the Austrian connection, moved partly by nostalgia for the Hapsburg Empire and partly by resentment of Rome; there are many German-speaking Triestini. There are also many Italian-speaking people who grew up in what is now Yugoslavia, like the writer Fulvio Tomizza, born near Capodistria in 1937, who went to the university in Belgrade and now lives in Trieste, giving personal voice in his writings to the mixed-up Austrian-Italian-Yugoslav-Triestrian feelings many residents of the city share. (The earlier Trieste writer Italo Svevo, author of *The Confessions of Zeno*, was the product of a slightly different mixture, his pen name—Italus the Swabian—disguising Ettore Schmitz, member of an Italianized Austrian Jewish merchant family.) Some 5 percent of Trieste's cosmopolitan population are Slovene, with their own schools, political groups and theater. And every day Slovene-speaking Yugoslavs flock into Trieste. Some work in places like the Gran Motore diesel factory, near the border; some come to clean homes and offices; most come to shop. In the open-air market off the Canale, the stalls are crowded with Yugoslavs, weighed down with shopping bags; the haberdashers and provision stores in the nearby streets indicate, with Slovene signs, their desire for Yugoslav custom. Some, with big bundles of jeans and jackets, seemed to have come to restock their own shops at home. Some, in native costume, crouching on the sidewalk as they waited for friends, seemed to have come from far afield, in Dalmatia or back-country Serbia. Yugoslavia, whatever its drawbacks as a haven of free speech, sets an example to the other Eastern-bloc countries; it has—at least when it can afford it—the confidence to let its people leave, knowing that they will return. And Trieste—out of all this— suggests that a place that was an international problem for years and a possible cause of conflict can quite drop out of the headlines and become a point where people meet rather than are parted.

One of the first people to recognize Svevo's literary talent was another writer living in Trieste, James Joyce. Joyce was a resident in the city for most of ten years, teaching English at the Berlitz School while writing

Dubliners and *Stephen Hero*, and starting *Ulysses*. Joyce, according to his biographer Richard Ellman, was thrown in jail one night when first in Trieste in 1904 for trying to stick up for three drunken British sailors. The British consul, with bad grace, got him out. On another occasion when the British fleet was in port he was invited aboard a battleship and— says Ellman—drank so much he became "magnificently unconscious." I refrained from visiting the U.S. warship. It was, for one thing, dry. For another, although its radar scanners and guided-missile launchers represented another aspect of Western European security, and the ship was a visible and mobile part of NATO's ability to deter aggression, Trieste had in a sense disarmed me—I was irritated by one more reminder of the weaponry that at once supports and threatens the long peace of our sundered world. Our dilemma is that disarmament—particularly nuclear disarmament—is recognizably important; we are tempted by the thought that some sort of unilateral first step in giving up arms should be made in Western Europe; and yet the whole physical structure of Soviet power as represented by the wall, the fence, the Vopos and the SM-70s makes evident what we do not want spreading into Western Europe: the terror of "psychiatric hospital" treatment and the Gulag labor camps. Cannot the tradeoff in East-West discussions be not only in missiles and tanks, in financial credits and energy supplies, but in an exchange—perhaps for Western technology or grain—in which the Soviet Union is forced to make genuine concessions in the liberties of human beings? For demanding which all we need is the will.

From my room, on the fifth floor of the hotel, I had a fine view of the old theater building across the street; just below its eaves were stone caryatids—in this case male figures with beards and a sort of beach towel or toga over one shoulder, one hand gripping it in mid-chest, another holding it where it was bunched at the waist. All the figures had the same gloomy expression, as if the job of supporting the eaves—perhaps at the same time as holding up their togas—was too much for them. Were they stranded sea gods? I also had a view down a narrow street alongside the theater to the harbor, to the Adriatic. I had begun this journey by one sea and was ending by another, which led south to Ithaca, homeland of the first Ulysses, the wily Odysseus. I, turning north again, meant not to be so long on the voyage home.

INDEX